Gendered Lives
Communication, Gender, & Culture

ELEVENTH EDITION

Gendered Lives
Communication, Gender, & Culture

Julia T. Wood
Lineberger Distinguished Professor of Humanities Emerita
The University of North Carolina at Chapel Hill

CENGAGE
Learning·

Australia • Brazil • Mexico • Singapore • United Kingdom • United States

Gendered Lives: Communication, Gender, & Culture, Eleventh Edition

Julia T. Wood

Product Director: Monica Eckman

Product Manager: Nicole Morinon

Content Coordinator: Alicia Landsberg

Product Assistant: Colin Solan

Media Developer: Jessica Badiner

Marketing Brand Manager: Lydia LeStar

Content Project Manager: Dan Saabye

Art Director: Linda May

Manufacturing Planner: Doug Bertke

Rights Acquisition Specialist: Ann Hoffman

Production Service: PreMediaGlobal

Text and Cover Designer: Chris Miller

Cover Image: Lynn Hughes

Compositor: PreMediaGlobal

For product information and technology assistance, contact us at **Cengage Learning Customer & Sales Support, 1-800-354-9706.**

For permission to use material from this text or product, submit all requests online at **www.cengage.com/permissions**. Further permissions questions can be emailed to **permissionrequest@cengage.com.**

Library of Congress Control Number: 2013944602

ISBN-13: 978-1-285-07593-8

ISBN-10: 1-285-07593-5

Cengage Learning
200 First Stamford Place, 4th Floor
Stamford, CT 06902
USA

Cengage Learning is a leading provider of customized learning solutions with office locations around the globe, including Singapore, the United Kingdom, Australia, Mexico, Brazil and Japan. Locate your local office at **www.cengage.com/global**.

Cengage Learning products are represented in Canada by Nelson Education, Ltd.

To learn more about Cengage Learning Solutions, visit **www.cengage.com.**

Purchase any of our products at your local college store or at our preferred online store **www.cengagebrain.com.**

Printed in the United States of America
1 2 3 4 5 6 7 17 16 15 14 13

This book is dedicated to Susan B. Anthony, Frederick Douglass, Charlotte Perkins Gilman, Emma Goldman, Alice Paul, Margaret Sanger, Elizabeth Cady Stanton, Sojourner Truth, Mary Wollstonecraft, and other women and men who began the conversation about gender in this country;

and to

Gloria Anzaldúa, Ella Baker, Robert Bly, Judith Butler, Karlyn Campbell, Mary Daly, Simone de Beauvoir, Marilyn French, Michael Kimmel, Betty Friedan, Ellen Goodman, bell hooks, Jackson Katz, Evelyn Fox Keller, Lady Gaga, Madonna, Bill McCartney, Gloria Steinem, and other women and men who have added to the cultural dialogue about gender;

and to

Malia Obama, Sasha Obama, Jason Muehlhoff, Niko Pezzullo Striphas, Michelle Wood Wilco, Daniel Wood Wilco, Harrison Wood Wilco, and other boys and girls whose voices will shape the next generation's understanding of women and men, masculinity and femininity, and the meaning of gender in our society.

Brief Contents

Contents

LIST OF EXPLORING GENDERED LIVES BOXES

Preface

I wrote *Gendered Lives* for two reasons. First, I wanted to introduce students to a rich body of research that informs us about the intricate connections among communication, gender, and culture. Second, I thought that learning about these connections would empower students to make more informed decisions about how they personally enact gender, address gender issues in their lives, and contribute to cultural attitudes, perspectives, and policies related to gender.

Since writing the first edition of this book in the early 1990s, our understandings of gender have changed and issues related to gender have mushroomed. Society has acknowledged a greater range of options for individual women and men—in the military, in the home, in professional life, and in politics. During the past 20 years, transgender awareness has grown, new women's and men's movements have emerged, mass media have challenged some gender stereotypes while creating others, and social media have added to the content and forms by which gender is continually negotiated. Academic researchers have continued to map the ways that communication, gender, and culture influence one another. This new edition responds to social changes in the United States and around the world, as well as to feedback from students and faculty who generously offered ideas for ways to improve this book.

I discuss this book's origins and features in the Introduction ("Opening the Conversation," pages 1–13). Here, I want to describe changes that make this edition different from the last and identify supplementary resources available for students and instructors.

Features of Gendered Lives, Eleventh Edition

This edition of *Gendered Lives* is the most substantive revision in the book's history. Five specific changes set this edition of *Gendered Lives* apart from its predecessors.

Enhanced Coverage of Social Media

One of the most significant changes in this edition is greater attention to social media. Although they pervade our everyday lives, that alone is not a reason to focus on them in a book about gender and communication. What does compel attention to social media in this book are the connections between social media and gender. Not only are social media—like mass media and society, in general—sources of gender socialization, but also they are powerful platforms for rethinking gender and for gender activism. Accordingly, Chapter 11 includes a major new section that details the use of social media and online communities to learn about gender issues; hold corporate interests accountable for actions that promote unhealthy and unrealistic views of gender; and engage in activism related to inequity and injustice. In addition to Chapter 11's concentrated attention to social media, I've incorporated discussion of social media into other chapters.

Revised Coverage of Women's and Men's Movements

A second significant change in this edition is more concise coverage of women's and men's movements. A number of faculty who use *Gendered Lives* have asked me to reduce the coverage given to these movements, particularly ones that are no longer active. Accordingly, Chapter 3 (Women's Movements) is 25% shorter than in the prior edition, and more of the chapter focuses on current activism among women.

I have also revised Chapter 4 (Men's Movements). New to this edition is the very current Good Man Project, which aims to facilitate a national conversation about what it means to be a (good) man today.

Attention to Emerging Issues

As I develop each new edition of *Gendered Lives*, I give particular attention to one or two issues that have emerged since the prior edition. For this edition, I give special emphasis to three. First, I've chosen to spotlight bullying, including cyberbullying. Bullying is gendered when it occurs because of a target's sex, gender, sexual orientation, or sexual or gender identity and/or when it reflects gender or sexuality discrimination by the perpetrator(s). The tragic suicide of Tyler Clementi and other suicides by young girls and boys who were targeted for online bullying make this issue one that calls for greater awareness. I've included discussion of it in Chapters 7 (Growing Up Gendered), 8 (Gendered Education), and 12 (Gendered Media). In addition, Chapter 10 (Gendered Organizational Communication) includes discussion of workplace bullying, including women's bullying of other women.

Second, this edition of *Gendered Lives* gives greater emphasis to work–life balance, which continues to be a major challenge and tension in many people's lives. Chapters 7 (Growing Up Gendered), 9 (Gendered Close Relationships), and 10 (Gendered Organizational Communication) call attention to multiple factors that contribute to tension over meeting responsibilities to paid labor and to other facets of life.

Third, this edition inaugurates coverage of reproductive violence, which is interference with an individual's free choice of whether, when, and with whom to reproduce, to become a parent and to parent existing children. Research by Natalie Fixmer-Oraiz (2013), among others, alerts us to the ways that new reproductive technologies can be used both to help and harm women. Accordingly, Chapter 12 features a new section that describes forms of reproductive violence ranging from forced abortion and eugenics to offering monetary incentives to low-income individuals in exchange for their consent to reproductive regulation.

Ongoing Attention to Cultural and Social Diversity

Beginning with the first edition of this book, I've aimed for content and a writing style that are inclusive. For example, I discuss diverse classes, ethnicities, races, ages, sexual orientations, and gender identities whenever research is available; I try to use language that includes all readers; and I punctuate my discussions throughout the book with comments from a wide range of students.

This edition extends my commitment to representing diversity by enlarging coverage of gender issues beyond the United States and beyond mainstream groups. I chose not to write a separate chapter on cultural gender beliefs and practices because I didn't want to separate cultural influences from the discussions about families, education, relationships, and so forth that are covered in this book. Instead, I've woven information about gender in a range of cultures and social groups into each chapter so that students can appreciate how profoundly culture shapes gender in multiple contexts. For instance, the introduction highlights different cultures' commitment to gender justice as measured by health, education, economics, and politics, and Chapter 9 highlights men's increasing participation in child care and home life. To Chapter 12, I've added new accounts of gendered violence around the globe and an entirely new section on reproductive violence.

In addition to covering differences across cultures, I also attend to differences within U.S. culture. It's no longer plausible to think of two sexes that equate to two genders; it's no longer reasonable to assume there are just two sexual orientations and two gender identities. Those binaries are collapsing under the weight of mounting evidence that human gender and sexuality are far more varied than we once realized or accepted. This edition of *Gendered Lives*, gives attention to the wide range of gender and sexual identities. There is more research relevant to people who do not fit neatly into conventional and approved categories for sex, gender, and sexual orientation, and there are more student voices from people who identify as transsexual, intersexed, gay, lesbian, bisexual, gender queer, or gender nonconforming.

Up-to-Date Research

A final focus of this revision is updating research. Understandings of gender and issues connected to it change at lightning speed. To keep up with these changes, a textbook must be continuously updated to reflect the most current research and events. To ensure the currency of this edition of *Gendered Lives*, I've incorporated more than 180 new references to publications that have appeared since the tenth edition went to press or that I had not read at that time.

Pedagogical Features to Engage Students

Five features are aimed to heighten students' engagement with the text and issues related to gender. First, each chapter opens with "Knowledge Challenge" questions, which focus on issues that are often misunderstood and which are covered in the chapter. Second, to encourage active engagement with material, selected Exploring Gendered Lives boxes conclude by asking students' opinion about issues raised in the feature. Third, each chapter concludes with questions for thought and discussion. These may be assigned for students to think about or as journal entries. They may also be prompts for class discussion. Fourth, "Gender Online," which appears after each chapter summary, invites students to visit websites related to chapter content and to search online for videos and information about concepts and ideas in the chapter. Finally, at the end of each chapter, I suggest two to four sources—films, articles, books. My criteria for selecting these are that (1) I consider them either classic or especially insightful and (2) they are accessible to undergraduate students.

In making these five changes, I've avoided "page creep"—the tendency of a book to grow longer with each new edition because old material is not deleted to make room for new material. I've eliminated dated coverage and references to make room for more current research and coverage of timely topics. I hope the changes I've described make this edition of *Gendered Lives* a valuable resource for instructors and students who want to explore the complex and fascinating ways in which communication, gender, and culture interact and affect our lives.

Supplementary Resources for Students and Instructors

Gendered Lives, Eleventh Edition, offers print and electronic supplements to assist in making the gender communication course as meaningful and enjoyable as possible for both students and instructors, and to help students succeed. Cengage Learning has prepared the following descriptions for your consideration.

Student Companion Website. This website provides chapter-by-chapter resources to help students understand and apply the text's instruction. The resources include live and updated web links for every URL mentioned in the book; self-quizzes written by Charles Goehring from San Diego State University; key term crossword puzzles and flashcards; and an online glossary.

Instructor Companion Website. The password-protected instructor's website includes electronic access to the Instructor's Resource Manual, PowerPoints, Testing Program, Comprehensive Video Program, and links to Cengage Learning technology resources.

Written by Emily Anzicek at Bowling Green State University, the Instructor's Resource Manual comprises two main parts, the first titled and addressing Special Issues in Teaching Communication, Gender & Culture, and the second a Chapter-by-Chapter Guide for Teaching Gendered Lives, which provides chapter outlines, activities and test questions.

PowerPoint® presentations prepared by Larry Edmonds at Arizona State University contain text and images, and can be used as is or customized to suit your course needs.

Communication Scenarios for Critique and Analysis videos includes communication scenarios covering interpersonal communication, group communication, gender, and culture. The BBC News and CBS News videos: Human Communication, Interpersonal Communication, and Public Speaking provide footage of news stories that relate to current topics in human and interpersonal communication, and footage of famous historical and contemporary public speeches, as well as clips that relate to current topics in speech communication.

Please consult your local Cengage Learning sales representative or cengage.com/login for more information, user names and passwords, examination copies, or a demonstration of these ancillary products. Available to qualified adopters.

Acknowledgments

One of the most gratifying aspects of writing a book is the opportunity to thank those who have offered support, insight, and advice. First and foremost, I thank my students. The women and men in my classes and whom I meet when I visit other campuses are unfailing sources of education for me. Their questions and ideas, their willingness to challenge some of my notions, and their generosity in sharing their perceptions and experiences have shaped the pages that follow in both obvious and subtle ways.

Among the undergraduate students who have pushed me to think in new ways about gender, communication, and culture are Jordana Adler, Cutler Andrews, Brandon Carter, Ethan Cicero, Alexis Dennis, Reuben Gelblum, Dimitri Martinez, and Nisha Verma. Among the graduate students who have influenced my thinking are J. Beckham, Walter Carl, Jen Cronin, Kate Harris, Naomi Johnson, Kristen Norwood, Tim Muehlhoff, Julia O'Grady, Phaedra Pezzullo, Stace Treat, and Grover Wehman.

My thinking and writing also reflect conversations with colleagues. I am particularly grateful to Professors Bonnie Dow, Vanderbilt University, and Steve W. Duck, the University of Iowa, for their unstinting interest in wrestling with questions about gender, communication, and culture. And I am especially indebted to two long-term colleagues on whom I rely for information, perspective, and critique. One is Lynn O'Brien Hallstein, Boston University, with whom I co-taught my first gender and communication class in 1989 and who remains an intellectual wellspring for me. The other is Natalie Fixmer-Oraiz, University of Iowa, with whom I team-taught gender and communication and who now teaches at the University of Iowa. Over our many years of talking and writing together, Natalie has deepened my understanding of the profound ways in which gender and power are imbricated.

I have benefited from the professional and personal support of the invincible Monica Eckman, executive editor for Communication Studies, and Julie Martinez, development editor, who made my job as an author far easier and far more satisfying than I had a right to expect. Along with Monica and Julie, others at

Cengage Learning have contributed in important ways to this edition of *Gendered Lives*. They are Colin Solan, production assistant; Alicia Landsberg, content coordinator; Jessica Badiner, media developer; Kara Kindstrom, senior marketing manager; Daniel Saabye, content product manager; and Ann Hoffman, permissions manager. As well I thank Samantha Ross-Miller, who managed the production of this book.

Finally, I am indebted to the reviewers for this edition: Emily Anzicek, Bowling Green State University; Janice Kelly, Molloy College; Nancy Tobler, Utah Valley University; and Esin C. Turk, Mississippi Valley State University.

And, always, I thank Robbie—the love of my life—for his support, criticism, and, most of all, his steadfast presence in my life.

Julia T. Wood
Chapel Hill, North Carolina
June 2013

About the Author

Julia T. Wood is Lineberger Distinguished Professor of Humanities Emerita at the University of North Carolina at Chapel Hill. She joined the faculty at that university at the age of 24. While on the faculty, she was named the Lineberger Distinguished Professor of Humanities and the Caroline H. and Thomas S. Royster Distinguished Professor of Graduate Education. She has authored 17 books and edited 10 others. In addition, she has published more than 100 articles and book chapters and has presented numerous papers at professional conferences. She has won 12 awards for undergraduate teaching and 15 awards for her scholarship.

Professor Wood lives with her partner, Robert Cox, who is Professor Emeritus of Communication Studies at the University of North Carolina at Chapel Hill. Filling out their immediate family are their dog, Cassidy, and two cats, Rigby and Rowdy.

When not teaching or writing, Professor Wood travels, works with victims of abuse, serves as a literacy tutor, and consults with attorneys on cases involving sex and gender issues.

Destiny is not a matter of chance, it is a matter of choice.
—William Jennings Bryan

Opening the Conversation

Knowledge Challenge:

- When was the term *feminism* first used?
- How many bras were burned in feminist protests in the 1960s?
- As a group, are heterosexual men happier in relationships with feminist or nonfeminist women?

Most textbooks open with a preview of chapters and features, but I'd like to launch our conversation a bit differently. I think you're entitled to know something about the person behind the words you'll be reading, so let me introduce myself and explain why I wrote this book.

We tend to think of books as impersonal sources of information. Like anything that people create, however, books reflect the experiences, identities, and historical context of the authors who write them. Authors influence books when they decide to include certain topics and omit others, to rely on particular theories, and to include some issues and exclude others. Authors' choices of topics, writing style, and theoretical stance shape the content and overall meaning of a book. This doesn't mean that books are not informative or reliable, but it does mean that authors' experiences and perspectives have an impact on books. By telling you a little about who I am and why I wrote this book, I am inviting you to think about how my background, experiences, beliefs, and values have shaped the book you're reading.

Let's start with some simple demographic information. I am a European-American, middle-aged, heterosexual, spiritually engaged, middle-class woman who has been in a committed relationship with Robbie (Robert) Cox for 41 years. Yet, if you think about it, this information isn't simple at all. It implies a great deal about my identity and my experiences. For instance, I became an adult when the second wave of the U.S. Women's Movement was ascending, and it influenced my personal life and my perspective on gender and culture. The "simple" demographic information about me also shows that I am privileged in many ways—my race, economic class, and sexual identity are approved by mainstream Western culture. Yet I am disadvantaged by my sex, because women continue to be valued less than men in Western culture. I did not earn the privileges conferred by my skin color, sexual orientation, and economic class, nor did I earn the inequities that come with being female. That is the nature of much privilege and inequity—they are unearned. They do not reflect the achievements, efforts, or failings of the individuals who enjoy or suffer them.

The Social Construction of Inequality

To speak of being privileged in some ways and disadvantaged in others does not mean that I assume these aspects of my life are fixed in stone. The fact that my sex makes me vulnerable to job discrimination, violence, and other injustices is not something I accept as unchangeable. Nor do I accept as unchangeable the fact that some people's sexual orientation or race or economic class or gender identity makes them vulnerable to inequity. In fact, one reason I wrote this book is because I believe we can bring about changes in our society. I also do not accept the privileges culture confers on me without reflection.

If we don't want to be limited by the horizon of our social positions, we can learn about the experiences, perspectives, and circumstances of people in other social positions: the anger and hurt experienced by transgendered people in a

Hola Images/Getty Images

Interacting with people who differ from us enhances our perspectives.

society that defines them as abnormal; the resentment felt by some heterosexual white men toward laws and policies that increase rights and opportunities available to women and minorities; what it means to be a person of color in a sea of whiteness; the sense of restriction many women feel knowing they cannot venture out at night without risking assault; the frustration felt by poor and working-class citizens whose needs and circumstances often are not represented in legislation that claims to help everyone.

Although we cannot fully understand the lives of people who differ from us, we can realize that our feelings, identities, values, and perspectives are not everyone's. Recognizing the limits of our own perspectives and experiences encourages us to learn from people who have different perspectives and experiences. We do this by respecting the specific conditions that shape their lives and by recognizing that only *they* can define the meanings of their experiences, feelings, thoughts, hopes, beliefs, problems, and needs. We cannot speak for them, cannot appropriate their voices as our own (González, Houston, & Chen, 2012). But to listen is to learn, and to learn is to broaden our appreciation of the range of human experiences and possibilities.

Realizing that inequality is socially constructed empowers us to be agents of change. We don't have to treat light skin, heterosexuality, maleness, and middle-class economic status as superior or normal. Instead, if we choose to, we can challenge social views that accord arbitrary and unequal value to people and that limit humans' opportunities and lives.

Feminism—Feminisms

Finally, in introducing myself to you, I should tell you that I am a feminist. Many people do not identify themselves as feminists. In some cases, people reject the label *feminist* because their understanding of the term has been shaped by media misrepresentations. The word *feminism* was coined in France in the late 1800s. It combined the French word for "woman," *femme*, with the suffix *ism*, meaning "political position." Thus, *feminism* means "a political position about women" (McCann & Kim, 2003). Ironically, although many people in their 20s do not call themselves feminists, they do think that the Women's Movement has improved the conditions and opportunities available to women. Also, many people—both male and female—believe women and men are equal and should have the same rights. This suggests that, for many people, there is greater reservation about the label *feminist* than about the actual goals, values, and achievements of feminism.

When I talk with students who say they aren't feminists, we often discover that we agree on most issues relevant to gender but disagree on the meaning of the word *feminism*. There's good reason for this. First, feminism is not one single belief or political position. Chapter 3 discusses a variety of feminist positions, and Chapter 4 explores the different stances—some feminist, some not—endorsed by men's movements. Second, most people's impressions of feminism have been shaped by bias in media portrayal of feminism and feminists. Beginning with the inaccurate report in the 1960s that feminists burned bras as a protest (which they did not do then), media have consistently misrepresented feminists as man-hating, tough, shrill extremists. Many people, like my student Andrea (see her commentary), say they aren't feminists because they associate feminism with media caricatures that emphasize male bashing, being unfeminine, and engaging in radical protests.

ANDREA

I would never call myself a feminist, because that word has so many negative connotations. I don't hate men or anything, and I'm not interested in protesting. I don't want to go around with hacked-off hair and no makeup and sit around bashing men. I do think women and men are equal and should have the same kinds of rights, including equal pay for equal work. But I wouldn't call myself a feminist.

Media stereotypes of feminists don't fit many women and men who define themselves as feminists. Like me, many feminists have good relationships with both women and men. In fact, research shows that heterosexual men in relationships with feminist women are happier and consider their relationships healthier than heterosexual men in heterosexual relationships with nonfeminist women. The converse is also true: Women in heterosexual relationships with feminist men are happier and more satisfied with their relationships than women in heterosexual relationships with nonfeminist men (Rudman & Fairchild, 2004; Rudman & Phelan, 2007). Also like me, many women who label themselves feminists are feminine in many ways: They enjoy wearing feminine clothes, experimenting with hairstyles and makeup, and engaging in traditionally feminine activities such as baking, watching chick flicks, and caring for children. Being a feminist does not conflict with being feminine, but it does mean being reflective about how women define and express femininity. Likewise, being a feminist does not conflict with being masculine, but it requires men to make conscious choices about how they define and express their masculinity.

Because feminism means different things to different people, I want to tell you how I define feminism. I see it as an active commitment to equality and respect for all forms of life. For me, this includes respecting all people, as well as nonhuman forms of life and the Earth itself. Simply put, my feminism means I am against oppression, be it the oppression of women, men, people with disabilities, people with any gender or sexual identity, people of any race, ethnicity or religion, elderly people, children, animals, or our planet. I don't think oppression and domination foster healthy lives for individuals or societies as a whole. I believe there are better, more humane, and enriching ways for us to live, and I am convinced we can be part of bringing these alternatives into existence. That is the core of feminism as I define it for myself. During the course of reading this book, you will encounter varied versions of feminism, which should shatter the myth that feminism is one position, and which should also invite you to consider where to locate yourself among diverse viewpoints.

Feminism does not just happen. It is an achievement and a process. I was not raised to be a feminist. In fact, quite the contrary. I was raised to be a traditional

Southern woman who deferred to men and devoted herself to home and family. In the 1970s when a friend first introduced me to some readings about discrimination against women, my initial response was denial. I tried to rationalize inequities or repress my knowledge of discrimination, perhaps because recognizing it was painful. When denial failed to work, I entered an angry phase. I was bitter about the ways in which women, including myself, were devalued and denied opportunities. I was also angry at myself for having been unaware of society's devaluation of women and for conforming to the roles assigned to women. This angry and embittered phase is natural in the process of becoming a feminist, but it doesn't lead us forward.

Finally, I was able to transform the anger into an abiding commitment to being part of change, not so much for myself as for future generations. I want our society to become fairer, to respect differences among human beings, and to affirm the entire range of identities that people have. When I began to study gender issues, I learned the path I traveled to achieve my feminist identity is not uncommon. Ignorance, denial, anger, internalization of new values and identities, and transformation to constructive commitment are stages that many individuals go through as they dislodge one identity and perspective on social life and embrace alternate ones.

Features of *Gendered Lives*

Three features distinguish this book and support the views I've just discussed. First, I include **discussion of diverse classes, ethnicities, races, gender identities, and sexual orientations** whenever research is available. For instance, the Exploring Gendered Lives box on page 8 identifies a range of ways in which cultures define gender and sexual identities. Although research on many races, sexual identities, and socioeconomic classes is still limited, I include the research that exists on the range of people who make up our world.

A second feature of this book is **language that aims to include all readers**. I use terms such as *he* and *she* and *women* and *men* in preference to *he, mankind,* and *men*. But inclusive language means more than including women; it also means using language that refuses to go along with cultural marginalization of any group. For instance, I refer to individuals in intimate relationships as *partners* rather than *spouses,* and I generally refer to *committed relationships* rather than *marriages*. I'm not entirely comfortable describing my sweetheart, Robbie, as my *partner*, because that sounds so businesslike. But I'm even less comfortable calling him my *spouse* or *husband*, because not everyone who is in a committed relationship can use those words. The terms *spouse, wife, husband,* and *marriage* exclude many lesbians, gay men, and transsexed, transgendered, and intersexed people because currently there are few places that allow same-sex couples the legal, material, and social legitimacy of marriage. The terms *spouse* and *marriage* also exclude cohabiting heterosexuals who choose not to marry.

A third feature of *Gendered Lives* is inclusion of different perspectives. I present not only research that reflects different views, but also **student voices**. In the pages that follow, you'll meet a lot of students—some like you, some quite different. In many courses on gender and communication, students keep journals or write reflection papers in which they discuss connections between ideas brought forth in their gender and communication classes and in their personal lives. Many of my own students gave me permission to include their reflections in this book. In addition, students at other campuses around the country have written to me in response to previous editions of *Gendered Lives*, and some of their comments appear in this edition. I've tried to return their generosity by including an array of individuals and viewpoints, including ones with which I personally disagree. In fact, including ideas with which I disagree, from both students and scholars, is necessary if this book is to reflect the variety of ideas about gender and communication that circulate in our culture. Hannah, a student from a northeastern college, makes a point in her commentary on this page.

Hannah's comment reflects open-mindedness, which fosters learning. As you read this book, I hope you will think about research findings and students' voices and reflect on how they are similar to or different from your own beliefs and values. I have refrained from evaluating or interpreting the reflections that appear in this book. The students write clearly and eloquently, and I don't want to muffle their voices with my analysis. The student commentaries, my ideas, and your responses to what you read create a tapestry of learning in which we collaboratively explore gender, communication, and culture.

HANNAH

When I was reading Gendered Lives, I had to keep reminding myself that you were presenting information and that not all points were your personal values and beliefs. I didn't agree with all of your statements or the ideas of others, like the students in their commentaries, but I learned a lot about the ways others see gender. I also learned a lot about how I think about gender by seeing what ideas I agreed with and disagreed with.

The **Exploring Gendered Lives** boxes in all chapters highlight important information about gender. These are meant to stimulate thought and go beyond the basic material in the chapter. Some of the Exploring Gendered Lives features include websites you can visit to learn more about particular topics.

Becoming Aware

Reading this book will expand your understanding of gender—how it is shaped and expressed in contexts ranging from the political arena to intimate relationships. The awareness you gain will enhance your insight into yourself and your society.

At the same time, you may feel unsettled as you read this book. If you are a woman, you may find it disturbing to learn the extent to which Western culture (and others) discounts women's experiences and limits their opportunities. I also realize that a number of people reading this book—both women and men—have been raped, sexually abused, sexually harassed, or battered. Some of you have eating disorders; some have suffered job discrimination; some of you have been taunted for not embodying current social expectations for males or females. Reading *Gendered Lives* is likely to stir up these issues. If you don't wish to deal with such difficult issues, then you may choose to forgo or delay study in this area. However, if you are ready to wrestle with serious personal and social matters, then this book should help you understand issues in your life as not only personal but also political. Such issues reflect widespread cultural biases and perspectives that limit us all.

If you are a man, reading this book may increase your awareness of the ways in which cultural views of masculinity constrain your life choices. You may be uncomfortable learning about social expectations for men to succeed, to be self-sufficient, to repress feelings, and to put work ahead of family. You may also be surprised to learn that your maleness benefits you in ways that you may not have noticed, particularly if you are white.

Becoming aware of inequities in social life may lead you to speak out against practices and attitudes that sustain discrimination and disadvantage. Realize that some people will respond negatively if you make thoughtful criticisms of current social attitudes and practices. Women who speak out against inequities and discrimination are sometimes accused of male-bashing. Men who speak out against discrimination against women are sometimes regarded as wimps or as disloyal to men. Such responses reflect an unwillingness to engage in the substance of the criticism. If you want to take an active role in shaping our shared world, you must anticipate struggles with those who are less willing to consider ideas that question familiar perspectives and behaviors.

PATRICK

I don't want to be lumped with all men. I am not sexist; I don't discriminate against women; I believe in gender equality and try to practice it in my relationships with women. It really makes me angry when people bash males as if we are all oppressors or something. I don't oppress women or anyone else, and I don't want to be blamed for unfair things that others do.

In his commentary, Patrick makes an important point when he says he personally doesn't discriminate against women. We need to distinguish between the actions and attitudes of individuals and the social practices and values of our culture. I do not believe that most individual men are bad, oppressive, or sexist. The point is that Western culture as a whole has constructed inequalities between women and men, and these inequalities continue in our era.

The problem, then, is not individual men or women. Rather, it is a social system that accords unequal value and opportunity on the basis of sex, skin color, sexual identity, and other factors. This kind of prejudice diminishes us all. It limits our appreciation of human diversity by falsely defining a very narrow zone of what is good, normal, and worthy of respect. Regardless of whether you are privileged or oppressed by social evaluations of what is normal and good, your study of gender, communication, and culture may be unsettling. If you are seriously disturbed by what you read, you might find it helpful to talk with your instructor or to visit the counseling center at your school.

Why I Wrote This Book

I wrote *Gendered Lives* because I believe that change is needed in how we view and enact gender. I also believe that knowledge can empower you to make more informed choices about your personal identity and our shared world. Since the first edition appeared, I've received many positive responses from students in my classes as well as from students around the nation. I've also received feedback that has helped me rethink and improve the book.

EXPLORING GENDERED LIVES Multicultural Perspectives on Sex and Sexual Orientation

What's feminine? What's masculine? What's gay? It depends on which culture's perspective you take.

- The Agta in the Philippines and the Tini Aborigines in Australia see keen hunting ability as a feminine ideal (Estioko-Griffin & Griffin, 1997).

- In Melanesia, young Sambian boys perform fellatio on adult men. The Sambia believe that swallowing the semen of adult men helps boys grow into healthy adult males (Herdt, 1997).

- The Society Islands of French Polynesia have three sex-based classifications: males, females, and *māhū*. A *māhū* is understood to be half woman, half man. Female-bodied *māhū* behave in masculine ways and have sexual relations with *non-māhū* females; male-bodied *māhū* behave in feminine ways and have sex with *non-māhū* males.

- Berdaches are members of approximately 150 North American societies, many of which are Native Americans. Although berdaches often enact the behaviors of a gender other than that associated with their birth sex, within their societies they are recognized as distinct third and fourth genders (Roscoe, 1993).

- In parts of South America, male homosexuality is defined not by male-to-male sex but by whether a man penetrates (not homosexual) or is penetrated by (homosexual) another man (Almaguer, 1993).

- In addition to male and female, India recognizes a *hijra*, who are female men. *Hijras* sometimes remove their external genitalia to appear more womanlike (Herdt, 1997; Nanda, 2004).

- In addition to males and females, Juchitán in Oaxaca, Mexico, recognizes muxes, who are biological males who, from an early age, identify as females and adopt the roles and practices assigned to females in their community. Muxes are accepted, and many residents of Juchitán believe they have special abilities (Lacey, 2008).

- In Samoa, there is a third gender called the Fa'afafine. It is believed that the first Fa'afafines were in families with only boys, so one of the boys was raised as a girl. Today, Samoans consider Fa'afafine a third gender. Fa'afafines engage in sexual relations almost exclusively with heterosexual males, who are not perceived as homosexual for having sex with Fa'afafines (Bartlett & Vasey, 2006).

I wrote this book because I believe we need to challenge and change persisting inequities in our society. In the chapters that follow, you'll learn about the extent to which gender inequities and discrimination persist and diminish individual and collective life. For instance:

- Is there any way to justify the fact that, each day in the United States, at least four women are killed by their partners or ex-partners?
- Is it fair that men who want to spend time with their families are often evaluated negatively in professional contexts?
- Is it acceptable that a Pakistani court sentenced a woman to be gang-raped because of an offense allegedly committed by her brother?
- Is it right that most of the advances won by women's movements have benefited white, middle-class women more than minority and poor women?
- Is there any reason why women still earn less than men, even when they do the same jobs?
- Is it fair that mothers have an advantage over fathers in gaining custody of children?

If you don't want inequities such as these to continue, read on. Becoming aware of how our culture establishes and communicates inequities is necessary, but that alone will not lead to changes. In fact, concentrating exclusively on what is wrong tends to depress us, which can paralyze impulses toward reform. Awareness of inequities must be coupled with realizing that change is possible.

Through individual action and social movements, many blatant sex inequities have been eliminated. In the 1800s, women weren't allowed to vote. They also had no access to a university education, could not own property if they married, and were barred from participating in most professions. Women can now vote, attend universities, own property, and pursue professional careers. Our culture once defined women as too frail and delicate for hard manual or intellectual work. Today, women pursue careers in business, construction, science, education, politics, and the military.

Views of men, too, have changed. In earlier eras, our society defined manliness in terms of physical strength and bravery. After the Industrial Revolution, the ability to earn a good salary became the social standard of manliness. Today, many men are challenging social definitions of men as income providers and are seeking greater opportunities to participate in personal relationships. Forty years ago, it would have been almost unthinkable for a man to have been a stay-at-home dad. Today, a number of men are stay-at-home dads. In recent decades, sexual harassment, acquaintance rape, and marital rape have been named and recognized as illegal.

Changes such as the ones we've discussed lead many people to think that gender equality has been achieved. Some commentators call our time a "post-feminist era" in which all the issues that feminism focused on have been resolved. Many of my students tell me that gender discrimination is history and that sexism has been overcome.

- They tell me that women now have freedom of choice, but they don't seem to recognize that some health insurance companies will not pay for contraceptives and that there are more barriers to reproductive choice in the United States than in some other countries.

- They tell me that sex discrimination is no longer a problem in the workplace, but they can't explain why women earn less than men for equivalent jobs (2011).
- They cite high-visibility politicians such as Barbara Boxer and Hillary Clinton as evidence that the playing field in politics is now level, but they don't seem to realize that women hold only 17% of seats in the Senate and House of Representatives (Bennetts, 2012).
- They tell me that the United States opposes discrimination against women, but they don't seem disturbed that the United States—along with a few other nations such as Somalia and Sudan—has refused to ratify the United Nations Convention on the Elimination of All Forms of Discrimination Against Women. Jimmy Carter signed the treaty in 1980, and the Senate has yet to act on it.
- They tell me that heterosexual women and men now have egalitarian relationships, but they don't seem concerned that, in two-worker families, women still spend twice as much time as men on housework and child care (Beck, 2011).

As the above listing shows, not all of the inequities based on sex and gender are history. Even in the United States, gender equity has not been fully achieved. In a ranking of measures that affect women's lives (health, education, economics, politics, and justice) the U.S. ranked eighth, behind Iceland, Sweden, Canada, Denmark, Finland, Switzerland, and Norway (Streib, 2011). Although we've made progress toward gender equity, there are more changes to be made before we have a truly level-playing field for everyone.

Communication as the Fulcrum of Change

Communication is the heart of social life and social change. Through communication, we can identify and challenge current cultural views that constrain individuals and create inequities. We also rely on communication to define alternatives to the status quo and to persuade others to share our visions. For example, in the mid-1800s Elizabeth Cady Stanton and other early feminists galvanized support for the women's rights movement through their eloquent speeches. Public discourse sparks and guides collective efforts at political reform.

More recently, we saw students persuade a university to reconsider its policy on transgender students. Hollins University in Virginia is a woman's college, which had a policy stating that any student who had hormone treatment, surgery, or changed her name as part of redefining her sex could no longer attend classes and could not graduate. Students at Hollins expressed concerns about this policy. Explaining why Hollins is revisiting its policy, a researcher who studied how a number of women's colleges perceive and treat transgender students, said, "This current generation of students has a lot of agency and empowerment" (Troop, 2011, p. A19).

Other kinds of communication also instigate change. Perhaps you talk with a friend about gender inequities, and as a result your friend sees injustices he previously had not noticed. Maybe a teacher discusses sexual harassment with his class, and a student is empowered to bring charges against her supervisor who has been harassing her. You talk with your father about ways in which current leave policies disadvantage working mothers, and he persuades his company to revise its policies. Wherever there is change, we find communication. Through your interpersonal, social, and public communication, you can be someone who transforms yourself and the society in which we jointly participate.

Information is the foundation of effectiveness as an agent of change. Before you can define what needs to be different, you must first know what exists and what it implies. Reading *Gendered Lives* will provide you with a great deal of information that you can use to develop knowledgeable stands on gender issues. Then, you can make informed choices about what you believe and about the identity you wish to fashion for yourself. You may decide to change how you define yourself, or you may be satisfied with your identity and the existing gender arrangements in our culture. Either stance is grounded if it is an *informed* choice—but no choice is wise if it is not based on information and serious reflection.

The Challenge of Studying Communication, Gender, and Culture

Studying communication, gender, and culture requires courage because it involves us in perplexing questions about our society and our personal identities. We must be willing to consider new ideas openly and to risk the turmoil of changing values and identities that are familiar to us. Further, with awareness comes responsibility. Once we are informed about gender and communication, we can no longer sit passively back as if they were not our concern. They *are* our concern, both because gender and communication affect each of us directly and because we are part of a collective world. Thus, how we act—or fail to act— influences our shared culture.

Although studying communication, gender, and culture is disturbing, it can be very worthwhile. By questioning constructed inequality, we empower ourselves to do more than unthinkingly reproduce the cultural patterns we grew up with. By communicating to increase others' awareness and challenge unfair cultural practices, we assume active roles in creating personal and collective lives that are fairer, more humane, and infinitely more enriching than what might otherwise be possible.

EXPLORING GENDERED LIVES About "Male-Bashing": Julia—the Author—Comments

Occasionally, a student tells me that *Gendered Lives* "bashes men." This comment puzzles me, because I don't see myself as a male-basher. For 41 years, I've been in a committed relationship with a man I love; I have many male friends and colleagues; and I've done as much to mentor male students as female ones. When I ask students to explain why they think the book bashes men, they tell me it gives more attention to discrimination against women than to discrimination against men and that it points out that some men harm women. They are correct in this observation, but the difference in attention to harms to women and men reflects findings from research rather than any personal views I hold.

Like any scholar, what I write depends largely on available information. Existing research shows that, although both men and women experience violence from intimate partners, 95% of people who are known to be physically abused by romantic partners are women (Haynes, 2009; Johnson, 2006). It would be inaccurate to give equal space to discussion of men who are physically abused by intimate partners. The same is true of sexual harassment: Although members of both sexes are sexually harassed, most victims are female and most perpetrators are male. The only way I could present a gender-balanced discussion of sexual harassment would be by misrepresenting facts.

You should also realize that this book includes more information about men and men's issues than any other textbook for a course in gender and communication. In the chapters that follow, you'll learn about men's movements, pressures men face to succeed and conform to stereotypes of masculinity, and consequences, such as depression, of social perspectives that limit men in the workplace and in personal relationships. You'll also learn that men, like women, can be victims of sexual violence. In addition, you'll discover that men find it stressful to balance work and family, yet men today are contributing more to raising children than previous generations of men.

Research throughout this book shows how social expectations of women and men can restrict all of us. I hope that, as you read this book, you'll perceive the coverage as fair.

GENDER ONLINE

The Organization for Research on Women and Communication (ORWAC) publishes the journal, *Women's Studies in Communication*. You can read back issues of the journal online at ORWAC's site: **http://www.cios.org/www/wommain.htm**

1.   Terms for online searches: "sex, cultural views of," "feminism," "hijras."

REFLECTION AND DISCUSSION

1.   Using my self-description as a guideline, consider how your identity influenced your choice to take this course, as well as how it may affect your perceptions of topics in the book and the course. Have you been privileged or disadvantaged by your race, class, sex, and sexual orientation? How have your privileges and disadvantages affected your opportunities, knowledge of issues, interests, abilities, goals, and so on?

2. What changes do you think are most needed related to communication, gender, and culture?

3. How do you define *feminism?* Write down your definition, and see if it changes during the course of reading this book and taking this class.

4. Interview two people who are from non-Western cultures. Ask them to explain what it means to be a man (or manly or masculine) and what it means to be a woman (or womanly or feminine) in their cultures. How do their cultures' definitions of gender cohere with and depart from those in the United States? Ask them what they find most interesting or surprising about American men and women.

RECOMMENDED RESOURCES

1. Peggy McIntosh. (2007). White Privilege: Unpacking the Invisible Knapsack. In P. Andersen and P. H. Collins (Eds.), *Race, Class, & Gender*, 6th ed. (pp. 98–102). Belmont, CA: Thomson-Cengage. This is a classic article that raises awareness of privileges many people enjoy without being conscious of them.

2. Megan Seely. (2007). The F-Word. Introduction to *Fight Like a Girl* (pp. 1–14). New York: New York University Press. Seely is a young woman who asks why so many of her peers say, "I'm not a feminist, but...."

3. Allan Johnson. (2006). *Privilege, Power, and Difference*, 2nd ed. New York: McGraw-Hill. This is an engaging and accessible introduction to thinking about inequalities and how they harm all of us, including those who seem to benefit from them.

1

The Study of Communication, Gender, and Culture

Knowledge Challenge:

- How many sexes are there?
- Do all males have the same sex chromosomes?
- Are transgender people attracted to members of their sex or the other sex?

If you watch TV talk shows, you'll see guests discussing gender and communication. Go to a bookstore, and you'll find dozens of popular advice books that promise to help you communicate better with the "opposite sex." Watch *America's Next Top Model*, and you're likely to see a transsexual contestant, such as Iris on the 11th season. Visit YouTube and you'll see videos that comment on gender and gender relations. Watch music videos and you'll see mini-dramas about gender dynamics in relationships such as in Beyonce's "If I Were a Man." The general public's fascination with gender and communication is mirrored by college students' interest. Around the United States and in other countries, many campuses cannot meet the student demand for courses on gender and communication.

In this chapter, we will consider how learning about relationships among gender, communication, and culture can empower you personally and professionally. Then, we will discuss key concepts and vocabulary that form the framework of this book.

Communication, Gender, and Culture as an Area of Study

Had you attended college in the early- to mid-1980s, you would not have found a textbook like this one, and it's highly unlikely you could have found a course such as the one in which you're now enrolled. Today, most colleges and universities offer courses on gender.

Research on Gender, Communication, and Culture

A major reason for the growth of courses in gender, communication, and culture is that researchers have created a knowledge base of thousands of articles and books to support academic courses (Dow & Wood, 2006). In *Gendered Lives*, you'll encounter much of this research on the profound connections among gender, communication, and culture.

Research on gender is conducted by scholars in multiple fields including anthropology, communication, history, neuroscience, philosophy, psychology, and sociology. To give you an understanding of the research that informs the field of gender and this book, I'll briefly describe different research methods used by scholars.

Quantitative research methods[1] gather data that can be quantified and analyze the data to draw conclusions. These methods are most closely associated with the social sciences. Three of the more common quantitative methods are descriptive statistics, surveys, and experiments. Descriptive statistics describe populations, proportions, and frequencies. They answer questions such as: How often do women and men interrupt in conversations? How much are men and women in the same professional positions paid?

Surveys, which may be written or oral (interviews), ask people to report their feelings, thoughts, experiences, and so forth. Surveys could ask women and men what they do with close friends or what kinds of online activities they prefer.

Experiments are controlled studies that manipulate one thing (called an independent variable) to determine how it affects another thing (called a dependent variable). Experiments can determine what happens to women's self-esteem when they look at fashion magazines and whether different teaching methods affect how much boys and girls learn.

Qualitative research methods, sometimes called interpretive methods, aim to understand the meaning of experiences that cannot be quantified. Two popular qualitative methods are textual analysis and ethnography. As the name implies, textual analysis involves describing communication texts, which may be written, oral, or nonverbal. Textual analyses have illuminated the meaning of the *Declaration of Sentiments* (the speech given at the first Women's Rights Convention) and compared political speeches of male and female figures.

Ethnography relies on extensive observation of human activity to discover what things mean to people. Ethnographic study has provided detailed descriptions

---

[1]Boldface terms appear at the glossary at the end of this book.

of different culture's views of genders and of U.S. women's and men's flirting behaviors.

Critical research methods identify and contest power dynamics that create inequities in social life. Critical research has given us insight into ways in which organizational structures and practices create work environments that women and minorities perceive as unwelcoming.

Mixed research methods are exactly what the name implies—a combination of two or more of the methods described above. For example, a scholar might document the frequency (descriptive statistic) of men's and women's smiling in social situations and then interview men and women (qualitative method) to learn why they smile.

Reasons to Learn about Communication, Gender, and Culture

Learning about relationships among communication, gender, and culture serves three important goals. First, it enhances your appreciation of complex ways in which cultural values and practices influence your views of masculinity and femininity and men and women. Differences between feminine and masculine communication often show up when men and women employ different approaches to problem-solving, when male and female supervisors differ in how direct and assertive they are, and when female and male political candidates say similar things but the public evaluates them differently. You can increase your understanding of personal, social, and professional life by learning about cultural views of gender.

Second, studying gender, communication, and culture will enhance insight into your own gender, both as it is now and as it might be if you choose to remake it. You will become more aware of ways cultural expectations of gender are communicated to you, which empowers you to think more critically about the extent to which you wish to identify with cultural prescriptions for gender.

Third, studying communication, gender, and culture should strengthen your effectiveness as a communicator. Learning about general differences in women's and men's communication will enlarge your ability to appreciate the validity of diverse communication styles. This allows you to understand and adapt to ways of communicating that may differ from your own. In addition, you will learn

EXPLORING GENDERED LIVES *Journals That Feature Research on Gender and Communication*

Communication Education	*Journal of Men's Studies*
Communication Monographs	*Journal of Social & Personal*
Communication Studies	*Relationships*
Critical Cultural Studies	*Men and Masculinities*
Gender and Society	*Sex Roles*
Journal of Applied Communication	*Sexuality and Culture*
Research	*Signs*
Journal of Cross-Cultural Research	*Women and Language*
Journal of Gender, Culture & Health	*Women's Studies in Communication*

how your own communication does or doesn't conform to prevailing cultural pre-scriptions for gender, and this allows you to make informed choices about how you want to communicate in the future.

Gender in a Transitional Era

Because cultural views of gender are in flux, we may be perplexed or conflicted about where we stand on issues about which people in earlier eras had more clear-cut views.

TRACY

The issue of women in combat really troubles me. I have a son who is 17 and a daughter who is 15. I don't want either of them in combat, but I've always known my son could be in combat. Would I argue that my son should be and my daughter shouldn't be? That's like saying I value her life more than his. I can't say that.

Confusing Attitudes

You probably don't subscribe to your grandparents' ideals of manhood and wom-anhood. You may believe that both women and men should be able to pursue careers and that both should be involved in homemaking and parenting. You are probably not surprised when a woman knows how to change a tire or when a man is a good cook. Yet, if you're like most of your peers, there are also a number of gender issues about which you feel conflicted.

- You may think that both parents should participate in child rearing, yet also assume that the mother, not the father, should stop working to be the primary caregiver during the early years of children's lives.
- You may support equal opportunity but still think that colleges and universities should be allowed to offer more scholarships to male athletes.
- You may believe that everyone has a right to define their own identity, but feel uneasy when you learn your roommate is transsexual.
- You may think it doesn't matter whether a man or woman in a heterosexual couple earns more, but want the man in your own relationship to be the primary wage earner.

When we grapple with issues like these, we realize that our attitudes aren't always clear, even to ourselves. On one level, many of us think that women and men are equal in most respects. Yet, on another level, we may hold some very traditional values and beliefs. Many of us no longer accept all traditional views, yet we haven't become comfortable with alternative views and their implications for our own identities and relationships. This makes our lives and our relationships interesting, unsettling—and sometimes very frustrating.

MICHAEL

The other day in class, we were talking about whether women should have combat duty. I'm really uncomfortable with where I stand on this, since I think one way, but I feel another. I do think women should have to serve just as much as men do. I've never thought it was right that they didn't have to fight. And I think women are just as competent as men at most things and could probably be good soldiers. But then when I think about my mom or my sister or my girlfriend being in the trenches, having to kill other people, maybe being a prisoner who is tortured and assaulted, I just feel that's wrong. It doesn't seem right for women to be involved in killing when they're the ones who give life. Then, too, I want to protect my girlfriend and sister and mom from the ugliness and danger of war.

But then, this other part of me says, "Hey, guy, you know that kind of protectiveness is a form of chauvinism." I just don't know where I stand on this except that I'm glad I don't have to decide whether to send women into combat!

Differences between Women and Men

Are women and men really as different as pop psychologists would have us believe? Certainly, there are some differences between the sexes. There is also substantial variation within each sex as a result of diversity in experience, heredity, sexual orientation, race, culture, economic class, and other factors. And there are many similarities between women and men—ways in which the two sexes are more alike than different.

KATHERINE

I am really skeptical of books that describe women and men as "opposite" sexes. They focus on a few ways that most women and most men are different. They totally ignore all of the ways that women and men are alike. Even worse is that they act like all women are the same and all men are the same. People are just such individuals that you can't sum them up as "man" or "woman."

Katherine's commentary is important. Terms such as *women* and *men* are troublesome because they imply that all women can be grouped into one category and all men can be grouped into another and different category. When we say, "Women's communication is more personal than men's," the statement is true of most, but not all, women and men. Certainly some women don't engage in much personal talk, and some men do. Many factors, including race, economic class, and sexual identity, shape how specific women and specific men communicate (Zinn, Hondagneu-Sotelo, & Messner, 2007).

Changing Names—Not Equal Opportunity

Although most people aren't surprised when a woman keeps her birth name when she marries, few men consider changing their names upon marrying. And those who do may be in for a surprise, as Elizabeth Batton and Garrett Sorenson discovered. The two New Yorkers each wanted to take the other's last name. Elizabeth had no problem changing her surname to Sorenson—she simply put her new name on the marriage certificate. For Garrett, changing names was not so easy. New York, like most states, assumes that men will not change their names when they marry. To do so, Garrett had to petition the court, advertise in a newspaper, and pay a significant sum in legal fees (Porter, 2007).

Thinking and speaking as if there is some stable, distinct essence that defines a phenomenon is referred to as **essentializing**, the tendency to reduce something or someone to certain characteristics that we assume are essential to its nature and present in every member of a category. When we essentialize, we mistakenly assume that all members of a sex are alike in key respects. Essentializing obscures the range of characteristics possessed by individual women and men and obscures differences among members of each sex. In this book, we will discuss generalizations about women and men, but this does not imply any essential qualities possessed by all members of a sex.

In these opening pages, I've used the words *gender* and *sex* several times, but we haven't yet defined them. The next section of this chapter provides definitions to give us a shared understanding of key concepts that inform the chapters that follow.

Relationships among Gender, Culture, and Communication

When asked to discuss a particular aspect of nature, John Muir, founder of the Sierra Club, said he could not discuss any single part of the natural world in isolation. He noted that each part is "hitched to the universe," meaning that every part of nature is connected to all other parts. Likewise, sex, gender, culture, and communication are hitched to the whole universe. We cannot really understand any one of them without grasping a good deal about the others.

Sex

Although many people use the terms *gender* and *sex* interchangeably, they have distinct meanings. **Sex** is a designation based on biology, whereas **gender** is socially constructed and expressed. In most cases, sex and gender go together; most men are primarily masculine, and most women are feminine. In some cases, however, a male expresses himself more femininely than most men, or a woman expresses herself in more masculine ways than most women. Sex and gender are inconsistent for transgendered individuals, who have the biological characteristics of one sex

Grown-Up Tomboys

University of Southern California professor Judith "Jack" Halberstam says many girls are tomboys because "a lot of the really fun activities get allocated to men. That's where the action is" (Williams, 2012, p. B13). But, says Halberstam, "tomboyism is tolerated as long as the child remains prepubescent; as soon as puberty begins, however, the full force of gender conformity descends on the girl" (1998, p. 6). Wanting to challenge the pressure for girls to become feminine, Halberstam (1998, 2011, 2012) argues that we have to separate masculinity from male bodies—and, by extension, femininity from female bodies. For Halberstam, the goal is to learn to think about female masculinity—and, by extension, male femininity. And don't make the mistake of equating masculine men with lesbians or transgender people. If you follow Halberstam's logic, those linkages are just as constructed and questionable as the ones between masculinity and male and femininity and female.

but identify as the other sex. Because sex is the less complex concept, we'll explain it first, and then discuss gender and sexuality.

We generally classify people as male or female based on external genitalia (penis and testes in males, clitoris and vagina in females) and internal sex organs (ovaries and uterus in females, prostate gland in males). Genitalia and other sex markers are determined by chromosomes. In most cases, human development is guided by 23 sets of chromosomes, one of which determines sex. Usually chromosomes occur in pairs. The presence or absence of a Y chromosome usually determines whether a fetus will develop into what we recognize as male or female. Thus, people labeled female usually have XX sex chromosomes.

Perhaps you noticed that I qualified discussion of genetic markers of sex by using terms such as "usually" and "in most cases." That's because there are variations. For every 10,000 individuals, 20 do not have XX or XY sex chromosomes (Ellis & Eriksen, 2002; Harper, 2007). This means that of the approximately 300 million individuals in the United States today, roughly 600,000 do not have XX or XY sex chromosomes.

There are several known variations. Some people have an XO chromosomal pair. In other cases, there are three sex chromosomes: XXX, XXY, or XYY (Blackless, Charuvastra, Derryek, Fausto-Sterling, Lauzanne, & Lee, 2000). Occasionally, an individual has some XY cells and some XX cells (Gorman & Cole, 2004).

The sex chromosomes in all fetuses (and people) have at least one X chromosome because it carries genes essential to life (Jegalian & Lahn, 2001). Because males typically have only a single X chromosome, they are more vulnerable to a number of X-linked recessive conditions than are females, who have two X chromosomes and are unlikely to have an X-linked recessive condition on both. As long as there is a single Y chromosome, a fetus will develop into what we generally classify as male.

Some children are born with some biological characteristics of each sex. Traditionally, people whose internal and external genitalia are inconsistent were called **hermaphrodites**, a term from Greek mythology. According to the myth, the god Hermes and the goddess Aphrodite had a son whom they named Hermaphroditos. When the young woman Salmacis saw Hermaphroditos, she immediately fell in love and begged the gods to join her with him so that they would never be apart.

Social Views of Intersexuality

For many years, infants who were born with ambiguous genitals routinely underwent "normalizing surgery" to reconstruct genitals to be more consistently male or female (Crouch, 1998; Lorber, 2001).

But is it possible that intersexed people don't need to be "fixed"? A number of scholars, scientists, doctors, and laypeople advocate acceptance of intersexuality (Gorman & Cole, 2004; Preves, 2004; Rosenberg, 2007). Adult intersexuals within the transgender movement believe that being intersexed is not a problem but just another form of human identity. In other words, maybe there are multiple—not just two—sexes and genders.

Intersexuality is not new. Deborah Rudacille (2006) found records from 1629 describing Thomas Hall, who lived in the Jamestown settlement and claimed to be both a man and a woman. A number of groups, including several Native American tribes, historically recognized and celebrated "two spirit" people, who were both male and female.

The Intersex Society of North America (ISNA) has three primary missions: (1) to affirm a positive identity for intersexed people; (2) to change social attitudes toward intersexuality; and (3) to stop "normalizing surgery."

Do you think intersexed individuals are a distinct sex?

Visit the website at **http://www.isna.org**. Another site that provides information on intersexed and transgendered people is **http://www.itpeople.org**.

Granting Salmacis's wish, the gods joined them into a single body that was both male and female. Today, the term **intersexed** is preferred by people who have biological qualities of each sex.

Sexual development is also influenced by hormones. When pregnancy proceeds routinely, fetuses with a Y chromosome are bathed in androgens that ensure development of male sex organs, and fetuses without a Y chromosome receive fewer androgens, so female sex organs develop. In some cases, however, a genetically female fetus (XX) is exposed to excessive progesterone and may not develop the usual female genitalia. The opposite is also true: If a male fetus is deprived of progesterone, his male genitalia may not develop, and he may appear physically female (Pinsky, Erickson, & Schimke, 1999).

The influence of hormones does not end at birth. They continue to affect our development by determining whether we will menstruate, how much body hair we will have and where it will grow, how much fat and muscle tissue we will develop, and so forth. Because male fetuses receive greater amounts of hormones than female fetuses, they are generally more sensitive than females to hormonal activity, especially during puberty (Tavris, 1992).

Biology *influences* how we develop, but it doesn't absolutely *determine* behavior, personality, and so on. Nor does biology stipulate the meaning that members of a culture assign to sex. This moves us into discussion of a second concept: gender.

Gender

Gender is a classification that society makes, and, for most people, it endures throughout their lives. Related to gender is the concept of **gender identity**, which is a personal perception of one's sex. Unlike sex, gender is neither innate nor stable. Most of us are born male or female (sex), but we have to learn to act in masculine and/or feminine ways (gender). Gender varies across cultures, over time within a given culture, over the course of individuals' life spans, and in relation to the other gender. We'll elaborate these aspects of gender.

Consider current meanings of masculinity and femininity in America. To be masculine is to be strong, ambitious, successful, rational, and emotionally controlled. Although these requirements are less rigid than they were in earlier eras, they remain largely intact. Those we regard as "real men" still don't cry in public, and "real men" are successful and powerful in their professional and public lives (Kimmel, 2000a, 2000b, 2005; Martin & Finn, 2010).

Femininity in our era is also relatively consistent with earlier views, although there is increasing latitude in what is considered appropriate for women. To be feminine is to be physically attractive, emotionally expressive, nurturing, interested in aesthetics, and concerned with people and relationships (Martin & Finn, 2010). Acting feminine means not outdoing men (especially partners) or putting personal needs ahead of others. "Real women" still look good, adore children, and care about homemaking.

Gender is learned. From infancy on, we are encouraged to embody the gender that society prescribes for us. Young girls are often cautioned, "Don't be selfish— share with others" and "Be careful—don't hurt yourself." They are praised for looking pretty, taking care of others (including dolls), and being nice. Young boys, in contrast, are more likely to be admonished, "Don't be a sissy," "Go after what you want," and "Don't cry." They are rewarded for strength, independence, and success, particularly in competitive arenas.

BISHETTA

I remember when I was very little, maybe 5 or so. My brother and I were playing outside in the garden, and Mom saw us. Both of us were coated with dirt—our clothes, our skin, everything.

Mom came up to the edge of the garden and shouted, "Bishetta, you get out of that garden right now. Just look at you. Now, what do you think folks will think of a dirty little girl? You don't want people to think you're not a lady, do you?" She didn't say a word to my brother, who was just as dirty.

Although individuals learn gender and embody it, gender is not strictly personal. Rather, gender grows out of cultural ideas that stipulate the social *meaning* and *expectation* of each sex. Because our society's views of gender permeate public and private life, we tend to see them as normal, natural, and right. When society constantly represents women and men in particular ways, it is difficult to imagine that masculinity and femininity could be defined differently. But, as we will see, gender varies widely across cultures and history.

Conventional views of both sex and gender are challenged by people who define themselves as transgendered, trans or genderqueer (Connell, 2010; Hirschfeld & Wolf, 2005; Shepard, 2008; Sloop, 2004, 2006). Although some transgender people identify with the sex other than the one that they were assigned at birth, others reject the binary categories of male and female, and still others self-identify as a third gender or a unique blending of femininity and masculinity (Ellis & Eriksen, 2002) or describe themselves as being without gender. In Chapter 2, we'll look more closely at queer theory, which gives insight into the entire range of gender identities and ways of performing gender.

Meanings of gender are also changed by personal communication. Role models, for instance, provide individuals with visible alternatives to traditional views. We also influence ideas about gender as we interact with friends. When one woman encourages another to confront her supervisor about inequitable treatment, she may instigate change in what her friend sees as appropriate behavior for women. Similarly, when one man tells another man that time with his family is a top priority, his friend may rethink, and perhaps change, his own views of men's roles. When one person announces that she or he is transgendered, that person may make it easier for others whose sex or gender identity doesn't fit neatly into conventional social categories. As these examples indicate, there is reciprocal influence between communication and cultural views of gender.

BOB

What I always thought was unfair in my family was the way my folks responded to failures my sisters and I had. Like once my sister Maryellen tried out for cheerleader, and she wasn't picked. So she was crying and upset, and Mom was telling her that it was okay and that she was a good person, and everyone knew that and that winning wasn't everything. And when Dad came home he said the same things—telling her she was okay even if she wasn't picked. But when I didn't make the junior varsity football team, Dad went bonkers! He asked me what had gone wrong. I told him nothing, that other guys were just better than I had been. But he'd have none of that. He told me I couldn't give up and had to work harder, and he expected me to make the team next season. He even offered to hire a coach for me. It just wasn't okay for me not to succeed.

A good example of the way we remake the meaning of gender is the concept of androgyny. In the 1970s, researchers coined the word **androgyny** by combining the Greek word *aner* or *andros*, which means "man," and the Greek word *gyne*, which means "woman." Androgynous individuals embody qualities that Western culture considers both feminine and masculine. For example, androgynous women and men are both nurturing and assertive, both strong and sensitive. As Miguel points out in his commentary, there is value in the full range of human qualities—those the culture labels feminine and those it labels masculine.

MIGUEL

I like to be strong and to stand up for myself and what I think, but I would not want to be only that. I am also sensitive to other people and how they feel. There are times to be hard and times to be softer; there are times to be strong and times to let others be strong.

To realize the arbitrariness of the meanings of gender, we need only to consider different cultures' views of masculinity and femininity. Many years ago, anthropologist Margaret Mead (1935/1968) reported three distinct gender patterns in the New Guinea societies she studied. Among Arapesh people, both women and men conformed closely to what we consider feminine behavior. Both were passive, peaceful, and deferential, and both nurtured others, especially young children. The Mundugumor tribe socialized both women and men to be aggressive, independent, and competitive. Mothers were not nurturing and spent very little time with newborn babies, weaning them early instead. Within the Tchambuli society, genders were the reverse of current ones in America: Women were domineering and sexually aggressive, whereas men were considered delicate and taught to wear decorative clothes and curl their hair so they would be attractive to women.

Body ideals for women provide another example of the constructed and arbitrary character of gender. Currently, Western culture regards thinness as desirable in women. Yet in the 1950s, fuller-figured women exemplified femininity and sexiness. Even today, some cultures regard heavier women as particularly beautiful and desirable. For example, in the Islamic Republic of Mauritania (sub-Saharan Africa), young girls are often overfed so that they become obese and thereby signify their family's wealth and status (LaFraniere, 2007).

Some cultures view gender as changeable, so someone born male may choose to live and be regarded as female and vice versa. In other societies, notably some Native American groups, more than two genders are recognized and celebrated (Brown, 1997; Nanda, 2004). In the United States, gender varies across racial-ethnic groups.

Even within a single culture or social group, the meaning of gender varies over time. Prior to the Industrial Revolution, men and women worked together to raise crops or run businesses, and both were involved in homemaking and child rearing. The Industrial Revolution gave rise to factories and to paid labor outside the home. With this came a division of life into separate spheres of work and home. As men took jobs outside the home, masculinity was redefined as earning income; as women increasingly assumed responsibility for family life, femininity was redefined as nurturing, depending on men for income, and making a good home (Cancian, 1989; Risman & Godwin, 2001). In her commentary, Emma, a 58-year-old part-time student, reflects on changes in how women see themselves.

EMMA

In my day, women were a lot different than they are today. We were quieter, and we put other people ahead of ourselves. We knew our place, and we didn't try to be equal with men. Today's women are very different. Some of the younger women in my classes put their careers ahead of marriage, some don't want children, and many think they should be as much the head of a family as the man. Sometimes, I feel they are all wrong in what they want and how they are, but I have to admit that a part of me envies them the options and opportunities I never had.

The meaning of gender also changes over the course of an individual's lifetime (Kimmel, 2003). Being masculine at 10 may mean being good at soccer or baseball. At 35, however, most men place high priority on a good job as a measure of their masculinity. Similarly, what a 10-year-old girl considers feminine may be bows in her hair, but a 35-year-old woman may define femininity as succeeding in her career and having children.

Finally, gender is a relational concept because femininity and masculinity make sense in relation to each other. As meanings of one gender change, so do meanings of the other.

Let's summarize this discussion of gender. We have noted that gender is the meanings that a society constructs and confers on biological sex. We've also seen that the meaning of gender varies across cultures and over time in particular cultures. This reminds us that, even though what our society defines as feminine and masculine may seem natural to us, there is nothing necessary or innate about any particular meaning for any gender. This suggests that we have more choice than we sometimes realize in how we enact gender in our lives.

Beyond Sex and Gender

Western culture classifies people by sex (male or female), gender (masculine or feminine), and sexual orientation (heterosexual, gay, lesbian, bisexual). Further, our society assumes connections between these categories such that male, masculine, and heterosexual are linked and female, feminine, and heterosexual are linked (Glover & Kaplan, 2009; Jagger, 2008).

Most people match social expectations for a neat linkage among sex, gender, and sexual orientation. For example, most males identify as male, act in masculine ways, and are sexually and emotionally attracted to females. Yet the three don't always go together. Think of these departures from the normalized pattern in our culture:

- A man who has a feminine gender identity
- A woman who has a masculine gender identity
- A man who behaves in feminine ways and is sexually attracted to women
- A woman who behaves in masculine ways and is sexually attracted to men
- A man who behaves in masculine ways and is sexually attracted to men
- A woman who behaves in feminine ways and is attracted to other women

Sexual orientation refers to a person's preferences for romantic and sexual partners. People who have heterosexual orientations are romantically and sexually attracted to members of the other sex while gays and lesbians are attracted to members of their own sex. Bisexuals are attracted to members of both sexes.

The term **cis** functions as a prefix—cisgendered, cisman, ciswoman—that designates a person who fits conventional categories. For instance a biological woman who identifies as female and feminine and who is attracted to men would be labeled cisgendered or ciswoman. "Cis" means "on the same side of." So people who stay on the side of the gender identity assigned at birth are cis. The use of this term disrupts the assumption that saying "woman" connotes someone who is female, feminine, and heterosexual. *Cis* calls attention to the category that society considers normal just as *gay* and *trans* call attention to those categories.

Changing views of gender and sex are evident in the increasing recognition of individuals who don't fit orthodox definitions of male or female, masculine or feminine. We've already noted that intersexed individuals have biological characteristics of both males and females. In addition, transgendered and transsexed individuals challenge the naturalness and permanence of biological sex. Although trans or transgender is sometimes used to refer to all gender nonconforming people, some researchers distinguish between transgender and transsexual. **Transgender** refers to individuals who feel that their biologically assigned sex doesn't match their true sexual identity—they are women, despite having male bodies, or men, despite having female bodies (Hines, 2006; Looy & Bouma, 2005; Tyre & Scelfo, 2006).

Transsexual refers to individuals who have had surgery and/or hormonal treatments to make their bodies more closely match the sex with which they identify. Researchers estimate that at least 1 in every 2,500 adult males in the United States has had sexual reassignment surgery (SRS) and has become a postoperative woman (Olyslager & Conway, 2007).

After surgery, transsexuals may describe themselves as *post-transition males to females* (MTF) or *post-transition females to males* (FTM). For example, 59-year-old Dr. Wally Bacon left his campus in Nebraska in the spring of 2005 and returned in the fall of 2005 as Dr. Meredith Bacon. Since making that decision, Dr. Bacon has had a number of surgeries so that her body conforms to her self-definition (Wilson, 2005). In 2012, Jenna Talackova, who was born male and underwent a sex change, was allowed to compete for Canada's spot in the Miss Universe pageant.

SEAN

In high school my closest friend was Megean. In our junior year she tried to kill herself and nobody knew why because she was pretty and popular and smart—the "girl who had everything." Later she told me that she had never felt she was female, that she'd always felt she was a guy and just didn't think she could keep going if she had to live as a girl. If I hadn't been so close to Megean, I would have found it totally weird, but we were close—still are, in fact, although now he's Mark—and what I mainly felt was sad that somebody I loved was so unhappy. He's a much happier person now that he's Mark.

EXPLORING GENDERED LIVES *Trans Athletes*

In 2011, the NCAA Executive Committee issued a policy that is intended to allow student-athletes to participate in athletics as the sex with which they identify. To preserve fairness, the NCAA specified that student-athletes' use of hormone therapy is consistent with current medical standards, which state:

• "A trans male (female to male) student-athlete who has received a medical exception for treatment with testosterone for gender transition may compete on a men's team but is no longer eligible to compete on a

women's team without changing the team status to a mixed team. A mixed team is eligible only for men's championships.

• "A trans female (male to female) student-athlete being treated with testosterone suppression medication for gender transition may continue to compete on a men's team but may not compete on a women's team without changing it to a mixed team status until completing one calendar year of documented testosterone-suppression treatment" (Lawrence, 2011).

Sexual orientation does not necessarily change just because a person transitions from one sex to another. Some transsexuals stay in their marriages or committed relationships after transitioning. An example of this can be found in Helen Boyd's 2007 book, *Not the Man I Married: My Life with a Transgender Husband.*

Deirdre (formerly Donald) McCloskey is a professor of economics. According to her, surgery and hormones changed her sex, but she had to learn gender, had to learn to be feminine. She studied all of the small actions—gestures, facial expressions, postures—that women use and practiced them until they were second nature to her. Reflecting on this, McCloskey (1999) wrote that gender is "an accretion of

EXPLORING GENDERED LIVES *Transgender Activism on Campus*

If Luke Woodward, a student at Brown University, had written a paper entitled "What I Did Last Summer" in 2003, he would have written that he had surgery to minimize the breasts that were incompatible with his self-identity as a man. Meanwhile, Paige Kruza, who attends Wesleyan University, is biologically female but does not identify as female. Paige prefers that people use transgender pronouns such as ze instead of *he* or *she* to refer to Paige (Bernstein, 2004). And Mykell Miller, a student at Northwestern who is biologically female but identifies as male, claims that not all men were born with male bodies (Rosenberg, 2007).

Recognition of transgendered and transsexed people calls for some

changes. In 2003, students at Smith College voted to eliminate female pronouns in the student constitution because some students who were biologically female did not identify as female. At Wesleyan, members of what had been the Women's Rugby team voted to delete the word *Women's* from its name so that students who are biologically female but who do not identify as female could be comfortable wearing the team sweatshirts. Wesleyan's student health services has replaced the boxes "M" and "F" that students once checked with the request, "Describe your gender identity history" (Bernstein, 2004).

To what extent does your campus recognize and accommodate transgender students?

learned habits, learned so well that they feel like external conditions, merely the way things are. It is a shell made by the snail and then confining it" (pp. 83–84). Because they have experience in being and being seen as more than one sex, transsexuals often gain keen insight into gendered dynamics in cultural life. For example, Ben Barres (2006), an FTM transgendered person wryly commented, "By far the main difference that I have noticed is that people who don't know I am transgendered (female to male) treat me with much more respect. I can even complete a whole sentence without being interrupted by a man" (p. 135).

In 2008 Thomas Beatie attracted a lot of attention when he gave birth to a girl; he later gave birth to a second child. You read the sentence right: *He* gave birth and he did so through vaginal delivery. How can this be? Thomas is a transgender FTM who is legally male and legally married to a woman named Nancy. Thomas's sex reassignment surgery was limited to chest reconstruction and testosterone therapy, but he kept his reproductive organs. Nancy had had a hysterectomy, so when she and Thomas wanted a child, they decided that Thomas would carry it (Beatie, 2008). Thomas later carried and gave birth to a second child. In Thomas's case we have a person whom the law defines as male relying on female sex organs to carry

Jennifer Finney Boylan was born James Richard Boylan but later had surgery to become female.

and deliver a baby. People like Thomas, who is not the first FTM to give birth, prove that the links between sex, gender, and sexual orientation are not always clear, stable, or absolute.

Before leaving this discussion, we need to discuss one other aspect of gender and sexual identity. Cross-dressers, or transvestites, enjoy wearing clothing of the other sex. A **transvestite** may wear just one or two articles of clothing associated with the other sex or may dress completely, from underwear to outerwear and accessories, in the other sex's clothing. Some cross-dressers wear the other sex's clothes to express gender identities inconsistent with their sex. Some find the novelty of cross-dressing fun or pleasurable; some find it sexually arousing to wear clothes generally worn by the other sex. The great majority of cross-dressers are biological, heterosexual males (Docter & Prince, 1997).

JOSH

I don't think there really is a category of transpeople. To me, it seems like if someone who is male is attracted to other men, he's gay. When men say they are trans and are really female in their identity and they then get together with other men, maybe they're just trying to avoid being seen as gay.

SLOAN

It's great that some people finally realize there are more than two sexes and two genders. Ever since I came to college, I found lots of people like me who don't identify as exactly male or female and not as straight or gay. There is so much gray area in between the dualities society has imposed.

Transgendered, transsexed, and intersexed people challenge the idea that sex and gender are dualities—that is, that male and female, masculine and feminine are opposite, stable, and the only two possibilities. Transpeople also disrupt society's assumption that sex, gender, and sexual orientation correlate in consistent and natural ways. Unlike what Josh says in his commentary, not all transsexuals are attracted to people of their own biological sex. An FTM or MTF person may be attracted to men or women. The links between sex, gender, and sexual orientation are not nearly as clear-cut as we sometimes believe.

Culture

A **culture** is made up of structures (also called institutions) and practices (also called activities) that reflect and uphold a particular social order. They do this by defining certain social groups, values, expectations, meanings, and patterns of behavior as natural and good and others as unnatural, bad, or wrong. Because gender is central to cultural life, society's views of gender are reflected in and promoted by a range of social structures and practices.

One of the primary practices that structures society is communication. We are surrounded by communication that announces social views of gender and seeks to persuade us that these are natural, correct ways for men and women to be and to behave. We open a magazine and see a beautiful, thin woman waiting on a man who looks successful and in charge; we turn on our television and see commercials showing women cleaning toilet bowls and kitchen floors and men going for the gusto after a pickup basketball game; we meet with a group of people on a volunteer project, and one of the men assumes leadership; we check out a new video game and don't even notice that it, like many videogames, includes women characters who are prostitutes and are supposed to be abused by game players; a working woman receives maternity leave, but her husband cannot get paternity leave. Each of these practices communicates our society's views of gender.

Consider additional examples of cultural practices that uphold Western views of gender. Although no longer universal, the custom whereby a woman gives up her name and takes her husband's on marriage still prevails. It signifies that a woman is defined by her relationship to a man but a man is not equivalently defined by his relationship with a woman. Within families, too, numerous practices reinforce social views of gender. Parents routinely allow sons greater freedom than they grant daughters, a practice that encourages males to be more independent. Daughters, much more than sons, are taught to do housework and care for younger siblings, thus reinforcing the idea that women are supposed to be concerned with home and family.

Now think about social structures, or institutions, which uphold gender ideology. One institution is the judicial system. Men's parental rights are abridged by judicial views of women as the primary caretakers of children who should have custody of children if divorce occurs. Thus, it is difficult for a father to gain child custody even when he might be the better parent or might be in a better situation to raise children.

In many respects Western culture, as well as many other cultures, is **patriarchal**. The word patriarchy means "rule by the fathers." In a patriarchal culture, the ideology, structures, and practices were created by men. Because America was defined by men, historically it reflected the perspectives and priorities of men more than those of women. For example, it would be consistent with men's interests to consider women property, which was the case early in America's life. Similarly, from men's point of view laws against marital rape would not be desirable. Today, some of the patriarchal tendencies and practices of American culture have been tempered.

DYMPNA

In 1974, I traveled to New York for my college education.... I'm a member of the Ibo tribe of Nigeria, and although I've lived in the United States most of my adult life, my consciousness remains fixed on the time and place of my upbringing.... When I left Nigeria at 18, I had no doubts about who and what I was. I was a woman. I was only a woman.... My role was to be a great asset to my husband.... I was, after all, raised within the context of child brides, polygamy, clitorectomies and arranged marriages.... I've struggled daily with how best to raise my daughter. Every decision involving Delia is a tug of war between Ibo and American traditions (Ugwu-Oju, 2000).

A culture's structures and practices create and sustain perspectives on what is normal and right for women and men. Because messages that reinforce cultural views of gender pervade our daily lives, most of us seldom pause to reflect on whether they are as natural as they have been made to seem. Like the air we breathe, they so continuously surround us that we tend not to notice them. Learning to reflect on cultural prescriptions for gender (and other matters) empowers you as an individual. It increases your freedom to choose your own courses of action and identity by enlarging your awareness of the arbitrary and not always desirable nature of cultural expectations.

Communication

The fourth key term we will discuss is **communication**. Communication is a dynamic, systemic process in which two levels of meanings are created and reflected in human interaction with symbols. To understand this rather complicated definition, we will focus on one part of it at a time.

Communication Is a Dynamic Process

Communication is dynamic, which means that it continually changes, evolves, and moves on. Because communication is a process, communicative interactions have no definite beginnings or endings. Suppose a friend drops by while you're reading this chapter and asks what you are doing. "Reading about gender, communication, and culture," you reply. Your friend then says, "Oh, you mean about how men and women talk differently." You respond, "Not exactly—you see, gender isn't really about males and females; it's about the meaning our culture attaches to each sex." Did this interaction begin with your friend's question, or with your instructor's assignment of the reading, or with other experiences that led you to enroll in this class?

Think also about when this communication ends. Does it stop when your friend leaves? Maybe not. What the two of you talk about may influence what you think and do later, so the impact of your conversation continues beyond the immediate encounter. All communication is like this: It is an ongoing, dynamic process without clear beginnings and endings.

Communication Is Systemic

Communication occurs in particular situations or systems that influence what and how we interact and what meanings we attach to messages. For example, suppose you observe the following interaction. In an office building where you are waiting for an appointment, you see a middle-aged man walk to the secretary's desk, put his arm around her shoulders, and say, "You really do drive me crazy when you wear that outfit." She doesn't look up from her work but responds, "You're crazy, period. It has nothing to do with what I'm wearing." How would you interpret this interaction? Is it an instance of sexual harassment? Are they coworkers who are comfortable joking about sexuality with each other? Is he perhaps not an employee but her friend or romantic partner? The only reasonable conclusion is that we cannot tell what is happening or what it means to the communicators, because we don't understand the systems within which this interaction takes place.

When we say communication is systemic, we mean more than that its contexts affect meaning. Recall John Muir's statement that each part of nature is "hitched to the universe." As a system, all aspects of communication are interlinked, so they interact with one another. Who is speaking affects what is said and what it means. In the foregoing example, the secretary would probably attach different meanings to the message "You really do drive me crazy when you wear that outfit," if it was said by a friend or by a coworker with a reputation for coming on to women. Communication is also influenced by how we feel: When you feel tired or irritable, you may take offense at a comment that ordinarily wouldn't bother you. The time of day and place of interaction may also affect what is communicated and how our words and actions are interpreted.

The largest system affecting communication is our culture, the context within which all our interactions take place. As we saw in our discussion of culture, a society's view and treatment of men and women changes over time. Thirty years ago, it would have been rude for a man not to open a car door for his date and not to stand when a woman entered a room. Today, most people would not regard either as rude. Just a few decades ago, sexual harassment did not have a name and was not considered cause for grievance or legal action. Today, laws and policies prohibit sexual harassment, and employees may bring charges against harassers. The same behavior now means something different from what it meant then. The systems within which communication occurs interact; each part affects all others.

Communication Has Two Levels of Meaning

Perhaps you noticed that our definition of communication referred to meanings, not just to a single meaning. That's because communication has two levels of meaning. Years ago, a group of clinical psychologists (Watzlawick, Beavin, & Jackson, 1967) noted that all communication has both a content level and a relationship level of meaning.

The **content level of meaning** is its literal meaning. If Ellen says to her partner, Ed, "You can't buy that car," the content level of the statement is that he can't buy a car. The content level also indicates a response that is expected to follow from a message. In this case, both Ellen and Ed may assume he will not buy the car. The content level of meaning involves a literal message and implies the appropriate response.

The **relationship level of meaning** is less obvious. It defines the relationship between communicators by indicating each person's identity and the communicators' relationship to each other. In our example, Ellen seems to be defining the relationship as one in which she calls the shots. The relationship level of meaning in her comment also suggests that she regards it as her prerogative to tell Ed what he can and cannot buy. Ed could respond by saying, "I certainly can buy it, and I will." Here, the content level is again clear. Ed is stating that he will buy the car. On the relationship level, however, he may be arguing about the power balance between himself and Ellen. He may be refusing to accept her control. If she says,

"Okay, then buy it," she accepts Ed's claim that she is not running the relationship. She affirms his right to buy what he wants and his prerogative to tell her how he'll spend money.

The relationship level of meaning is the primary level that reflects and influences how people feel about each other. It provides a context for the content level of meaning because it tells us how to interpret the literal message. Perhaps, when Ed says he is going to buy the car, he uses a teasing tone and grins, in which case the relationship level of meaning is that Ellen should not take the content level seriously, because he's joking. If, however, he makes his statement in a belligerent voice and glares at her, the relationship level of meaning is that he does mean the content level. Relationship levels of meaning tell us how to interpret content meaning and how communicators see themselves in relation to each other.

Relationship levels of meaning are particularly important when we try to understand gendered patterns of communication. A good example is interruption. Elyse is telling Jed how her day went. He interrupts and says, "Let's head out to the soccer game." The content level of meaning of this interruption is simply what Jed said. The more important level of meaning is usually the relationship level, which in this case declares that Jed has the right to interrupt Elyse, dismiss her topic, and initiate his own. If he interrupts, and she does not protest, they agree to let him control the conversation. If she does object, then the two may wind up in extended negotiations over how to define their relationship. In communication, all messages have two levels of meaning.

Meanings Are Created through Human Interaction with Symbols

This premise highlights two final, important understandings about communication. First, it calls our attention to the fact that humans are symbol-using creatures. Symbols are abstract, arbitrary, and often ambiguous ways of representing phenomena. For example, ♀ and ♂ are symbols for *female* and *male*, respectively. Words are also symbols, so *woman* and *man* are symbols for certain physical beings. We rely on symbols to communicate and create meanings in our lives.

Because human communication is symbolic, we have to think about it to figure out what it means. Rather than reacting in automatic or instinctive ways to communication, we usually reflect on what was said and what it means before we respond. To be interpreted, symbols require thought. Symbols can also be ambiguous; that is, their meanings may not be clear. Recall our earlier example, in which a man tells a secretary, "You really do drive me crazy when you wear that outfit." To interpret what he said, she has to think about their relationship, what she knows about him, and what has occurred in their prior interactions. After thinking about all these things, she'll decide whether his comment was a joke in poor taste, a compliment, sexual harassment, or a flirtatious show of interest from someone with whom she is romantically involved. Sometimes, people interpret what we say in a manner other than what we intended because symbols are so abstract and ambiguous that more than one meaning is plausible.

The fact that symbols are abstract, ambiguous, and arbitrary makes it impossible to think of meaning as inherent in symbols themselves. Each of us constructs an interpretation of communication by drawing on our past experiences, our knowledge of the people with whom we are interacting, and other factors in a communication system that influence our interpretations. Because the meaning we attach to communication is rooted in our own perspectives, we are inclined to project our own thoughts, feelings, desires, and so forth onto others' messages. Differences in interpretation are the source of much misunderstanding between people. However, you can become a more effective communicator if you keep in mind that people's perceptions and interpretations differ. Reminding yourself of this should prompt you to ask for clarification of another person's meaning rather than assuming your interpretation is correct. Similarly, we should check with others more often than we do to see how they are interpreting our verbal and nonverbal communication.

SUMMARY

In this chapter, we began to explore the nature of communication, gender, and culture. Because each of us is a gendered being, it's important to understand what gender means and how we can be more effective in our interactions within a culture that is also gendered. The primary focus of this chapter was to introduce four central concepts: sex, gender, culture, and communication.

Sex is a biological classification, whereas gender is a social, symbolic system through which a culture attaches significance to biological sex. Gender is something individuals learn; yet, because it is constructed by cultures, it is more than an individual quality. It is a whole system of social meanings that specify what is associated with men and women in a given society at a particular time. We also noted that meanings of gender vary over time and across cultures. Finally, we found that gender is relational, because femininity and masculinity gain much of their meaning from the fact that our society juxtaposes them.

The third key concept, culture, refers to structures and practices, particularly communicative ones, through which a society announces and sustains its values. Abundant structures and practices serve to reinforce our society's prescriptions for women's and men's identities and behaviors. To understand what gender means and how meanings of gender change, we must explore the cultural values, institutions, and activities through which the meanings of gender are expressed and promoted.

Finally, we defined communication as a dynamic, systemic process in which meanings are created and reflected in human interaction with symbols. In examining the dimensions of this definition, we emphasized that communication is a symbolic activity, which implies that meanings are variable and constructed rather than inherent in symbols themselves. We also saw that communication can be understood only within its contexts, including culture.

Building on the foundations we've established in this chapter, other chapters will examine how we learn gender, how we perform feminine and masculine identities, and the range of ways in which gender, communication, and culture interact in our lives.

KEY TERMS

The terms following are defined in this chapter on the pages indicated, as well as in alphabetical order in the book's glossary, which begins on page 283. The text's companion website (**http://www.cengage.com/communication/wood/genderedlives11e**) also provides interactive flash cards and crossword puzzles to help you learn these terms and the concepts they represent.

androgyny 23
cis 26
communication 31
content level of meaning 32
critical research methods 16
culture 29
essentializing 19
gender 19
gender identity 21
hermaphrodites 20
intersexed 21

mixed research methods 16
patriarchal 30
qualitative research methods 15
quantitative research methods 15
relationship level of meaning 32
sex 19
sexual orientation 26
transgendered 26
transsexual 26
transvestite 29

GENDER ONLINE

1. Wikipedia offers a summary of various research on different cultural norms and personal choices for married names: **http://en.wikipedia.org/wiki/Married_and_maiden_names**. Be sure to check out the "references" section for the works cited, which includes several informative articles.

2. Online search terms: "cross-sex communication," "genderqueer," "androgyny."

REFLECTION AND DISCUSSION

1. If you have traveled to other countries and experienced other cultures, what differences from U.S. views of women and men and masculinity and femininity did you notice?

2. How comfortable are you with current views of masculinity and femininity? Which ones, if any, do you find restrictive? Are you doing anything to change them in society's views or to resist them in how you personally embody gender? Talk with grandparents or with people of their generations. Ask them what it meant to be a woman or man when they were your age. Analyze how their views differ from yours.

3. Conduct a survey on your campus. Ask 10 people whom you know at least casually:

   • Should the campus provide separate bathrooms for people who are transsexed or transgendered? (Be prepared to define these terms.)

   • Why do you think separate bathrooms should or should not be provided?

Combine the results of your survey with those of classmates' surveys. What do the data tell you about attitudes on your campus?

4. Scott Turner Schofield is a critically praised performance artist who defines himself as a "gender renegade" (Cooper, 2006). His theater pieces include *Debutante Balls* and *The Southern Gents Tour*. Visit his website: **http://www .undergroundtransit.com/**

RECOMMENDED RESOURCES

1. *Boys Don't Cry*. (1999). Directed by Kimberly Pierce. Distributed by Fox. Even if you have seen this film, watch it again after reading this chapter. It offers a stunning portrait of how social linkage of sex, gender, and sexual orientation can oppress individuals.

2. Diane Levin and Jean Kilbourne. (2008). *So Sexy, So Soon*. New York: Ballantine. This book shows how media teach children about sex, gender, and sexuality.

There is nothing so practical as good theory.
—Kurt Lewin

2

Theoretical Approaches to Gender Development

Knowledge Challenge:

- When do most children understand that they are male or female and that their sex is not going to change?
- How does a person develop a standpoint?
- Which sex has a documented hormonal cycle?

A student of mine named Jenna told me that theory bores her because it has nothing to do with "real life." But the premier social scientist Kurt Lewin disagreed when he insisted, "There is nothing so practical as good theory." What he meant, and what I tried to explain to Jenna, is that theories are very practical. They help us understand, explain, and predict what happens in our real lives and in the world around us.

Theoretical Approaches to Gender

A **theory** is a way to describe, explain, and predict relationships among phenomena. Each of us uses theories to make sense of our lives, to guide our attitudes and actions, and to predict others' behavior. Although we're not always aware of the theories we hold, they still shape how we act, how we expect others to act, and how we explain, or make sense of, what we and others say and do. In this sense, theories are very practical.

Among the theories that each of us has are ones we use to make sense of men's and women's behaviors. For instance, assume that you know Kevin and Carlene, who are 11-year-old identical twins. In many ways, they are alike; yet they also differ.

Carlene is more articulate than Kevin, and she tends to think in more integrative ways. Kevin is better at solving analytic problems, especially ones that involve spatial relations. He also has better-developed muscles, although he and Carlene spend equal time playing sports. How you explain the differences between these twins reflects your implicit theory of gender.

If put a lot of trust in biology, you might say that different cognitive strengths result from hemispheric specialization in male and female brains. You might also assume that Kevin's greater muscle development results from testosterone, which boosts musculature, whereas estrogen programs the body to develop less muscle and more fat and soft tissue.

Then again, if you believe socialization shapes development, you might explain the twins' different cognitive skills as the result of what parents reward. Similarly, you might explain the disparity in their muscle development by assuming that Kevin is more encouraged and more rewarded than Carlene for engaging in activities that build muscles.

These are only two of the many ways we could explain the differences between Kevin and Carlene. Each represents a particular theoretical viewpoint—a way of understanding the relationship between gender and people's behaviors and abilities. Neither is the right theory or even more right than the other. Each viewpoint makes sense, yet each is limited, which suggests that a full understanding of gender relies on multiple theories.

Our theories about sex and gender affect our thoughts and behaviors. How we explain the twins' differences is likely to influence how we treat them. If you think the differences in muscle development are determined by biology, then you probably would not push Carlene to work out more in order to develop muscles. On the other hand, if you think differences result from socialization, you might encourage Carlene to build her muscles and Kevin to think more integratively.

There are many theories about how we develop gendered identities. Because each theory attempts to explain only selected dimensions of gender, different theories are not competing to be the definitive explanation of how gender develops and what it means. Instead, theories often complement one another by sharpening our awareness of multiple ways in which communication, sex, gender, and culture interact. Thus, as we discuss alternative theories, you shouldn't try to pick the best one. Instead, appreciate the strengths of each one and realize how they fit together to provide a richly layered account of how we become gendered.

Theories of gender development and behavior can be classified into four broad types: (1) biological, (2) interpersonal, (3) cultural, and (4) critical. Within these broad categories, a number of specific theories focus on particular factors and processes that contribute to the gendering of individuals. As we discuss these, you will probably notice both how they differ in focus and how they work together to create an overall understanding of gender.

Biological Theories of Gender

Biological theory maintains that biological characteristics such as chromosomes, hormonal activities, and brain specialization account for gender differences.

One focus of biological theories is the influence of sex chromosomes. As we saw in Chapter 1, most males have an XY chromosomal structure. Most females have

EXPLORING GENDERED LIVES *Chromosomal Variations*

Although most humans have either XX or XY sex chromosomes, there are variations.

- About 1 in 2,500 females has Turner's syndrome, in which there is a single X chromosome instead of the usual two in most cells. Some people with Turner's syndrome have Y chromosomes in their blood cells (Wade, 2009). Girls with Turner's syndrome do not undergo the usual changes at puberty and they are usually unable to have children. They tend to be shorter than average and have normal intelligence.
- About 1 in 700 males has Klinefelter's syndrome, which is determined by the presence of two or more X chromosomes instead of a single X. Boys with Klinefelter's syndrome tend to be taller than average and have normal levels of intelligence. They usually produce less testosterone and have less impulse control than XY males.
- Approximately 1 in 1,500 females is born with three X chromosomes. Triple X girls tend to be taller than XX girls and have normal intelligence and normal puberty. Without genetic testing, triple X girls are unlikely to be identified (March of Dimes, 2006).

an XX chromosome structure, because they inherit an X chromosome from each parent. Men are more prone to a number of hereditary conditions than women because the single Y chromosome that has the gene for a condition is not corrected by a second Y chromosome that does not carry that gene. A person with two X chromosomes, on the other hand, is more likely to have one that overrides a gene for a condition.

X and Y chromosomes are distinct. Larger than the Y, the X holds 1,100 genes whereas the Y holds only about 50 genes (Angier, 2007a, b). In part because of the larger number of genes carried on the X chromosome, it is more of a multitasker than the Y. Yet, the Y chromosome is evolving faster than any other human chromosome (Borenstein, 2010). The Y chromosome's primary function is determining that a fertilized egg will evolve into a male. The X chromosome, however, controls a lot more than sex determination; it influences intelligence, some hereditary conditions, and sociability (Angier, 2007a).

As we've noted, women typically have two X chromosomes. Scientists had assumed that one of the X chromosomes was silenced to avoid toxic effects of double X genes. However, more recent research shows that the second X chromosome is not entirely shut down (Dowd, 2005; "Study Reveals," 2005). Instead, 15% of the genes (between 200 and 300 genes) on the second X remain active. And in some women, another 10% of the second X's genes showed some level of activity.

A second focus of biological theories is hormonal activity. For instance, estrogen, the primary female hormone, causes women's bodies to produce "good" cholesterol and to make blood vessels flexible (Ferraro, 2001). Estrogen strengthens the immune system, making women generally less susceptible to immune disorders, infections, and viruses. Estrogen causes fat tissue to form around women's hips, which provides cushioning for a fetus during pregnancy. And estrogen seems to impede liver functioning so women eliminate alcohol more slowly than men and thus may react more quickly to alcohol consumption (Lang, 1991).

EXPLORING GENDERED LIVES *Determining Athletes' Sex*

A person's sex is not always obvious. At the 2009 Olympics, South African runner Caster Semenya was challenged after she won the women's 400 meter race (Bearak, 2009; Clarey & Kolata, 2009). A poor woman from a remote, rural village in South Africa, Caster was stunned. Her birth certificate said she was a female; she had been raised as a girl; and her aunt and mother, who had changed her diapers, said she was female. After winning the women's 2009 world title, she was sidelined for 11 months while her sex was debated. Eventually, she was cleared to compete.

Semenya is not the only Olympic athlete whose sex has been contested. At Olympics hosted in Beijing, Sidney, and Athens, female athletes have been forced to submit to testing in a sex-determination laboratory to prove they were females. In 1967 Ewa Klo-bukowska, a sprinter from Poland, was not allowed to compete because she failed the chromosomal test even though she passed the nude test. Some years later Maria José Martínez, a hurdler from Spain, was barred when tests showed she had a Y chromosome. A later ruling restored her eligibility to compete as a woman.

When the chromosomal tests disqualified eight athletes at the 1996 Atlanta Olympics, the tests themselves came under scrutiny. All eight athletes were allowed to compete as women because they had a rare congenital condition which gave them a Y chromosome but did not make them male. People who appear female and have a Y chromosome may live their lives as women, never suspecting that they, like some Olympic athletes, would fail the sex-determination test.

If it were up to you to set policy for the Olympics, would you require sex testing? If so, what sort of test would you require?

Like women, men have hormonal cycles that affect their behavior (Federman & Walford, 2007). Research shows that males who use drugs, engage in violent and abusive behavior, and have behavior problems tend to be at their cycle's peak level of testosterone. A 2011 study reported that testosterone levels tend to decrease markedly when a man becomes a father. Scientists think this may be an evolutionary pattern aimed to lessen men's aggression and interest in other mates while increasing their tendencies to nurture (Belluck, 2011).

Beginning around the age of 30, men's testosterone level starts declining. Unlike the more abrupt change that women experience with menopause, men's hormonal change is gradual with testosterone levels dropping about 1% a year after age 30 (Federman & Walford, 2007). Researchers estimate that about 10 million American men over the age of 50 have testosterone levels sufficiently low to decrease muscle, bone strength, and interest in sex and to increase body fat, moodiness, and depression (Federman & Walford, 2007).

Hormones influence some tendencies that we associate with gender. Research shows that girls favor trucks over dolls if their mothers had atypically high levels of testosterone during pregnancy, and that males who are given estrogen experience declines in normally strong spatial skills and increases in usually less strong verbal skills (Gurian & Stevens, 2007; Tyre, 2006). Men who are given a spray of oxytocin, known as the "cuddle" hormone, show more empathy and sensitivity to others' feelings (Hurleman, Patin, Onur, Cohen, Baumgartner, Metzler, Dziobek, Gallinat, Wagner, Maier, & Kendrick, 2010).

EXPLORING GENDERED LIVES *The Claims of Sociobiology*

One of the more controversial theories of sex and gender differences is sociobiology (also called evolutionary psychology) (Barash, 2002; Wilson, 1975). According to sociobiology, differences between women and men result from genetic factors that aim to ensure survival of the fittest.

A key claim of sociobiology is that women and men follow distinct reproductive strategies in an effort to maximize the chance that their genetic lines will continue (Barash & Lipton, 2002; Buss, 1994, 1995, 1996, 1999; Buss & Kenrick, 1998). For men, the best strategy is to have sex with as many women as possible in order to father many children who continue their genetic line. Because men produce millions of sperm, they risk little by impregnating multiple women. Women, however, usually produce only one egg during each menstrual cycle during their fertile years, so the best evolutionary strategy for them is to be highly selective in choosing sex partners and potential fathers of their children.

Sociobiology has at least as many critics as proponents. One criticism is that the theory fails to account for sexual behavior that occurs without the goal of reproduction—and sometimes in an active effort to avoid that outcome! Another criticism is that sociobiology ignores the ways in which social influences mitigate biological drives (Newcombe, 2002).

Behavioral ecology advances a less extreme view. According to behavioral ecology, factors in the environment influence—but do not determine—sexual behaviors and preferences (Begley, 2009). That's why extremely thin women are considered ideal in some cultures and very heavy women are viewed as ideal in other cultures. This may also explain the "cougar phenomenon" in which older, successful women pick younger men as mates. This emergent pattern reflects changes in women's earning power and social status.

A third focus of biological theories is brain structure and development. Although there are some inconsistencies in research findings, many studies indicate that, although both women and men use both lobes of the brain, each sex tends to specialize in one. Men tend to have better development in the left lobe, which controls linear thinking, sequential information, spatial skills, and abstract, analytic reasoning (Andersen, 2006; Mealy, 2000). Women tend to have greater development of the right lobe, which controls imaginative and artistic activity, holistic and intuitive thinking, and some visual tasks (Joseph, 2000; Mealy, 2000). In women, the prefrontal cortex, which restrains aggression, is larger and develops earlier than in men (Brizendine, 2007; Tyre, 2006), and the insula, which affects intuition and empathy, is larger (Brizendine, 2007). In men, the amygdala, which is the center of emotions such as anger and fear, is larger (Brizendine, 2007).

A bundle of nerves and connecting tissues called the corpus callosum links the two lobes of the brain. Women generally have greater ability to use this structure, which allows crossing from one lobe to the other (Fausto-Sterling, 2000). The splenium, which is part of the corpus callosum, becomes stronger with use, which implies that we can develop it by using it, just as we use exercise to develop other muscles in our bodies.

Although much of our discussion suggests that biological influences are moderated by socialization, it would be a mistake to dismiss the biology's power to affect our lives. The force of biology is evident in cases where doctors try to change a child's biological sex. Perhaps the most famous case is that of David Reimer,

Used by permission of John L. Hart FLP, and Creator's Syndicate, Inc.

which is often called "the case of David/Brenda" (Butler, 2004; Colapinto, 2006; McClelland, 2004). When David was eight months old, a surgeon mistakenly amputated his penis during surgery to correct phimosis, a condition in which the foreskin of the penis interferes with urination. Following doctors' advice, the parents authorized "normalizing surgery" so the testicles were removed, hormones were given to induce female characteristics, and the child was renamed Brenda. Brenda did not take to being a girl. Her preferred toys were trucks and guns; she routinely ripped off the dresses her parents made her wear; and, despite not having a penis, Brenda preferred to stand to urinate. Even hormonal treatments and therapists could not convince Brenda to identify as female. Finally, when Brenda was about 15, her father told her that she had been born a boy. For Brenda/David, things now made sense. David had his breasts removed and a penis constructed using muscle tissue and cartilage, took male hormone shots, and began to live as a male. At age 25, David married a woman with children, and he helped raise his three stepchildren. In June of 2004, at age 38, David took his own life.

LUANNE

When I was in high school, I wanted to play football. My folks were really cool about it, since they'd always told me being a girl didn't mean I couldn't do anything I wanted to. But the school coach vetoed the idea. I appealed his decision to the principal as sex discrimination (my mother's a lawyer), and we had a meeting. The coach said girls couldn't play football as well as guys because girls are less muscular, weigh less, and have less dense bodies to absorb the force of momentum. He said this means girls can be hurt more than guys by tackles and stuff. He also said that girls have smaller heads and necks, which is a problem in head-to-head contact on the field. My dad said the coach was talking in generalizations, and he should judge my ability by me as an individual. But the coach's arguments convinced the principal, and I didn't get to play, just because women's bodies are generally less equipped for contact sports.

In summary, biological theories focus on the ways that chromosomes, hormones, and brain structure may affect physiology, thinking, and behavior. Biological theory is valuable in informing us about genetic and biological factors that may influence

EXPLORING GENDERED LIVES *Biological Differences That Make a Difference*

Although men and women are alike in many respects, there are some significant biological sex differences (Duenwald, 2005; Fisher, 2000; Wartik, 2002):

- Women are more likely than men to suffer from migraine headaches and lupus; men are more likely than women to suffer from cluster headaches.

- On average, women's brains are smaller than men's; women's brains are also more densely packed with neurons than men's.

- Men's livers metabolize most drugs, including alcohol, more quickly than women's.

- Daily use of low-dose aspirin is helpful in preventing first heart attacks in men but not in women; low-dosage aspirin does seem to offer women some protection against stroke, which is not a benefit that has been demonstrated for men.

- Men tend to experience heart disease 10 to 15 years earlier than women. Also, the sexes typically have different symptoms of heart attack. Women's symptoms include shortness of breath, jaw pain, backache, and extreme fatigue. Men's primary symptom is usually chest or arm pain.

- Women are more likely to develop melanoma, but men are more likely to die from this cancer.

our abilities and options. Yet, biological theories tell us only about physiological and genetic qualities of men and women in general. They don't necessarily describe individual men and women. Some men may be holistic, creative thinkers, whereas some women, like Luanne, may excel at football.

There is substantial controversy about the strength of biology. Increasing evidence (Rivers & Barnett, 2011) indicates that biological differences other than reproductive ones are actually quite small and do not explain most behavioral differences between women and men. That's why a majority of researchers believe that biology is substantially edited by environmental factors (Fausto-Sterling, 2000; Kolata, 2012). To consider how environmental forces may shape gender, we turn now to interpersonal theories of gender.

Interpersonal Theories of Gender

Three theories focus on interpersonal factors that influence the development of masculinity and femininity. Psychodynamic theory emphasizes interpersonal relationships within the family while social learning and cognitive development theories stress learning and role modeling between children and a variety of other people.

Psychodynamic Theories of Gender Development

Psychodynamic theories claim that the first relationship we have fundamentally influences how we define our identity, including gender. Most infants are cared for by women, often mothers. Because the mother or mothering figure herself is gendered and may subscribe to social views of girls and boys, she may act differently toward sons and daughters. This explains why male and female infants typically follow distinct developmental paths.

Between mother and daughter, there is a fundamental likeness that encourages close identification (Chodorow, 1989). Mothers generally interact more with daughters, keeping them physically and psychologically closer than sons. In addition, mothers tend to be more nurturing and to talk more about emotions and relationships with daughters than with sons. Because of the identification with the mother, young girls may first understand their gender identity in relation to their mothers.

Theorists suggest that infant boys recognize in a primitive way that they differ from their mothers (Chodorow, 1978, 1999). More importantly, mothers realize the difference, and they reflect it in their interactions with sons. In general, mothers encourage more and earlier independence in sons than in daughters, and they talk less with sons about emotional and relationship matters (Galvin, 2006).

ABE

I remember something that happened when I was a little kid. Mom had taken me to the playground, and we were playing together. Some other boys started teasing me, calling me "Mama's boy." I remember thinking I had to stop playing with Mom if I wanted those other boys to accept me.

To establish his independent identity, a boy must distinguish himself from his mother or other female caregiver—he must define himself as distinct from her. Whether he rejects his female caregiver or merely differentiates himself from her, defining himself as different from her is central to most boys' initial development of a masculine identity (Kaschak, 1992).

Identity, of course, is not fixed in the early years of life. We continue to grow and change throughout life. Yet, psychodynamic theorists maintain that the identity formed in infancy is fundamental. Thus, as infants mature, they carry with them the basic identity formed in the pivotal first relationship. As girls become women, many tend to elaborate their identities in connections with others, giving relationships high priority in their lives. As boys grow into men, many build on the basic identity formed in infancy, making independence central in their lives. Thus, for someone who identifies as feminine, intimate relationships may be a source of security and comfort, and they may affirm her (or his) view of self as connected with others. In contrast, someone who identifies as masculine may feel that really close relationships threaten the autonomy needed for a strong identity (Gurian, 2006).

Psychological Theories of Gender Development

Psychological theories focus on the interpersonal bases of gender, but they do not emphasize intrapsychic processes at the center of psychodynamic explanations. Instead, psychological theories of gender highlight the influence of interaction within families and social contexts.

Social Learning Theory

Developed by Walter Mischel (1966) and others (Bandura, 2002; Bandura & Walters, 1963; Burn, 1996), **social learning theory** claims that individuals learn to be masculine and feminine by imitating others and getting responses from others to their behaviors. Children imitate the communication they see on television, online, and on DVDs as well as the communication of people around them. At first, young children are likely to mimic almost anything. However, others reward only some of children's behaviors, and the behaviors that are rewarded tend to be repeated. Thus, social learning suggests that rewards from others teach boys and girls which behaviors are appropriate for them (Kunkel, Hummert, & Dennis, 2006; Morrow, 2006; Wood, 2013).

As parents and others reward girls for what is considered feminine and discourage behaviors and attitudes that parents perceive as masculine, they shape little girls into femininity. Similarly, as parents communicate approval to boys for behaving in masculine ways and curb them for acting feminine—for instance, for crying—they influence little boys to become masculine. Even people who claim to treat boys and girls the same often have unconscious gender biases. When told an infant is a boy (but is really a girl), adults describe the infant as angry. When told an infant is a girl (but is really a boy), adults describe the infant as happy and socially engaged (Elliott, 2009).

VICTORIA

When I was little—like four or five maybe—if I got dirty or was too loud, Mama would say, "That's no way for a lady to act." When I was quiet and nice, she'd say, "Now, you're being a lady." I remember wanting Mama to approve of me and trying to act like a lady. But sometimes it was hard to figure out what was and wasn't ladylike in her book. I had to just keep doing things and seeing how she responded until I learned the rules.

DERRICK

Over break, I was visiting my sister's family, and her little boy attached himself to me. Wherever I went, he was my shadow. Whatever I did, he copied. At one point, I was dribbling a basketball out in the driveway, and he got it and started dribbling. I egged him on, saying, "Attaboy! What a star!" and stuff like that, and he just grinned real big. The more I praised him for playing with the ball, the harder he played. It was really weird to see how much influence I had over him.

Media also play a role in teaching children what activities and roles are rewarded for each sex (Jamieson & Romer, 2008). If children watch TV programs that show only women caring for children, traditional sex roles are reinforced. However, if children watch TV programs that show men being rewarded for caring for children, children learn that it's appropriate for men to engage in caregiving.

Gendered behaviors are developed by imitating role models.

My students called my attention to *Toddlers and Tiaras* on which the very young girls who win usually dress and act sexy. This teaches girls who watch that being sexy is the key to success. Media characters give boys and girls images of appropriate behavior in certain situations. When those children later encounter similar situations in their own lives, they may act as they saw television characters act.

Cognitive Development Theory

Unlike social learning theory, **cognitive development theory** assumes that children play *active* roles in developing their gender identities. They do this by picking models of competent masculine or feminine behavior.

Children go through several stages in developing gender identities (Gilligan & Pollack, 1988; Kohlberg, 1958; Piaget, 1932/1965). From birth until about 24 to 30 months, they notice the ways others label and describe them. When they hear others call them a "girl" or "boy," they learn the labels for themselves. "My sweet little lady" and "my strong man" are distinct gendered descriptions that children may hear.

Gender constancy is a person's understanding that he or she is a male or female and this will not change. Gender constancy may develop as early as age three and almost certainly by age six (Miller-Day & Fisher, 2006; Rivers & Barnett, 2011). Once gender constancy is established, most children are motivated to learn how to be competent in the sex and gender assigned to them. Same-sex models become important gauges as young children figure out what behaviors, attitudes, and feelings go with their gender. Many young girls study and see their mothers and key women in their lives as models of femininity, whereas little boys often study their fathers and men in their lives as models of masculinity (Tyre, 2006).

Related to cognitive development theory is **gender schema theory** (Bern, 1983; Frawley, 2008; Meyers, 2007). According to gender schema theory, even before reaching the first birthday, an infant distinguishes between male and female faces and voices. By the age of two, gender schema theorists claim that children use the concept or schema of gender to organize their understandings. A **gender schema** is an internal mental framework that organizes perceptions and directs behavior related to gender. Using gender schemata, children organize clothes, activities, toys, traits, and roles into those appropriate for boys and men and those appropriate for girls and women. They apply gender schemata to guide their choices of activities, roles, clothes, and so forth.

LINDSAY

The gender constancy that we read about doesn't happen so easily or "naturally" for everyone. Long before I started kindergarten I knew that I was a boy, but I also knew that I wasn't. Everyone called me a boy, and I knew I had boy genitals, but I also knew that I identified more with girls and women and with girl things like dolls and dresses. So, for me, gender constancy didn't happen—I was caught on a fence between how everyone else saw me and how I saw myself.

As children mature, they continue to seek role models to guide them in becoming masculine and feminine. Perhaps you watched music videos and slightly older people to figure out how to be a boy or girl. We learn it's feminine to squeal or scream at the sight of bugs and mice, but boys who do so are sissies. It's acceptable—if not pleasant to everyone—for adolescent boys to belch, but a teenage girl who belches would most likely be criticized.

Cultural Theories of Gender

Cultural theorists do not dismiss biological and interpersonal factors, but they do assume that these are qualified by the influence of culture.

Of the many cultural contributions to knowledge about gender, we will focus on two. First, we'll look at findings from anthropology to appreciate the range of ways that societies define gender. Second, we will explore symbolic interactionism, which explains how individuals acquire their culture's views of gender in the process of interaction.

Anthropology

Anyone who has been outside the United States knows that traveling prompts you to learn not only about other countries but also about your own. Our views of gender in twenty-first-century America are clarified by considering what it means elsewhere—how other cultures view gender and how women and men in other cultures express gendered identities.

Many societies have views of gender that differ from those currently prevalent in the United States. Tahitian men tend to be gentle, mild-tempered, and nonaggressive, and it is entirely acceptable for them to cry, show fear, and express pain (Coltrane, 1996). Australian Aboriginal fathers have no say in their daughters' marriages; mothers have that authority. Many Samoan males tattoo their bodies from waist to below the knees to mark the transition from boyhood to manhood. A male is not considered a man until he has undergone the painful process of extensive tattooing (Channell, 2002; Cote, 1997). The Mbuti, a tribe of pygmies in central Africa, don't discriminate strongly between the sexes. Both women and men gather roots, berries, and nuts, and both hunt (Coltrane, 1996). The Mukogodo people in Kenya place a higher value on females than on males; as a result, daughters are given greater care than sons (Cronk, 1993). And on Orango Island on the western shore of Africa, women choose mates and a man cannot refuse without dishonoring his family (Callimachi, 2007).

LYNN

At school, I've gotten to know a woman from the Congo. She can't believe how American girls break up with their boyfriends and wives divorce husbands. She says she could never do that, because she was raised to believe a woman can't leave her man and remain good. I know she is not happy in her marriage, but I also know she'll never leave it.

What fathering means varies among cultures. Hazda fathers in Tanzania, spend about 5% of their time holding infants; Aka fathers in the Congo Basin hold their

EXPLORING GENDERED LIVES *Learning from Other Species*

Meet Roy and Silo, two chinstrap penguins at a Manhattan zoo. To the frustration of zookeepers, they rejected close relationships with female chinstrap penguins. But Roy and Silo longed for a family. They once put a rock in their nest and sat on it, keeping the rock toasty warm in the folds of their abdomens. A zookeeper finally gave them a fertilized egg that needed to be sat on to hatch. After the usual 34 days of sitting on the egg, a female chick was born, and Roy and Silo devoted the usual two and one-half months to raising her (Smith, 2004a). In the spring of 2004, Silo's eye began to wander and early in the 2005 mating season he forsook Roy, his partner of six years, and took up with Scrappy, a female penguin.

Roy and Silo's relationship isn't unique in the animal kingdom. In fact, nonheterosexual behavior has been documented in 450 species (Bagemihl, 2000).

EXPLORING GENDERED LIVES *Varied Cultural Approaches to Fathering*

Many countries have done more than the United States to link parenting to manhood. In 1990, only 4% of Swedish men took any time off when a child was born. The Swedish government decided to use public policy to encourage men to be more involved in fathering. In 1995 the Swedish govern-ment set aside 30 leave days for fathers only; if fathers didn't take them, their families lost the leave. In 2002 the state added a second month of leave that new fathers could either take or lose.

Now more than 80% of fathers take four months of leave for the birth of a child (Beck, 2011; Romano & Dokoupil, 2010).

Or consider Germany. In 2007, the country passed a law that new fathers were entitled to leave. The percentage of new fathers who take family leave soared 700%. Japan also provides paid leave to new fathers and honors men who devote themselves to child care as "stars of ikumen" (men who rear children) (Romano & Dokoupil, 2010).

children for as much as 22% of the time; fathers in India are typically near their children three to five hours a day; and Japanese fathers spend an average of 20 minutes near children each day (Gray, 2010).

Another example of how cultural attitudes vary comes from a group of villages in the Dominican Republic where it is common for males to be born with undescended testes and an underdeveloped penis. Because this condition is not rare, the society doesn't regard it as abnormal. Instead, boys born with this condition are raised as "conditional girls," who wear dresses and are treated as girls. At puberty, a secondary tide of androgens causes the testes to descend, the penis to grow, and muscle and hair typical of males to appear. At that point, the child is considered a boy—his dresses are discarded, and he is treated as a male. Members of the society call the condition *guevedoces,* which means "testes at 12" (Blum, 1998).

Some Native American tribes recognize the category of "two-spirit" for indivi-duals who preferred to mate with others of the same sex. Within Native American traditions, these people were not "gay" or "lesbian," but two-spirit people who were particularly admired (Gilley, 2006). Similarly, in Kruje, an isolated rural society in rural Albania, gender swapping is the solution for families that do not have males. When Pashe Kequi's father was killed 60 years ago, she whacked off her long hair, dressed in her father's clothes, and vowed to live as a man and be a virgin for life, giving up marriage and children. Kequi's community accepted her as a man because it's the custom in Kruje (Bilefsky, 2008).

SHENG

Growing up, when guests came to our home, my mother and I served them drinks, then went to the kitchen to fix food while the men talked. If another woman was a guest, she came to the kitchen with us. Men ate at their own table. The women either stay in the kitchen or eat at a separate table.

Symbolic Interactionism

Symbolic interactionism claims that through communication with others we learn who we are. Parents describe a child as big or dainty, delicate or tough, active or quiet, and so on. With each label, others offer the child a self-image, and children internalize others' views to develop their own understandings of who they are.

Cultural views of gender are also communicated through play activities with peers (Maccoby, 1998; Powlishta, Serbin, & Moller, 1993) and through teachers' interactions with students (Sandler, 2004; Wood, 1996b). For example, when young boys move furniture in classrooms, teachers often praise them by saying, "You're such a strong little man." This links strength with being male.

At school, young girls are likely to be reprimanded for roughhousing as a teacher tells them, "That's not very ladylike." Boys engaged in similar mischief more often hear the teacher say with some amusement, "You boys really are rowdy today." Notice that responses from others, such as teachers, not only reflect broad cultural values but also provide positive and negative rewards, consistent with social learning theory. In play with peers, gender messages continue. When a young girl tries to tell a boy what to do, she may be told, "You can't boss me around. You're just a girl." Girls who fail to share their toys or show consideration to others may be told, "You're not being nice," yet this is considerably less likely to be said to young boys.

An important contribution to a cultural theory of gender is the concept of **role**—specifically, roles for women and men. A role is a set of expected behaviors and the values associated with them. In a classic book, Elizabeth Janeway (1971) identified two dimensions of roles. First, roles are external to individuals because a society defines roles in general ways that transcend particular individuals. Thus, for each of us there are certain roles that society expects us to fulfill and others that society deems inappropriate for us.

Within our culture, one primary way to classify social life is through gender roles. Women are still regarded as caretakers and they are expected to provide most of the care for infants, elderly relatives, and others who are sick or disabled. Even in work outside the home, cultural views of femininity are evident. Women remain disproportionately represented in service and clerical jobs, whereas men are moved into executive positions in for-profit sectors of the economy. Women are still asked to take care of social activities on the job, but men in equivalent positions are seldom expected to do this.

Men are still regarded by many as the primary breadwinners. Thus, it is seen as acceptable for a woman not to have an income-producing job, but to fulfill the masculine role, a man must produce income. The current recession in which more men than women have been laid off is challenging these traditional roles.

Postpartum depression, which is feelings of profound sadness following the birth of a child, has been associated with women because society links women to children. However, 10.4% of men suffer from depression three to six months after the birth of a child (Ostrow, 2010). The symptoms of men's depression have been evident before this research, but social views of men may have prevented us from recognizing postpartum depression in them.

My father is in the Air Force, so he's away a lot of the time. Mom has had to become the head of our family. She does everything from work and take care of us to pay bills and cook. Normally, she sits at the head of the table for meals. But when Dad comes home, he sits at the head of the table. Mom still does everything— he says he's on vacation—but they both seem to think the man should be at the head of the table when he's home.

Not only does society assign roles, but it also assigns value to the roles. Western culture teaches women to accept the role of supporting, caring for, and responding to others. Yet that is a role clearly devalued in the United States. Competing and succeeding in work life and public affairs are primary roles assigned to men, and to those roles prestige is attached.

A second important dimension of role is that it is internalized. As we internalize our culture's gender roles, we learn not only that there are different roles for men and women but also that unequal values are assigned to them. This can be very frustrating for those who are encouraged to conform to roles that are less esteemed.

Critical Theories of Gender

Two theories go beyond the standard goals of theory, which are description, explanation, and prediction. Critical theories do something else—they direct our attention to structures and practices by which societies accord more or less privilege to different groups. Critical theorists identify how dominant groups manage to privilege their interests and perspectives. At the same time, critical theorists look for ways to empower oppressed groups and change dominant ideologies. In this sense, critical theories have a political edge.

Standpoint Theory

Standpoint theory complements symbolic interactionism by noting that societies are made up of different groups that have different amounts of power and privilege. Standpoint theory focuses on how membership in groups, such as those designated by gender, race, class, and sexual identity, shapes what individuals experience, know, feel, and do, as well as how individuals understand social life as a whole (Collins, 1986; Harding, 1991, 1998; McClish & Bacon, 2002; Wood, 2005; Wood, in press). Standpoint theory dates back to the writings of nineteenth-century German philosopher Georg Wilhelm Friedrich Hegel (1770–1831) and Karl Marx (1818–1883). Hegel (1807) noted that society as a whole recognized the existence of slavery but that its nature was perceived quite differently depending on whether one's social location was that of master or slave. From this insight, Hegel reasoned that, in any society where power relationships exist, there can be no single perspective on social life. Marx's (1867/1975, 1977) contribution was to emphasize that social location regulates the work we do—our activities and labor—which shapes consciousness, knowledge, and identity.

But social location is *not* standpoint. A standpoint is earned through critical reflection on power relations and through engaging in the struggle required to construct an oppositional stance to the dominant one. Being a woman (social location) does not necessarily confer a feminist standpoint, and being Hispanic (social location) does not necessarily lead to a Hispanic standpoint. Because social location and standpoint are so frequently conflated, let me emphasize the distinction one more time: A standpoint can grow out of the social location of group members' lives. Thus, a feminist standpoint can, *but does not necessarily*, arise from the conditions that shape most women's lives.

Standpoint theory claims that marginalized groups can generate unique insights into how a society works. Women, minorities, gays and lesbians, people of lower socio-economic class, intersexuals, transgendered people, and others who are outside the cultural center may see the society from perspectives that are less biased than those who occupy more privileged social locations. Marginalized perspectives can inform all of us about how our society operates. María Lugones and Elizabeth Spelman (1983) point out that dominant groups have the luxury of not having to understand the perspective of less privileged groups. They don't need to learn about others in order to survive.

TIFFANY

I attended a predominantly white middle-school. My mother made me check my homework twice before I turned it in. I asked her why I had to do that when most of the other kids in the school didn't. She said, "the number of times you check your homework is the same as the number of limitations set up against you— one for being black and two for being a girl." I said that was unfair and she said fairness had nothing to do with succeeding if you're black. I think that was my first lesson in standpoint.

Patricia Hill Collins (1986, 1998) uses standpoint theory to show that black women scholars have special insights into Western culture because of their dual standpoints as "outsiders within," that is, as members of a minority group (African Americans) who hold membership in majority institutions (higher education). Similarly, in his *Autobiography of an Ex-Coloured Man* (1912/1989), James Weldon Johnson reflected, "I believe it to be a fact that the coloured people of this country know and understand the white people better than the white people know and understand them" (p. 22).

An intriguing application of standpoint logic came from Sara Ruddick's (1989) study of mothers. Ruddick concluded that the social location of mothers facilitates the development of "maternal thinking," which is values, priorities, and understandings that are specifically promoted by taking care of dependent young children. Ruddick argues that what we often assume is a maternal instinct that comes naturally to women is actually a set of attitudes and behaviors that arise out of women's frequent location in domestic, caregiving roles.

The impact of social location on nurturing ability is further demonstrated by research on men in caregiving roles. In her research on single fathers, Barbara Risman (1989) found that men who are primary parents are more nurturing, attentive to others' needs, patient, and emotionally expressive than men in general and as much so as most women. Armin Brott, an ex-Marine and business consultant, is widely known as "Mr. Dad," the author of eight books for men like him who are stay-at-home dads. According to Brott, women are not born knowing how to take care of babies and children. They learn how to do it by doing it. The same goes for men, says Brott: They learn how to nurture, comfort, and guide children by engaging in the labor of doing so (Lelchuk, 2007). That's the standpoint argument that social location shapes our identities and skills, including our ability to parent well.

Each of us occupies multiple social locations and can earn or develop multiple standpoints that overlap and interact. For example, a heterosexual, middle-class, African-American man's social locations are different from those of a gay, working-class, European-American man.

Standpoint theory's major contribution to understanding gender is calling our attention to how membership in particular groups shapes individuals' experiences, perspectives, identities, and abilities. Our different social locations provide the possibility of developing standpoints that reflect a political awareness of social hierarchy, privilege, and oppression.

Queer Performative Theory

Perhaps the best way to introduce **queer performative theory** is with three examples.

1. Munroe identifies as a transgender person, or—in Munroe's words—"the hottest and coolest drag queen in town." Before going out, Munroe shaves twice to remove all stubble, spends an hour applying makeup, chooses one of four wigs, and selects an ensemble from the closet, hoping to hook up with an interesting man.

   • Is Munroe female or male?
   • Is Munroe feminine or masculine?
   • Is Munroe straight or gay?
   • Are men who hook up with Munroe straight or gay?

2. Two years ago, Aimee began hormone therapy to stimulate growth of facial hair, increase muscle mass, and decrease breast size. Over the summer, Aimee had sex reassignment surgery. Now, with a new name to match the new body, Andy has set up an appointment with the coach for the men's track team at the university in the hope of joining the team. Later, Andy will share the news with his boyfriend.

   • Is Andy male or female?
   • Is Andy masculine or feminine?
   • Is Andy gay or straight?
   • Is Andy's boyfriend gay or straight?

3. Jada, who was born with a penis, testes, and a prostate gland, identifies as female. Since the age of 15, Jada has had several romantic and sexual relationships, all with women.
   - Is Jada male or female?
   - Is Jada masculine or feminine?
   - Is Jada gay or straight?
   - Are Jada's girlfriends gay or straight?

Munroe, Jada, and Andy illustrate the focus and value of queer performative theories. Each of them defies conventional categories. Each slips beyond and outside of binary views of identity as male or female, masculine or feminine, gay or straight. The identities that they claim and perform don't fit neatly with our taken-for-granted understandings of sex, gender, and sexual identity. According to queer performative theories, Munroe, Jada, and Andy trouble our thinking, and the trouble they provoke is very productive.

Queer theory and performative theory are distinct, yet closely allied. We'll define each theory and then explore how they interact and how, working together, they offer unique insights into gender, sex, sexual orientation, and cultural life.

Queer theory is a critique of conventional categories of identity and cultural views of "normal" and "abnormal," particularly in relation to sexuality. Queer theory argues that identities are not fixed, but somewhat fluid. In our first example, Munroe invests significant effort in creating and performing a female identity. In our second example, Aimee becomes Andy, thereby illustrating the fluidity of identity. In the third example, Jada identifies as female, despite having biological features that fit society's category of male.

Queer theory arose in the context of gay and lesbian studies (Butler, 1990, 1993a, b, 2004; Foucault, 1978; Halperin, 2007; Sedgwick, 1990). The initial focus of queer theory was **heternormativity**, which is the assumption that heterosexuality is normal and all other sexual identities are abnormal. Yet, it would be a mistake to think queer theory is relevant only to gays and lesbians. Almost as soon as queer theory emerged, scholars realized that it has important implications for our understanding of many aspects of identity (Sloop, 2006; Zimmerman & Geist-Martin, 2006). Within the context of queer theory, the word *queer* does not refer only or necessarily to gays and lesbians, but to anything that departs from what society considers normal (Halperin, 2004, 2007). Queer theory challenges the ways that a culture defines and polices what is considered normal and abnormal.

Two ideas are central to queer theory. First, queer theory claims that terms such as "women," "men," "gay," and "straight" are not useful. How much does it tell us about someone if we know that the person is biologically male or female? Identities are shaped by numerous factors, so naming somebody according to any one factor is unavoidably misleading. As well, such terms erase the variation among those who are placed into the categories. Queer theorists point out that there are many different ways of being a woman or man, multiple ways of being gay, straight, or trans. Using the term *man* to describe Zac Effron, Barack Obama, and Kanye West obscures the very different ways that these three people enact their identities as men.

Second, queer theory assumes that identities are not fixed, but are relatively fluid. Any of us may perform our identities one way in this moment and context and another way in a different moment and context. As with Jada, Munroe, and Andy, features such as sex organs don't determine our identities. Rather, according to queer theory, identities arise from choices of how to express or perform ourselves within the particular contexts of our lives.

Fluidity of identity means more than being able to switch from one sex or gender to the other. It can also mean refusing to accept any stable sexual identity. Some trans people will not specify their sex or specify being of multiple sexes. For them, defining themselves in terms of the existing categories (male, female, heterosexual, gay) would simply reinforce those unhelpful categories (Valentine, 2007).

Performative theory argues that humans generate identities, including gender, through performance or expression. A key theorist, Judith Butler (1990, 2004), explains that gender comes into being only as it is expressed, or performed. The performance, she says, is the thing we call gender. Butler's point is that gender is not a thing we have, but rather something that we do at specific times and in specific circumstances. In other words, for Butler and other performative theorists, gender is more appropriately regarded as a verb than a noun. Gender is doing. Without doing—without the action of performance—there is no gender.

According to performative theorists, all of us perform gender, although we may do so in quite diverse ways (Butler, 1990, 1993a, b, 2004; Halberstam, 2012). We express, or perform, conventional gender through everyday practices such as dominating or deferring in conversations and crossing our legs so that one ankle rests on the knee of our other leg or so that one knee rests over the other knee. Conversely, we resist conventional views of gender if we act in ways that are inconsistent with the sex and gender society assigns to us. Some researchers suggest that gender performances also shed light on why women generally do more housework than men. It is possible that women perform domestic labor as a way of demonstrating their femininity (DeVault, 1990) while men refuse to perform household labor as a way to demonstrate masculinity (De Ruijter, Treas & Cohen, 2005; DeVault, 1990; Natalier, 2003).

But—and this is the second key claim of performative theory—our performances are not solo acts. They are always collaborative, because however we express gender, we do so in a context of social meanings that transcend any individual. For instance, a woman who defers to men and tilts her head when talking to men (two behaviors more often exhibited by women than men) is acting individually, but her individual actions are stylized performances of femininity that are coded into cultural life. Our choices of how to act assume and respond to other people who are either physically or mentally present in particular contexts and times.

Queer performative theories integrate the views of queer and performative theory. The result is a view of queer (remember, in this context that means anything other than what is considered "normal") performances as means of challenging and destabilizing cultural categories and the values attached to them. As communication scholar John Sloop (2006) explains, "queer scholarship works against the ways in which gender/sexuality is disciplined ideologically and institutionally and works toward a culture in which a wider variety of genders/sexualities might be performed" (p. 320).

Which of the following is true of Lady Gaga?

A. When asked if she was intersexed, she said, "I think this is society's reaction to a strong woman" (Williams, 2010).

B. She has appeared as ultrafeminine and as entirely unfeminine.

C. In 2010, she told an audience, "If anyone ever tells you you're not good enough, not pretty enough, not smart enough, you tell them, 'Fuck you! I'm gonna be a star!' " (Gray, 2012 p. 3).

D. Is a self-described humanitarian who, with her mother, founded the Born this Way Foundation in 2012.

If you select all of the above, you're correct. Lady Gaga, who says her art is her performance (Gray, 2012), defies gender categorization and does so quite deliberately.

Lady Gaga has often been compared to Madonna who presented herself as a material girl, traditionally feminine, erotically charged, a submissive victim of male power, a dominatrix, and a devoted mother. Both Madonna and Lady Gaga have performed traditional femininity and also parodied it; they have performed heterosexuality and homosexuality. They have courted the male gaze, disrupted it, and used it to look at both women and men.

Both Lady Gaga's and Madonna's performances subvert any stable notion of femininity. In so doing, they insist that a person can be both dominating and docile, both masculine and feminine, both gay and straight, both "good girl" and "bad girl."

How would you describe Lady Gaga, Madonna, or other popular culture figures who perform different gender identities? Can you identify other artists who perform different sex and gender identities?

To disrupt social categories and valuations, performances aim to queer normal. For instance, a person who wears a lace blouse, necktie, combat fatigues, and stilettos cannot be reduced to only feminine or only masculine. This choice of dress is a performance that challenges and undermines conventional gender categories. Two women who perform disagreement with fist fights instead of verbal arguments queer normative views of femininity. A heterosexual man who gives mouth kisses to other men queers cultural views of heterosexuality and—by extension—of homosexuality. Everyday performances such as these become political tools that unsettle taken-for-granted categories of identity that structure social life and label individuals as "normal" or "abnormal."

In sum, queer performative theories allow us to understand deliberately transgressive presentations of self as political acts that aim to point out the insufficiency of binary categories of male/female, masculine/feminine, gay/straight, and normal/abnormal.

Theories Working Together

We've discussed seven theories discretely, but often theories work together to shed light on how we develop and enact gendered identities. For instance, women basketball players are nearly three times as likely to suffer anterior cruciate ligament

(ACL) injuries as men. For soccer players, the risk for females can be eight times greater than for men (Jacobson, 2001; Miller, 2012; Scelfo, 2002). The fact that women suffer more ACL injuries than men suggests that there may be a sex difference—a biologically based difference between women's and men's knees. However, socialization may also be a factor.

Dr. William Garrett (2001), a sports medicine surgeon, notes that women and men athletes hold their bodies differently. Men, he says, are looser and tend to move and stand with their knees slightly bent. Women are more likely to keep their legs and knees straight and to maintain more rigid posture. Loose posture and bent knees reduce stress on the knee and thus reduce the risk of ACL injury. In addition, early socialization teaches girls and boys how to sit, run, and so forth. Thus, what seems a purely biological effect may also reflect interpersonal and social factors.

Let's consider another example that shows how theories we've discussed work together in complementary ways. In 2008, Hillary Rodham Clinton ran a strong and nearly successful campaign to be the Democratic nominee for President. Prior to that, she had excelled in a legal career, participated in policy making during the eight years that Bill Clinton was President, and been elected a Senator for the state of New York. After Barack Obama was elected President, Hillary assumed the top-ranking position of Secretary of State. How do we explain Hillary Clinton's interest and success in arenas that are male dominated?

Social learning and cognitive development theories shed light on Clinton's interests and her success in pursuing them. Growing up, she was rewarded for learning, ambition, living by her faith, and contributing to her community. Clinton also chose strong women and men as role models. Being born in the late 1940s allowed Clinton to see that women had fewer professional opportunities than men and that blacks were denied basic rights in America. These insights, combined with analysis of them, allowed her to develop an oppositional standpoint that led her to challenge institutional discrimination based on race and sex.

Hillary Clinton went to law school at a time when few women did. She was passionately involved in civil rights struggles through which she learned a great deal about blacks' social location in America. Once she had influence, she fought for equity for blacks, women, and other groups that have historically been marginalized. You can see that multiple theories offer insight into Hillary Clinton's career choices and her achievements. Multiple theories often work together to give us a fuller, more complete understanding of gendered phenomena than any single theory could.

SUMMARY

In this chapter, we have considered different theories offering explanations of relationships among communication, gender, and culture. Rather than asking which is the right theory, we have tried to discover how each viewpoint contributes to an overall understanding of how gender develops. By weaving different theories together, we gain a powerful appreciation of the complex individual, interpersonal, and cultural origins of gender identity. Adding to this, queer performative theory invites us to understand and perhaps appreciate the ways we can create performances that deliberately provoke and destabilize culturally constructed categories of identity and normalcy.

The next two chapters build on this one by exploring how communication within rhetorical movements has challenged and changed social views of men and women.

KEY TERMS

The following terms are defined in this chapter on the pages indicated, as well as in alphabetical order in the book's glossary, which begins on page 283. The text's companion website (**http://www.cengage.com/communication/wood/genderedlives11e**) also provides interactive flash cards and crossword puzzles to help you learn these terms and the concepts they represent.

biological theory 38
cognitive development theory 46
gender constancy 47
gender schema 47
gender schema theory 47
heternormativity 54
performative theory 55
psychodynamic theories 43

queer performative theory 53
queer theory 54
role 50
social learning theory 45
standpoint theory 51
symbolic interactionism 50
theory 37

GENDER ONLINE

1. The Urban Dictionary offers definitions of many terms related to gender, communication, and culture. Visit the site and look up terms such as "cis," "genderqueer," and "ze": http://www.urbandictionary.com/

2. Online search terms: "brain, sex differences," "guevedoces," "Lady Gaga."

REFLECTION AND DISCUSSION

1. Distinguished anthropologist Ruth Benedict said that "the purpose of anthropology is to make the world safe for difference." Having read this chapter, how would you explain Benedict's statement?

2. Think about your relationship with your parents. How were your connections to your father and mother similar and different? If you have siblings of a different sex, how were their relationships with your parents different from yours?

3. How might you engage in queer performance? Describe one way that you could express yourself that would challenge conventional understandings of sex and gender, and the "normal" or "abnormal" judgments that are attached to them.

4. Now that you've read about a range of theories that describe and explain gender, how much do you think gender is due to nature and how much to nurture?

5. Psychodynamic theories assume the mother is the primary caregiver and that this accounts for different gender development in boys and girls. How would you extend psychodynamic theory to explain the effects of fathers who are primary caregivers?

RECOMMENDED RESOURCES

1. John Colapinto. (2006). *As Nature Made Him*. New York: Harper Perennial. This is a very readable account of the life of David/Brenda, who was born male and then medically altered and socialized as a female.

2. Caryl Rivers and Rosalind Barnett. (2011). *The Truth about Girls and Boys: Challenging Toxic Stereotypes about our Children*. New York: Columbia University Press. Coauthored by a journalist and a scientist, this well-written book shows that many claims of sex difference are wildly exaggerated and undermined by looking closely at research.

3. bell hooks. (1990). The politics of radical black subjectivity. In *Yearning: Race, Gender, and Cultural Politics*. Boston: South End Press. This seven-page chapter provides an example of how some blacks move from black social location to political standpoint.

3

The Rhetorical Shaping of Gender: Competing Images of Women

Knowledge Challenge:

- To what extent have women's movements in the United States fought for the rights of all women?
- Are all feminists pro-choice?
- To what degree is third-wave feminism a movement for social change?

What are your dreams for the future? Do you imagine working with an NGO, playing professional sports, earning a graduate or professional degree, or running your own business? Do you intend to accumulate some property and some savings? Is there an age at which you plan to have children? Turning to the more immediate future, have you taken out loans in your name? Do you have your own credit card? Whom do you plan to vote for in the next election? Have you ever considered running for office yourself?

Thinking about these questions isn't odd to you, is it? For men, these are unsurprising questions. Yet entertaining any one of the foregoing questions would have been impossible for a woman in the 1800s, and many of them would have been improbable for most women in the United States even in the 1950s. Until 1920, women could not vote, own property, attend college, or pursue professional education. Until the latter part of the twentieth century, women found it difficult and often impossible to get loans or credit in their own names; they had no legal control over their reproductive health; they were routinely and *legally* discriminated against in the workplace; and they had no hope of scholarship support for athletic ability. Changes in the status and rights of women didn't just happen. They came about because ordinary people thought the status quo was wrong and took active roles in challenging and changing it.

This and the next chapter allow us to appreciate the profound ways that individuals and groups have transformed cultural views of gender and sex.

We will explore rhetorical, or persuasive, efforts to challenge and change existing attitudes, laws, and policies that affect how women and men are understood and how they are treated. In this chapter, we will consider women's movements that have advanced different images of women in the United States. In Chapter 4, we'll explore men's efforts to safeguard or change the images of men in the United States. As we discuss these rhetorical movements, you'll discover that they are anything but uniform. They advocate diverse images of gender and pursue a range of goals, not all of which are compatible. Knowledge of varying activism about gender may allow you to more clearly define your own ideas about gender, as well as how you personally express your gender. Even if you choose not to become politically active, learning about these movements will enhance your understanding of the dynamism of U.S. culture.

The Three Waves of Women's Movements in the United States

Many people think the activism about women began in the 1960s. This, however, disregards more than a century of intense activism about women. It also implies that there is a single women's movement, when actually there have been and are multiple women's movements.

Rhetorical movements to define women's nature and rights have occurred in three waves. During each wave, two distinct ideologies have informed movement goals and efforts for change. One ideology, **liberal feminism**, holds that women and men are alike and equal in most respects. Therefore, goes the reasoning, they should have equal rights, roles, and opportunities. A second, quite different ideology, **cultural feminism**, holds that women and men are fundamentally different and, therefore, should have different rights, roles, and opportunities. These two ideologies coexist, reflecting different images of women and their rights. Also, as we'll learn later in this chapter, each wave of activism for women has witnessed a reactionary backlash against efforts to change images of women.

You should realize that the wave metaphor for women's movements has limits (Hewitt, 2010). Although it's helpful to organize the movements chronologically, they don't really fit neatly into generational compartments. Many themes that were in the first wave—reproductive rights, for example—were also in the second wave and are now part of the third wave. Likewise, some of the goals and tactics of third-wave feminists echo those of the feminists during the second wave (Dow & Wood, in press; Fixmer & Wood, 2005). Thus, as you read about three waves of women's movements, keep in mind that specific concerns and ideologies are not restricted to any single chronological point.

The First Wave of Women's Movements in the United States

Roughly spanning the years from 1840 to 1925, the first wave of women's movements included both liberal and cultural branches. Ironically, the conflicting views of these two movements worked together to change the status and rights of women in U.S. society.

Liberal Ideology: The Women's Rights Movement

The most well-known women's activism during the first wave endorsed a decisively liberal ideology. The **women's rights movement** came into being to gain basic civil rights for women. Scholars date the start of this movement as 1840 (Campbell, 1989a). Between 1840 and 1848, Lucretia Coffin Mott and Elizabeth Cady Stanton, in collaboration with others, organized the first women's rights convention, the Seneca Falls Convention, which was held in New York in 1848. The keynote address, entitled "Declaration of Sentiments," was ingeniously modeled on the Declaration of Independence (Campbell, 1989b, p. 34):

> We hold these truths to be self-evident: that all men and women are created equal; that they are endowed by their Creator with certain inalienable rights, that among these are life, liberty, and the pursuit of happiness.

Continuing in the language of the Declaration of Independence, the Declaration of Sentiments catalogued specific grievances women had suffered, including not being allowed to vote, exclusion from most forms of higher education, restrictions on employment, and loss of property rights upon marriage. At Senaca Falls, 32 men and 68 women signed a petition supporting women's rights. Instrumental to passage of the petition was the support of the former slave Frederick Douglass (Campbell, 1989b).

Douglass' support of women's rights does not signify widespread participation of blacks in the women's rights movement. Initially, there were strong links between abolitionist, or antislavery, efforts and women's rights (Beck, 2008). However, those ties dissolved as many abolitionists became convinced that attaining voting rights for black men had to precede gaining them for women. In addition, many black women thought that the women's rights movement focused on white women's circumstances and ignored grievous differences caused by race (Breines, 2006). Forced to choose between allegiance to their race and allegiance to their sex, most black women of the era chose race. Thus, the women's rights movement became almost exclusively white in its membership and interests.

Women's rights activists marched and spoke at rallies, enduring stinging social disapproval for stepping out of their domestic roles. First-wave activists engaged in peaceful nonviolent protests and hunger strikes. They were jailed, mistreated, and violently force fed. The fight for rights is splendidly documented in the HBO film *Iron Jawed Angels*. A long 72 years after the Senaca Falls Convention, women won the right to vote.

A'n't I a Woman?

Isabella Van Wagenen was born as a slave in Ulster County, New York, in the late 1700s. After she was emancipated, Van Wagenen moved to New York City and became a Pentecostal preacher at the age of 46. She preached throughout the Northern states, using the new name she had given herself: Sojourner of God's Truth. She preached in favor of temperance, women's rights, and the abolition of slavery.

On May 28, 1851, Truth attended a women's rights meeting in Akron, Ohio. Throughout the morning, she listened to speeches that focused on white women's concerns. Moved to point out what was missing, Truth rose and gave her own speech, "A'n't I a Woman?," which pointed out the ways in which white women's situations and oppression

differed from those of black women (Campbell, 2005; Clift, 2003; Hine & Thompson, 1998). Truth had been owned by a Dutch master, so English was a second language for her, one in which she was not fully fluent. The following excerpt from the speech is based on Frances Dana Gage's transcription (Stanton, Anthony, & Gage, 1882, p. 116).

Dat man over dar say dat womin needs to be helped into carriages, and lifted ober ditches, and to hab de best place everywhar. Nobody eber helps me into carriages, or ober mud-puddles, or gives me any best place! And a'n't I a woman? ... I have borne thirteen chilern and seen 'em mos' all sold off to slavery, and when I cried out with my mother's grief, none but Jesus heart me! And a'n't I a woman?

Cultural Ideology: The Cult of Domesticity

Although the Women's Rights Movement is often assumed to represent the interests of most women in the 1800s, actually most women of the time did not agree with women's rights activists that women and men are fundamentally alike and equal. Instead, they thought that women were suited to the domestic sphere because they were more moral, nurturing, concerned about others, and committed to harmony than men. Because they believed that women were suited to domesticity, these women belong to what has been called the **cult of domesticity** (Welter, 1966).

Yet women who were devoted to home, family, and community felt a need to represent those interests in matters of public life. This is why they felt compelled to crusade to end slavery (breaks up family, cruel), ban the consumption of alcohol (causes strife in families, undercuts support for families) (Fields, 2003; Million, 2003), and enact child labor laws (unkind to children). Their desire to right injustices required them to have a public voice, including the right to vote. Thus, for quite different reasons than the women's rights activists, women in the cult of domesticity also worked for women's enfranchisement (Baker, 2006; Sarkela, Ross, & Lowe, 2003).

Antisuffrage Activism in the First Wave

Challenging and changing women's roles and rights did not happen without dissent. Beginning with the first wave, there have been intense antifeminist efforts, also called the **backlash** against feminism (Superson & Cudd, 2002). **Antifeminism** opposes changes in women's roles, status, rights, or opportunities.

The first example of antifeminism was the **antisuffrage movement**, which aimed to prevent women from gaining the right to vote. Immediately following the Seneca Falls Convention, antisuffragists organized, arguing that allowing women to vote, pursue higher education, and own property conflicted with women's natural roles as wives and mothers.

The antisuffrage movement reached its apex between 1911 and 1916 and disbanded after women won the right to vote in 1920.

After passage of the 19th amendment, giving franchise to women, women's movements in the United States were relatively dormant for about 40 years. This time of quiescence resulted from several factors. First, America's attention was concentrated on two world wars. While men were at war, women joined the labor force in record numbers to maintain the economy and support the war effort. Between 1940 and 1944, six million women went to work—a 500% increase in the number of women in paid labor (Harrison, 1988).

Women's participation in the paid labor workforce was halted when men came home from war. More than two million women who had held jobs during the wars were fired, and their positions were given to male veterans (Barnett & Rivers, 1996). With limited career options, the average woman in the 1940s married at 20 and had three children before turning 30. By the time she was 40, mothering did not fully occupy her. By the time she was 50, the children had left home (Collins, 2009b). The lack of opportunities beyond home and family that this era afforded women sowed the seeds for the second wave of U.S. feminism.

Although there was no major feminist activism between the 1920s and the 1960s, there were changes that affected women's lives. Amelia Earhart showed that women could be daring and adventurous; women's sports teams were established and gained a limited following; and more effective and available methods of birth control were developed.

The Second Wave of Women's Movements in the United States

Starting in 1963, a second wave of women's movements emerged in the United States. As in the first wave of U.S. women's movements, the second wave included liberal feminists, cultural feminists, and antifeminists.

Liberal Ideology

The second wave of U.S. feminism included a number of groups that endorsed a liberal ideology. The first feminist activism to emerge during the second wave was **radical feminism**, also called the **women's liberation movement**. Not surprisingly, college campuses provided fertile ground for the emergence of radical feminism. It grew out of New Left politics that protested the Vietnam War and fought for civil rights. Women in the New Left movement did the same work as their male peers and risked the same hazards of arrest and physical assault, but New Left men treated women as subordinates, telling them to make coffee, type news releases, do the menial work of organizing, and be ever available for sex.

In 1964 and 1965, women in several New Left groups challenged the sexism of their male peers, but there was little response to their demands for equality (Stansell, 2010). Outraged by men's refusal to extend to women the democratic, egalitarian principles they advocated for minorities, many women withdrew from the New Left and formed their own organizations.

Radical feminists relied on "rap" groups, or consciousness-raising groups, in which women gathered to talk informally about personal experiences with sexism and to link those personal experiences to larger social and political structures. Radical feminists' commitment to equality and their deep suspicion of hierarchy led them to insist on leaderless discussions so that participants would have equal power.

Radical feminists relied on revolutionary analysis and politics along with high-profile public events to call attention to the oppression of women and to demand changes (Barry, 1998; Freeman, 2002). Examples of public events they staged include:

- Occupation of the *Ladies' Home Journal* office.
- Speak-outs about silenced issues such as rape and abortion.
- Protests against the Miss America pageants in 1968 and 1969, in which women threw cosmetics and constrictive underwear for women into a "Freedom Trash Can" to protest the view of women as sex objects.
- Guerrilla theater, in which they engaged in public communication to dramatize issues and arguments.

JES

My grandmother was a radical feminist. I grew up hearing stories about how badly the guys treated her and other women who were working for civil rights. It's totally weird that the guys couldn't see women were their equals when they were all about blacks being equal and that's why they were in the Civil Rights movement. Grandma has told me about her rap groups and stuff like that. She says they changed her life.

EXPLORING GENDERED LIVES *The Famous Bra Burning (That Didn't Happen!)*

One of the most widespread misperceptions is that feminists burned bras in 1968 to protest the Miss America pageant. That never happened. Here's what did. In planning a response to the pageant, protesters considered a number of strategies to dramatize their disapproval of what the pageant stood for and how it portrayed women. They decided to protest by throwing false eyelashes, bras, and girdles into what they called the Freedom Trash Can. They also put a crown on an animal labeled Miss America and led it around the pageant. In early planning for the protest, some members suggested burning bras, but this idea was abandoned (Collins, 2009a; Hanisch, 1970). However, a reporter heard of the plan and reported it as fact on national media. Millions of Americans accepted the report as accurate, and even today many people refer to feminists as "bra burners."

Demonstrations are one communication tool of rhetorical movements.

Perhaps the most important outcome of radical feminism was the identification of the structural basis of women's oppression. The connection between social practices and individual women's situations was captured in radical feminists' declaration that "the personal is political." Through consciousness raising and collective efforts, radical feminists launched a women's health movement that taught women to resist sexist attitudes from some doctors and become knowledgeable about their own bodies (Boston Women's Health Club Book Collective, 1976; The Diagram Group, 1977). Although radical feminists' refusal to formally organize limited their ability to affect public policies and structures, they offered—and continue to offer—a profound and far-reaching critique of sexual inequality.

Roughly at the same time that radical feminism arose, another second-wave feminist group was coming to life in the suburbs of America. Liberal feminism, which advocates women's equality in all spheres of life, was ignited in 1963 with publication of Betty Friedan's landmark book, *The Feminine Mystique*. The book's title was Friedan's way of naming what she called "the problem that has no name." The problem that hadn't been named was the discontent that many white, middle-class American women felt because they had no opportunities beyond home and family. Friedan named the problem and declared that this seemingly personal issue was actually also a political issue. She pointed out that women were not able to pursue personal development because of political or structural factors: American institutions, especially laws, kept many women confined to domestic roles with no opportunity for fulfillment in arenas outside of home life. Although most suburban stay-at-home moms loved their families and homes, they also longed for an identity outside of home, particularly in the 30 to 50 years of life after children left home (Collins, 2009b).

Also fueling changes in women's lives were economic factors. The robust economic boom that followed WWII moved unprecedented numbers of families into the middle class, and all of these new middle-class families wanted their own homes, central heating, appliances, and other advantages of wealth. Marketers in the 1960s began emphasizing the two-income family as the American ideal because both incomes were needed to sustain the consumption patterns Americans had developed.

Liberal feminism is embodied in NOW, the National Organization for Women. Founded in 1966, NOW works to secure political, professional, and educational equality for women and has become one of the most influential public voices for women's rights.

Although second-wave liberal feminism was characterized by more focus on and leadership by white, middle-class women, it would be a mistake to buy the stereotype that second-wave liberal feminism was "lily white." As scholars (Dow, in press; Lumsden, 2009; McDonald, 2012) of the second wave have pointed out, the truth is more nuanced. From the start, concerns about race and racism were negotiated alongside concerns about sex and sexism. Most liberal feminist as well as radical feminists fought for Civil Rights, and second-wave liberal

---

EXPLORING GENDERED LIVES   *About NOW*

The NOW was established on June 30, 1966, at the Third National Conference on the Commission on the Status of Women. Betty Friedan, NOW's first president, and the Reverend Pauli Murray, an African-American woman who was an attorney and poet, coauthored NOW's original mission statement, which begins with this sentence: "The purpose of NOW is to take action to bring women into full participation in the mainstream of American society now, exercising all privileges and responsibilities thereof in truly equal partnership with men." Among NOW's achievements:

- Executive Order 11375, which prohibits sex discrimination by federal contractors.

- Amending the Civil Rights Act of 1965 to include sex, along with race, religion, and nationality, as an illegal basis for employment discrimination.

- Support of federally financed child-care centers to enable women to work outside the home.

- Documenting sexism in media.

- Identification of and publicity about sexism in children's books and programs to enable parents and teachers to make informed choices about media for their children.

- Reform of credit and banking practices that disadvantage women.

- Enlargement of women's opportunities to participate in sports.

- The Equal Employment Opportunity Commission's adoption of a rule that sex-segregated want ads are discriminatory.

- Support for women who seek elective and appointive public office.

- Highlighting gender inequities worldwide, particularly in poorer countries.

feminism benefited from strong voices of non-white women, such as Flo Kennedy, Pauli Murray, bell hooks (Gallagher, 2012). In 1970, Jamaican-American Aileen Fernandez became NOW's second president. Liberal feminism today is inclusive of diverse women and the issues in their lives. NOW's homepage has a link to its work against racism.

Liberal feminism is not confined to the United States. Feminist groups around the world are committed to equal rights for women. Spain, the country that gave birth to the word *machismo*, is responding to the influence of liberal feminism. Activist work, particularly work done by feminist NGOs (nongovernment organizations) in the third world at the grassroots level, has contributed substantially to global awareness of particular forms of oppression of women, such as sex trafficking (Hegde, 2006; Townsley, 2006). In 2004 in Mumbai, India, record numbers of women participated in The World Social Forum and drew worldwide attention to the urgent and continuing issues of violence against women (Sen & Saini, 2005). In Iraq, women today have fewer rights than before U.S. troops invaded the country. Women there have created The Organization of Women's Freedom in Iraq (OWFI: **http://www.equalityiniraq.com**) to fight for women's rights to education, employment, marital choice, and inheritance (McKee, 2006). After a long struggle for suffrage, Kuwaiti women gained the right to vote in 2006 (Fattah, 2006).

CASS

I really like what NOW is about and how it works. It's not as cool as some of the radical groups, but it makes change happen by working within the system. NOW has changed laws and policies. It's given a national platform for fighting racism and women's self-hatred. It's gotten women elected to office. You can't have that kind of impact unless you get inside the system and figure out how to change it from the inside.

Although many liberal feminists of different races in the 1960s and 1970s grappled with issues of race, some women of color formed their own activist organizations. A group of black women founded **womanism** to highlight the ways in which gender and racial oppression intersect in the lives of women of color. Womanists point out that, compared to white women, black women as a group are more often single, bear more children, are paid less, and assume more financial responsibility for families (Walker, 1992; Parks, 2010).

In addition to focusing on race, womanists attend to ways in which class intersects race and sex to create inequality. Womanist organizations often include working-class women and address issues that keenly affect lower-class African-American women. Their goals include reforming social services to be more responsive to poor women, and increasing training and job opportunities so that women of color can improve the material conditions of their lives.

In 1997, African-American women held a **Million Woman March** in Philadelphia. Powered by grassroots volunteers who built support in their localities, the steering committee of the Million Woman March was made up not of celebrities but of average women who worked at unglamorous jobs and lived outside the spotlight. Perhaps the spirit of the Million Woman March is best summed up by Irma Jones, a 74-year-old woman who had marched with Dr. Martin Luther King Jr. from Selma to Montgomery. After the Million Woman March, Jones said, "I'm glad we did this before I died. People say black women can never get together. Today, we got together, sister" (Logwood, 1998, p. 19).

EXPLORING GENDERED LIVES To Be Womanish, To Be a Womanist

Alice Walker is credited with coining the term womanism as a label for black women who believe in women's rights, and opportunities. According to Walker, Southern black women often said to their daughters, "You acting womanish," which meant the daughters were being bold, courageous, and wilful. To be womanish is to demand to know more than others say is good for you—to stretch beyond what is prescribed for a woman or girl (Collins, 1998). In her 1983 book *In Search of Our Mothers' Gardens*, Walker writes, "Womanist is to feminist as purple is to lavender" (p. xii).

Building on womanism's focus on equality for black women, **multiracial feminism** emphasizes multiple systems of domination that shape people's lives (Anzaldúa, 2002; Anzaldúa & Keating, 2002; Collins, 1998; Ryan, 2004). Although race is especially important from multiracial feminists' perspective, race is intertwined with other systems of domination. Multiracial feminists insist that gender does not have universal meaning—instead, what gender means and how it affects our lives varies as a result of race, economic class, sexual orientation, gender identity, and so forth.

KATIE

I like the ideas of the multiracial feminists. I agree that race cuts across everything else. I'm middle-class, but my life isn't the same as a white, middle-class girl's, because I'm Asian American. It's like the issues in my life aren't just about my sex; they're also about my race. I can talk to black or Hispanic girls, and we have a lot in common—more than I have in common with most white girls. You just can't get away from the issue of race unless you're white.

Central to both womanism and multiracial feminism is emphasis on women's agency. Despite the constraints imposed by systems of domination, women of color have often resisted their oppressions. Even when they operated within abhorrent systems of domination such as slavery, women of color found ways to care for themselves and their families and to contribute to their communities. In recognizing that women of color have resisted oppression, multiracial feminists highlight the strengths of women.

A final strand in liberal feminism is **ecofeminism**. In both Europe and America, ecofeminists assert there is a connection between the effort to control and subordinate women and the struggle to dominate nature (perhaps not coincidentally called "Mother Earth"). Rosemary Radford Reuther (1974, 1983, 2001), a theological scholar, argues that the lust to dominate has brought the world to the brink of a moral and ecological crisis in which there can be no winners. Ecofeminists believe that, as long as oppression is culturally valued, it will be imposed on anyone and anything that is unable or unwilling to resist.

For ecofeminists, women's oppression is best understood as a specific example of an overarching cultural ideology that esteems oppression. Believing in humans' profound interdependence with all other life forms, ecofeminists argue that exploitation, domination, and aggression oppress women, men, children, animals, and the planet itself. In *Feminism Is for Everybody*, author bell hooks (2002) says it's a mistake to think that feminism is about only women or women's rights. She says feminism is about justice, which she thinks is achieved by ending all kinds of domination and oppression, including but not limited to sexism and racism. For her, all forms of oppression are linked.

Some of my strongest values involve ending the oppression of animals and living a sustainable lifestyle. Until I read about ecofeminism, I never saw the connection between those beliefs and feminism. But it makes sense, once you think about it, that if it's wrong to oppress animals and the earth, it's wrong to oppress women … or anyone …or anything.

The 1990s gave birth to **power feminism**, which contends that society doesn't oppress women because women have the power to control what happens to them. Naomi Wolf (1993) tells women that the only thing holding them back from equality is their own belief that they are victims. Similarly, power feminist Katie Roiphe (1993) claimed that Take Back the Night marches, annual nonviolent protests to speak out against rape, are self-defeating because "proclaiming victimhood" does not project strength.

The only people I know who talk the power feminist talk have never been raped and never been slapped in the face with discrimination. They think their success and safety is a result of their own efforts and that any woman or minority person who hasn't achieved what they have just didn't try. I'll bet a lot of them would drop the power feminist line if they got raped. That might make them see that women and minorities don't have as much power as people like Wolf and Roiphe. As for me, I don't think of myself as a victim, but I know I'm vulnerable just because I'm black and a woman.

Power feminism ignores the difference between being a victim at one moment, on the one hand, and adopting the status of victim as an identity, on the other hand. Power feminism may appeal to women who are financially comfortable, successful, well educated, and living in safe neighborhoods. It is less helpful to women who do not enjoy those privileges. Perhaps that is why power feminism is embraced mainly by white, heterosexual, middle- and upper-class women who have little or no personal experience with discrimination and violation.

Cultural Ideology

We've looked at second-wave feminist groups that subscribe to the liberal ideology that regards women and men as fundamentally alike and, thus, as entitled to the same rights and roles. Just as in the first wave, the second wave includes groups

EXPLORING GENDERED LIVES | *Reproductive Rights*

Birth control was and is a priority in many women's movements. In the nineteenth century, Elizabeth Cady Stanton insisted that "voluntary motherhood" was a prerequisite of women's freedom (Gordon, 1976; Schiff, 2006). Margaret Sanger's work as a nurse and midwife made her painfully aware that many women, particularly immigrants and poor women, died in childbirth or as a result of illegal abortions (Chesler, 1992). She insisted that a woman's body belongs to herself, not the Church or government.

During the second wave of feminism in the United States, feminists again protested for safe, accessible birth control and abortion for all women. In 1973, the landmark case *Roe v. Wade* established abortion as a woman's right. Yet, abortion is still not available to all women who are citizens of the United States.

Reproductive rights have also emerged as a focus of the third wave. The March for Women's Lives, held on April 25, 2004, on the Capitol Mall in Washington, DC, drew hundreds of thousands of marchers who were concerned that *Roe v. Wade* might be reversed. Voicing their support for the right of women to be in charge of their own reproductive health, the marchers included young men and women, grandmothers, and mothers with babies.

Reproductive rights are central to feminist movements, but not all feminist movements are pro-choice. Groups such as Feminists for Life are firmly against abortion. They argue that choosing not to have a child is antithetical to feminine values.

There is a widespread assumption that birth control is liberatory for women. In reality, however, efforts to control reproduction have been liberatory only for some women, and they have been decisively disempowering for other women (Fixmer-Oraiz, 2012; Gordon, 2007; Rose, 2007). For instance, throughout much of the twentieth century in the United States, many women who were black, immigrant, poor, mentally challenged, or otherwise "undesirable" were sterilized without their consent.

that disagree with that view and, instead, believe that women and men are different in important ways and, thus, should have different rights and roles.

Separatism was developed to provide communities for women to live independently of men. Separatists believe that women are fundamentally different from men in the value they place on life, equality, harmony, nurturance, and peace. Finding that these values gain little hearing in a patriarchal, capitalist society, separatists form all-women communities in which feminine values can flourish without the aggressive, individualistic, oppressive values these women associate with Western masculinity.

In choosing to exit mainstream society and form sequestered communities, separatists limit their potential to alter dominant social values. Because they do not assume a public voice to critique the values they find objectionable, they exercise little political influence. Yet, their very existence defines an alternative vision of how we might live—one that speaks of harmony, cooperation, and peaceful coexistence of all life forms.

I don't see much to be gained by having equal rights to participate in institutions that are themselves all wrong. I don't believe dog-eat-dog ethics are right. I don't want to be part of a system where I can advance only if I slit somebody else's throat or step on him or her. I don't want to prostitute myself for bits of power in a business. I would rather work for different ways of living, ones that are more cooperative, like win-win strategies. Maybe that means I'm a dreamer, but I just can't motivate myself to work at gaining status in a system that I don't respect.

Revalorism highlights women's traditional activities and contributions and increasing society's appreciation of women and their contributions to society. The broad goal of revalorists is to increase the value that society places on women and on the skills, art, and philosophies associated with women's traditional roles.

It saddens me that so few young women knit or crochet or even sew. Nearly all women of my generation knew how to sew, and many of us knew how to knit or weave or quilt. Historically, women have made beautiful clothing and linens for their families—the kind you can't buy in a store. Women today seem so focused on career that they are cutting off their links to their own histories. Does it have to be either or?

Drawing on standpoint theory, which we discussed in Chapter 2, revalorists believe that women's traditional involvement in homemaking and caregiving makes most women more nurturing, supportive, cooperative, and life-giving than most men. Sara Ruddick (1989), for instance, claims that the process of mothering young children cultivates "maternal thinking," which is marked by attentiveness to others and commitment to others' health, happiness, and development. In documenting women's contributions, revalorists aim to render a more complete history of the United States and the people who comprise it.

Antifeminist Activism in the Second Wave

Antifeminist activism resurged in the 1970s when Marabel Morgan (1973) launched the Total Woman movement and Helen Andelin (1975) founded the Fascinating Womanhood movement, both of which advocated women's return to traditional attitudes, values, and roles. Primary support for women's return to traditional roles came from women who were economically dependent on husbands and who embraced conservative values.

EXPLORING GENDERED LIVES *The Text of the Equal Rights Amendment*

Equality of the rights under the law shall not be denied or abridged by the United States or by any State on account of sex.

A more significant form of antifeminism was the STOP ERA movement, which also emerged in the 1970s. This movement was a direct response to the 1972 and 1973 campaign to ratify the Equal Rights Amendment (ERA).

The most prominent spokesperson for STOP ERA, Phyllis Schlafly, traveled around the nation announcing that feminism was destroying femininity by encouraging women to leave traditional roles and be more like men. Ironically, although Schlafly argued that women's place was in the home, her speaking schedule kept her on the road constantly, so she was unable to devote much time to her own home and family. The STOP ERA movement was successful in blocking passage of the bill. To this day, America has not passed the ERA.

LYLE

I'm a lot older than most students. I've had a career and my wife and I raised four kids. I should say she raised them because that was her job. Mine was to earn an income for the family. That system worked fine for us, and our kids turned out just fine. I don't understand why so many young people don't want to follow traditional roles. We approve of division of labor in business and government; what's wrong with division of labor (he makes the money, she takes care of family) in our personal lives?

The Third Wave of Feminism in the United States

Many branches of second-wave feminism continue to be active today. Alongside them, a third wave of feminism emerged in the mid-90s. Influenced by multiple branches of second-wave feminism, especially radical and multiracial feminism, **third-wave feminism** includes women of different ethnicities, abilities and disabilities, classes, appearances, sexual orientations, and gender identities. Perhaps because it is new, this wave of feminism has not yet defined a clear center. On the other hand, it could be that the third wave will be characterized by multiplicity and the resistance to any single center (Henry, 2004).

Although the newest generation of feminists draws on earlier movements, third-wave feminism is not simply an extension of the second wave (Fixmer, 2003;

Fixmer & Wood, 2005; Johnson, 2007). Third-wave feminists have a distinct historical location and consciousness that inform their politics and goals. We'll discuss features of third-wave feminism as it appears at this early point in its development.

Intersectionality

Informed by multiracial feminists' attention to differences among women, third-wave feminists recognize that women differ in many ways, including race, class, sexual orientation, body shape and size, and (dis)ability. Coming of age in an era sharply infused with awareness of differences, third wavers are trying to figure out how to speak about and for women as a group while simultaneously recognizing differences among women (Fixmer, 2003; Zack, 2005). Drawing on the insights of multiracial feminists, third wavers focus on the intersectionality of oppression, pointing out that race, class, sex, sexual orientation, and gender identity are intricately woven together and must be addressed holistically. Eve Ensler's latest book, *I Am an Emotional Creature* (2011), includes monologues from girls all over the world, showing both how they are different and how they have commonalities.

Coalitions and Alliances

Because third-wave feminists recognize the intersectionality of oppression, they are committed to building alliances with other groups that work against various kinds of oppression. As third-wave writer, Mocha Jean Herrup (1995) explains, "to fight AIDS we must fight homophobia, and to fight homophobia we must fight racism, and so on…. Oppression is interrelated" (p. 247).

NATALIE

I really appreciate what the sixties women's movement did to make my life better, but I can't identify with it. My life is different than my mother's, and so are the issues that matter to me. Mom fought to get a job. I want a job that pays well and lets me advance. Mom worked really hard to find day care for her children. I want to have a marriage and a job that allow me not to have to rely on day care. Her generation fought to make it okay for women not to marry. My generation wants to figure out how to make marriages work better, more fairly. Different generations. Different issues.

Everyday Resistance

Third-wave feminists point out that many of the reforms won by the second wave have not been woven into everyday life. Sexism is often more subtle today than in 1960 or 1980, but it still exists; in fact, its subtlety is what makes it so challenging (Bennett, Ellison, & Ball, 2010). This motivates third wavers to embrace grassroots organizing and to challenge racist comments in the workplace and on the street, confront homophobic attitudes, and be willing to reject class privileges, including those that benefit us. Third wavers Jennifer Baumgardner and Amy Richards (2000) declare that, for third-wave feminists, "our politics emerge from our everyday lives" (p. 18). Personal acts in local contexts are seen as a key way to instigate change (Bodey & Wood, 2009; Fixmer & Wood, 2005; Sheridan-Rabideau, 2009).

Third-wave feminists insist that their politics must be rooted in personal, bodily resistance to oppressive ideologies (Babel & Kwan, 2011). In a stunning essay that explicitly links social constructions of female beauty to eating disorders that jeopardize millions of women's health, Abra Fortune Chernik (1995) writes, "Gazing in the mirror at my emaciated body, I observed a woman held up by her culture as the physical ideal because she was starving, self-obsessed and powerless, a woman called beautiful because she threatened no one except herself" (p. 81). After recognizing the connection between cultural codes for femininity and her own body, Chernik responded in a way that was both personal and political: "Gaining weight and getting my head out of the toilet bowl was the most political act I have ever committed" (p. 81).

Media Savvy

Third-wave feminism is also media savvy and media engaged. Third-wave feminists, like other members of their generation, tend to be wired, plugged in, and virtually networked so that they gain information from numerous sources and also create media of their own (Harris, 2004; Kearney, 2006; Johnson, 2007). Whereas second-wave feminists waited for the 6 p.m. news on TV to learn about the day's events, third-wavers are likely to learn immediately of new developments from text messages and blogs, and they often post their own videos of rallies and other events on YouTube and other websites. They also organize online as was the case when The Komen Foundation, which fights against breast cancer, announced it would no longer provide support to Planned Parenthood. Using social media, feminists got the word out, fueled outrage toward Komen's announced action, and forced Komen to reverse its position and continue funding Planned Parenthood.

Consumerist

Some, but not all, women who identify as third-wave feminists embrace traditional "girl culture" by placing a premium on being pretty, feminine, sexy, and having the latest fashions. They argue that there is no contradiction between being feminist and being sexy. Critics point out that while being sexy and being feminist aren't mutually exclusive, embodying society's ideal of womanhood is not equally possible

EXPLORING GENDERED LIVES | "Don't Tell Us How to Dress. Tell Men Not to Rape."

On January 24, 2011, at York University in Toronto, Canada, Toronto Police Constable Michael Sanguinetti spoke to a group of women about crime prevention. He advised them to "avoid dressing like **sluts**" if they wished to prevent sexual assault (Stampler, 2011). Some women who heard Sanguinetti's comment were angry about what they perceived as yet another instance of blaming victims and excusing perpetrators of sexual violence. Two women who took offense decided to take their grievance to the streets by organizing the first SlutWalk protest, which took place on April 3, 2011, at Queen's Park in Toronto.

Although the organizers asked participants to dress in their everyday clothing to symbolize the fact that women in ordinary dress are assaulted, some participants chose to wear lingerie, stilettos, and other provocative clothing to symbolize their right to dress "like sluts" without being becoming victims of sexual violence. Some of the marchers scrawled messages on their bodies or carried signs reading "My dress is not a yes" and "Don't tell us how to dress. Tell men not to rape" (Valenti, 2011).

Since the movement's inception, Slutwalk protests have emerged organically in Asia, Australia, Denmark, New Zealand, Germany, Czechoslovakia, Finland, Argentina, Mexico, Morocco, India, Honduras, Brazil, and South Africa as well as majorly in the United States.

Opinions of SlutWalks vary widely (see Dow & Wood, in press). One social critic cheers, "Here at last is that bold, original, do-it-yourself protest movement we've been waiting for, a rock-hard wall of female solidarity ... presented as media-savvy street theater that connects the personal and the political" (Pollitt, 2011). Yet another social critic sees SlutWalks as "narcissistic stunts," that "are yet another frivolous distraction by those who take advantage of the unprecedented freedoms won by others as they wrap themselves in the mantle of victim" (Phillips. 2011).

Go online to learn more about SlutWalks. After doing so, what do you think of these protests? Are they effective grassroots feminist organizing? Are they proof that women themselves have bought into sexist objectification of women? Are they something else?

for all women. It takes a lot of energy and money to meet society's current ideals for women. Thus, third-wave feminists who have sufficient time and money can embrace consumerism—spending money to be seen at the "right" restaurants, bars, spas, and stores and to acquire designer clothes, name-brand products, and cosmetic procedures (Chaudhry, 2005; Levy, 2005). Women who have less time and money to spare will lack the resources to meet the ideals, yet many will struggle to "stay in the race."

The pressure to meet the unrealistic and unhealthy ideals for women is relentless. Sexually explicit and endlessly digitalized photos of perfection create a pressure for women to accept and emulate sexual images of women in order to feel that they are liberated (Paul, 2006). Exposed to the endless stream of air-brushed photos of ideal women, many young women today objectify themselves, particularly by making themselves into sex objects for others' consumption (Gender in Media, 2012; Levy, 2005; Newsome, 2011).

Individualism

A final characteristic of third-wave feminism reflects its personal politics: a focus on individuals and individualism—individual goals, strategies, and identities (Crawford, 2007; Henry, 2004). Third wavers claim that because women are so different and their issues are so diverse, there can be no collective political agenda. Life and identity become DIY (do it yourself) projects in which each woman defines feminism on her own terms and lives her life on the principle that every woman can choose to be whatever she wants to be.

One example of third wavers' emphasis on individualism is autobiographical essays, often posted on blogs or social network pages. Astrid Henry (2004), whose research focuses on women's movements, notes that while autobiographical essays can be a first step in consciousness raising, third-wave feminists have gotten stuck and are unable or unwilling to move "from this beginning consciousness-raising stage of self-expression to developing a larger analysis of the relationship between individual and collective experience, culminating in theory and political action … for the third wave, identity politics is limited to expression of individual identity" (pp. 43–44).

The third wave's emphasis on individualism does not cultivate a cohesive political agenda that can help build the structures that will support their individual choices. For example, many women in my classes believe that if they do well in school and work hard, they can succeed in any career they choose. Yet, I worry that they may confront obstacles such as lower pay than male peers and discrimination against mothers (Hayden & O'Brien Hallstein, 2010). Obstacles such as these cannot be overcome by individual effort. They require structural change, and structural change grows out of collective political action.

In sum, third-wave feminists use media, particularly social media, to build a feminism that is more inclusive, more engaged with everyday life, and more individualistic. It is clear that a new generation of feminists is engaging issues that affect women's lives. What remains unclear is whether third-wave feminists will move beyond personal reflection and practice and into some form of public activism that remakes feminism as a political movement that resonates with the priorities of their generation.

EXPLORING GENDERED LIVES *Twenty-First-Century Feminism*

In a July 9, 2009, interview, a *The Seattle Times* reporter asked Gloria Steinem what twenty-first-century feminism looks like. Here's Steinem's answer: "It looks like you. It looks like each self-respecting woman in the twenty-first century. It's not for me to define; the message of feminism is that each of us, as female human beings, define ourselves. There are some generalities that you can see. It's much more international, I'm happy to say. I think clearly most of the country now understands that women can do what men can do; the problem is that they don't understand that men can do what women can do, which as I was saying, is the reason why women still suffer from having two jobs" (*Seattle Times*, 2009).

Antifeminism in the Third Wave

Remember the Total Woman and Fascinating Womanhood movements in the second wave? The same idea resurfaced in the 2001 book *The Surrendered Wife: A Practical Guide for Finding Intimacy, Passion, and Peace with a Man* (L. Doyle). This book, like the earlier two antifeminist movements that it echoes, counsels women to abandon the quest for equality if they want happy marriages (Clinton, 2001). Women are advised to let their husbands lead the family and to accommodate their husbands. Another book, *The War Against Men* (Hise, 2004), claims that women have gained power at the expense of men and that this is contrary to God's commandments, which define the proper relationship between women and men.

Many feminists charge that claims advanced by antifeminists are misrepresentations and exaggerations. There is truth to that charge. At the same time, some of the claims made by some feminists have been exaggerated, too. It is productive to have different voices, including feminist and antifeminist ones, to act as checks and balances on each other.

SUMMARY

This chapter demonstrates that there are competing images of women that circulate in society. Through activist efforts, people argue for the images they think are most true, right, fair, or useful. And others argue back in an ongoing dialogue about who women are and what that means for their rights, roles, and opportunities.

The issue of whether a person is a feminist is considerably more complicated than it first appears. The "women's movement" is really a collage of many movements that span more than 170 years and include a range of political and social ideologies. Whether or not you define yourself as a feminist, you have some views on women's identities, rights, and nature. Much of the analysis in various women's movements should inform your thinking about women's roles and lives.

KEY TERMS

The following terms are defined in this chapter on the indicated pages, as well as in alphabetical order in the book's glossary, which begins on page 283. The text's companion website (**http://www.cengage.com/communication/wood/gendered lives11e**) also provides interactive flash cards and crossword puzzles to help you learn these terms and the concepts they represent.

antifeminism 63
antisuffrage movement 64
backlash 63
cult of domesticity 63
cultural feminism 61
ecofeminism 70
liberal feminism 61
Million Woman March 69
multiracial feminism 70

power feminism 71
radical feminism 64
revalorism 73
separatism 72
third-wave feminism 74
womanism 69
women's liberation movement 64
women's rights movement 62

GENDER ONLINE

1. To learn more about ecofeminism, visit Eve Online at: **http://eve.enviroweb .org** or visit the home page of the ecofeminist organization at: **http://www .ecofem.org/ecofeminism**

2. Visit NOW at: **http://www.now.org**

3. To learn more about the third wave and differences and commonalities between it and earlier waves, visit this website: **http://www.thirdwavefoundation.org/**

4. Online search terms: "ecofeminism," "eve ensler," "third wave feminism."

REFLECTION AND DISCUSSION

1. How have your views of feminism changed as a result of reading this chapter?

2. With which of the feminist movements discussed in this chapter do you most identify? To what extent do you think we should work to ensure that women have equal rights and opportunities within existing systems (liberal feminism) or should work to change the systems to incorporate traditionally feminine values and concerns (cultural feminism)?

3. Write or act out a discussion about whether women should serve in combat roles, which takes place between three feminists: an ecofeminist, a power feminist, and a separatist.

4. To what extent do you think it is possible for women to be both politically engaged feminists and sexy and conventionally feminine?

RECOMMENDED RESOURCES

1. Michael Kaufman & Michael Kimmell. (2011). The Guy's Guide to *Feminism*. Berkeley, CA: Seal Press. In this short, very accessible book, Kaufman and Kimmel explain why, in their own words, "in spite of all the garbage jokes and media stereotypes, feminism is also an amazing gift to us guys" (p. 9).

2. *Iron Jawed Angels*. (2004). Directed by Katja von Garnier. Distributed by HBO. This film dramatizes the final stage of the fight for women's right to vote.

3. Marilyn French. (1977). *The Women's Room*. New York: Ballantine. This novel's protagonist engages in consciousness raising that allows her to see and challenge her own oppression. The novel represents what many women in the 1960s and 1970s experienced.

4. Gail Collins. (2009). *When Everything Changed: The Amazing Journey of American Women from 1960 to the Present*. New York: Little, Brown & Co. This is one of the most comprehensive and readable histories of the second wave of American feminism. Trained as a journalist, Collins writes in an engaging, accessible style.

You must be the change that you wish to see in the world.
—Mahatma Gandhi

4

The Rhetorical Shaping of Gender: Competing Images of Men

Knowledge Challenge:

- What does it mean to perform traitorous identity?
- Which men's groups ally themselves with feminism?
- What is the Good Men Project?

MATT

It's really weird when I go home and see the guys I used to hang with who stayed there. I used to fit in with them. We played baseball as kids. When we were in high school, we hunted, played video games, and lied about sex. We were so much alike we could complete each other's sentences. But now it's really awkward. They're still playing video games and trash talking girls and their idea of a good night is to watch a game and drink beer. I tried talking to them about some of the stuff I'm learning, but they're not interested in anything other than what they've grown up with. We don't have much in common except history.

JENNA

When my dad got laid off in 2009, it hit him like a ton of bricks. At first, he was sure he'd get another great job. Didn't happen. After a year, he really hit bottom. Some days, he didn't even get up. Mom said he was depressed, but he refused to see a doctor or even talk to us. The most he says is that he feels like nobody because he can't support his family. He could do a lot to support us that doesn't have anything to do with making money, but he doesn't see that.

Matt's and Jenna's reflections give us insight into different understandings of man-hood that circulate in the United States. Matt, who took a class with me, grew up in a small, rural town in the South. Like many rural communities, Matt's leaned toward conservative politics and fairly traditional views of women and men (McMahan, 2011). Coming to the University of North Carolina at Chapel Hill was a culture shock for him. He encountered liberal ideas that he'd not thought about at home, met people who were invested in politics and passionate about issues, and dated women who were more professionally ambitious than he was. As Matt explored his new context, he reconsidered what he had taken for granted grow-ing up. He continued to be steadfast in his faith, yet gradually distanced himself from some of the conservative social views in his hometown. Only when Matt went home did he realize how much his views, including his view of men, had changed.

Jenna's reflection on her father gives us insight into how conditions beyond our individual lives can affect our gendered self-images. Jenna's dad isn't alone in feeling that he's not a successful man because he's not bringing in a salary. The recession that started in 2008 threw many men out of work. Since a majority of men in the United States regard being a good provider as central to being a man, losing jobs also affected their sense of their manhood.

Images of men as breadwinners and hunters coexist with views of men as engaged fathers and family cooks. Competing images of manhood are not new; they've existed throughout history. Although one image tends to dominate at any given time, alternative images are always in the mix and often serve as catalysts for changing how we understand manhood and masculinity.

Historically, American men have been less involved than women in organized efforts to change images of their gender. Although many men have not given sustained thought to their identity as men, some men have. In this chapter, we examine those men's efforts to define what manhood means. Like women's activism, men's has reflected diverse, sometimes deeply conflicting, political and personal values and goals. Some men's groups aim to usher in new images of mas-culinity, whereas others want to reinvigorate traditional images of masculinity and safeguard or increase men's privileges. Also like women's activism, men's activism is evolving, with new groups arising as once-prominent groups fade away. In the 1990s, the Promise Keepers and the Million Man March were high-profile efforts to shape images of manhood. Today, both appear to be waning, yet a new group has emerged to ask what it means to be a good man today.

Men's efforts to define manhood are not independent of women's activism. As we will see in this chapter, some men's groups ally themselves with feminist orga-nizations, particularly the liberal branches of feminism. Other men's groups fiercely reject feminism and feminists, and they work to bolster traditionally masculine roles, status, and the privileges.

BILL

I can't remember when I wasn't a feminist. It's as much a part of me as being a man or a Christian. My parents both work, Mom as a lawyer and Dad as an accountant. I grew up seeing my mother as strong and achieving and loving, just as Dad was. I grew up seeing my mother express her ideas articulately and seeing my father respect what she said and did. She listened when he talked; he listened when she did. When I was a kid, sometimes Mom worked late, and Dad was in charge of fixing dinner for me and my brother. Other times, Dad worked late, and Mom was in charge. Both of them took care of us. Both of them were successful outside of the home. I grew up seeing that women and men are equal. How could I not be a feminist?

Profeminist Men's Groups

Referred to as **profeminists**, *progressive men*, or **male feminists**, these groups emerged in the 1960s. Although many men in New Left organizations like Student Nonviolent Coordinating Committee (SNCC) and Students for a Democratic Society (SDS) ignored women who accused them of sexism, some men involved in the New Left thought the women's criticism was on target, and they were ashamed when confronted with the hypocrisy of their political efforts to end discrimination against blacks while discriminating against women.

Progressive men worked to bring their attitudes and behavior in line with the egalitarian ideology they espoused. They joined forces with women to work for women's rights. Profeminist men's close relationship with mainstream liberal feminism generated two distinct foci, one related to women and the other to men.

Because they believe in the equality of the sexes, male feminists support women's battles for equitable treatment in society and participate in efforts to increase women's rights. For instance, during the 1972 campaign to ratify the Equal Rights Amendment (ERA), many men gave time, effort, and money to the battle for legal recognition of women's equality. Today, most male feminists endorse equal pay for equal work, hiring and promoting qualified women, and parental leaves and affordable child care (White, 2008).

One strategy used by some profeminist men is performing a **traitorous identity**. In performing a traitorous identity, a group member criticizes attitudes or actions that are common and accepted among members of that group. An example comes from Larry May, author of *Masculinity and Morality* (1998). May notes that, at meetings he attends, male speakers sometimes make sexist jokes or comments. May points out that, if a woman objects to the sexist comments, many men roll their eyes or dismiss her as being overly sensitive or "unable to take a joke." However, when he or other men criticize the sexism, both the speaker and other men in the group find it difficult to ignore. The other men can't dismiss the criticism easily when it comes from "one of us." People who perform traitorous identity are not really "traitors" to their group. Rather, by questioning certain behaviors, they are challenging the group to become better.

Male feminists also engage in interpersonal persuasion to convince friends and coworkers to alter discriminatory attitudes and practices. For instance, Scott Straus (2004) used his voice on campus to criticize fraternities. Later, he wrote an article in which he criticized men in the fraternity to which he had belonged for practices such as bragging about who had sex with whom and rating females' attractiveness.

RAYMOND

When one guy isn't playing well, others on the team will say he's playing like a girl. I don't know where that started, but you hear it a lot when a guy's game is off. My girlfriend gets really ticked off about that. She's in sports, too, and she says it's really disrespectful to talk like girls aren't any good at sports. So, last week I was off my game, and one of the other guys shouted that I was playing like a girl; I said "Like Venus Williams? Thanks, bro."

Another interest of male feminists is their personal growth beyond society's pre-scriptions for masculinity. Endorsing the liberal belief that men and women are alike in most ways, male feminists want to develop the emotional capacities that society approves in women but discourages in men. Whereas social codes have restricted women's professional development and civic rights, they have tended to force men to repress many emotions. Male feminists encourage men to be more sensitive, caring, open, and able to engage in meaningful, close relationships with women and with other men. In her study of black men who define themselves as feminist, Aaronette White (2008) showed how these men's feminism enriches their parenting, friendships, and self-identity.

Formal, public profeminist activism dates back to 1975, when the first Men and Masculinity Conference was held in Tennessee. The conference explores the meaning of masculinity and provides a network of support for men who want to talk about problems and frustrations inherent in our culture's definition of mas-culinity and the roles and activities appropriate for men (Doyle, 1997; Messner, 2001). We will look more closely at the National Organization for Men Against Sexism (NOMAS) and men's antiviolence groups as prototypes of the profeminist movement.

NOMAS

One of the most prominent and long-lasting male feminist organizations is **NOMAS**. NOMAS sponsors workshops to expand men's awareness of ways in which their emotional development has been hindered by restrictive social views of masculinity. In addition, the workshops offer men guidance in becoming more feeling and sensitive. Often, these groups serve as safe testing grounds in which men experiment with talking about their feelings, needs, and problems.

Although members of NOMAS believe that some qualities traditionally associ-ated with masculinity, such as courage and ambition, are valuable in men, NOMAS condemns other conventionally masculine qualities, such as aggression, violence, and emotional insensitivity. One of the major achievements of NOMAS is its Fathering Task Group. This group issues a newsletter called *Brother*, which promotes strong, supportive ties between men.

EXPLORING GENDERED LIVES *Building Men for Others*

"What is our job as coaches?" asks Joe Ehrmann, former NFL star and current football coach for the Greyhounds at Gilman School in Baltimore. "To love us," chant the football players. "What is your job?" Ehrmann demands. "To love each other!" the players shout back (Marx, 2004, p. 4). Not exactly a typical exchange between coaches and players. But then, Ehrmann is definitely not a typical football coach.

Joe Ehrmann thinks society does a terrible job of helping boys become men. It teaches three flawed criteria for manhood: athletic ability, sexual conquest, and economic success. When boys are taught to strive for these three things, they wind up constantly competing with each other. According to Ehrmann, this "leaves most men feeling isolated and alone. And it destroys any concept of community" (p. 5). In place of what he calls "false masculinity," Ehrmann teaches his players that to be a man is to develop "strategic masculinity," which is defined by relationships with

others and having a cause beyond yourself.

He teaches his players that, on the field and in real life, success comes from building and sustaining good relationships, which require men to be able to love and be loved. One of Ehrmann's rules is that no Greyhound player should ever let another student, whether a teammate or a stranger, sit alone in the school lunchroom. Instead, they are taught to think about how bad it would feel to be eating all alone and to invite that student to their table.

Ehrmann's record suggests that his approach can build winning teams. In many seasons, the Greyhounds were undefeated; in 2002 they were number one in Maryland and number 14 in national rankings. Ehrmann explains that "winning is only a by-product of everything else that we do—and it is certainly not the way we evaluate ourselves" (p. 7).

Do you think Ehrmann's approach would work for men's competitive sports at the college level? Why or why not?

NOMAS hosts an annual conference on men and masculinity. Four issues consistently arise as priorities for discussion and action at these conferences. The first is recognizing and resisting the power and privilege that accompany being men. The second is ending violence against women by analyzing the relationship between cultural codes for masculinity and men's violence against women. A third issue is working to end men's homophobic attitudes and the resulting cruel, sometimes deadly, attacks on gays and trans people. The fourth issue is continuing to develop men's studies at colleges and universities.

Modeled on the consciousness-raising groups popular with many second-wave feminists, NOMAS discussion groups encourage men to talk about what our society expects of men and the problems these expectations create. In this supportive context, men learn to talk openly with other men about feelings, fears, and ways to change attitudes and behaviors they find unworthy in themselves as individual men and in society overall.

Members of NOMAS voice public support of women's rights and men's personal development. In addition, NOMAS members are often involved in educational outreach programs that aim to raise other men's awareness of the constraints of traditional images of masculinity. Finally, members of NOMAS often enact traitorous identities to challenge everyday incidents of homophobia, sexism, and devaluation of women.

Men's Antiviolence Groups

As we saw in our discussion of NOMAS, profeminists are committed to ending violence against women. Like Kevin, whose commentary appears on this page, profeminists believe that violence against women is not just a "woman's issue." These men reason that, because the majority of violence against women (as well as men) is enacted by men, it is an issue for men. Two specific men's antiviolence programs deserve our attention.

The White Ribbon Campaign

Perhaps you've noticed that some men wear white ribbons between November 25 and December 6. Those who do are stating that they identify with the **White Ribbon Campaign (WRC)**, an international group of men who work to end men's violence against women (**http://www.whiteribbon.com,** n.d.). Formed in 1991, the WRC is the largest men's antiviolence group in the world.

The WRC began when a group of Canadian men felt they had to respond to an appalling incidence of violence against women. On December 6, 1991, 14 women were slaughtered in what came to be called the Montreal Massacre. They were students in the Engineering School at the Université de Montreal. The murderer, who had failed to be admitted to the engineering school (Kaufmann & Kimmel, 2011), felt that engineering was a man's field in which women had no rightful place, so he removed the women students from the school—and from life. Some male students at the Université de Montreal felt compelled to speak out and make it clear that not all men hate women, and not all men condone violence against women.

KEVIN

If someone had told me five years ago I would say I'm a feminist, I wouldn't have believed it. Four years ago, my little sister was raped. I was enraged, and I felt totally powerless to help her, which was hard for me to deal with. I thought I was supposed to solve the problem, make things right, get the guy who did it. But I couldn't. I went with my sister to the rape crisis center and began to learn how bad the problem is. I began to see that the problem wasn't just the guy who raped her. It's the way that most men are socialized, including me—my wanting to be in control and get the guy who raped her. Gradually, I got more involved with others who want to end violence against women. Ending it has to start with men.

At first, only a handful of men met about the issue, but the group grew. They defined their mission as taking the responsibility as men to speak out against men's violence against women. Designating a white ribbon as the symbol of men's opposition to men's violence against women, in six weeks this small group convinced more than 100,000 Canadian men to wear white ribbons. According to the White Ribbon website, "wearing a white ribbon is a symbol of a personal pledge never to commit, condone, nor remain silent about violence against women" (**http://www .whiteribbon.com**, n.d.).

Since the WRC was founded in Canada in 1991, it has spread to many other countries. Local chapters in some countries select Father's Day and Valentine's Day for WRC events that emphasize men's caring and investment in positive, loving relationships. Many college campuses have local WRC groups. Although not often in the limelight, the WRC continues in resolute, steadfast pursuit of its mission to persuade men to take responsibility for ending men's violence against women.

Wearing a white ribbon for one or two weeks a year is not the WRC's only rhetorical strategy. Members also present antiviolence workshops in schools, communities, and places of employment. In the workshops, WRC members encourage men to become part of the solution to men's violence by speaking out against men's violence and by talking with other men about the issue. The workshops focus not only on physical violence such as battering and rape, but also on emotional violence, sexual harassment, sexist humor, and other practices that devalue and harm women.

EXPLORING GENDERED LIVES *Men Can Stop Rape*

Men Can Stop Rape is the name of a group that focuses primarily on raising college age men's awareness of rape culture, encouraging them to resist it and to stop sexual assault by other men. The group's mission is to mobilize men to create cultures free from violence, especially men's violence against women. The group's web site that explains its mission and provides videos and texts of interviews on a range of topics related to rape and, more generally, gendered violence: **http://www .mencanstoprape.org/**

WRC emphasizes that it is not "bashing men." On its website, **http://www .whiteribbon.com/about_us/#1**, this statement appears:

> The majority of men are not violent. At the same time … many men have come to believe that violence against a woman, child or another man is an acceptable way to control another person. By remaining silent about these things, we allow other men to poison our working and learning environments.

The WRC has been praised by both men and women. A number of men agree with WRC that, because men commit most of the violence against women, men need to take responsibility for stopping it. In addition, many women's groups welcome men's groups as allies in their efforts to end men's violence (Lansberg, 2000).

One criticism that has been voiced is that the WRC doesn't go far enough in its analysis of men's violence. Some of the most prominent spokespeople (Johnson, 2006; Katz, 2000) for ending men's violence argue that the problem is not a few men who are violent, but rather it is that violence is intimately woven into how society defines men and masculinity.

Mentors in Violence Prevention

Jackson Katz is one of the leaders in men's effort to end male violence against women. The program he developed, **Mentors in Violence Prevention (MVP)**, aims to educate men about socialization that links masculinity to violence and aggression and to motivate men to reject violence in themselves and other men (Katz, 2000).

Many young boys want to be kind to others, but peer pressure keeps them from showing any tenderness. Gail Williamson and Jay Silverman (2001) conducted a study to find out whether peer influence is also a factor in heterosexual men's violence against women they date. They reported that men are more likely to be violent toward dates if they associate with peers who verbally endorse or actually engage in violence against female partners. In Michael Kaufmann and Michael Kimmel's (2011) words, "Men look to other guys to define what it means to be a man" (p. 167).

The MVP program seeks to use the power of peer influence to instill antiviolence attitudes in men who then teach their male peers not to be violent. The program has two foci. The first is to teach men that aggression and violence are closely linked to cultural views of masculinity and thus part of routine masculine socialization. In other words, the MVP program focuses on normative masculinity—on the ways in which violence is seen as a normal part of manhood in our society (Katz & Jhally, 1999, 2000). From sports to the military, masculine socialization teaches boys that violence is an appropriate means of gaining and maintaining control over others and winning—whether it's winning on the football field or on the battlefield or a personal relationship. Becoming aware of normative masculine socialization is the first step in challenging and changing it.

The second focus of the MVP program is to call attention to the role of bystanders in preventing violence. Jackson and other MVP trainers reject the idea that only those who actually commit violence are blameworthy. In many cases, for violence to be committed there must be bystanders who approve, encourage, condone, or just remain silent, Katz insists (2000). MVP encourages men to take responsibility not only for refraining from violence themselves, but also for refusing to allow, condone, or be silent in the face of other men's violence.

Profeminist men's groups, including NOMAS, the WRC, and MVP, share the belief that current views of masculinity in Western culture are toxic for all of us, men and women alike. They also share a commitment to challenge and change how the culture and individuals in it define and enact masculinity. In stark contrast are masculinist groups. We turn now to those.

Masculinist Men's Groups

A number of men's groups embrace cultural ideology, which holds that women and men are fundamentally different and, therefore, should have different roles and rights. Men's groups that believe this are called **masculinist** (Fiebert, 1987), or *promasculine*. They assert that men suffer from discrimination and that men need to reclaim their rightful status as men (Mansfield, 2007).

Masculinists also differ from profeminist men in attitudes toward gay men. The issue of gay rights is not a primary concern for most masculinist men, who tend to either ignore or denounce gay men. Profeminist men, in contrast, are committed to supporting gay concerns, challenging men's homophobic attitudes, and eliminating discrimination against gay men.

Men's Rights

Among the most conservative men's groups are **men's rights activists**, whose goal is to restore the traditional roles of men and women and, with that, the privileges men historically enjoyed. Men's rights groups include MR, Inc. (Men's Rights, Incorporated); the National Coalition for Free Men; and NOM (the National Organization of Men).

One of the more extreme men's rights groups is **Free Men**, a small group that aims to restore men's pride in being "real men," who are tough, rugged, invulnerable, and self-reliant. Free Men regard male feminists as soft and unmanly and refer to them as "the men's auxiliary to the women's movement" (Gross, 1990, p. 12). According to Free Men, the primary burden of masculinity is the provider role, which makes men little more than meal tickets whose worth is measured by the size of their paychecks and their professional titles.

Free Men want men to regain their rightful places as heads of families and unquestioned authorities. At the same time, they think their status should not be tied to the breadwinner role. Free Men oppose affirmative action and believe men should not have to pay alimony and child support (Kimmel, 1996).

SAM

I know it's not politically correct these days to say it, but I agree with a lot of what masculinist men believe. I think families were stronger when the man was the head and the woman knew to follow. Families can't work if both spouses want to lead. There can be only one leader. I think the country was a lot stronger, too, before women started getting into business and government. I think women and men have different abilities. They're equal, but they're different. As far as gays go, I'm not homophobic or anything, but I don't see protecting their rights as a priority.

Men's rights groups, including the Free Men, think that it's more important to address discrimination against men than discrimination against women. To support their claim that men are oppressed, men's rights groups point to issues such as the military draft, shorter life spans, more health problems, and child custody laws that favor women (Whitaker, 2001).

EXPLORING GENDERED LIVES Time for a New Men's Group?

Does the traditional script for masculinity still work in contemporary America? The recession that began in 2008 resulted in massive job losses. The losses, however, were not evenly distributed. Initially, the hardest hit sectors were manufacturing and construction, two of the sectors that remain heavily male dominated. And many of those jobs aren't coming back. Over the next 10 years, more than 15 million new jobs will be created, and a majority of them will be ones that women have traditionally held—nursing, primary and secondary teachers, home health assistants (Romano & Dokoupil, 2010).

Younger men may be taking heed. In 2012, the Pew Research Center reported that for the first time in America's history, more 18- to 34-year-old women (66%) than men (59%) say succeeding in a high-paying career is one of the most important things in life (Blow, 2012). Men of this era may find it useful to do what women did during the second wave: consider new ways of defining their identities, figure ways to balance paid labor and contributions to home and family, think outside of the conventional boxes about careers, and reinvent themselves to fit changing constraints and opportunities.

Father's Rights Groups

Fathers' rights groups are angry and hurt that men don't have at least 50% custody of their children after divorce. They claim that courts discriminate against men by assuming that women should be the primary parents.

The highest-profile fathers' rights group is in England. **Fathers 4 Justice** performs dramatic stunts that attract publicity. In one stunt, 33-year-old Jason Hatch, whose wife had left him and taken their two children with her, dressed as Batman, climbed the front wall of Buckingham Palace, perched on a ledge, unfurled a Fathers 4 Justice banner, and held it for more than five hours ("Batman," 2004).

Fathers 4 Justice isn't the only group fighting for fathers' rights. In the United States, there are dozens, including the American Coalition for Fathers, Fathers and Families, and Children and Dads Against Discrimination. These groups file class-action custody suits to argue that a father has a constitutional right to be a parent, and thus he is guaranteed nothing less than 50% of the time with his children (Dominus, 2005). The key questions fathers' rights groups ask are these:

- Can fathers love their children as much as mothers?
- Do children need their fathers as much as they need their mothers?
- Is it sex discrimination to give mothers an advantage when it comes to custody rights?

Father's rights groups call attention to bias against fathers in granting custody and other matters.

Many of us would answer "yes" to these questions. However, the issues are a bit more complicated than these questions suggest. Not all fathers make the legally required child-support payments, and a number of fathers don't even contact children following a divorce. This makes it difficult for judges and family-service agencies to be confident that all or most fathers will accept the responsibilities that accompany the rights they seek.

Mythopoetic Men

Another men's group that gained a lot of attention in the late 1980s and early 1990s is the **mythopoetic movement**, founded by poet and former peace activist Robert Bly. Bly blended neoconservative politics with traditional gender ideology to shape the mythopoetic movement, which aimed to foster men's personal growth, wholeness, and bonding in all-male gatherings (Bonnett, 1996; Silverstein, Auerbach, Grieco, & Dunkel, 1999).

Mythopoetics claimed that ideal manhood existed in ancient times and in the Middle Ages, when men were self-confident, strong, emotionally alive, and sensitive. As exemplars of ideal manhood, mythopoetics cited the Knights of the Round Table, Henry David Thoreau, Walt Whitman, and Johnny Appleseed (Gross, 1990).

Mythopoetics thought that men's formerly profound connections to the earth and to comradeship with other men were ripped asunder by modernization and the Industrial Revolution. Men were taken away from their land and, with that, from ongoing contact with natural life itself and their roles as stewards of the land (Kimbrell, 1991). At the same time that men were isolated from their earthy, natural masculinity (Gross, 1990), industrialization separated men from their families. When men began to work outside the home, young boys lost fathers who could initiate them into manhood and teach them how to relate spiritually and emotionally to other men.

Although mythopoetics believe that men have been separated from their feelings, their views depart dramatically from those of profeminist men (Keen, 1991; Mechling & Mechling, 1994). Like Free Men, Bly and his followers laid much of the blame for men's emotional deficits on feminism. Bly said that in male feminists "there's not much energy" (Wagenheim, 1990, p. 42). Stating this view more strongly, some mythopoetics charge that "feminists have been busy castrating American males. They poured this country's testosterone out the window in the 1960s" (Allis, 1990, p. 80).

Mythopoetics urge men to recover the *distinctly male mode of feeling*, which is fundamentally different from the female feelings endorsed by profeminist men. Mythopoetics think men need to reclaim courage, aggression, and virility as masculine birthrights and as qualities that can be put to the service of bold and worthy goals, as they were when knights and soldiers fought for grand causes.

Central to modern man's emotional emptiness, argued Bly, is **father hunger**, a grief born of yearning to be close both to actual fathers and other men and to build deep, spiritual bonds between men. To help men who experience father hunger, Bly and other leaders of the movement urged men to get in touch with their grief and, from there, to begin to rediscover their deep masculine feelings and spiritual energies. To facilitate this process, Bly and other movement leaders held

Rites of Manhood

Men's rites may be as important as women's rights. Prior to the Industrial Revolution, most American fathers worked at or near their homes, so they spent a great deal of time with their sons, teaching them what it means to be a man. The same sort of mentoring of young boys existed in African tribes. When a boy reached a certain age, the men of the tribe—not just the father—would take the boy away from the village and teach him the tribe's values. When the boy returned to the village, he was recognized as a man.

Building on traditions of mentoring boys into manhood, Rites of Passage is a program that pairs African-American boys with a male elder in the community, who serves as a mentor and role model (McDonald, 2005). The elder teaches the boy to take responsibility for caring for himself and his community, to eschew violence, drugs, and other things that weaken self and community, and to keep promises to himself and others. When the elder is satisfied that the boy understands what it means to be a man, he gives the boy an African name, which symbolizes that he has become a man.

Do you think rites to mark the passage into manhood are valuable? Why or why not?

workshops and nature retreats where men gather in the woods to beat drums, chant, and listen to poetry and mythic stories, all designed to help them get in touch with their father hunger and move beyond it to positive masculine feeling.

The mythopoetic movement received both praise and blame. Naming father hunger highlights the anguish many men feel because they have or had distant relationships with their fathers (Chethik, 2001; Schwalbe, 1996). At the same time, mythopoetics have been charged with unwillingness to confront issues of gender inequality and with participation in sustaining that inequality (Schwalbe, 1996). In addition, some think the mythopoetics were elitist, as the membership was largely white and middle class.

You may have noticed that the majority of references in this discussion of mythopoetics were published in the early 1990s. Although there are still weekend nature retreats, the group is attracting few new members. It is possible that mythopoetics' focus on personal growth wasn't enough to sustain a movement. Without a political agenda, it's difficult to keep a movement charged and vital. Even so, the mythopoetic movement contributed to the dialogue about masculinity by naming father hunger.

Promise Keepers

In 1990, Bill McCartney, who was then head football coach at the University of Colorado, and his friend Dave Wardell were on a three-hour car trip to a meeting of Christian athletes in Pueblo, Colorado. On that trip, the two men conceived the idea of filling a stadium with Christian men. Later that year, McCartney and Wardell motivated 72 men to pray and fast about the idea of men coming together in Christian fellowship. The first **Promise Keepers** event in 1991 drew 4,200 men. Two years later, McCartney achieved his goal of filling the 50,000-seat Folsom Field. In 1994, the Promise Keepers spread out to seven sites, at which more than 278,000 men came together to pray and commit themselves to a Christ-centered life. Promise Keeper events, such as "Stand in the Gap," "Storm the Gates," and "The Challenge," drew thousands of men each year (Shimron, 1997, 2002; Wagenheim, 1996).

| SOPHIA |

A few years ago my dad went to a Promise Keepers event, and it changed him and our whole family. Before he went, he was the stereotype of the absent or uninvolved husband and father. After he went, he totally turned around—he was there for mom and for me and my brother. He started making the family the center of his life. For us, Promise Keepers has been a good thing.

Whereas mythopoetics saw reconnecting with nature as the way for men to regain their wholeness, Promise Keepers see reconnection to God's commandments as the path. The movement urges men to be the leaders of their families because it reflects the "God-given division of labor between women and men" (Messner, 1997b, p. 30). Following the Christian path requires men to be good husbands, fathers, and members of communities. Each Promise Keeper makes seven promises (Shimron, 1997):

1. To honor Jesus Christ through worship, prayer, and obedience to God's word through the power of the Holy Spirit.
2. To pursue vital relationships with other men, understanding that they need brothers to help them keep their promises.
3. To practice spiritual, moral, ethical, and sexual purity.
4. To build strong marriages and families through love, protection, and biblical values.
5. To support the mission of his church by honoring and praying for his pastor and by actively giving his time and resources.
6. To reach beyond any racial and denominational barriers to demonstrate the power of biblical unity.
7. To influence his world for good, being obedient to the Great Commandment (see Mark 12:30–31) and the Great Commission (see Matthew 28:19–20).

Supporters of Promise Keepers believe that the movement promotes values that build strong families and strong communities. In their opinion, Promise Keepers is a call for male responsibility (Whitehead, 1997). Furthermore, a number of women who are married to Promise Keepers say their marriages have improved since their husbands joined the movement (Cose, 1997; Griffith, 1997; Shimron, 2002; Whitehead, 1997).

Yet, others voice reservations about the Promise Keepers. They ask why women can't attend Promise Keepers' meetings. The Promise Keepers' answer is to quote Proverbs 27:17: "Iron sharpens iron, and one man sharpens another." This reflects Promise Keepers' belief that men should lean on each other, not on women, in their quest to be good men; men can hold each other accountable in ways women can't (Shimron, 2002).

Another question asked by people who have reservations about the Promise Keepers is, "Why can't husbands and wives be equals?" (Ingraham, 1997). McCartney responds, "When there is a final decision that needs to be made and they can't arrive at one, the man needs to take responsibility" ("Promise Keepers," 1997, p. 14A). Critics charge that "taking responsibility" is a code term for denying women's equality, voices, and rights.

KATHY

I really don't know what to think of the Promise Keepers. I like what they say about men committing to family values and strong spirituality. I'm Christian, so I agree with a lot of what they stand for. But I don't like the idea that men have to be the leader in relationships. I won't be led by a man, and I don't want to lead a man, either. I want a relationship where we're equal in all respects. This makes me identify with only parts of what the Promise Keepers stand for.

Another frequently expressed criticism is that Promise Keepers are elitist. The great majority of Promise Keepers are white and economically middle or upper class. In response to criticism, Promise Keepers has tried to broaden its membership to include men of different races and to soften its rhetoric about husbands leading wives. In a move to symbolize the group's racial diversity, in 2003 when McCartney retired from the presidency, the group chose Thomas Fortson, an African American, to head Promise Keepers (Gorski, 2003).

But racial inclusiveness doesn't help Promise Keepers respond to charges of another kind of exclusion. Promise Keepers assert that homosexuality is a sin and that gays therefore are leading immoral lives. Naturally, this makes gays and their allies uncomfortable with the movement. A final criticism is that Promise Keepers is more a conservative political movement than a social and spiritual movement (Cose, 1997; Whitaker, 2001).

The Promise Keepers reached its peak in 1997 with the "Stand in the Gap" rally at the National Mall in Washington, DC. In 1997, the group had a budget of $117 million. By 2003, the budget was $27 million, reflecting a steep decline in membership (Gorski, 2003). In 2004, President Fortson announced that Promise Keepers intended to take its message beyond the borders of the United States. Following in the missionary tradition, Promise Keepers hope to establish a presence in places such as South Africa, New Zealand, and South America.

TONY

The PKs really frustrate me. I am a born-again Christian. I'm also gay. I believe everything that PKs stand for except their condemnation of gays. I'll put my Christian values up against those of any PK, but there's no room for me in the organization.

Whether Promise Keepers reinvigorates itself or not, its impact continues. Some men who were involved with Promise Keepers in the 1990s have used the movement as a model for building grassroots men's ministries in churches around the United States

(Murphy, 2005). Men's ministries work to make local churches relevant to men. For instance, one group sponsors Saturday morning sports and prayer meetings. Another group has once-a-month "God's Weekend Warriors" retreats, at which men meet for breakfast and prayers followed by two hours of community service (Murphy, 2005).

After attending Promise Keepers' trademark two-day events, many men did not maintain contact with churches (Shimron, 2007). Some male Christian leaders believe that men's low involvement in churches results from what they call the "feminization of the church" (Caughlin & Caughlin, 2005; Pinsky, 2007). In his book, *Why Men Hate Going to Church*, David Murrow asserts that the modern church service is weak and emasculated and represents Jesus as a sweet, loving person instead of a warrior whom men would regard as a hero worthy of following. To rekindle men's interest in Christian worship, some churches are replacing praise music with martial hymns such as "Onward Christian Soldiers," giving sermons about a rebellious, courageous Jesus, and stressing action over reflection and aggression over gentility.

The Million Man March

Just as many African-American women feel that feminism doesn't speak to or for them, many African-American men feel that most of the men's movements don't fit their histories and lives (Hammer, 2001). In the fall of 1995, Minister Louis Farrakhan, leader of the Nation of Islam, and the Reverend Benjamin Chavis, Jr., organized the first **Million Man March**. Their goal was for black men to fill the mall of the nation's capital. The goals of the 1995 meeting were for black men to atone for sins and reconcile with one another. Spike Lee's film *Get on the Bus* (1997) offers a dramatic documentation of this first march.

At the march, organizers encouraged men to pledge themselves to spiritual transformation and political action. Specifically, organizers called for the men to register

EXPLORING GENDERED LIVES | *Grassroots Men's Ministries*

Would you like to learn more about grassroots men's ministries? Would you like to start one in your community? Two model groups are the Washington Area Coalition of Men's Ministries and the National Coalition of Men's Ministries. On its website, **http://www.wacmm.org**, the Washington Area Coalition of Men's Ministries offers this description of itself:

> We join together as men from local churches and organizations in the Washington D.C. Metro area to encourage every man within the sphere of our influence to pursue a vital relationship with God and with one another, to equip them for servant leadership in the home,

workplace, community and world, and to enable them to gather for corporate celebration and edification.

The National Coalition of Men's Ministries (**http://www.ncmm.org**) includes more than 100 grassroots groups that work to connect men with local churches. The group states its mission thusly:

> The National Coalition of Men's Ministries welcomes inquiries from people who are interested in starting a men's ministry in their communities. Contact the group at 180 Wilshire Blvd., Casselberry, FL 32707. Phone Number: (407) 332-7703. Toll Free: (877) MAN-NCMM (626-6266). E-mail: **office@ncmm.org**.

to vote, to fight drugs in their lives and communities, and to stand against unemployment and violence. Men were asked to recommit themselves to their wives and families and to active involvement in their churches and communities.

MICHAEL

I attended a Million Man March years ago, and it was the most important event of my life. It was wonderful to see so many black men in one place—all there to unite with one another and to change our world. The whole mood was one of total brotherhood. It strengthened my pride in being a black man and my feeling that I can build a life around strong spiritual values.

The Million Man March was not a one-time event. Additional marches were held in years following the first one; each time, the crowd stretched from the steps of the Capitol nearly to the Washington Monument. Those who attended found something they could identify with in this movement—something that could guide their lives and give them meaning. The Million Man March has been widely praised as a positive, uplifting movement for black men. Yet, criticisms have also been voiced. One is that women are excluded from Million Man Marches. Some critics find it ironic that men leave home and get together with other men in order to commit to their wives and families.

Another criticism was advanced by Glenn Loury (1996), an African-American professor of economics. He is concerned that Million Man encourages black men to base their rage on the racial identity of those who suffer rather than to rage against suffering and inequity no matter who is the victim. Finally, Million Man March is criticized for being antifeminist and antigay and for holding overly conservative views of families and women (Messner, 1997b).

The inaugural Million Man March in 1995 became a model for other groups. Since that march, America has seen a Million Woman March in Philadelphia, a Million Youth March in Harlem, a Million Mom March in Washington, and, in 2000, a Million Family March ("Million Family March," 2000). Most recently, in October 2005, the Millions More Movement was launched in the nation's capital. Conceived by Minister Louis Farrakhan, who also led the Million Man March, the Millions More Movement learned from criticisms of Millions marches. From the start, it was defined as an ongoing movement rather than a march. The mission statement focuses on educational, political, spiritual, social, and economic aspects of community development. Also, unlike the Million Man March, the Millions More Movement is inclusive of all sexes, races, and sexualities, although its focus remains on racial disparities that continue to affect blacks negatively (Muwakkil, 2005).

The Good Men Project

Most of the men's groups we've discussed in this chapter currently have limited memberships and impact. Even some of the more prominent groups such as Promise Keepers and Million Man March haven't been able to sustain their memberships or influence. Given this, it's not surprising that many men today don't identify with any of the groups we've discussed. Does this mean that men today don't have issues?

Not if you ask Tom Matlack. By outside measures, his life was a huge success. Barely 30, he was earning a large salary and was even featured in a story in the *Wall Street Journal*. He had a stunning home and a wife and children. But Matlack's outward success wasn't matched by inward happiness. His dependence on alcohol contributed to ending his marriage and almost cost him his life. When he reached his personal bottom, Matlack began reflecting on his life and how he could make it a life that he respected.

That was the start of the **Good Men Project**, which is a multifaceted effort to stimulate a national conversation about what it means to be a good man today. Partnering with James Houghton and Larry Bean, Matlack published a book, *The Good Men Project* (Houghton, Bean, & Matlack, 2009), whose royalties are donated to groups that work with at-risk boys. The book is a collection of stories by 31 men who are black and white, gay and straight, rich and poor, NFL Hall of Fame Linebackers, and ex-cons. Each man's story describes a defining moment in his life. Accompanying the book is a DVD (Gannon, 2009) in which men talk

EXPLORING GENDERED LIVES   *"If You Don't Like What's Being Said, Change the Conversation."*

Tom Matlack knows something about being at risk. More than once, his drinking endangered his life, including time when a rollover car accident threw him through windows. Looking back on that time, Matlack says he had "this perfect, superficial picture—two kids, a big house, a wife. I had everything and yet I was ashamed of my behavior—drinking, cheating. At 31, I was a professional success and personal failure all at once" (Weigel, 2010).

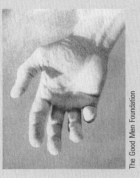

The Good Men Foundation

Matlack's efforts to come to grips with his own life led him to realize he wasn't alone—there are lots of men trying to figure out how to live lives of integrity. With James Houghton, Matlack set up The Good Men Foundation, which has two goals: funding organizations that help at-risk boys and launching a national discussion about what it means to be a good man. Proceeds from the book and a portion of proceeds from the media arm of the foundation go to organizations that help at-risk boys.

The *Good Men Project* magazine encourages participation—comment on others' ideas, initiate your own, and help shape the dialogue. As the site says, "If you don't like what's being said, change the conversation."

Tumblr: **http://goodmenproject .tumblr.com/**

Twitter: @GoodMenProject

The Good Men Project resists providing any general definition of "good" or "good men." How would you define a "good man"?

honestly about spiritual crises, watershed moments in fathering, turning points in relationships, and struggles with infidelity, alcohol, and drugs. According to Matlack, the stories are effective because "Men are more open to listening to issues in male ways, like being in the locker room. It's not talking about emotion directly but talking about emotion in terms of a story of a guy dying in combat" (Weigel, 2010).

Although the men featured in the book and DVD have widely varying life experiences and circumstances, what they have in common is that they are all trying to figure out what it means to be good men today. In introducing the book, Matlack states "there is no definitive way to be 'good'" (Houghton et al., p. 8). But, he continues, reading other men's stories and thoughts can help each man formulate his own definition of what it means to be good. Not only has the book sold well, not only are men reading and talking about it, but it has propelled creation of an online community for thinking about manhood today.

In 2010, the Good Men Foundation (**http://goodmenproject.com/foundation**) launched the *Good Men Magazine* (**http://goodmenproject.com**), whose readers and contributors represent diverse ages, ethnicities, races, religions, economic classes, and sexualities. This online magazine features stories and columns that address issues that surface in men's lives: sex and relationships (Mark Greene, "Why I Hate Porn"), sports (open thread, "Should Penn State's Football Team Be Shut Down?"), dads, (Al Watts, "The Reality of Being an At-Home Dad"), and advice ("Dear John" responds to readers' questions on everything from wearing hairpieces to dealing with difficult neighbors). In addition, the magazine facilitates an ongoing conversation about what masculinity does and might mean. Perry Glasser, prizewinning author, says the magazine is an alternative to "media images of masculinity that are dangerously repellent and full of rage" (Bergeron, 2009).

The magazine tells readers, "Guys today are neither the mindless, sex-obsessed buffoons nor the stoic automatons our culture so often makes them out to be.... We explore the world of men and manhood in a way that no media company ever has, tackling the issues and questions that are most relevant to men's lives. We write about fatherhood, family, sex, ethics, war, gender, politics, sports, pornography, and aging. We shy away from nothing."

The magazine is a place for men to talk openly about their lives without fear of being reproached for their thoughts, feelings, and experiences. But the magazine steers clear of prescriptions and proselytizing. It doesn't tell men *how* to be good; it simply provides a forum for discussing issues so that each man can figure out his own definition of good.

Men aren't the only readers of *The Good Men Project Magazine*. A third of the readers are women who want to understand men's perspectives and who find the magazine offers something more real and more interesting than the superficial stereotypes in *Sports Illustrated, Maxim,* and *GQ.* Senior Editor Henry Belanger says that men today "are trying to do more things than their fathers did." As men try to figure out how to do that, many of them find it helpful to be part of a community of other men who are struggling with similar issues.

SUMMARY

Men's efforts to define gender, like that of women, are diverse and even contradictory. Some men consider themselves feminists, work with women for gender equality in society, and attempt to become more comfortable expressing their feelings. Other men think feminism has destroyed families, twisted women, and caused diminished men. Men's activism ranges from efforts to advance women's rights and status to vigorous attacks on women's resistance to traditional, subservient roles. Men's groups contribute to the cultural conversation about gender—its meaning and its effect on the individual men and women who live under its edicts.

In this chapter and the preceding one, we discussed a wide range of groups that give voice to diverse images of women and men. As the conversation evolves, some of the current voices will fade out and new voices will emerge. Some people will tune out the conversation. Others will reflect thoughtfully on what different groups say about men and women. Still others will join the conversation and take active roles in defining masculinity, femininity, and the host of issues linked to gender. It's up to you to define your role in the cultural conversation about gender.

KEY TERMS

The terms following are defined in this chapter on the pages indicated, as well as in alphabetical order in the book's glossary, which begins on page 283. The text's companion website (**http://www.cengage.com/communication/wood/genderedlives11e**) also provides interactive flash cards and crossword puzzles to help you learn these terms and the concepts they represent.

father hunger 92
Fathers 4 Justice 91
Free Men 89
Good Men Project 98
male feminists 83
masculinists 89
Mentors in Violence Prevention
   (MVP) 88

men's rights activists 89
Million Man March 96
mythopoetic movement 92
NOMAS 84
profeminists 83
Promise Keepers 93
traitorous identity 83
White Ribbon Campaign (WRC) 86

GENDER ONLINE

1. To learn about the range of men's movements and issues and resources on all of them, visit the Voice of the Shuttle's directory for these: **http://vos.ucsb.edu /browse.asp?id=1810**

2. If you wish to learn more, visit NOMAS's website at: **http://www.nomas.org**

3. If you want to learn more about Free Men, visit this website: **http://www .ncfm.org**

4. To find out more about the Promise Keepers, visit their website: **http://www
.promisekeepers.org**

5. Check out the Good Men Project's online magazine: **http://goodmenproject.com**

6. Online search terms: "fathers' rights," "male feminist," "mentors in violence
prevention."

REFLECTION AND DISCUSSION

1. Before you read this chapter, did you know that there were so many men's
groups with such diverse goals? What does limited knowledge of men's
groups imply about biases in media and education in America?

2. Which of the men's groups are most and least consistent with your values
and your views of masculinity?

3. Write or act out a discussion of whether men should pay alimony and child
support as that discussion might transpire between a Free Man, a mythopoetic,
and a Promise Keeper.

RECOMMENDED RESOURCES

1. Paul Kivel. (2007). The Act Like a Man Box. In Michael Messner (Ed.), *Men's
Lives,* 7th ed. (pp. 148–150). Cranbury, NJ: Pearson/Allyn & Bacon. This short
article provides a clear way of thinking about how Western society's view
of masculinity boxes men into social prescriptions.

2. *Get on the Bus.* Directed by Spike Lee. (1996). Distributed by Sony. This award-
winning film provides a dramatic representation of the first Million Man
March and what it meant to black men.

3. Michael Messner. (2008). *Guyland: The Perilous World Where Boys Become Men.*
New York: Harper. Long-standing feminist Michael Messner examines the
pressures, fears, and anxieties facing many young men today.

4. The Good Men Project DVD. This is available with the book of the same title
or separately from: **http://goodmenproject.com/foundation**

5

Gendered Verbal Communication

Knowledge Challenge:

- Do women or men generally talk more?
- How do childhood games affect adult communication styles?
- What is *conversational maintenance work* and who generally does it?

Consider these three statements:

I now pronounce you man and wife.
Bob babysat his son while his wife attended a meeting.
Freshmen find it difficult to adjust to college life.

What do these sentences reflect about Western culture's views of women and men? The first sentence designates *man* an individual, whereas *wife* is defined only by her relationship to the man. In the second sentence, the word *babysat* implies that the father was performing a special service, one for which we usually pay people who are not related to the children. Have you ever heard someone say that a mother babysat her children? Unless the third sentence refers to first-year students at an all-male school, the word *freshmen* erases first-year female students.

In this chapter and the one that follows, we look closely at relationships between communication and gender. This chapter focuses on verbal communication, and Chapter 6 concentrates on nonverbal communication. We will explore how communication reflects cultural views of sex and gender. In addition, we will consider how individual women's and men's communication embodies or challenges cultural prescriptions for femininity and masculinity.

Verbal Communication Expresses Cultural Views of Gender

Language is one of our most complex symbol systems. The language we learn and use both reflects and reinforces cultural views and values, including those about gender. We'll discuss ways that language and gender are connected.

Male Generic Language Excludes Women

One way that language erases women is through the use of **male generic language**, which purports to include both women and men yet literally refers only to men. Examples of male generic language are nouns such as *congressman, spokesman, mailman,* and *mankind,* and pronouns such as *he and his* used to refer to both women and men. Some people think that there is no problem with male generic language and that using inclusive language is just about political correctness.

Research makes it clear that inclusive language is about something far more substantial than political correctness. In a classic study (Schneider & Hacker, 1973), children were asked to select photographs for a textbook with chapters entitled "Urban Man" and "Man in Politics" or "Urban Life" and "Political Behavior." The children almost always chose pictures of men when the titles included male generic language. When the titles did not refer only to men, the children chose more photographs that portrayed both sexes. The language of the titles shaped what the children thought was appropriate to include in the chapters.

Later research confirmed the finding that male generic language leads many people to assume that only males are included (Gastil, 1990; Hamilton, 1991; Switzer, 1990). In a particularly interesting study, students from first grade through college were asked to make up a story about an average student. When the instructions referred to the average student as *he*, only 12% of students composed a story about a female. However, when the instructions defined the average student as *he* or *she*, 42% of the stories were about females (Hyde, 1984).

Because there is convincing evidence that male language is not perceived as generic, all the major dictionaries and national newspapers now have policies requiring inclusive language. In addition, new dictionaries and writing style manuals caution against other using male generic language.

Language Defines Men and Women Differently

Women are frequently defined by appearance and by relationships with others, whereas men are more typically defined by activities, accomplishments, and positions. For instance, coverage of women's sports frequently focuses more on women athletes' appearance than on their athletic skills. Commentators' descriptions of women athletes routinely focus on outfits, bodies, and hairstyles, whereas their descriptions of male athletes more typically focus on athletic skills.

ANDY

For a long time, it seemed really clear to me that a word like mankind obviously includes women or that chairman can refer to a girl or a guy who chairs something. I thought it was pretty stupid to hassle about this. Then, last semester I had a woman teacher who taught the whole class using she or her or women whenever she was referring to people, as well as when she meant just women. I realized how confusing it is. I had to figure out each time whether she meant women only or women and men. And when she meant women to be general, I guess you'd say generic for all people, it still made me feel left out. A lot of the guys in the class got pretty hostile about what she was doing, but I kind of think it was a good way to make the point.

Watching Maria Sharapova play, a commentator remarked that her outfit's "asymmetrical hemline was slit to the hip, adding a little sauce" (Cassidy, 2004, p. 3B). Can you imagine such a comment about a male athlete? Another example of the emphasis placed on appearance for girls and women came from the Beijing Olympics. Based on talent, Yang Peiyi won the competition to sing "Ode to the Motherland" at the opening ceremony. Officials, however, decided that although Yang Pei had the best voice, she was not attractive enough. The officials chose third grader Lin Miaoke to stand on stage and lip sync the song while Yang Pei, hidden from view, sang (Yardley, 2008).

Language also reflects social views of women as passive and men as active participants in sexual activity. Have you noticed that people say, "He laid her," "He balled her," "He screwed her," "She got laid," and "He made love to her?" Each of these phrases suggests that, in sexual activity, men are active, whereas women are passive. Perhaps because men are expected to be sexual initiators, inappropriate sexual initiative by men is sometimes described in language that makes it seem acceptable. For instance, why did no one challenge Arnold Schwarzenegger's use of "playful" and "rowdy" to describe the multiple incidents of sexual harassment? And why did Fox news commentator Greta Van Susteren refer to Kobe Bryant's rape trial as a "sex scandal" (Morgan, 2003/2004, p. 95)? A sex scandal refers to unconventional but consensual sexual activity; rape refers to violation and violence.

EXPLORING GENDERED LIVES   *Parallel Language?*

Parallel language means equivalent terms. For instance, male and female are equivalent, or parallel. But what about some other allegedly parallel terms?

Masculine Term	Feminine Term
Master	Mistress
Sir	Madam
Wizard	Witch
Patron	Matron

Our language also reflects society's view of women as more defined by their relationships than men are. On prime-time television, even professional women are often depicted primarily in interpersonal contexts, and their appearance is highlighted (Dow & Wood, 2006). Throughout the 2008 Democratic primary contest, commentators commented on Hillary Clinton's appearance—she was being suggestive when she wore a v-necked top; her pantsuits were dowdy; she had crow's feet (Mandziuk, 2008). The male contenders' appearance was not scrutinized in the same way.

Historically, women who don't marry have been viewed with pity and referred to as *spinsters* or *old maids* (contrast this with the nonpejorative term *bachelor* for men). In Japan, unmarried women are called *leftover* and *parasite single* (Onishi, 1998; Retherford, Ogawa, & Matsukura, 2001). Underlining the view that women are supposed to marry and have children, Japan's Health Minister Hakuo Yanagisawa referred to Japanese women as "birth-giving machines and devices" (Dyer, 2007).

BRIAN

I never considered whether my wife would take my name. I just assumed she would. I'm proud of my family, and I feel tied to who we are, and my family name represents that. I always thought it would be a great honor for a woman to have my family name. But my fiancé doesn't feel the same way. She says she's proud of her name, too, that it's who she is, too. I can understand that in a way, but still it seems like she should want to take my name. She turned the tables on me by asking if I would take her name.

There are a number of alternatives to the traditional ways of naming ourselves (Foss, Edson, & Linde, 2000). Some heterosexual women choose to retain their birth names when they marry. A number of men and women adopt hyphenated names, such as Johnson-Smith, to symbolize the family heritage of both partners. In some countries, such as Spain, both the mother's and father's family names are used to construct children's family names. Another alternative, one less often practiced so far, is renaming oneself to reflect **matriarchal** rather than patriarchal lineage. (The term *matriarchy* means "rule by the mothers" and generally refers to systems of ideology, social structures, and practices that are created by women and reflect the values, priorities, and views of women as a group.) This involves changing a last name from that of the father's family to that of the mother's. Because that course of action, however, still reflects male lineage—that of the mother's father—some women use their mothers' first names to create a matrilineal last name: for example, Lynn Franklin's daughter, Barbara, might rename herself Barbara Lynnschild.

Language Shapes Awareness of Gendered Issues

Naming is important. We give names to things that matter to us. We don't bother to name what doesn't matter (Spender, 1984a, 1984b). The power of naming is clear with sexual harassment and date rape (Wood, 2008, 2009a). For most of

EXPLORING GENDERED LIVES   *What's in a Name?*

During the 1970s, several states did not require women to assume their husbands' last names on marrying. Other states, however, insisted that a woman must assume her husband's last name on marrying. In 1975, the issue resolved when a Hawaiian statute requiring women to give up their birth names on marriage was ruled unconstitutional (Schroeder, 1986).

Research by Laura Stafford and Susan Kline (1996) shows that some men say they would question a woman's commitment if she did not adopt her partner's name. Although men felt more strongly than women about this, a majority of both sexes surveyed favored a woman's taking her partner's last name.

Elizabeth Suter and Ramona Oswald (2003) conducted a study to find out how lesbian couples chose names. They found that, like heterosexual couples, women who placed high priority on social recognition of their relationship preferred that one or both partners change her name. For women who kept their names, individual identity was a higher priority.

Do you have different perceptions of women who choose to keep their birth names and women who choose to take their partners' names on marrying?

history, sexual harassment occurred frequently but was unnamed. Because it wasn't named, sexual harassment was not visible, making it difficult to recognize, discipline, or stop. If sexual harassment was discussed at all, it was described as *making advances*, *getting out of line*, or *being pushy*. None of these phrases conveys the abusiveness of sexual harassment. Only when the term *sexual harassment* was coined was it recognized as unwanted behavior that ties sexuality to security and advancement. With recognition came efforts to redress sexual harassment.

Similarly, for many years women who were raped by their dates had no socially recognized way to name what had happened to them. Until we coined the term *date rape*, women had to deal with their experiences without the language to define grievous violations that often had lifelong repercussions. Even today, not all women are comfortable using the term *date rape* to refer to nonconsensual sex with friends and dates. Drawing on its historical meaning, they associate rape with violent assault by a stranger (Harris, 2011).

As our discussion suggests, language is not static. Instead, we continually change language to reflect our changing understandings of ourselves and our world. We

EXPLORING GENDERED LIVES   *Seeing the Unseen/Naming the Unnamed*

Naming helps us notice things we otherwise don't see. Scholars from America and Germany collaborated to see whether people became less tolerant of sexist behavior when they were given names that allowed them to detect it. Results showed that learning to name sexism made women, but not men, less tolerant of the behavior. Of particular interest to the researchers was participants' learned ability to detect **benevolent sexism**, which is a paternalistic attitude that describes women affectionately but assumes they aren't competent to do particular tasks. For instance, "that sweet little thing can't change a tire" is benevolent sexism (Swim & Becker, 2011).

reject terms we find objectionable (male generics), and we create new terms to define realities we think are important (*sexual harassment, Ms., womanism*). As we modify language, we change how we see ourselves and our world. Further, we shape meanings of our culture.

TRISHA

As a nontraditional student, I remember when language was very different. I was sexually harassed when I first started college in the 80s, but I didn't know what was happening because there was no name. A man I dated for a long time tried to rape me, but I would never have called it rape then. No one would have. I just thought he "went too far." You really do see situations differently when you have different language to describe them.

Language Organizes Perceptions of Gender

Two ways in which language organizes perceptions of gender are stereotyping men and women and encouraging polarized perceptions of sex and gender.

A **stereotype** is a generalization about an entire class of phenomena based on some knowledge of some members of the class. For example, if most women you know aren't interested in sports, you might stereotype women as uninterested in sports. This stereotype could keep you from noticing that many women engage in sports and enjoy attending athletic events. Relying on stereotypes can lead us to overlook important qualities of individuals and to perceive them only in terms of what we consider common to a general category.

Many people stereotype women as emotional and weak and men as rational and strong. Stereotypes such as these can distort our perceptions. For instance, women's arguments are sometimes dismissed as emotional when, in fact, they involve evidence and reasoning (Mapstone, 1998). Women who use assertive speech are frequently described as rude or bitchy (O'Neill & O'Reilly, 2011), whereas men who employ emotional language may be described to be wimps or weak (Rasmussen & Moley, 1986).

The English language may also encourage **polarized thinking**, which is conceiving of things as absolute opposites. Something is right or wrong; a person is male or female or masculine or feminine. Our commonly used vocabulary emphasizes all-or-none terms and thus all-or-none thinking. English includes few words that indicate degrees and increments.

Queer performative theory challenges polarized language for sex, gender, and sexual orientation, claiming that the polar—or binary—terms obscure the range of genders, sexes, and sexual orientations that humans express. Our culture's binary labels for sex, gender, and sexual orientation encourage us not to notice how much variation there is among women and among men. The polar categories of men and women erase transgendered people. Likewise, people who are intersexed or who do not identify with any gender don't fit into the male-female polarity. Awareness of our language's polarizing tendencies allows us to notice what dichotomous conceptions of sex and gender exclude or misrepresent.

Language Evaluates Gender

Language reflects cultural values and is a powerful influence on our perceptions. Women are often described in trivializing terms. Numerous terms label women as immature or juvenile (*baby doll, girlie, little darling*) or equate them with food (*dish, feast for the eyes, good enough to eat, sugar, sweet thing, cookie, cupcake, hot tomato*) and animals (*kitten, catty, chick, pig, dog, cow, bitch*). Diminutive suffixes designate women as reduced forms of the standard (male) form of the word: *suffragette, majorette*. Calling women *girls* (defined as a female who has not gone through puberty) defines them as children, not as adults. Women who are sexually active may be called derogatory names such as *slut*, whereas men who are equally sexually active are described with terms such as *stud* or *man whore*, which my students say is a compliment.

ANTHONY

Until we talked about language in class, I hadn't really thought about the double standard for sexually active girls and guys. Or if I had thought about it, I probably would have said that the double standard doesn't exist anymore. Our discussion got me thinking, and that's not really true. Guys who have sex with a lot of girls are studs or players. Girls who have sex with a lot of guys are sluts or easy. It's not as bad as it used to be, but I guess there still is kind of a double standard.

Language Allows Self-Reflection

We use symbols to name and evaluate not only the phenomena around us, but also ourselves. Self-reflection is thinking about yourself—how you name and evaluate yourself. Yet, self-reflection is not just personal. Each of us has society's values in our heads, so we tend to reflect on ourselves from society's perspective. In the 1950s, a 5-foot 5-inch woman who weighed 140 pounds would have been considered slender. In 2010, some might see a 5-foot 5-inch woman who weighs 140 pounds as overweight. In 1950, a man would not feel pressure to be as muscular as is the current masculine ideal. We live in a celebrity culture (Lamb & Brown, 2006; Levin & Kilbourne, 2008),

---

EXPLORING GENDERED LIVES *Fat Talk*

"I'm fat." "You're not half as fat as I am. Look at my big butt." "I need to give up eating." Fat talk is common. In fact, it's almost obsessive among some people, both male and female (Martz, Petroff, Curtin, & Bazzini, 2009). Almost always fat talk is negative, self-critical comments about how the speakers' bodies don't measure up to ideals advanced by media.

Fat talk isn't harmless. Engaging in fat talk predicts lower body satisfaction and greater depression and increases perceived pressure to be thinner (Arroyo & Harwood, 2012). At the same time, people who have lower satisfaction with their bodies are more likely to engage in fat talk. In other words, fat talk and body dissatisfaction make up a self-defeating cycle (Arroyo & Harwood, 2012).

which makes it tempting to define ourselves in comparison to celebrities—or the air-brushed, digitally manipulated images of them. According to Michael Rich (2008), Director of the Center on Media and Child Health, "exposure to body ideals of impossibly thin women and unrealistically muscular men can contribute to negative self-images and viewers' attempts to alter their bodies through restrictive eating, exercise, or drugs or surgery" (p. 90).

"Masculine" and "feminine" are not the only ways we can label our gender. We may also label ourselves androgynous, a concept we first mentioned in Chapter 1. Androgynous people possess qualities the culture defines as masculine *and* feminine instead of only those assigned to one sex. Androgynous women and men are, for example, both assertive *and* sensitive, both ambitious *and* compassionate. Likewise, people who define themselves as gender queer or gender nonconforming choose not to place themselves in a single, narrow gendered identity.

Gendered Styles of Verbal Communication

In addition to expressing cultural views of gender, language is a primary means by which we express our gendered identities. In the pages that follow, we'll explore the ways we use verbal communication to perform masculinity and femininity. Keep in mind that we're looking at *gendered* styles of communicating, not necessarily sex-based styles. In other words, although most girls are socialized to communicate primarily in feminine ways, some boys learn feminine modes of communicating; although most boys are encouraged to cultivate primarily masculine styles of communicating, some girls learn masculine modes as well. Also, as queer performative theorists would remind us, some people perform genders other than the two conventionally recognized in our society.

Gendered Speech Communities

Philosopher Suzanne Langer (1953, 1979) asserted that culture, or collective life, is possible only to the extent that a group of people share a symbol system and the meanings encapsulated in it. Langer's attention to the ways in which language sustains cultural life is consistent with the symbolic interactionist and cultural theories that we discussed in Chapter 2. William Labov (1972) extended Langer's ideas by defining a *speech community* as a group of people who share norms about communication. By this, he meant that a **speech community** exists when people share understandings about goals of communication, strategies for enacting those goals, and ways of interpreting communication.

It's obvious that we have entered a different speech community when we are in countries whose languages differ from our own. Distinct speech communities are less apparent when they rely on the same language but use it in different ways and attach different meanings to it. Yet, as we noted in Chapter 2, belonging to a particular race-ethnicity, economic class, and gender influences what we know and how we communicate.

Males and females are typically socialized into gendered speech communities. To understand these different communities, we will first consider how we are socialized into feminine and masculine speech communities. After this, we will explore divergence in feminine and masculine speech communities. Please note the importance of the word *typically* and other words that indicate we are discussing general differences, not absolute ones. Not all women learn or choose to perform a feminine style of communication, not all men learn or choose to perform a masculine style of communication, and not everyone accepts the idea that there are two "opposite" genders with associated communication styles.

The Lessons of Children's Play

A classic study by Daniel Maltz and Ruth Borker (1982) gave us initial insight into the importance of children's play in shaping patterns of communication. As they watched young children engaged in recreation, the researchers were struck by two observations: Young children almost always played in sex-segregated groups, and girls and boys tended to play different kinds of games. Maltz and Borker found that boys' games (football, baseball, war) and girls' games (school, house, tea party) cultivate distinct communication styles.

More recent research on children's play confirms Maltz and Borker's original findings. Sex-segregated groups and forms of play remain the norm for children in the United States (Clark, 1998; Gray & Feldman, 1997; Kovacs, Parker, & Hoffman, 1996; McGuffey & Rich, 2004; Moller & Serbin, 1996; Wood, 2009a). Even children as young as two or three years old (about the time that gender constancy develops) show a preference for same-sex playmates (Ruble & Martin, 1998).

Boys' Games

Boys' games usually involve fairly large groups—nine individuals for each baseball team, for instance. Most boys' games are competitive, have clear goals, involve physically rough play and are organized by rules and roles that specify who does what and how to play (Pollack, 2000; Rudman & Glick, 2008).

Because the games boys typically play are structured by goals, rules, and roles, there is limited need to discuss how to play, although there may be talk about strategies to reach goals. In playing games, boys learn to communicate to accomplish goals, compete for and maintain status, exert control over others, get attention, and stand out. Specifically, boys' games cultivate four communication rules:

1. Use communication to assert your ideas, opinions, and identity.
2. Use talk to achieve something, such as solving problems or developing strategies.
3. Use communication to attract and maintain others' attention.
4. Use communication to compete for the "talk stage." Make yourself stand out, take attention away from others, and get others to pay attention to you.

These communication rules are consistent with other aspects of masculine socialization. For instance, notice the emphasis on individuality and competition.

Also, we see that these rules accent achievement—doing something, accomplishing a goal. Boys learn that they must do things in order to be valued members of the team. Finally, we see the undercurrent of masculinity's emphasis on invulnerability: If your goal is to control and to be better than others, you cannot let them know too much about yourself and your weaknesses.

Girls' Games

Many girls today also play competitive games like those that boys favor. In addition, most girls play some games that few boys play. The games played primarily by girls cultivate distinct ways of communicating. Girls tend to play in pairs or in small groups rather than large ones (Benenson, Del Bianco, Philippoussis, & Apostoleris, 1997). Also, games such as house and school do not have preset, clear-cut goals and roles. There is no touchdown in playing house, and the roles of daddy and mommy aren't fixed like the roles of guard and forward. Because traditional girls' games are not highly structured by external goals and roles, players have to talk among themselves to decide what to do and what roles to play.

When playing, young girls spend more time talking than doing anything else—a pattern that is not true of young boys (Goodwin, 2006). Playing house, for instance, typically begins with a discussion about who is going to be the daddy and who the mommy. The lack of stipulated goals for the games is also important because it tends to cultivate girls' skill in interpersonal processes. The games generally played by girls teach four basic rules for communication:

1. Use communication to create and maintain relationships. The process of communication, not its content, is the heart of relationships.

2. Use communication to establish egalitarian relations with others. Don't outdo, criticize, or put down others. If you have to criticize, be gentle.

3. Use communication to include others—bring them into conversations, respond to their ideas.

4. Use communication to show sensitivity to others and relationships.

The typically small size of girls' play groups fosters cooperative play (Rudman & Glick, 2008) and an open-ended process of talking to organize activity, whereas the larger groups in which boys usually play encourage competition and external rules to structure activity (Campbell, 1993). In a study of preschoolers, boys gave orders and attempted to control others, whereas girls were more likely to make requests and cooperate with others (Weiss & Sachs, 1991). In another investigation, 9- to 14-year-old African-American girls typically used inclusive and nondirective language, whereas African-American boys tended to issue commands and compete for status in their groups (Goodwin, 1990).

The conclusion from much research is that girls tend to engage in more cooperative play, whereas boys tend to engage in more instrumental and competitive play (Harris, 1998; Leaper, 1994, 1996). The lessons of children's play are carried forward. The basic rules of communication that many adult women and men employ are refined and elaborated versions of those learned in childhood games (Clark, 1998; Mulac, 1998, 2006). Even in the virtual world, boys tend to favor competitive games and girls favor relationship-oriented games.

Children's games teach gendered rules of communicating.

ERIN

I played house and school, but I also played softball and soccer. Most of my friends did too. We learned to compete and work with external rules and be goal oriented just as much as boys did. The games children play aren't sex segregated anymore.

Erin made the above comment when she was a student in my class. She's right that young girls today often play competitive sports and that doing so allows them to learn and use the rules of masculine speech communities. This is consistent with standpoint theory's premise that members of subordinated groups are motivated to learn the standpoint of dominant groups. However, Erin is not entirely correct in saying that children's games are no longer sex segregated. How many boys play house and school? It is much more acceptable and much more common for girls to play traditional boy games than vice versa.

Gendered Communication Practices

We will consider features of feminine and masculine speech that have been identified by researchers. We'll also explore some of the complications that arise when people of different genders operate by different rules in conversations with each other.

Feminine Communication

People who are socialized in feminine speech communities—most women and some men—tend to regard communication as a primary way to establish and maintain relationships with others. They engage in conversation to share about themselves and to learn about others (Wood, 2011a). Consistent with this primary goal, feminine people use language to foster connections, support closeness, and mutual understanding.

Establishing equality between people is a second important feature of feminine communication. To achieve symmetry, communicators often match experiences to indicate "You're not alone in how you feel." Typical ways to communicate equality would be saying, "I've felt just like that" or "Something like that happened to me, too, and I felt like you do." Growing out of the quest for equality is a participatory mode of interacting in which communicators respond to and build on each other's ideas in the process of conversing. Rather than a rigid "You tell your ideas, then I'll tell mine" sequence, feminine speech more characteristically follows an interactive pattern in people to collaboratively create conversations.

A third characteristic of feminine speech is support for others. To demonstrate support, communicators often express emotions (Guerrero, Jones, & Boburka, 2006; Mulac, 2006) to show understanding of another's situation or feelings. "Oh, you must feel terrible" communicates that we understand and support how another feels. Related to these first two features is attention to the relationship level of communication (Eisenberg, 2002; MacGeorge, Gillihan, Samter, & Clark, 2003). You will recall that the relationship level of talk focuses on feelings and on the relationship between communicators rather than on the content of messages. Conversations between feminine people tend to be characterized by intensive adverbs ("That's *really* exciting") (Mulac, 2006) and questions that probe for greater understanding of feelings and perceptions surrounding the subject of talk (Dunn, 1999). "How did you feel when it occurred?" "How does this fit into the overall relationship?" are probes that help a listener understand a speaker's perspective.

YOLANDA

With my boyfriend, I am always asking, "How was your day? Your class? Your jam session? Did you get such-and-such done? Did you talk to so-and-so?" He answers my questions, usually with just a few words, but he almost never asks questions about my day and my life. When I do talk about myself, he often interrupts and sometimes listens, but he doesn't say much in response. I'm tired of doing all the work to keep a conversation going in our relationship.

A fourth feature of feminine speech style is conversational "maintenance work" (Fishman, 1978; Taylor, 2002). This involves efforts to sustain conversation by inviting others to speak and by prompting them to elaborate their ideas. Questions are often used to include others: "How was your day?" "Did anything interesting happen on your trip?" "Do you have anything to add?" (Mulac, 2006). Communication of this sort maintains interaction and opens the conversational door to others.

A fifth quality of feminine speech is responsiveness. A feminine person might make eye contact, nod, or say, "Tell me more" or "That's interesting." Responsiveness affirms the other person and encourages elaboration by showing interest in what was said.

A sixth quality of feminine talk is personal, concrete style. Typical of feminine talk are details, personal disclosures, and concrete reasoning. These features cultivate a personal tone, and they facilitate feelings of closeness by connecting communicators' lives.

A final feature of feminine speech is tentativeness (Mulac, 2006). This may be expressed in a number of forms. Sometimes people use verbal hedges, such as "I kind of feel you may be overreacting." In other situations, they qualify statements by saying, "I'm probably not the best judge of this, but...." Another way to keep talk provisional is to tag a question onto a statement in a way that invites another to respond: "*Midnight in Paris* was a pretty good movie, wasn't it?" Tentative communication leaves the door open for others to respond and express their opinions.

There is controversy about tentativeness associated with feminine speech. Robin Lakoff (1975), who first reported that women use more hedges, qualifiers, and tag questions than men, claimed that these indicate uncertainty and lack of confidence. Calling women's speech "powerless," Lakoff argued that it reflects women's low self-esteem and socialization into subordinate roles. It's important to note that Lakoff's judgment that feminine speech is powerless was based on her assumption that masculine speech is the standard. If we use feminine speech as the standard, the use of hedges, qualifiers, and tag questions may reflect not powerlessness but the desire to keep conversations open and to include others. You should realize, however, that people outside feminine speech communities may use masculine standards, as Lakoff did, to interpret tentative speech.

Masculine Communication

Masculine speech communities tend to regard talk as a way to accomplish concrete goals, exert control, preserve independence, entertain, and enhance status. Conversation is often seen as an arena for proving oneself and negotiating prestige.

The first feature of masculine speech is the effort to establish status and control. Masculine speakers do this by asserting their ideas and authority, telling jokes and stories, or challenging others. Also, men maintain both control and independence by disclosing less than women. Men and boys typically use more I-references ("I have a plan," "I had a good game") than women and girls (Mulac, 2006). One way to exhibit knowledge and control is to give advice. For example, a person might say, "The way you should handle that is ...," or "Don't let your boss get to you." On the relationship level of meaning, people socialized in feminine speech communities may interpret advice as the speaker saying she or he is superior—smarter, more experienced, etc.,—in comparison to the other person.

A second prominent feature of masculine speech is instrumentality—the use of speech to accomplish instrumental objectives. Particularly when men think they are knowledgeable about a topic, they may want to show their knowledge to others (Leaper & Ayres, 2007). In conversation, this is often expressed through problem-solving efforts to get information, discover facts, and suggest solutions. Conversations between women and men are often derailed by the lack of agreement on the meaning of this informational, instrumental focus. To people socialized in feminine speech communities, it may feel as if men don't care about their feelings. When a man focuses on the content level of meaning after a woman has disclosed a problem, she may feel that he is disregarding her emotions. He, on the other hand, thinks he is supporting her in the way that he has learned to show support—by suggesting how to solve the problem.

JOANNE

My boyfriend is the worst at throwing solutions in my face when I try to talk to him about a problem. I know he cares about me; if he didn't, he wouldn't use up all that energy thinking up solutions for me. But I'm the kind of person who prefers a good ear (and maybe a shoulder) when I have a problem. I would like it so much better if he would forget about solutions and just listen and let me know he hears what's bothering me.

A third feature of masculine communication is conversational command. Despite jokes about women's talkativeness, research indicates that, in most contexts, men tend to talk more often and at greater length than women (Mulac, 2006). Compared with girls and women, boys and men talk more frequently and for longer periods of time in face-to-face conversation and on the Internet (Crowston & Kammeres, 1998). Further, masculine speakers may reroute conversations by using what another says as a jumping-off point for their own topics, or they may interrupt. Although both sexes interrupt, most research suggests that men do it more frequently (Johnson, 2000; West & Zimmerman, 1983).

Not only do men generally interrupt more than women, they may do so for different reasons. Research indicates that men are more likely to interrupt to control conversation by challenging other speakers or wresting the talk stage from them, whereas women interrupt to indicate interest and respond to others. A different explanation is that men generally interrupt more than women because interruptions are considered normal and good-natured within the norms of masculine speech communities (Wood, 1998). Whereas interruptions that reroute conversation might be viewed as impolite and intrusive in feminine speech communities, the outgoing, give-and-take character of masculine speech may render interruptions as just part of normal conversation.

Fourth, masculine speech tends to be direct and assertive. Compared with women's language, men's is typically more forceful and authoritative (Mulac, 2006). An exception to this pattern is when men talk with someone of high status. In this situation, men with lower status may be less assertive and commanding (O'Neill & Colley, 2006; Palomares, 2008, 2010).

Fifth, masculine speech tends to be more abstract than feminine speech. Men frequently speak in general or conceptual terms that are removed from concrete experiences and personal feelings. Within public environments, norms for speaking call for theoretical, conceptual, and general thought and communication. Yet, within more personal relationships, abstract talk sometimes creates barriers to intimacy.

CHRIS

Once I decided to live as a woman, I had to learn a whole different way of communicating. Even though I've always identified as female, I've always hung out with guys and I learned pretty much what our textbook describes as masculine speech patterns. To be accepted as a woman, I've had to relearn how to communicate—ask more questions about others, express more feelings, describe my experiences with a lot more detail, be more indirect like saying "Maybe we need to do such and such" instead of "Do such and such."

Finally, masculine speech tends to be less emotionally responsive than feminine speech, especially on the relationship level of meaning (Guerrero et al., 2006). Men, more than women, give what are called **minimal response cues** (Parlee, 1979), which are verbalizations such as "yeah" or "umhmm." People socialized into feminine speech communities may perceive minimal response cues as indicating lack of involvement (Fishman, 1978). Men's conversation also often lacks self-disclosure as well as expressed sympathy and understanding (Eisenberg, 2002). Within the rules of masculine speech communities, sympathy is a sign of condescension, and the revealing of personal problems is seen as making one vulnerable. Yet, within feminine speech communities, sympathy and disclosure are understood as demonstrations of equality and support. This creates potential for misunderstanding between people who express themselves in masculine and feminine ways.

The Gender-Linked Language Effect

We've discussed some gendered tendencies in communication. However, these are not as hard and fast as they may seem. Recent study identifies the **gender-linked language effect** (Mulac, 1998; Palomares, 2008), which notes that language differences between women and men are influenced by a variety of factors including topics, speaker status, salience of gender in a communication situation, and other people present. One study (Palomares, 2008) found that women tend to speak more tentatively when speaking about masculine topics (sports and automotive matters were the topics in the study), but men speak more tentatively than women when speaking about feminine topics (shopping and fashion in the study). Another study showed that women communicate in more typically feminine ways when they're assigned feminine avatars than when they're assigned masculine avatars. The same is true of men: They communicate in more typically masculine ways when assigned masculine avatars. Research on the gender-linked language effect reminds us that gender is not static, but is highly dynamic. The extent to which our communication reflects our gender varies according to context and other factors.

Gender-Based Misinterpretations in Communication

In this final section, we explore what happens when gendered communication styles meet in conversations. We'll consider five communication misunderstandings that can arise.

Showing Support

Martha tells her coworker George that she is worried about Angie, who has been late to work several days recently. George gives a minimal response cue, saying only, "Oh." To Martha, this suggests he isn't interested, because she perceives verbal responses as signals of interest. Yet, operating by norms of masculine speech communities, George assumes that if Martha wants to say anything further or ask his opinion, she will. Masculine rules of speech assume people use talk to assert themselves.

Even without much encouragement, Martha continues by saying she knows Angie has a teenage daughter that has been causing some worries lately. She says, "I feel so bad for Angie, and I want to help her, but I don't know what to do." George then says, "It's her problem, not yours. Just butt out." At this, Martha explodes: "Who asked for your advice?" George is now completely confused. He thought Martha wanted advice, so he gave it. She is hurt that George didn't tune into her feelings. Both are frustrated.

The problem is not so much what George and Martha say and don't say. Rather, it's how they interpret each other's communication—actually, how they *misinterpret* it, because they fail to understand that they are operating by different rules of communication. George is respecting Martha's independence by not pushing her to talk. When he thinks she wants advice, he offers it in an effort to help. Martha, on the other hand, wants comfort and a connection with George—that's her primary purpose in talking with him. To her, George's advice seems to dismiss her feelings. He doesn't offer sympathy, because masculine rules for communication define this as condescending. Yet, the feminine speech community in which Martha was socialized taught her that giving sympathy is a way to show support.

Troubles Talk

Talk about troubles, or personal problems, is a kind of interaction in which hurt feelings may result from differences between masculine and feminine styles of communicating. Naomi tells her partner, Greg, that she is feeling down because she didn't get a job she wanted. In an effort to be supportive, Greg responds by saying, "You shouldn't feel bad. Lots of people don't get jobs they want." To Naomi, this seems to dismiss her feelings—to belittle them by saying lots of people experience her situation. Yet within masculine speech communities, you show respect by assuming that others don't need sympathy.

Now, let's turn the tables and see what happens when Greg feels troubled. When he meets Naomi, Greg is unusually quiet because he feels down about not

EXPLORING GENDERED LIVES *Scholarship versus Popular Psychology*

Deborah Tannen (1990a, 1990b, 1995) declares that "communication between men and women can be like cross-cultural communication" (1990b, p. 42). John Gray goes even further, claiming that women and men are so different that it's as though they are from different planets (1992, 1995, 1996a, 1996b, 1998). Both Tannen and Gray have sold millions of books. Should we believe what they say about communication between the sexes?

When trying to determine the worth of their claims, we might first ask about their credentials as experts in communication. Tannen is a linguist who holds a PhD. Gray has no graduate degree from an accredited school. Tannen bases her claims on research that she and others have conducted. Gray relies on anecdotes from his personal experience.

Second, we should compare their claims to findings from sound research.

Tannen's claims fare better than Gray's. Although Tannen sometimes generalizes too broadly from limited and unrepresentative samples, her claims do have some credible support. Gray, on the other hand, portrays women and men in extreme and dichotomous stereotypes that are not supported by credible research.

If you want to learn about how these popular psychology books measure up to research, read these articles: Goldsmith, D., & Fulfs, P. (1999). "You just don't have the evidence": An analysis of claims and evidence in Deborah Tannen's *You Just Don't Understand*. In M. Roloff (Ed.), *Communication Yearbook*, 22 (pp. 1–49). Thousand Oaks, CA: Sage; and Wood, J. T. (2001a). A critical response to Gray's portrayals of men, women, and relationships. *Southern Communication Journal*, 67, 201–210.

getting a job offer. Sensing that something is wrong, Naomi tries to show interest by asking, "Are you okay? What's bothering you?" Greg feels she is imposing and pushing him to expose his vulnerability. Naomi probes further to show she cares. As a result, he feels intruded on and withdraws further. Then Naomi feels shut out.

But perhaps Greg does decide to tell Naomi why he feels down. After hearing about his rejection letter, Naomi says, "I know how you feel. I felt so low when I didn't get that position at DataNet." She is matching experiences to show Greg that she understands his feelings and that he's not alone (Basow & Rubenfeld, 2003). According to a masculine speech community, however, Naomi's comment about her own experience is an effort to steal the center stage from him and focus the conversation on herself.

JAY

Finally, I understand this thing that keeps happening between my girlfriend and me. She is always worrying about something or feeling bad about what's happening with one of her friends. I've been trying to be supportive by telling her things like she shouldn't worry, or not to let it get her down, or not to obsess about other people's problems. I was trying to help her feel better. That's what guys do for each other— kind of distract our attention from problems. But Teresa just gets all huffy and angry when I do that. She tells me to stuff my advice and says if I cared about her I would show more concern. Finally, it makes sense. Well, sort of.

When I broke up with Tommy, my dad tried so hard to help me through it. He took me to games and movies, offered to pay for it if I wanted to take horseback riding lessons. He just kept trying to DO something to make me feel better. That's how he's always been. If Mom's down about something, he takes her out or buys her flowers or something. It used to really bother me that he won't talk to me about what I'm feeling, but now I understand better what he's doing. I get it that this is his way of showing love and support for me.

The Point of the Story

Another instance in which feminine and masculine communication rules often clash is in relating experiences. Masculine speech tends to follow a linear pattern, in which major points in a story are presented sequentially to get to the climax. Talk tends to be straightforward without a great many details. The rules of feminine speech, however, call for more detailed, less linear storytelling. Whereas a man is likely to provide rather bare information about what happened, a woman is more likely to embed the information within a larger context of the people involved and other things going on (Wood, 1998, 2011a). Women include details not because they are important at the content level of meaning, but because they matter at the relationship level of meaning. Recounting details is meant to increase involvement between people and to invite a conversational partner to be fully engaged in the situation being described.

Because feminine and masculine rules about details differ, men often find feminine accounts wandering and tedious. Conversely, the masculine style of storytelling may strike women as leaving out all the interesting details. Many a discussion between women and men has ended either with his exasperated demand, "Can't you get to the point?" or with her frustrated question, "Why don't you tell me how you were feeling and what else was going on?" She wants more details than his rules call for; he is interested in fewer details than she has learned to supply.

Relationship Talk

"Can we talk about us?" is the opening of innumerable conversations that end in misunderstanding and hurt. In general, people who are socialized into masculine style are interested in discussing relationships only if there is a problem to be addressed. However, people socialized into feminine style generally find it pleasurable to talk about important relationships even—or perhaps especially—when there are no problems (Acitelli, 1988).

Masculine speech communities view communication as a means to doing things and solving problems, whereas feminine speech communities regard the *process* of communicating as a primary way to create and sustain relationships. No wonder many men duck when their partners want to "discuss the relationship," and women often feel a relationship is in trouble when their partners don't want to talk about it.

Public Speaking

Differences in feminine and masculine communication patterns also surface in public contexts. Historically, men have dominated politics. Thus, it's not surprising that the assertive, dominant, confident masculine style is the standard for public speaking. Women who are effective in politics tend to manage a fine balance in which they are sufficiently feminine to be perceived as acting appropriately for women and sufficiently masculine to be perceived as acting appropriately for politicians. Women who are considered effective public speakers, such as former Texas governor Ann Richards, manage to combine the traditionally feminine and masculine communication styles (Dow & Tonn, 1993).

These are only five of many situations in which differences between feminine and masculine communication styles may lead to misunderstandings. Many people find they can improve their relationships by understanding and using both gendered communication styles. When partners understand how to interpret each other's rules, they are less likely to misread motives. In addition, when they learn to speak the other's language, they become more gratifying conversational partners, and they enhance the quality of their relationships.

SUMMARY

In this chapter, we have explored relationships among verbal communication, gender, and culture. We first looked at how language reflects and sustains cultural views of masculinity and femininity. By defining, organizing, and evaluating gender, language reinforces social views of sex and gender. From generic male terms to language that demeans and diminishes women, verbal communication is a powerful agent of cultural expression. We also saw, however, that symbolic abilities allow us to be self-reflective about our definitions of masculinity and femininity in general and our own gender identities in particular.

The second theme of this chapter is that we express gendered identities through our communication. Because males and females tend to be socialized into different gender communities, they learn different rules for expressing support, interest, and involvement. This can lead to misunderstanding, frustration, hurt, and tension. Appreciation of and respect for the distinctive validity of each style of communication are foundations for better understanding between people. Further, learning to use different styles of communication allows all of us to be more flexible and effective in our interactions with a range of people.

KEY TERMS

The terms following are defined in this chapter on the pages indicated, as well as in alphabetical order in the book's glossary, which begins on page 283. The text's companion website (**http://www.cengage.com/communication/wood/genderedlives11e**) also provides interactive flash cards and crossword puzzles to help you learn these terms and the concepts they represent.

benevolent sexism 106
gender-linked language effect 116
male generic language 103
matriarchal 105

minimal response cues 116
polarized thinking 107
speech community 109
stereotype 107

GENDER ONLINE

1. Visit this site to learn what sexist language is and why it matters: **http://www .sexistlanguage.com**

2. Online search terms: "gender-linked language effect," "generic language," "speech community."

REFLECTION AND DISCUSSION

1. Think about naming—specifically, about naming yourself. If you are a heterosexual woman, how important is it to you to keep your name or take your partner's name if you marry? If you are a heterosexual man, how much do you expect (or want) your partner to change hers? What are your preferences if you are gay, lesbian, or trans?

2. Think back to your childhood games. What games did you play? Do you think the games you played affected your style of verbal communication?

3. Read several newspapers. To what extent are women and men represented differently in stories? Are women described by appearance, marital status, and family life more often than men? Are men described in terms of accomplishments and action more than women?

4. The next time you have a conversation in which you feel that gendered rules of talk are creating misunderstandings, try to explicate your expectations to the person with whom you are talking. For instance, if you are a woman talking with a man about a problem, he might try to help by offering advice. Instead of becoming frustrated that he doesn't focus on your feelings, say, "I appreciate your suggestions, but I'm not ready to think about how to fix things yet. Right now, I wish you would help me work through my feelings about this issue." Discuss what happens when you explain what you want from others.

RECOMMENDED RESOURCES

1. Dale Spender. (1984). *Man-made language.* London: Routledge and Kegan Paul. This classic book provides strong evidence that the English language was developed more by men and represents men's experiences better than women's experiences.

2. Jessica Valenti. (2008). *He's a Stud, She's a Slut, and 49 Other Double Standards Every Woman Should Know.* New York: Seal Press. This is a somewhat humorous look at a serious issue—double standards in how behaviors are named for women and men.

3. Nora Vincent. (2006). *Self-Made Man: One Woman's Journey into Manhood and Back.* New York: Viking. Nora Vincent spent a year and a half posing as a man, "Ned." As Ned, she discovered that the freedoms and privileges men enjoy come at the cost of suppressing emotions and enduring constant testing.

We first make our habits, and then our habits make us.
—John Dryden

6

Gendered Nonverbal Communication

Knowledge Challenge:

- How do women and men differ in their typical use of nonverbal communication to regulate interaction?
- To what extent does physiology explain men's typically lower vocal pitch?
- How accurately do women and men interpret others' emotions?

The nonverbal dimension of communication is extensive and important. Scholars estimate that nonverbal behaviors carry from 65 (Birdwhistell, 1970) to 93% (Mehrabian, 1981) of the total meaning of communication. That's not surprising when we realize that **nonverbal communication** is all about elements of communication other than words themselves. It includes not only gestures and movement but also inflection, volume, physical appearance, and environmental factors, such as space and color.

Like language, nonverbal communication is learned through interaction with others. Also like language, nonverbal communication is related to gender and culture in two ways: It expresses cultural meanings of gender, and men and women use nonverbal communication to present themselves as gendered people. In other words, nonverbal communication continually reproduces or challenges images of femininity and masculinity (Butler, 1990, 2004).

Functions of Nonverbal Communication

The three primary functions of nonverbal communication are (1) to supplement verbal communication, (2) to regulate interaction, and (3) to convey the bulk of the relationship level of meaning.

To Supplement Verbal Communication

Nonverbal behavior supplements verbal messages in five ways. First, nonverbal communication may *repeat* words, as when you say, "Right!" while pointing to the right. Second, we may nonverbally *contradict* a verbal message. For example, you say, "I'm fine" while weeping. Third, nonverbal behavior may also *complement* verbal communication by underlining a verbal message. The statement "I never want to see you again" is more forceful if accompanied by a threatening glare. Fourth, sometimes we use nonverbal behaviors to *replace* verbal ones. Rather than saying, "I don't know," you might shrug your shoulders. Finally, nonverbal communication may *accent* verbal messages, telling us which parts are important. "I love *you*" means something different from "*I* love you" or "I *love* you."

To Regulate Interaction

Nonverbal communication can also regulate interaction. We use body posture, eye contact, and vocal inflection to signal others that we wish to speak or that we are done speaking.

There are some sex-related differences in patterns of regulating interaction. Women frequently use nonverbal communication to invite others into conversation—looking at someone who hasn't spoken, smiling when a new person sits down in a group. Men, in general, are more likely to use nonverbal communication to hold onto the talk stage. For instance, a man who is talking avoids eye contact with others to signal he doesn't want them to jump into the conversation.

To Establish the Relationship Level of Meaning

A final and particularly important function of nonverbal communication is to convey the relationship level of meaning that expresses relationships between communicators. The three primary dimensions of relationship-level meaning are *responsiveness*, *liking*, and *power*, each of which is linked to gender.

Responsiveness

The first dimension of the relationship level of meaning is **responsiveness**, which is showing attentiveness to others and interest in what they say and do. Nonverbal cues of responsiveness include inflection, eye contact, and attentive body posture. Lack of responsiveness may be signaled by yawns or averted eyes.

Research shows that women generally are more responsive communicators than men. If you recall the lessons learned in gender speech communities, you'll realize that greater responsiveness is cultivated in feminine speech communities. Socialized to be affiliative, many women use nonverbal behaviors to indicate engagement with others, emotional involvement, and empathy. Females tend to smile more, maintain more eye contact and direct body orientation, whereas males lean forward, display, and adopt postures congruent with those of the persons speaking (Guerrero, 1997; Hall, 2006; Miller, 2011).

Race-ethnicity interacts with gender to influence responsiveness. For instance, traditional Japanese women usually refrain from smiling in formal contexts, including weddings. The norms of Japanese culture regard smiling as indicating a lack of seriousness (Dresser, 1996). In the United States, African-American women generally don't smile as much as Caucasian women. In general, if a white woman does not smile and maintain eye contact, others are likely to think she is angry, upset, or stuck up. Conversely, people may be suspicious of a man who smiles a lot because he is deviating from norms for masculinity.

Liking

A second dimension of the relationship level of meaning is **liking**. We use nonverbal behaviors to signal that we like or dislike others. Nonverbal cues of liking include vocal warmth, standing close to others, touching, and holding eye contact. Because most females are socialized to be nice to others and to form relationships, they tend to employ more nonverbal communication that signals liking, acceptance, and friendliness than do men (Miller, 2011). For instance, when conversing, two women typically stand or sit closer together and engage in more eye contact than two men.

We can also use nonverbal behaviors to signal that we do not like others. A frown or glare communicates dislike, as does turning your back on someone.

Power or Control

The third aspect of the relationship level of meaning is **power**, or control. Power refers to the degree to which people are equal to, dominant over, or deferential to others. Control is exercised in conversations by those who define topics, direct conversation, and interrupt. Although many nonverbal behaviors convey control messages, three are especially important: vocal qualities, touch, and use of space. In all three categories, men generally exceed women in efforts to exert control (Major, Schmidlin, & Williams, 1990). For instance, compared with women, men tend to use greater volume and inflection to add force to their words. In addition, men generally take up more personal space than women.

Nonverbal behaviors may also assert or defer when it comes to territoriality. Women generally are more likely than men to surrender their territory, or space. You can confirm this for yourself by watching people on campus and elsewhere. Notice what men and women do when walking toward each other on a sidewalk. Usually, the woman moves to one side and she often does so well in advance.

Now that we have seen how nonverbal communication functions to supplement verbal communication, to regulate interaction, and to define the relationship level of meaning, we are ready to explore how it reflects and expresses cultural definitions of gender.

Forms of Nonverbal Communication

We'll consider six forms of nonverbal communication that reflect or express gender.

Artifacts

An **artifact** is a personal object that can both express identity and influence how we see ourselves. Beginning with the pink and blue blankets used with babies in many hospitals, personal objects for children define them as feminine or masculine. Parents send artifactual messages through the toys they give to sons and daughters. Typically, boys are given toys that invite competition and active, rough play, whereas girls are more likely to be given toys that encourage nurturing, domestic activities, and attention to appearance (Messner, 2000a).

Toy catalogues offer clear messages about cultural meanings attached to the sexes. Even in 2012, as I was writing this book, catalogues for children's toys featured pastel-colored pages titled "For Girls," with play kitchen appliances, makeup, hair accessories, and pink tutu outfits. The pages labeled "For Boys" had bolder colors and showed soldiers, science equipment, swords, shields, and building sets. Researchers Sharon Lamb and Lyn Brown (2006) drew three conclusions from their survey of toy sections in stores: (1) Toys are sex-segregated—different aisles for girls' and boys' toys; (2) the boys' section features action toys (Spider-Man, NEO-Shifters), whereas the girls' section features toys that involve fashion (wigs and make up), taking care of homes (toy vacuums), and nurturing (dolls); and (3) toys for boys usually come in darker, bolder colors than do toys for girls.

Toys and other artifacts have colors and many colors are associated with a specific gender. How many men do you know who have pink wallets, lime green laptops, and chartreuse watchbands? How many men do you know who wear lavender shirts and powder blue socks? Pay attention to the colors on packaging and marketing for products ranging from those for personal care (deodorants, shampoos, cologne) to those for recreation (bikes, video games, running clothes). You'll notice that there are clear and patterned differences in how the same products are packaged for men and women.

EXPLORING GENDERED LIVES | *Guns Are for Girls; Tea Parties Are for Boys*

Even at very young ages, boys are more likely than girls to want to play with guns and girls are more likely than boys to want to play with tea sets.
BUT
Research suggests there's nothing about guns or tea sets themselves that makes them differently attractive to boys and girls. Researchers created a gun that was purple and covered with rhinestones and a tea set that was dark and covered with spikes. Guess which toy children preferred? Boys went for the spiked tea set and girls went for the sparkling gun. Researchers concluded that the children had learned from others that "boy stuff"

is dark and angular and "girl stuff" is glittery (Rivers & Barnett, 2011).

For years *Dora the Explorer* was the top commercial television program for girls and boys aged 2 to 5. But then Dora started getting more, well, girly. The new Dora lives in town so she doesn't go on adventures in nature. Dora's shorts and shirts have been replaced by miniskirts and lots of pink. Products to go with Dora as she changed include a magic kitchen, a shopping cart, younger siblings to care for, jewelry, and flower lip gloss. Boys, who had loved Dora the Explorer as much as girls, lost interest (Wade, 2009).

Guys Can Take Anything

Well, anything except diet drinks, it seems. When diet soft-drink manufacturers decided to go after the male market, they knew they had to create very different advertising campaigns than those aimed at the female market. First up to bat was Pepsi Max, which was introduced in a 2009 Super Bowl commercial. Commercials for Pepsi Max feature buffed men listing the ingredients in Pepsi Max that made it a tough, manly drink: pepper spray, scorpion venom, crushed bones.

Not to be outdone, Dr. Pepper came out with Dr. Pepper Ten. The commercials emphasize that Dr. Pepper Ten has 10 calories because "dudes don't drink diet." Ramping up the it's-a-man-thing advertising, the ads for Dr. Pepper Ten proclaim, "It's not for women" and have a Facebook page for men only. And the packaging? Steely gray color with images of bullets—quite a contrast with delicate tan bubbles on the diet Dr. Pepper that's presumably for women.

Although clothing has become less sex-distinctive than in former eras, fashions for women and men still differ in the world beyond college. Men's clothes generally are not as colorful or bright as women's, and they are designed to be more functional. Pockets in jackets and trousers allow men to carry wallets, change, keys, and miscellany. The relatively loose fit of men's clothes and the design of men's shoes allow them to move quickly and with assurance. Thus, men's clothing enables activity.

Women's clothing is quite different. Reflecting social expectations of femininity, women's clothing is designed to call attention to women's bodies and to make them maximally attractive to viewers. Form-fitting styles, clingy materials, and revealing cuts encourage women to perform femininity and sexuality. Formal women's clothing often has no pockets to hold wallets and keys. Further, most women's shoes are designed to flatter legs at the cost of comfort and safety—how fast can you run in stilettos?

Artifacts and what they mean depend on cultural context. This point is well made by Zainab, an international student in California, who e-mailed me a comment about the meaning that she, as a Muslim woman, attaches to wearing a hijab, a headscarf that many Western women regard as a symbol of the oppression of Muslim women.

Indecent Dress for Women

Lubna Hussein, a 30-something Sudanese journalist was arrested for violating Islamic law by wearing "indecent clothing." Her offence? Wearing trousers. In July of 2009, Ms. Hussein and 12 other trouser-wearing women were apprehended in a café and sentenced to a fine and lashing with whips that leave permanent scars. Most of the accused women pleaded guilty and

accepted the punishment, but Ms. Hussein pleaded not guilty. For defying the court, she was sentenced to more lashes. Ms. Hussein printed invitations and sent e-vites asking people to come to witness her whipping. Embarrassed, the government offered to drop the charges if Ms. Hussein would agree not to wear trousers. She refused (Gettleman, 2009b).

ZAINAB

Most Americans I have met think that the hijab [head covering] worn by Muslim women is oppressive. I must disagree with that. Muslim women who choose to wear the hijab are liberated from the stereotypes of women as sex objects. We are not oppressed by the standards of our culture, which are the standards that we should be judged by.

Other artifacts communicate cultural views of women and men. Advertisements for food, homemaking, and child rearing feature women, reiterating the view of women as homemakers and mothers and the view of men as uninvolved in parenting. Products associated with heavy work, cars, and outdoor sports feature men (or women in seductive poses who are admiring the strong men), underlining the assumption that men are strong and daring. Also, consider the artifacts that women are encouraged to buy to meet the cultural command to be attractive: The cosmetics industry is a multimillion-dollar business in the United States. Girls and women scramble to find products to straighten, curl, color, and extend hair and products to create "natural-looking" faces by covering up blemishes, coloring skin, and thickening and curling lashes.

EMILY

Why do girls have to look nice all the time? My boyfriend rolls out of bed and goes to class or the mall or wherever. He doesn't have to shampoo and blow his hair or dress in clean, ironed clothes. His clothes are rumpled and his hair isn't even combed some days. Once when I had a really bad cold, I felt so bad I didn't do what I usually do before going out. I showered, but I didn't do my hair or put on blush and eye shadow, and I wore workout clothes. My boyfriend told me I looked like a slob just because for once I looked like he did.

Some people use artifacts to challenge existing perceptions of masculinity and femininity. For example, some men wear one or more earrings, either because they like the adornment or to signal support of people who aren't straight. Women may wear military boots or may dress in other ways that defy conventional performances of femininity.

RAQUEL

As a Puerto Rican I often felt like I was always different as a child. My skin was darker and there seemed to be no Puerto Ricans in the media to make me feel more pride in my ethnicity as a child.

I think it's very sad the things we do to conform to the ideal beauty. I have a friend who is Vietnamese who hates her eyes. She is very beautiful but she would rather have the Western eyes. I have another friend who is Italian and had the large

Roman nose but right after high school she had rhinoplasty to "fix" it. When I was younger I wanted lighter skin even though all of my white friends said they were jealous of my "tan."

Proximity and Personal Space

Proxemics refers to space and our use of it. Space is a primary means by which a culture designates who is important and who has privilege. In strongly patriarchal societies, women are not allowed to own property; thus, they are denied literal, physical space. Only in the mid-1990s did India begin to allow daughters to inherit property from parents.

Consider who gets more and less space in our society. Executives have large offices, although there is little functional need for so much room. Secretaries, however, are crowded into cubicles that overflow with file cabinets and computers. Generally, there is a close correlation between status and the size of a person's home, car, office, and so forth. Who gets space and how much space they get indicate power.

Think about the home in which you grew up. Who sat at the head of the table—the place typically associated with being head of the household? Did your father or stepfather have his own room, space, or chair? Did your mother or stepmother? Many men have private studies, workshops, or other spaces, but fewer women with families have such spaces. My students initially disagreed with this observation and informed me that their mothers have spaces. When we discussed this, however, it turned out that many of their mothers' spaces were kitchens and sewing rooms—places where they do things for other people. Students whose mothers had spaces for their own work in the home, reported their mothers generally used parts of other rooms (a corner in the living room) or temporary spaces (using the dining room table when it's not needed for meals).

EXPLORING GENDERED LIVES *Gendered Proxemics*

Virginia Valian (1998) is a professor of psychology and linguistics who is interested in how gender stereotypes shape perceptions. She conducted an experiment to find out whether college students are equally likely to perceive women and men as leaders. Students were asked to identify the leader in photos of people seated around a conference table. When the people in the photo were all men or all women, students overwhelmingly chose the person at the head of the table as the leader. Students also selected the person at the head of the table as the leader when the photo showed both women and men and a man was seated at the head of the table. However, when both women and men were in the photo and a woman was at the head of the table, students selected the woman at the head as the leader only half the time.

Create pictures like those in Valian's experiment, show them to friends, and ask friends to identify the leader in each picture. Do your results concur with those of Valian?

Territoriality is personal space. Yet, not everyone's territory is equally respected. People with power tend to enter the spaces of those with less power, but the converse is not true. In general, men go into women's spaces more than women enter men's spaces and more than men enter other men's spaces. Also, men are more likely than women to challenge those who enter their territory (LePoire, Burgoon, & Parrott, 1992).

Haptics (Touch)

Haptics, or touch, from parents and other adults communicates different messages to boys and girls. Parents tend to touch daughters more often and more gently than they do sons, which teaches girls to expect touching from others and to view touching as an affiliative behavior. Boys are more likely to learn to associate touching with control and power and not to expect nurturing touches from others. This may explain why members of female softball teams exchange more team hugs and hand piles than members of male softball teams, particularly after negative game events (Kneidinger, Maple, & Tross, 2001).

ROSEANNE

A few months ago, I was out with this guy I'd been seeing for a while. We weren't serious or anything, but we had gone out a few times. Well, we were at his place listening to music when he started coming on to me. After a while, I told him to stop because I didn't want to go any further. He grinned and pinned my arms back and asked what I was going to do to stop him. Well, I didn't have to, thank goodness, because he didn't really push, but just the same I had to think there really wasn't anything I could have done if he had. That's always there when I'm with a guy—he could overpower me if he wanted to.

Because men are generally larger and stronger than women, they tend to have more physical confidence and to be more willing to use physical force than women. Some men are unaware of how imposing their strength is, especially in relation to others who are less so.

Kinesics (Facial and Body Motion)

Kinesics are face and body movements. Kinesic behaviors more typical of women than men include tilting heads, smiling, and condensing their bodies to take up less space. Kinesic behaviors more typical of men than women include using large gestures, taking up space, and entering others' territories. In combination, these gender-differentiated patterns suggest that women's facial and body motions generally signal that they are approachable, friendly, and unassuming. Men's facial and body communications, in contrast, tend to indicate that they are reserved and in control.

ELAINE

I never thought it would be so hard not to smile. When you challenged us in class to go one day without smiling except when we really felt happy, I thought that would be easy. I couldn't do it. I smile when I meet people, I smile when I purchase things, I even smile when someone bumps into me. I never realized how much I smile. What was most interesting about the experiment was how my boyfriend reacted. We got together last night, and I was still working on not smiling. He asked me what was wrong. I told him, "Nothing." I was being perfectly nice and talkative and everything, but I wasn't smiling all the time like I usually do. He kept asking what was wrong, was I unhappy, had something happened—even was I mad. I pointed out that I was being as friendly as usual. Then he said, yeah, but I wasn't smiling. I told him that I just didn't see anything particular to smile about, and he said it wasn't like me. I talked with several other women in our class, and they had the same experience. I just never realized how automatic smiling is for me.

DUNCAN

When I was in high school, I played on the football team. On the day we were taking the team photograph, one of the seniors on the team yelled out before the photo, "if anyone smiles, I'm going to beat your ass." Football is a tough, aggressive game, so you're not supposed to smile when you're playing or having a photo in your uniform.

Males are more likely than females to use facial and body movements aggressively in social, business, and other contexts (Kinney, Smith, & Donzella, 2001; Timmers, Fischer, & Manstead, 1998). Male athletes engage in nonverbal confrontations with teammates, whereas female athletes are more likely to talk through tensions than engage in physical confrontations (Sullivan & Short, 2001).

Called by poets the "windows to the soul," eyes can express love, anger, fear, interest, challenge—a great range of emotions. Many women have learned to signal interest and involvement by sustaining eye contact, whereas men generally do not sustain eye contact during conversations. An exception to this rule is using eye contact to meet a perceived challenge. Men in my classes tell me that they would lose face and come across as wimps if they didn't return a stare.

RANDALL

It sounds kind of stupid when we talk about it, but it's true that a guy has to return another guy's stare if he wants to hold his own. It's like a staring contest. Sometimes, on a street another guy will meet my eyes. When I notice, then he's locked into holding the stare, and that means that I have to, too. It's like that old joke about the first one to blink loses. It's kind of dumb, but I'd feel strange not returning another guy's gaze. Like a wimp or something.

Paralanguage

Vocal cues that accompany verbal communication are called **paralanguage**. Although there are physiological differences in male and female vocal organs (the larynx and pharynx), these do not account fully for gender differences in paralanguage. For instance, the larger, thicker vocal folds of male larynxes do result in lower pitch, but the difference between the average pitch of male speakers and female speakers exceeds that explained by physiology.

To understand why women and men tend to have divergent paralanguage, we must once again consider socialization. What vocal cues would you expect of someone taught to be deferential and caring? What would you expect of someone taught to be assertive, emotionally reserved, and independent? Your expectations probably closely match identified differences in male and female paralanguage. In general, women use higher pitch, softer volume, and more inflection. Men tend to use lower pitch and greater volume in order to assert themselves and command the conversational stage.

Physical Appearance

Western culture as well as many other cultures places high priority on physical appearance. Although striving to meet physical ideals is typically associated with girls and women, men are not immune. Members of both sexes often feel pressured to meet current cultural criteria for being physically attractive.

An increasing number of men feel pressure to measure up to social prescriptions for ideal masculinity. For them, the goal tends to be having buff, muscular bodies rather than losing weight (Boodman, 2007; Roosevelt, 2010). Action figures socialize boys at an early age to understand that the ripped look is the current body ideal for masculinity. Consider one example: the 1973 G.I Joe action figure, if a real

---

EXPLORING GENDERED LIVES *A New Model for Models?*

The fashion industry has long favored models who are alarmingly thin. For many years, critics have charged that using emaciated models encouraged eating disorders among women. The critics were largely ignored until 2006 when two South American models died: one from anorexia, and one from heart failure, which can be caused by excessive thinness.

In September 2006, Spain's top fashion show—Pasarela Cibeles in Madrid—required women who wanted to model to have a body mass index of 18 or higher. As a result, 30% of the models who expected to be in the show were rejected as too thin (Woolls, 2006). In

December 2006, Milan pledged that it would keep dangerously thin models off its runways (Givhan, 2006). Taking note, in January 2007, the Council of Fashion Designers of America, based in New York, issued a memo suggesting that models be educated about eating disorders and that healthy snacks be provided for models backstage during fashion shows.

Currently, Crystal Renn is the reigning plus-size model. But what is "plus-size?" Renn is a size 12; the average American woman is a size 14. Says Renn, "It's simply bizarre that 'normal' is the new overweight" (Wilson, 2010, p. E1).

Do you prefer to see a range of body sizes or a single size in advertisements?

EXPLORING GENDERED LIVES *Beauty for Sale*

Q: Isn't it mainly women who have cosmetic surgery?

A: Today, both sexes have cosmetic surgery. Women most often have breast augmentation, tummy tuck, liposuction, eyelid surgery, and breast lift (American Society of Plastic Surgeons, 2012). The most popular surgeries for men are liposuction, eyelid surgery, rhinoplasty, and face lifts (American Society of Plastic Surgeons, 2012). Both sexes also increasingly rely on treatments such as Botox injections—4,030,318 in 2011.

Q: Isn't cosmetic surgery for people with lots of discretionary income?

A: Not anymore. One in three people having cosmetic surgery makes less than $30,000 a year, and fewer than one in three make more than $70,000 a year (Dana, 2011). Even when the United States was in a deep recession and many people were unemployed, the cosmetic surgery industry grew. While Americans spent approximately 4% less on food and 7% less on entertainment, they spent 5% more on liposuction, 8% more on eyelid surgery, and 24% more on butt lifts. It helps that cosmetic surgery patients can now finance their body work—with interest rates on loans of over 25% (Dana, 2011). In 2011, Americans spent nearly $10 billion on cosmetic procedures (American Society of Plastic Surgeons, 2012).

Q: But adults are entitled to make their own choices, right?

A: Perhaps, but cosmetic surgery is not adults only. Increasingly Americans between 13 and 19 years old are having injections of botulinum toxin, which goes by the brand names Botox and Dysport. In 2009, 12,000 injections were sold to people in this age group (Louis, 2010b). Consider Charice Pempengco, a 18-year-old Filipino singer. Before her appearance on Glee in 2010, Pempengco had Botox injections and a skin firming treatment "to look fresh" (Louis, 2010).

Q: So what's the big deal? Maybe appearance shouldn't matter so much, but if you can afford to have cosmetic surgery, why not do it?

A: All of us care about our looks. However, too many people seeking cosmetic surgery have unrealistic expectations that breast augmentation or a face lift will make their lives better. Many think others will like them better if they "fix" how they look. That's unlikely. Also, there can be complications that are painful and sometimes disfiguring or disabling. Injections to hide wrinkles and lines can shrink and distort the face. Skin resurfacing can cause inflammation and discoloration of skin. Eyelift surgeries can make it difficult or even impossible to close the eyes completely. Breast implants decrease breasts' sensitivity to touch. Scarring, chronic pain, and nerve damage are other possible complications. Botox and Dysport injections in facial areas can result in facial nerve paralysis, an asymmetrical smile, and speech impairments (Louis, 2010b).

Another reason to think carefully about surgery that changes your appearance is that body ideals change. Years ago, when small-breasted Twiggy was a supermodel, women had breast-reduction surgeries in record numbers. Larger breasts are part of the current physical ideal for women, which goes a long way toward explaining why breast enlargement surgery has increased more than 700% since 1992 (Levy, 2005; Rives, 2005). And it's probably no coincidence that record numbers of women are paying for lip augmentation at a time when Angelina Jolie is a superstar (Louis, 2010a). When ideals for breast and lip size change, fashion-conscious people may need more procedures to reverse the earlier ones.

man, would be 5-foot 10-inches tall, have a 31.7-inch waist, a 44.4-inch chest, and 12.2-inch biceps, but the more recent G.I. Joe Extreme, if a real man, would be 5-foot 10-inches tall, have a 36.5-inch waist, a 54.8-inch chest, and 26.8-inch biceps (Harrison, 2008).

Action figures aren't the only role models offered to boys and men. The most successful male actors have toned bodies and good musculature. Even male news reporters such as Anderson Cooper and Jason Carroll and expert consultants such as Sanjay Gupta (medical expert on CNN) increasingly have toned bodies (Trebay, 2010).

Girls and women are more likely to allow concerns about appearance to affect their general sense of self-worth (Bulik & Taylor, 2005; Davies-Popelka, 2011). Many women, particularly young ones, find it nearly impossible to resist the pervasive pressure to be thin (Hesse-Biber & Leavy, 2006; Rhode, 2010). Many young women say they know that models are digitally altered and not "real," but still they dislike their own bodies for not measuring up to the manufactured perfection (Rhode, 2010).

For many girls and women concern about weight starts early. By third grade, 50 to 80% of girls say they want to lose weight (Rhode, 2010), and by the fourth grade, 40% of girls diet (Kilbourne, 2004, 2007, 2010). By age 13, 53% of American girls say they are "unhappy with their bodies"; and by age 17, 78% say this (National Institute on Media & the Family, 2007). Pressure to be thin contributes to the epidemic of eating disorders, which affect 7 to 10 million Americans of which 90 to 95% are girls and women. Today, 10% of college students suffer from an eating disorder and 15% of women have unhealthy attitudes and behaviors regarding food (National Association of Anorexia Nervosa and Associated Disorders, 2010; National Institute of Mental Health, 2010). Without treatment, as many as 20% of anorexics die within 20 years of developing the disease as a direct result of the disease, but with treatment only 2 to 3% die (National Association of Anorexia Nervosa and Associated Disorders, 2010; National Institute of Mental Health, 2010).

NIKKI

When I was growing up, my mother and grandmother were always on diets. They think being ultra-thin is essential. Four years ago, when I came to college, I gained the "freshman 15." When I went home for the summer, my mother and grandmother commented on how much weight I'd gained and how bad I looked.

Mother got her doctor to put me on FenPhen, the diet pill. I'd heard it could be dangerous (you've probably read about the lawsuits against it), but I took the pills for two months and lost a lot of weight—more than the 15 pounds I'd gained. Then, I started having echoing sounds in my ears. I went to a doctor, and he said it was the result of taking FenPhen. The ringing is with me all the time, even though I've quit taking that pill. Being thin is fine, but it's not worth risking your health. I actually feel sorry for my mother and grandmother because they obsess over their weight and never enjoy eating food.

When women are encouraged to focus so intensely on their bodies, they may give less attention to more important aspects of identity. For many young women in America, the body has become an all-consuming project that takes precedence over developing character, integrity, and other components of identity (Barash, 2006; Davies-Popelka, 2011).

Karl Prouse/Catwalking/ Getty Images

Many current models are anorexic.

| KYLE |

For me, the issue of physical appearance is really complicated because I'm trans-
gendered. Biologically, I am female, but psychologically and spiritually I am male.
Every time I see my naked body or have my period, it's totally unsettling because
I'm really a man and shouldn't have breasts or periods. Surgery scares me, but
I may have it one day so that my body matches my self-concept.

Perhaps you are wondering who is most likely to become obsessed with weight. Approximately 40% of new cases of anorexia are females between the ages of 15 and 19 (Boodman, 2007; Bulik & Taylor, 2005; Strout, 2007). Female athletes are vulnerable to eating disorders, particularly anorexia (Strout, 2007). Women who have internalized the culture's views of femininity are more susceptible than androgynous women to cultural ideals for women's weight (McRobbie, 2009; Mernissi, 2004; Northrup, 1995).

In general, African-American women tend to be less critical of their bodies, less prone to eating disorders, and less extreme in pursuing unrealistic physical ideals (Banks, 2000; Walker, 2007). African-American women who identify strongly with their ethnic heritage are less vulnerable to obsession with thinness than are African-American women who leave their communities or who don't have strong black identities. In a letter to me, Daneen, a black student from a northern college, described the ideology behind the views of physical beauty that she and other black women in her community learned:

> My family and my African American culture instilled pride in me. I was told that my full lips, round body, and rough hair encompassed the beauty and pride of my history. To want to be skinny or have straight hair or thin lips would be to deny my identity as a Black woman.

Because our culture is increasingly emphasizing men's bodies, more and more men are exercising, working out with weights, taking fitness supplements, and using potentially lethal steroids to develop muscularity (Roosevelt, 2010). One eating disorder, binge eating, seems to be increasing among men. Male model Ron Saxen (2007) details his battle with binge eating in his book, *The Good Eater*. Gay men are particularly likely to be concerned about appearance and to develop eating disorders because physical appearance is linked more closely to self-worth for gay than straight men (Beren, Hayden, Wilfey, & Grilo, 1996).

In summary, sex-related differences in nonverbal behavior reflect culturally constructed views of masculinity and femininity. In general, women are more sensitive to nonverbal communication; display more overt interest, attention, and affiliation; constrict themselves physically; are given and use less space; use touch for affiliative purposes but are touched more; and restrict body gestures more than men. Reflecting cultural messages about how to enact masculinity, men tend to use nonverbal communication to signal power and status, to assert themselves and their agendas, to command territories, and to veil their emotions from public display.

EXPLORING GENDERED LIVES *Race and Views of Physical Beauty*

What's thin? What's fat? Is weight attractive on women? It turns out that the answers often depend on the race of the person answering. There is growing evidence that black and white girls and women have different ideals of feminine beauty.

At early ages, many white girls learn that being slender or even thin is considered desirable. When asked to describe a perfectly shaped female, young white women respond that she would be 5 feet 7 inches tall and weigh 100 to 110 pounds. Young black women's descriptions of physical ideals typically include full hips and thick thighs. Young black women also tend to emphasize that beauty is about more than appearance: It's having the "right attitude." These differences in feminine ideals shed light on reasons why

anorexia and bulimia are less common among black girls and women, especially those who are strongly identified with African-American culture (Bocella, 2001; Molloy & Herzberger, 1998).

Thinness is not the only aspect of physical attractiveness that is race related. For years, European-American features have been represented as the only standard of female beauty. Tyra Banks, Naomi Campbell, and other women of color who are successful models have skin color, hair, and features that are more like those of European Americans than like members of their own ethnic groups. But Campbell is trying to change that—working with other black models, she's pushing the fashion industry to feature more black models on the runway and in magazines (Samuels, 2008).

Interpreting Nonverbal Behavior

Before leaving our discussion of gender and nonverbal communication, we should ask whether there are sex- or gender-related differences in skill at decoding others' nonverbal behaviors. The research that has addressed this question reports that women are generally more skilled than men at interpreting others' nonverbal communication to identify the emotions they are experiencing (Hall, 2006; Miller, 2011). There is one exception to this generalization, and it's one that calls our attention to both biological and sociological influences on our gendered identities. Although overall women exceed men in their ability to decipher facial cues, in an experiment men were notably faster than women at noticing angry faces (Bakalar, 2006). One explanation for this is that historically men's survival depended on having a keen ability to detect anger and other signs of possible aggression.

Although researchers agree that women are generally more skilled than men at interpreting nonverbal behavior, they disagree on why this is so. One explanation of women's generally strong ability to read feelings is sex-related brain differences—females' right brain specialization—may make them more adept at decoding emotions. Second, both cognitive development and social learning theories explain that, from childhood on, most females are encouraged to be sensitive to others and to relationships. Related to this is the third explanation: women's social location encourages them to develop a standpoint that prioritizes attending to others and being able to read their feelings and needs.

> KRISTA
>
> *I buy the power explanation for women's decoding skill. I know that I learned to do this from my mother. My father is very moody, and you have to know how to read him, or there's trouble ahead. I remember, when I was a little girl, my mother would tell me not to ask Daddy for something or not to tell him about things at certain times because he was in a bad mood. I asked her how she knew, and she gave me a blueprint for reading him. She told me, when he was mad he fidgeted and mumbled more and that he got real quiet when he was upset. Later, she taught me other things, like how to tell when he's getting angry about something—his eyebrows twitch. She made it seem like a science, and I guess it was in a way. But she sure knew how to read his moods, and that's how we stayed out of his way when he was on the warpath.*

Standpoint theory also suggests that women's decoding skill results from their standpoint as subordinate members of society. Those who are oppressed or who have little power learn to interpret others in order to survive. For members of oppressed groups, decoding is a survival skill. Women's decoding skills probably result from a combination of biology, socialization, and historic and current power discrepancies between the sexes.

You might think about your experiences and observations of others and ask which explanation of women's decoding ability makes most sense to you.

Cultural Values Associated with Gendered Nonverbal Communication

Nonverbal behaviors expected of women emphasize communality—building and sustaining relationships and community. Nonverbal behaviors considered appropriate for men emphasize agency—displaying power and initiative, achieving. How are these prescriptions for feminine and masculine nonverbal communication valued in Western culture?

We begin by noting that Western society values agency more than communality. In other words, Western culture places higher value on the behaviors associated with masculinity than on those associated with femininity.

But cultural beliefs are not etched in stone. Instead, they are constructed, sustained, and sometimes altered as members of a society interact in ways that constantly remake social views of gender. We can resist our culture's unequal views of agency and communality if we recognize that different nonverbal styles are simply different—not better or worse, just different. We can also choose not to embody the gendered nonverbal style prescribed for our gender. If we find that social expectations restrict us, we may resist them. In doing so, we act as agents of change who alter cultural understandings of women's and men's behavior.

Respecting Gendered Styles of Nonverbal Communication

What we've learned in this chapter also empowers us to be more effective in our communication and in our interpretation of others' communication. People who have been socialized in conventionally masculine speech communities may perceive a woman who defers as less confident of her ideas than a man who advances his views assertively. Similarly, someone socialized in conventionally feminine speech communities might view a man as insensitive and domineering if he looks impassive, offers little response to her talk, and promotes his agenda. And some people make negative judgments of anyone who defies conventional expectations of gender and performs outside of the usual identity categories. Yet, such judgments reflect the communication rules we have learned, ones that may not apply to others' ways of expressing themselves. If we impose our values on behaviors that emanate from an alternative standpoint that is not guided by the rules we take for granted, then we distort what others mean to communicate. Greater accuracy in interpreting others' nonverbal communication results from understanding and respecting differences in how people use it.

Respecting differences calls on us to suspend judgment based on our own perspectives and to consider more thoughtfully what others mean in their own terms, not ours. This might lead you to ask for clarification of intent from conversational partners whose nonverbal communication patterns diverge from yours. For example, it might be constructive to say to someone less facially expressive than you, "I don't know how you're feeling about what I just said, because your face doesn't show any reaction. Could you tell me what you feel?" Conversely, understanding may be enhanced when someone with a masculine, assertive, nonverbal style says to his or her more deferential partner, "I'm not sure where you stand, because you seem to be responding to my ideas rather than expressing your own. I'm interested in your opinion." Communicative techniques such as these allow you to minimize the potential for misunderstandings that grow out of gendered communication styles.

Understanding and respecting different forms of nonverbal communication require us to make an honest effort to appreciate what another says on his or her own terms. At first, this is difficult because we have to get past our own egocentric ways of perceiving the world in order to interpret other people from their standpoints. People who commit to doing this say that it becomes easier with practice.

There's another benefit to learning to understand and respect alternative styles of nonverbal communication. It enhances your personal effectiveness by increasing the range of options you have for communicating with different people in diverse contexts and for varied reasons. Now that you are aware of gendered patterns in nonverbal communication, you may reflect on your own behaviors. Do you fit the patterns associated with your gender? Are you comfortable with your style and its effects, or would you like to alter your nonverbal behavior in some respects? By reflecting on your own nonverbal communication, you empower yourself to consciously create a style that reflects the identity you assign to yourself.

SUMMARY

In this chapter, we have seen that nonverbal communication expresses cultural views of gender. Social definitions of women as deferential, decorative, and relationship-centered are reinforced through nonverbal communication that emphasizes their appearance, limits their space, and defines them as touchable. Views of men as independent, powerful, and in control are reflected in nonverbal behaviors that accord them larger territories and greater normative rights to touch others, particularly women, and to invade their space. Consistent with how nonverbal communication defines men and women are differences in how they use it. Whereas many women embody femininity by speaking softly, condensing themselves, yielding territory, and displaying responsive facial expressions, men are likely to command space and volume, defend their turf, and display little facial expression to keep feelings camouflaged.

Recognizing the value of alternative styles of communication, both verbal and nonverbal, enables you to reflect critically on the patterns esteemed in our society. In turn, this empowers you to resist those social meanings that you find unconstructive, to revise your own nonverbal communication to reflect the identity you want, and to work toward changing the values our society assigns to masculine and feminine modes of expression. In doing this, you participate in the processes of constructing the meanings of masculinity and femininity and the values assigned to different forms of communication.

KEY TERMS

The terms following are defined in this chapter on the pages indicated, as well as in alphabetical order in the book's glossary, which begins on page 283. The text's companion website (**http://www.cengage.com/communication/wood/gendered lives11e**) also provides interactive flash cards and crossword puzzles to help you learn these terms and the concepts they represent.

artifact 126	*paralanguage 132*
haptics 130	*power 125*
kinesics 130	*proxemics 129*
liking 125	*responsiveness 124*
nonverbal communication 123	*territoriality 130*

GENDER ONLINE

1. To learn more about race and cultural representations of female beauty visit this site: **http://www.pale-reflections.com**

2. Online search terms: "cosmetic surgery, side effects," "gender, nonverbal communication," "ideal bmi."

3. Check out online responses to changes in Dora the Explorer by googling Dora the Explorer, make over.

REFLECTION AND DISCUSSION

1. Look at the ads in magazines you enjoy reading. Describe the feminine and masculine ideals that are reflected in them.

2. Observe people in your classes, in restaurants and stores, and walking around campus. To what extent do you see gendered patterns of nonverbal communication that were identified in this chapter? For example, do women smile and hold eye contact more than men? Do men use larger motions and command more space than women?

3. Visit a store and study the packaging on products marketed to men and women. What differences are there in color, images, size, and so forth of the products?

4. Violate an expectation for nonverbal communication for your sex. Analyze how people respond both verbally and nonverbally.

5. Conduct an informal survey to learn how students on your campus define the physical ideal for women and men:

    •   Ask five men and five women of a single race (preferably your own race so they feel comfortable talking with you) to describe their physical ideal for women and men.

    •   Record their answers, and share your findings with those of classmates.

    •   Compare physical ideals stated by people of different races and sexes.

    •   To what extent are your findings consistent with those reported in this chapter?

RECOMMENDED RESOURCES

1. *Tootsie.* (1994). Burbank, CA: RCA/Columbia Pictures. This is a classic film, featuring Dustin Hoffman as Michael Dorsey who adopts the persona of Dorothy Michaels in order to get work. Hoffman does a superb job of changing his nonverbal behaviors from masculine when he is Michael to feminine when he is Dorothy.

2. Sandra Metts. (2006). Gendered Communication in Dating Relationships. In B. Dow & J. T. Wood (Eds.), *Handbook of Gender & Communication* (pp. 25–40). Thousand Oaks, CA: Sage. This chapter offers a wealth of information on gendered patterns of nonverbal communication. Especially interesting are the detailed descriptions of nonverbal flirting behaviors.

7

The individual has always had to struggle to keep from being overwhelmed by the tribe. If you try it, you will be lonely often, and sometimes frightened. But no price is too high to pay for the privilege of owning yourself.

—Fredrich Nietzsche

Becoming Gendered: The Early Years

Knowledge Challenge:

- To what extent do mothers and fathers interact differently with children?
- How do today's fathers compare with their fathers in terms of involvement in parenting?
- How do ego boundaries affect women's and men's comfort in relationships?

What does it mean to be the sex and gender you are in America today? Write one or two paragraphs describing what it means to you personally to be the sex and gender that you are. Later in this chapter, we'll return to what you've written.

In this chapter, we explore the critically important early years of our lives. Our experiences as infants, children, and adolescents profoundly influence who we are. Although we continue to evolve throughout our lives, the foundations of our identities, including gender, are keenly shaped by the first few years of life.

Because parents are such a key influence on our identities, we will examine at length how parents' communication teaches children the cultural gender code. We will also consider contemporary college students' views of what it means to be a man, woman, gay, or transsexual in America today. Their descriptions give rich insight into current prescriptions for gender—and, equally, some of the difficulties those prescriptions pose.

Gendering Communication in the Family

Families, particularly parents and stepparents, are primary influences on gender identity. To understand how families contribute to gendering children, we will first elaborate on the largely unconscious dynamics at work in gender development, which we discussed briefly in Chapter 2. Second, we will draw on social learning, cognitive development, and symbolic interaction theories to examine more overt ways in which children learn gender in families.

Unconscious Processes

The conscious realm of human experience does not fully explain human development. Insight into unobservable, yet very important, unconscious dynamics comes primarily from psychoanalytic theories, which claim that core identity, including **gender identity**, is shaped in the early years of life.

GABE/GABBY

Growing up was not a piece of cake for me. My father was in the Army and he embraced a very rigid code of masculinity. Since I was five, I liked to dress up in my sister's clothes. By the time I was 12, I was stuffing tissues in my shirt so I looked like I had breasts—always in the privacy of my own room, of course. Dad expected me to be a fullback and I wanted to be a ballerina.
As I said, not easy.

Gender Identity

As part of developing an overall identity, each of us has to achieve a gender identity, which is a person's private sense of, and subjective experience of, his or her gender. Psychoanalytic theory originated with Sigmund Freud, who lived from 1856 until 1939. Freud claimed that "anatomy is destiny," by which he meant that biology, particularly the genitals, determines with which parent a child will identify and, thus, how the child's psyche will develop. According to Freudian theory, from an early age, children of both sexes focus on the penis. Boys identify with their fathers, who have penises, whereas girls recognize their similarity to their mothers, who do not have penises. Freud theorized that girls regard their mothers as responsible for their "lack" of penises, whereas boys view their fathers as having the power to castrate them. Both children see the father and the penis as power.

EILEEN

I don't buy this stuff about penis envy. I've never envied my brother, his penis. I remember, when we were both little, we took baths together sometimes, and I saw that he was made differently than I was. I thought it looked strange, but I didn't want it myself. But I do remember being jealous of him, or of the freedoms my parents allowed him but not me. They let him go off all day long to play, but I had to stay in the yard unless my mother was with me. He could play rough

and get dirty, but I'd get a real fussin' if I did it. I remember wishing
I were a boy so that I could do all of the fun things, but I didn't wish
I had a penis. Definitely not.

As interesting as Freud's theory is, there is limited empirical support for his beliefs about penis envy and fear of castration. Despite rejecting some of Freud's ideas, current psychoanalytic theorists agree with the basic claim that families are critical to the formation of gender identity. In infancy, children of both sexes tend to depend on and identify with the person who takes care of them. Usually, this is a woman, often the mother. Thus, children of both sexes generally form their first identification with an adult woman.

Yet, their common identification with a female does not mean that boys and girls pursue similar paths to develop gender identity. Around the age of three, male development and female development diverge dramatically. You'll recall from cognitive development theory that this is the time at which gender constancy is usually secured, such that children realize that their sex is an unchanging, continuous part of their identity. For most girls, concrete, daily interactions with her mother or another female caregiver crystallize her sense of self within a close relationship.

To develop masculine gender identity, however, boys need to identify with a male. This process is complicated for boys whose fathers are not highly involved in their everyday lives. Although fathers in our era say they have closer relationships with their sons than their fathers had with them, the sons perceive their fathers as less affectionate than their fathers perceive themselves (Floyd & Morman, 2005).

ADRIENNE

I remember watching my mother fix her hair and makeup in the morning. I thought she was the most beautiful woman in the world, and I wanted to be just like her. Many days, I went into her dressing room when she was busy downstairs and practiced putting on makeup and fixing my hair just like she did.

For boys who lack a strong, personal relationship with an adult male, masculine gender can be elusive and difficult to grasp (Tyre, 2009). This may help explain why many boys define their masculinity predominantly in negative terms—as not feminine, not female, not like mother. By extension, this may be the source of young boys' tendency to devalue the feminine in general ("Ugh, girls are icky"), a pattern not paralleled by young girls' views of masculinity. Young boys' vigorous contempt for anything feminine may be a way to assure themselves that they are truly masculine (Chodorow, 1989).

RICH

My father left us before I was even a year old, so I didn't know him at all. My mom worked all day and was too tired to date or anything else, so there wasn't a man around. I tried to help Mom, but she'd tell me I didn't have to do this stuff, because

*I was "her little man." I used to watch Mom doing stuff around the house, and
I'd think, "That's not what I'm supposed to do," but I had a lot of trouble figuring
out what it was that I was supposed to do. I just knew it wasn't girl stuff. Then, I got
a Big Brother through a program at school. He was 17, and he spent most every
Saturday with me and sometimes a while after school during the week. Michael was
great. He'd let me hang out with him, and he'd show me how to do stuff like play
ball and use tools to make things. Finally, I had a sense of what I was supposed to
be like and what I should do. Michael really helped me figure out who I was.*

As development continues, girls are often given positive rewards for being
"Mommy's helper" and interacting with their mothers at home. Boys, on the
other hand, are more likely to be rewarded for being independent, so they tend
to roam away from home. Boys' social development typically occurs in larger
groups with temporary and changing memberships, whereas for many girls it
unfolds within continuing, personal relationships with individuals, including
mothers. These different developmental paths encourage boys to become achieving and independent and girls to become nurturing and relationally oriented
(Chodorow, 1989).

Because most girls develop feminine identity within personal, ongoing
relationships, they continue to seek close relationships and place importance on
personal communication with others throughout their lives. Because most boys
develop masculine identities that require separating from their initial relationship with their mothers, and because they tend to interact in activity-specific
groups with changing members, they learn to define themselves relatively
independently of others and to maintain some distance between themselves
and others.

Children in single-parent families may have difficulty finding available models
of both sexes. There has been little research on what happens when men, not
women, are solo parents, perhaps because there are fewer single-father families.
Preliminary research suggests that single-father families can be highly cohesive

EXPLORING GENDERED LIVES *Superheroes and Slackers*

When searching for role models, boys
are not limited to the men who are
actually in their lives. They also
have media, which offers images of
men. But how diverse are these
images? According to recent
research (Lamb, Brown, & Tappan,
2009), media offer boys pretty
limited role models. Interviews
with nearly 700 boys aged 4 to
18 allowed the researchers to
identify the media characters with

which the boys most identified. Two
were dominant:

The superhero, who is aggressive and
often violent, has high-powered weapons, and is disrespectful, if not exploitive
of women.

The slacker, who is amusing and
doesn't like school or responsibility and
has no plans for his life.

**To what extent do your experiences
confirm or challenge these as dominant
media images of men today?**

and that father-child discussions are more elaborate and less competitive than discussions between fathers and children in families with mothers as well as fathers (Galvin, 2006).

Ego Boundaries

At the same time that we construct our gender identity, we simultaneously form **ego boundaries** (Chodorow, 1989; Surrey, 1983). An ego boundary is the point at which an individual stops and the rest of the world begins. They distinguish the self—more or less distinctly—from everyone and everything else. Because they are linked to gender identity and evolve concurrently with it, masculine and feminine ego boundaries tend to differ. Individuals who develop feminine gender identities, which emphasize interrelatedness with others, tend to have relatively permeable ego boundaries. Because girls do not need to differentiate sharply from their mothers in order to develop a feminine gender identity, they often do not perceive clear-cut or absolute lines between themselves and others.

VINCE

My girlfriend is so strange about her friends. Like, the other night I went by her apartment, and she was all upset and crying. When I asked her what was wrong, she told me Linda, her best friend, had just been dumped by her boyfriend. I said she acted like it was her who'd broken up, not Linda, and she didn't need to be so upset. She got even more upset and said it felt like her problem too; couldn't I understand what Linda was going through? I said I could, but that she wasn't going through it; Linda was. She told me it was the same thing because when you're really close to somebody else you hurt when they hurt. It didn't make sense to me, but maybe this concept of ego boundaries is what that's all about.

The relatively permeable ego boundaries associated with femininity may partially explain why many girls and women tend to experience the feelings of those close to them almost as their own (Hall, 2006; Hartman, 1993). It may also explain why some women become so engaged in helping others that they neglect their own needs. Finally, this may shed light on the tendency of many women to feel responsible for others and for situations that are not their own doing. When the lines between self and others are blurred, it's hard to make a clear distinction between your own responsibilities and needs and those of others.

Conventional masculine gender identity is premised on differentiating from a female caregiver and defining the self as "not like her." It makes sense, then, that masculine individuals tend to have relatively firm ego boundaries. They generally have a clear sense of where they stop and others begin; they may sympathize with others but not experience others' feelings as their own. People with masculine gender identities and firm ego boundaries tend to feel secure when autonomy is high, and they may feel smothered in relationships that are extremely close. The firmer ego boundaries that usually accompany a masculine gender identity explain why,

later in life, many men have fewer emotionally intimate relationships than women typically do.

Parental Communication about Gender

From Chapter 2, you'll recall that one way children learn gender roles is by receiving rewards and punishments for various behaviors (social learning theory) and through observing and emulating others whom they see as models (cognitive development theory). Typically, girls are rewarded for being cooperative, helpful, nurturing, and deferential—all qualities consistent with social views of femininity. Parents may also reward—or at least not punish—girls for being sensitive, athletic, and smart. For boys, rewards are more likely to come for behaving competitively, independently, and assertively.

Parents' communication toward sons and daughters often reflects the parents' gender stereotypes. A classic study showed that in just 24 hours of birth, parents responded to their babies in terms of gender stereotypes (Rubin, Provenzano, & Luria, 1974). Although male and female babies were matched for size, weight, and level of activity, parents described boys as *strong, big, active,* and *alert,* and described the equally large, active girls as *small, dainty, quiet,* and *delicate.* These findings have been replicated in more recent studies (Elliott, 2009).

MELISSA

In my family, I learned that thinking about boys was not a high priority. If I told my mama that I liked a boy or that I was afraid a boy I was dating was going to break up with me, she'd say "Get your mind off boys and on books." Mama made it very clear that I was supposed to get my education and learn to take care of myself. Period.

Some parents convey distinct messages about assertiveness and aggressiveness to sons and daughters. Research shows that parents, particularly white middle-class parents, reward verbal and physical activity, including aggression, in sons and reward interpersonal and social skills in daughters (Mills, Nazar, & Farrell, 2002; Morrow, 2006). Because many girls are discouraged from direct, overt aggression yet still feel aggressive at times, they develop other, less direct ways of expressing

EXPLORING GENDERED LIVES *Pink Is for Boys*

If you had been a boy born in 1900, chances are you would have worn pink—and lots of it. It was only around the turn of the century that children's dress became gendered in America. Prior to that time, society regarded male and female children pretty much the same, and infants of both sexes typically wore white dresses.

When gendered clothing first emerged, pink was viewed as a stronger color than blue so pink was prescribed for boys and blue for girls. Starting in the 1950s, pink began its reinvention as feminine and blue was recast as masculine (Glenn, 2012; Paoletti, 2012).

aggression. We'll explore girls' ways of expressing aggression later in this chapter when we discuss gender dynamics among peers.

Parents, especially fathers, encourage in children what they perceive to be gender-appropriate behaviors, fostering more independence, competitiveness, and aggression in sons and more emotional expressiveness and gentleness in daughters (Bryant & Check, 2000; Fivush, Brotman, Buckner, & Goodman, 2000; Galvin, 2006). Heterosexual fathers are particularly clear in encouraging sons to be heterosexual (Solebello & Elliott, 2011).

Mothers tend to communicate with children more than fathers (Bianchi, Robinson, & Milkie, 2006; Galvin, 2006). Mothers use talk to build connections with children and to give information, advice, encouragement, and emotional support to children (Galvin, 2006; Segrin & Flora, 2005). Mothers surpass fathers in talking with children, particularly daughters, about feelings and relationships, guiding them in how to build social connections, and become emotionally competent (Galvin, 2006; Segrin & Flora, 2005). Recent research (Chang, Sandhofer, & Brown, 2012) also shows that even when children are less than two years old, mothers call sons' attention to numbers and talk with sons about numbers more than they talk with daughters.

MARK

My father took me hunting and coached me in football. He taught me to be strong around other men and to treat any woman with respect. He taught me that a real man is tough when he needs to be, loyal to friends, and protective of women.

When interacting with children, mothers typically focus on providing comfort, security, and emotional development. They engage in more eye contact and face-to-face interaction with children than do fathers. More than fathers, mothers tend to play with children at the children's level, which develops children's confidence and security in play.

Although fathers spend less time than mothers in one-on-one communication with children, today's fathers talk more with children than did fathers in previous generations (Bianchi et al., 2006; Pruett & Pruett, 2009; Tarkan, 2009). Fathers tend to engage in play that is physically stimulating and exciting, and they encourage children, especially sons, to develop skills and meet challenges. Fathers, more than mothers, stretch children by urging them to compete, achieve, take risks, act independently, and move beyond their current levels of ability (Luster & Okagaki, 2005; Popenoe, 1996; Stacey, 1996).

Another notable difference between communication typical of mothers and fathers concerns talk about sexual activity. Mothers are much more likely than fathers to discuss sex topics with children, particularly daughters (Dennis & Wood, 2012; Wilson & Koo, 2010). When mothers talk with daughters about sex, the daughters are more likely to delay sexual activity and to engage in safer sex when they decide to be sexual (Weinman, Small, Buzi, & Smith, 2008; Wilson & Koo, 2010). Research also shows that when mothers encourage condom use if their daughters choose to engage in sex, their daughters are more likely to use condoms consistently (Aronowitz, Rennells, & Todd, 2005; Weinman et al., 2008). Although mothers do most of the sex education of children, both fathers and mothers are more likely to talk about sex with daughters than with sons.

Parents also communicate gender expectations through the toys and activities they encourage for sons and daughters. Although many parents encourage their children to play with a range of toys, some parents actively discourage their children's interest in toys and games that are associated with the other sex. For instance, boys may be persuaded not to play house, and girls may be dissuaded from engaging in physically aggressive sports.

Our childhood toys and activities affect our thought and social patterns. Different types of toys and activities promote distinct kinds of thinking and interaction. More "feminine" toys, such as dolls, encourage quiet, nurturing interaction with another, physical closeness, and verbal communication. More typically "masculine" toys, such as sports equipment and train sets, promote independent or competitive activities that require less verbal interaction. Parents who don't want to limit their children to sex-typed toys may encounter challenges. Many stores sell girls' bikes in pink and other pastels and boys' bikes in darker colors (Orenstein, 2011a, 2011b; Rivers & Barnett, 2011). Halloween costumes are also very sex-typed. Typical costumes for boys are characters with supernatural powers and great strength whereas costumes for girls are ball gowns, bridal gowns, and highly sexualized outfits.

Another way parents communicate gender expectations is through the household chores they assign to sons and daughters. Like toys, various tasks cultivate particular types of thinking and activity. Domestic chores, which are more often assigned to girls, emphasize taking care of others (e.g., washing clothes, cooking, and making beds), whereas outdoor work and repair jobs, more typically assigned to boys, encourage independent activity (e.g., mowing the lawn, taking garbage to the curb, and raking).

In general, gender socialization is more rigid for boys than for girls (DeFrancisco & Chatham-Carpenter, 2000), and fathers are more insistent on gender-stereotyped toys and activities, especially for sons, than are mothers. It's much more acceptable for girls to play baseball or football than for boys to play house or to cuddle dolls. Similarly, it's considered more suitable for girls to be strong than for boys to cry, and more acceptable for girls to act independently than for boys to need others. Overall, boys are more intensively and rigidly pushed to be masculine than girls are pushed to be feminine.

TAYLOR

My father always tried to encourage me to be strong, play sports, and do things that girls were not supposedly good at doing, like working on carpentry for example. I tried my best to meet my father's expectations, but I often failed. Peers often teased me and called me names like "faggot," "wuss," because I was never good at playing sports and because of my size. I really enjoyed watching sports, but I was afraid to even try to get on teams in middle school because I was setting myself up for failure.

Parental Modeling

Another way parents communicate gender is through modeling masculinity, femininity, and, for heterosexual parents, male-female relationships. As you will recall from Chapter 2, cognitive development theory tells us that, once children have gender constancy, they actively look for role models of their sex and use those models to develop masculine or feminine qualities, behaviors, and so forth. For most children, parents are the single most visible and available models of masculinity and femininity. By observing parents, children often learn the roles socially prescribed for women and men. In heterosexual families that adhere to traditional sex roles, children of both sexes are likely to learn that women are supposed to nurture others, clean, cook, and show emotional sensitivity, and that men are supposed to earn money, make decisions, and be strong and emotionally controlled.

Not all families, however, adopt traditional sex roles; in fact, families in our era are highly diverse (Galvin, 2006). Many children have a single parent, at least for part of their lives. Single mothers provide children with multifaceted models of women's roles, and single fathers provide children with multifaceted models of manhood.

Another departure from tradition has to do with the breadwinner role. In the mid-1970s, only about 40% of married women worked outside the home (Galvin, 2006). By 2000, 60% of married women were employed outside the home (Bond, Thompson, Galinsky, & Prottas, 2002). The recession that began in 2008 further affected proportions of women and men in the paid labor force. Today, 70% of children in the United States live in households in which all adults work (Coonz, 2013), and 26% of American women who are in the paid labor force and are in two-earner marriages earn more money than their male partners (Ream, 2012). Kathleen Gerson (2010), who tracks changes in gender roles in families, reports that 80% of women and 70% of men in America today want egalitarian relationships in which both partners share breadwinning and family responsibilities.

Gay, lesbian, and transgender parents are also increasing. Whereas some same-sex partners choose to be child free, others have children or parent older children from former heterosexual unions. Nearly half of first marriages end within 20 years (Stobbe, 2012). Parents who remarry often create blended families. Being part of more than one family and being able to observe multiple models of gender gives these children more diverse ideas about how families can work and how gender can be embodied.

Parents model attitudes about gender. Fathers who work out and engage in vigorous physical activities and who encourage their sons to play sports may impart the message that physical strength is masculine. Mothers who make disparaging remarks about their weight communicate that to be feminine is to be thin.

The Personal Side of the Gender Drama

So far, this chapter has summarized research on gender socialization in the early years of life. Yet, gender is also deeply personal. Let's now translate the research we've considered into personal portraits of becoming gendered in contemporary Western society.

At the beginning of this chapter, I asked you what it means to the sex and gender that you are. In the pages that follow, you'll learn how other college students answer that question. As you read their responses, consider how their ideas harmonize with and depart from your own.

Growing Up Masculine

What does it mean to identify as a man in America in the twenty-first century? A first answer is that there is no single form of manhood or masculinity as we saw in Chapter 4. Although there is a dominant model of masculinity, there are also many variations on and challenges to that (Jackson & Balaji, 2011; Zinn, Hondagneu-Sotelo, & Messner, 2007). To understand the advantages, challenges, and issues of various masculinities, let's consider what five college men have to say. In their commentaries, Mark, Aaron, Steve, Clifford, and Derek focus as much on the pressures, expectations, and constraints of manhood as they do on its prerogatives and privileges. What these five men tell us is consistent with research (Coonz, 2013; Doyle, 1997; Lindgren & Lélièvre, 2009). We'll discuss six themes of manhood in America today. Five of these were first identified by Doyle (1997).

Don't Be Female

For many men, the most fundamental requirement for manhood is not to be feminine. At young ages many boys talk openly and expressively with friends about serious topics, including feelings (Way, 2010). Yet, as boys mature, many of them encounter pressure to "grow up," by embodying traditional norms of masculinity. To be accepted by peers, they become more closed off and less expressive. Any male who shows sensitivity or vulnerability is likely to be called a sissy, a mama's boy, or a wimp. Peer groups pressure males to be tough, aggressive, and not feminine. The antifemale directive is at least as strong for African-American men as for European-American men (Messner, 2007).

Not being like a girl means learning to "suck it up." Youths of both sexes engage in sports and sustain injuries, yet males are less likely than females to report pain or symptoms of injuries, including life-threatening brain injuries. Recent research reports that the most prominent features of ideal masculinity today are courage, risk-taking, and the ability to withstand pain without crying, whining, or quitting

(Lindgren & Lélièvre, 2009). From an early age "we teach boys they have to be tough" and they have to "play through the pain" (Gregory, 2007, p. 70).

MARK

Being a man means being strong and able to take care of yourself without whining or asking for help. Guys learn early not to be sissies. A kid who cries when the ball hits him will be called a girl. You learn or you don't have friends. It's not a big deal, just how it is.

Be Successful

This is the second requirement for men. From boyhood through the teen years, boys are expected to be successful at sports and other activities. Sports train boys to compete and be aggressive and to focus on winning (Messner, 2007; Messner & Sabo, 2006). As adults, men are expected to achieve status in their professions, to "make it."

The theme of success translates into not just being good at what you do but being better than others, more powerful than your friends, pulling in a bigger salary than your colleagues, and having a more expensive home and car than your neighbors. Many men today, like Aaron, say that being a good provider is the primary requirement for manhood—an internalized requirement that appears to cut across lines of race and economic class. Not all men who marry will be the sole or primary breadwinner for their families. Even the group that has historically fared best economically, college-educated white men, is not immune to economic downturns. In 2011, over one million white men who worked in nonsales positions were unemployed (Marin & Dokoupil, 2011). That same year, a record number of out-of-work fathers were caring for children: 32% regularly caring for children under 15 and 20% being the primary caregivers for preschool children (Stonington, 2011). In his commentary, Steve expresses some anger about the breadwinner expectation.

AARON

The one thing I know for sure is that a man takes care of his family. My dad had no respect—zero—for his cousin who had to go on unemployment and then got a job but didn't earn enough to support his family. My dad called him "lazy," "no 'count," and "freeloader." The whole reason I'm majoring in business is because students who graduate from the business school have higher starting salaries and higher salaries down the line.

STEVE

I am sick of hearing about "male privilege." Where is it? That's what I'd like to know. I'm expected to pay for dates; girls get a free ride. I have to pay a cover charge to get into a bar; ladies nights are freebies for girls. If the draft comes back, I could be drafted and shipped to a war; women aren't subject to the draft. I have to get

a job and make money; a woman can do that, but she doesn't have to.
So tell me where male privilege is in all of this.

Be Aggressive

A third injunction for masculinity is to be aggressive. Boys and men are expected to take stands, be tough, and not run from confrontations. Many boys first learn this lesson in sports as coaches psych teams up with demands that they "make the other team hurt, hurt, hurt" or "make them bleed." Messner (2005) also found that, in addition to reproducing men's power over women, sports are a way for higher-status men to exert dominance over other men. As adults, men are expected to be aggressive in their careers.

Be Sexual

The fourth element of the male role is to be interested in sex—all the time, any time. The more partners a man has and the more casually he treats them, the more of a stud he is. During rush, a fraternity sent out invitations with the notation "B.Y.O.A.," which one of my students translated for me: Bring your own ass, meaning female date. Cornell West (2007) notes that for black males, sexuality is particularly associated with a machismo identity and with being powerful. A man who doesn't want a lot of sex with a lot of women may find his manhood questioned by other men (Kimmel, 2008).

The pressure to be highly sexual with women is difficult for many men. Those who are gay or trans may not be attracted to women. In addition, a number of younger men don't want constant casual sex anytime with anyone. National

Contact sports encourage aggressiveness and self-confidence.

surveys (Schalet, 2011, 2012) report that romantic relationships matter to young men, and that 40% of men between 15 and 19 have not had sex because they are waiting for the right relationship. For these men, peer pressure to measure up to the stud image is particularly troublesome.

Be Self-Reliant

Many men feel that a "real man" depends on himself, not others. Both physically and emotionally, men are expected to be controlled and self-sufficient.

CLIFFORD

Black men face their own issues with masculinity. You have to present yourself as manly and powerful. If you don't get that down, you won't be seen as a man by any other black men. For black men, being a man also means knowing that you're expected to be violent, not to support your family, and to know everything about music and sports. That's what whites expect and they put that on me all the time. But black women are looking for men who will stand their ground—be strong and be there for them all the time. So what it means to be a black man depends on whether you look from a white or black perspective.

Michael Shelton coordinates youth camp programs for Philadelphia and is a national consultant on best practices for youth agencies. Shelton (2008) observes that when boys at residential camps get homesick, both counselors and parents expect and sometimes coerce them to stick it out and "become a man" by staying at camp. According to Shelton, "when a male child begins to exhibit signs of homesickness, he breaks many of the cardinal rules of masculinity. He exhibits emotions of vulnerability, he does not display expected toughness, and perhaps most damaging, he shows that he has not achieved independence" (p. 44).

Embody and Transcend Traditional Views of Masculinity

The sixth theme highlights the confusing messages about masculinity that confront many boys and men today. In his commentary, Derek expresses his frustration with the paradoxical expectations to be a "real man" in traditional ways and simultaneously to defy traditional views of men.

DEREK

It's really frustrating to be a man today. My girlfriend wants me to open up and show my feelings and talk about them and stuff like that. But the guys on the team get on my case whenever I show any feelings other than about winning a game. I'm supposed to be sensitive and not. I'm supposed to keep my feelings to myself and not. I'm supposed to open doors for girls and pay for dates but then respect them as equals. A lot of times it feels like a no-win situation.

For many males, a primary source of pressure to be conventionally masculine is peers—other boys and, later, men—who enforce the masculine code (Archer & Coyne, 2005; Messner, 2005). At the same time, many men feel other pressures—often from romantic partners, female friends, sisters, and mothers—to be more sensitive and emotionally open and to be a full partner in relationships. It's hard to be both traditionally masculine and not traditionally masculine.

Media are another source of masculine socialization. Media put forward images of extreme masculinity such as the oversized, inhumanly muscled male figures in video games and the TV characters who are dropped into wilderness locales and must forage and use survival techniques. These images of "real men" lead many young boys to decide they have to toughen up to make it (Brown, Lamb, & Tappan, 2009). A recent study (Vokey, Tefft, & Tysianczny, 2013) of advertising images in magazines targeted at men, such as *Fortune, Field & Stream, Playboy,* and *Game Informer,* found that men are most often portrayed as "hyper-masculine"—violent, tough, sexually aggressive, and dangerous.

Some counselors believe that men's struggles to live up to social ideals of masculinity have produced an epidemic of hidden male depression. Because masculine socialization stresses emotional control and self-reliance, many men who are depressed are unwilling to seek help. They "equate seeking assistance with weakness, or the appearance of not being able to handle their own problems" (Freed & Freed, 2012, p. 36). Depression that is untreated and that does not go away on its own can be deadly—men account for nearly 80% of suicides in the United States (Freed & Freed, 2012).

Other researchers (Cross, 2008; Garcia, 2008; Kimmel, 2008) identify a new trend among young men: A resistance to growing up and maturing in the ways that their fathers and grandfathers did. In his recent book *Guyland,* sociologist Michael Kimmel (2008) says that the rising generation of men is extending adolescence. Whereas their fathers left home, finished their educations, got married, started work, and became parents by age 30, increasing numbers of men today have not reached or wanted to reach those milestones by age 30. Based on interviews with hundreds of men in their 20s, most of whom had at least some college education, Kimmel concluded that many men today spend years—even a decade—drinking, smoking, having sex, and avoiding commitments to partners, causes, or jobs.

The first five themes of masculinity clearly reflect gender socialization in early life and lay out a blueprint for what being a man means. Yet, the sixth theme points out the contradictions between traditional and emerging views of masculinity. Individual men have options for how they define and embody masculinity in an era where gender is in flux.

Growing Up Feminine

What does it mean to be a woman in America in the twenty-first century? Two quite different narratives of femininity coexist today. One suggests that women now have it all. They can get jobs that were formerly closed to them, have egalitarian marriages with men who share in homemaking and child care, and raise amazing children (Sandberg, 2013).

Simultaneously, there is a very different narrative that tells women they may be able to get jobs, but fewer than 20% will be given opportunities to advance to the highest levels of professional life. Even women graduating today with M.B.A.s make $4,600 less per year than men (Bennett, Ellison, & Ball, 2010). Overall, male physicians make 26% more than female physicians who work the same amount and in the same specialty (Esteves-Sorenson & Snyder, 2012). Married women may have careers, but most of them still do the majority of housework and child care (Coonz, 2013; Gerson, 2010). And some women who have high power careers find that their workplaces don't accommodate their family responsibilities (Slaughter, 2013).

And media relentlessly carry the message that youth and beauty are women's tickets to success (Barash, 2006; Lamb & Brown, 2006). Prevailing images of women are conflicting and confusing, as the commentaries by Jeanne, Mala, Bonita, Rebecca, Emily, and Sharon demonstrate. We can identify five themes in current views of femininity and womanhood.

JEANNE

Hungry. That's what being a woman means to me. I am hungry all of the time. Either I'm dieting, or I'm throwing up because I ate too much. I am scared to death of being fat, and I'm just not made to be thin. I gain weight just by smelling food. I think about food all the time—wanting it but being afraid to eat, eating but feeling guilty. It's a no-win situation. I'm obsessed, and I know it, but I can't help it. How can I not think about my weight all the time, when every magazine, every movie, every television show I see screams at me that I have to be thin to be desirable?

Appearance Still Counts

This is the first theme. As Jeanne notes in her commentary, women are still judged by their looks. To be desirable, they are urged to be pretty, slim, and well dressed. The focus on appearance begins in the early years of life, when girls are given dolls and clothes, both of which invite them to attend to appearance. Gift catalogues for children regularly feature makeup kits, adornments for hair, and even wigs, so girls learn early to spend time and effort on looking good. Teen magazines for girls are saturated with ads for makeup, diet aids, and hair products. Romance novels send the message that popularity depends on wearing the right clothes, engaging in casual sex, and being rich, thin, and sexy (Johnson, 2007, 2011; Wolf, 2006).

The ideals of feminine appearance are communicated to women when they enter retail stores. Mannequins are often size 2, 4, 0, or minus sizes. Managers of stores that market to young women hire people who are young, sexy, and good-looking. According to Antonio Serrano, a former assistant store manager for Abercrombie & Fitch, he and other employees were told by upper management "to approach someone in the mall who we think will look attractive in our store. But if someone came in who had lots of retail experience and not a pretty face, we were told not to hire them at all" (Greenhouse, 2003, p. 10 YT).

Angela McRobbie (2009) notes that disorders related to body image have become so common that they are considered normal in young women. The make-over genre of television programs feature a person, most often a woman, who begins as unattractive and is made over to be very attractive. To maintain the new "improved" image, she must become active in consumer culture—spending her money to continue buying the products and services that make her acceptable.

Consumption is unending and never sufficient to secure lasting success (Johnson, 2007; Levin & Kilbourne, 2008; Levy, 2005). As Susan Barash notes in her insightful book, *Tripping the Prom Queen* (2006), "in the perpetual beauty contest any woman who wins the contest today must expect to lose it—if not tomorrow, then the day after, or the day after that" because "beauty is bound up inextricably with youth" (p. 110).

Women athletes sometimes feel special pressure to look and act feminine. Women athletes in my classes tell me that, if they don't look ultrafeminine, others assume they are lesbians. Female Olympic competitors increasingly pose nude or nearly nude in *Sports Illustrated*, *FHM* (*For Him Magazine*), or *Playboy*, which resoundingly performs femininity (Levy, 2005). And let's not forget lingerie football. To be successful both as athletes and as women, women athletes have to violate some facets of the traditional image of women while also conforming to other facets of it (Gilenstam, Karp, & Henriksson-Larsen, 2008; Meân & Kassing, 2008).

Be Sensitive and Caring

A majority of women feel they are expected to be nice, deferential, and helpful and to care about and for others. From assuming primary responsibility for young children to taking care of elderly, sick, and disabled relatives, women do the preponderance of hands-on caring in America.

In addition, many girls learn that being outspoken and smart does not win them prizes in the quest to be seen as feminine. They are encouraged to soften their opinions and to accommodate others, particularly males (Berger, 2006; Deveny, 2009). Girls learn not to stand up to boys at school because they fear being called "bitch" (Bennett et al., 2010; Deveny, 2009). The bottom line is that, for many girls, adolescence is the start of shifting attention from developing and asserting identity to pleasing others.

MALA

Males are favored over females in Indian culture. It is custom for a girl's family to give a dowry to a man who marries the girl to make it worth his while. As a result, many poor families in India kill a newborn baby if it is female and rejoice if the baby is male. When my third sister was born, my great grandmother expressed her disappointment that we had no boys and so many girls.

Negative Treatment by Others

This is a third persistent theme of femininity for women. Men students in my class sometimes challenge this as a theme of femininity. They say women are treated better than men. They point out that women—but not men—get free drinks at

"Ladies' Night," they get their meals paid for by dates, and they can cry their way out of speeding tickets. However, these rather minor advantages of being female don't compensate for more significant disadvantages such as being more subject to sexual assault, more likely to live in poverty, and more likely to face job and salary discrimination.

Early in life, many children learn how society values each sex. In the United States, parents generally prefer sons, although the preference seems less strong than in former eras. In some cultures the preference for males is so strong that female fetuses are often aborted, and female infants are sometimes killed after birth (see Chapter 12).

BONITA

You asked us to think about whether we ever got the message that males are more valued than females. I know I did. I guess I got it in a lot of ways, but one really stands out. I remember, when I was nine, my mother was pregnant for the third time. When she went into labor, Daddy took her to the hospital with me and my sister. We all sat in the waiting room while they took Mom down the hall. Later, the doctor came in and went to my father. I still remember his exact words. He said, "I'm sorry, Mr. Chavis, it's another girl. Guess you'll have to try again."

Devaluation and mistreatment of females is pervasive in Western culture. The Web teems with sites that feature beatings and sexual assaults on women. Gangsta rap refers to women as bitches and "hos," and routinely shows men abusing them. Highly popular video games allow players to earn points by mauling women.

Devaluation of femininity is not only built into cultural views but typically is internalized by individuals, including women. Negative treatment of females begins early and can be especially intense in girls' peer groups (Simmons, 2002; Tavris, 2002; Wilier, 2011). Girls can be highly critical of other girls who are not pretty, thin, and otherwise feminine, as the Exploring Gendered Lives feature on page 159 demonstrates.

REBECCA

"Sugar and spice and everything nice" is not the whole picture about girls. They can be really mean, especially to other girls. In middle school, there was one girl who was a real bully. Sherry and I were friends until 7th grade, and then out of nowhere she started ignoring me and spreading rumors about me to make other people not want to be friends with me. Boys may fight physically with each other, but at least that's direct and honest. When Sherry decided she didn't like me, she was really underhanded and indirect in how she hurt me.

Rebecca is right when she says that sugar and spice is not a full description of girls. Research (Archer & Coyne, 2005; Levy, 2005; Simmons, 2002, 2004) shows

Sisterhood?

Sororities claim to be sisterhoods—communities in which unrelated women become caring sisters to one another. Carolyn Thatcher might disagree. In 2007, she and 22 other members of DePauw University's chapter of Delta Zeta were dropped from the sorority. Why? Some members of the chapter were upset that fewer students were pledging Delta Zeta, so they decided that the sorority would be more attractive if all members met what one of the remaining sisters called standards of "social image, appearance, and weight" (Adler, 2007, p. 47). The only black member of the sorority was ousted, as were two of the three Asian members, and all members who wore a size larger than eight. Only 12 of the original 35 members were allowed to stay. However, only half of those—six women—chose to stay. The other six left to show solidarity with their ousted sisters.

Do you think sororities have a right to exclude girls who don't meet a specific physical ideal?

that many young girls engage in social aggression toward other girls. As the term implies, social aggression involves attacking others using social, rather than physical, strategies. It takes forms such as spreading hurtful rumors, excluding a girl from groups, and encouraging others to turn against a particular girl.

Why do young girls rely on indirect strategies of aggression? One reason appears to be that, even at young ages, girls understand that they are supposed to be nice to everyone, so they fear that being overtly mean or competitive would lead to disapproval or punishment (Barash, 2006; Simmons, 2002). Instead of learning how to work through feelings of anger, dislike, and so forth, young girls learn to hide those feelings and express them only indirectly.

Be Superwoman

This is a fourth theme emerging in cultural expectations of women (Sandberg, 2013). Sharon's exhilaration (see box on page 160) over the choices open to her is tempered by Emily's impression that women feel they are required to try to have it all. It's not enough to be just a homemaker and mother or just a career woman. Many young women today seem to feel they are expected to do it all.

EMILY

Women are expected to want to climb the business ladder, yet they are also expected to pick up the kids after school, make dinner, help with homework, and be a loving wife. I do not want a career that will ruin my family life or a family life that will ruin my career. How am I supposed to pick between my personal life and my career goals? Why is it that women are expected to sacrifice their careers or be superwomen who do it all but men don't have to be that way?

Women students talk with me frequently about the tension they feel trying to figure out how to have a full family life and a successful career. They tell me that they want both careers and families and don't see how they can make it all work.

EXPLORING GENDERED LIVES *Careers for Women: Gendered, Raced, and Classed*

What do gender, race, and class have to do with expectations about working? In-depth interviews revealed that expectations about who works full time are shaped by gender, race, and socioeconomic class (Damaske, 2011). Roughly half of women who grew up in working-class white and/or Latino families expected to work, whereas nearly all working-class black women expected to work in the paid labor market. The clear majority of middle-class white, Asian, African-American, and Latina families expect to work continually.

The physical and psychological toll on women who try to do it all is well documented, and it shows no signs of abating (Coonz, 2013; Galvin, 2006; Kantor, 2012; Traister, 2012).

There Is No Single Meaning of Feminine Anymore

This is the final theme of femininity in the current era. This theme reflects all the others and the contradictions inherent in them. A woman who is assertive and ambitious in a career is likely to meet with approval, disapproval, and curiosity from some people and to be applauded by others. At the same time, a woman who chooses to stay home while her children are young will be criticized by some women and men, envied by others, and respected by still others. Perhaps, as Sharon suggests in her commentary, there are many ways to be feminine, and we can respect all of them.

Prevailing themes of femininity in Western culture reveal both constancy and change. Traditional expectations of attractiveness and caring for others persist, as does the greater likelihood of negative treatment by others. Yet, today there are options that allow women with different talents, interests, and identities to define themselves in diverse ways and to chart life courses that suit them as individuals.

SHARON

My mother and I talk about women, and she tells me that she's glad she didn't have so many options. She says it was easier for her than it is for me because she knew what she was supposed to do—marry and raise a family—and she didn't have to go through the identity crisis that I do. I see her point, yet I kind of like having alternatives. I know I wouldn't be happy investing my total self in a home and family. I just have to be out doing things in the world. But my best friend really wants to do that. She's marrying a guy who wants that, too, so as soon as they've saved enough to be secure, they plan for her to quit work to raise a family. I know someone else who says she just flat out doesn't want to marry. She wants to be a doctor, and she doesn't think she can do that plus take care of a home and family, so she wants to stay single. I don't really know yet if I will or won't have kids, but it's nice to know I can choose to go either way. My mother couldn't.

Growing Up Outside Conventional Gender Roles

Not every person grows up identifying with socially prescribed gender, sex, or sexual orientation. For people who do not identify with and perform normative gender, sex, and sexuality, growing up can be particularly difficult. Gay men are often socially ostracized because they are perceived as feminine, and lesbians may be scorned because they are perceived as masculine.

Social isolation also greets many people who are (or are thought to be) transgendered. They find themselves trapped in a society that rigidly pairs males with masculinity and females with femininity. There are no in-between spaces, no means of blurring the rigid lines, and no options beyond the binary choices of male/female, masculine/feminine, and straight/gay. Consider this blog post from a 17-year-old (Kellerman, 2012):

> I'm CJ, formerly known as Chana. I'm also "genderqueer," which, in my case, means that I feel part-female and part-male. I'm not sure yet whether I will transition or not…. My mother requested to list me on Facebook as her daughter, but I didn't feel that that was totally right, but neither was "son." But there was no other choice. I either have to be a brother or a sister to my sisters on Facebook. And that's not me. It's troubling that I can't be Facebook friends with my family and correctly identify my relationships with them, because according to Facebook those relationships don't exist. Or maybe I don't exist. How strange is that?

For people who do not fit the conventional sex and gender roles, it is hard to find role models and equally difficult to find acceptance from family, peers, and society. Of the students who have studied gender and communication with me over the years, a few have volunteered commentaries on growing up outside of conventional gender roles. Ben, Zena, and Mike's commentaries appear on this page and the next.

BEN

What it means to be a man depends totally on whether you're gay or straight. I'm gay—knew that since I was 9 or 10. And being gay is hell for a teenager. Other guys, the straight ones, called me names all through middle school and high school—fag, queer, girlie. It didn't matter that I was big and toned and good at baseball. They totally excluded me because I was gay.

In 2007, a cover story of the mainstream magazine *Newsweek* was about transgendered people. The author of the story, Deborah Rosenberg, wrote that most people "have no quarrel with the 'M' or the 'F' on our birth certificates…. But to those who consider themselves transgender, there's a disconnect between the sex they were assigned at birth and the way they see or express themselves" (2007, p. 50). Until very recently, transgendered (as well as transsexed and intersexed) people seldom made their identities or struggles public. That's changing as more and more people who don't fit in conventional identity boxes demand to be recognized and accepted on their own terms. One sign of changing attitudes toward transgender people is campus policies. Many colleges have added gender identity and expression to their nondiscrimination policies and passed gender-neutral housing policies so that transgender students can choose appropriate roommates (Tilsley, 2010).

ZENA

I wear a tie always and a dress never. If I go to a doctor, I'm labeled "female," but in everyday life, most people think I'm a "male." The problem is, neither of those labels is right. Neither fits me. I'm both or neither or maybe something that is totally different than those stupid categories. Sexually, I'm attracted to both "males" and "females," although more often to "females." I have no interest in girlie things, but I'm sensitive to others and a very caring person. All I can say is that I'm Zena, and that's a name I gave myself.

Individuals who don't fit into conventional categories for sex, gender, and sexual orientation face challenges that most gender-conforming people can't imagine. For those of you who fit comfortably in the existing gender system, imagine this: You visit a doctor and learn that you are actually a different sex than you have believed yourself to be and that you identify with. If you think of yourself as a woman, you discover that genetically you are a man. If you think of yourself as a man, you learn that genetically you are a woman. Your body doesn't match your self-concept. Everything from how you dress to whom you date to which bathroom you can use suddenly becomes an issue that you have to negotiate.

MIKE

I have no idea what it means to be a man. I've never felt I was one, never identified with men. As a kid, I liked to dress in my mother's clothes until my dad caught me and beat the—out of me! I still identify more with women, and I think that I was meant to be a woman. Growing up looking like a male but feeling like a female meant that I didn't belong anywhere, didn't fit with anyone. It's better now that I'm in college and have found some people like me, but there was nobody in my rural Southern hometown!

Stay with this hypothetical situation. Would you want to have hormone treatments and surgery so that your body was consistent with the sex and gender you feel that you are? The surgery is expensive and painful. Are you willing to tolerate that in order to fit into society's categories and be considered "normal?" Or would you choose, instead, to change how you dress, style your hair, move, speak, and so forth in order to perform more credibly as your genetic sex? Or would you continue living as you have, looking and acting as the sex and gender you identify with while knowing that by medical criteria you are actually a different sex and perhaps a different gender?

EXPLORING GENDERED LIVES *Job (Dis)Qualification*

When he reached his mid-40s, Steven Stanton, the former city manager of Largo, Florida, could no longer tolerate feeling that he was a female trapped in a male body. He decided to become the woman he had always felt he was. He began hormone treatments and planned to have sex reassignment surgery. Then the roof fell in when a newspaper published a story about his planned sex-change. Almost immediately, on March 12, 2007, the city commissioners voted five to two to fire Stanton despite his 14 years of service and consistently excellent job evaluations. On May 30, Stanton—now Susan, wearing a skirt, high heels, and makeup—applied for the job from which Steven Stanton had been fired. Susan was not hired (Waddell & Campo-Flores, 2007).

Stanton isn't the only one to find that the professional world values men more than women even if they are the same person. Researchers Kristen Schilt and Matthew Wiswall studied the career implications of changing one's sex (Cloud, 2008). They found that men who become women earn significantly less after they change sex than women who become men. Even people who stayed in the same job after transitioning were regarded as more competent if they had become men than if they had become women.

SUMMARY

We are born into a gendered society that shapes our personal gendered identities. At birth, many hospitals provide pink blankets for baby girls and blue blankets for baby boys. As children grow up, they interact with parents and siblings who see them and treat them as gendered. They see boy characters on television engaging in more adventurous, rugged play than girl characters. They see cereal boxes that feature girls with dolls and boys with guns. They play with peers who, because of their own socialization, exert pressure to conform to gender norms. For instance, research shows that young boys use mockery and name-calling to punish a boy who doesn't play with masculine toys.

But socialization is not as deterministic as it may seem. Clearly, we are influenced by the expectations of our culture, yet these expectations endure only to the extent that individuals and institutions sustain them. Through our own communication and the ways we act, we reinforce or challenge existing views of gender. As we do so, we contribute to forming social views that affect the extent to which each of us can define ourselves and live our lives on our own terms.

KEY TERMS

The terms following are defined in this chapter on the pages indicated, as well as in alphabetical order in the book's glossary, which begins on page 283. The text's companion website (**http://www.cengage.com/communication/wood/genderedlives11e**) also provides interactive flash cards and crossword puzzles to help you learn these terms and the concepts they represent.

ego boundaries 146   gender identity 143

GENDER ONLINE

1. Go to Youtube.com and search for videos on "gender socialization children."

2. Statistics about diverse family forms are available from the Census Bureau at: **http://www.census.gov/population/www/socdemo/hh-fam.html**

3. Online search terms: "father role," "feminine socialization," masculine socialization," "parental models, gender."

REFLECTION AND DISCUSSION

1. How did your parents and/or stepparents model masculinity and femininity? Does your own embodiment of gender reflect their influences?

2. Analyze how your ego boundaries work in one particular relationship in your life. How do your ego boundaries both enhance and constrain that relationship?

3. I opened this chapter by asking you to write what it means to you to be a man or a woman today in America. How does your response echo or differ from themes in the responses of student commentaries presented in this chapter? How does your response differ from or contradict themes in the commentaries presented in this chapter?

4. Return to the hypothetical scenario presented on page 162. What choices would you make if the sex and gender you identify with were inconsistent with your genetics?

RECOMMENDED RESOURCES

1. *Tough Guise*. (1999). Media Education Foundation, 26 Center Street, Northampton, MA. This video offers a critical perspective on socialization that links masculinity with aggression and violence. It is a disturbing video and an important one.

2. Michael Messner is a scholar who studies gender, particularly as it relates to athletics. Visit his blog at Huffington Post: http://www.huffingtonpost.com

3. Michael Kimmel. (2008). *Guyland: The Perilous World Where Boys Become Men*. New York: Macmillan. Kimmel argues that many young men today are postponing the responsibilities that have traditionally accompanied manhood.

4. Susan Barash. (2006). *Tripping the Prom Queen*. New York: St. Martin's Griffin. This is a funny, sassy, and very insightful analysis of social expectations of girls and women and the competition between them that those expectations fuel.

Education is the most powerful weapon which you can use to change the world.
—Nelson Mandela

8

Gendered Education: Communication in Schools

Knowledge Challenge:

- Are girls or boys disadvantaged in schools?
- Are female and male college athletes given equal support?
- What differences are there in how college students evaluate male and female instructors?

America's schools are failing boys. Fewer men than women graduate from high school, college, or graduate school. That is largely because schools are hostile environments for boys and men.	America's schools are failing girls. Although girls and women exceed boys and men in grades and graduation rates, they still get less good jobs and make less than men because schools don't prepare them to succeed.

Which of the above claims seems more accurate to you? If you think schools are biased against boys, there's evidence to support you. Particularly in the early grades, the demands of school—sit in your seat, be quiet, work in a focused way—frustrate many young boys whose developmental stage makes it difficult for them to be still and to concentrate (Tyre, 2009; Whitmire, 2011).

Perhaps you think that schools discriminate against girls. If so, there's evidence to support that belief too. Persisting biases discourage women from studying science and math, and there is less support for women athletes than male athletes (Hattery, 2012). There's also evidence showing that teachers favor male students (Riegle-Crumb & Humphries, 2012), and that education benefits male students more than female students.

The two claims are like many that media have spotlighted: They contain some truth and much exaggeration. In this chapter, we want to gain an accurate picture of how schools support—or fail to support—students of all sexes and genders. We will first discuss distinct expectations and pressures that confront students of different sexes, genders, and sexual orientations. Second, we will explore gendered attitudes and practices that affect male and female students. As we will see, although American schools no longer discriminate blatantly and primarily based on sex, gendered biases and issues continue to infuse educational institutions.

As you read this chapter, keep in mind what's at stake. Schools do more than instruct us in various subjects. They are also powerful agents of gender socialization. They teach us what each sex is expected to be and to do and which careers are appropriate for women and men. As social views of gender have changed, so have educational opportunities for women and men. As social views continue to change in the years ahead, so will educational practices.

Gendered Expectations and Pressures Facing Students

To understand the range of gendered dynamics facing students today, we'll examine academics, athletics, and peer cultures at colleges and universities.

Academics

Both males and females encounter gendered expectations and pressures in schools from kindergarten through graduate and professional school. We'll consider gendered expectations affecting boys and men, girls and women, and gay and transgendered students.

Males

Most boys are developmentally disadvantaged in the early grades. Compared to same-aged girls, young boys tend to have more physical energy and less impulse control, so many young boys have difficulty adjusting to school contexts where they are supposed to sit quietly, follow instructions, and not deviate from lesson plans (Garloch, 2009; Whitmire, 2011). This means that elementary classrooms may not be boy friendly, which can render the early years of school a time of frustration and often of failure for boys (Tyre, 2009). This provides a poor foundation for success later in school.

The mismatch between young boys' development and the demands of school may contribute to a significant difference in the sexes' academic success. In kindergarten and elementary school, boys lag behind girls in reading and other verbal skills (Strauss, 2008; Tyre, 2006). Boys' verbal skills mature later than those of girls so young boys may be understandably frustrated by the strong emphasis on reading and writing that is central to the first years of school.

The mismatch between boys' development and typical early school curricula may explain why more boys than girls tune out and turn off when it comes to school. Boys are less likely than girls to complete high school (Knapp, Kelly-Reid, & Ginder, 2011). Currently, women comprise 57% of undergraduate enrollment and 59% of graduate enrollment (Knapp et al., 2011). When 20.1 million women have college degrees, only 18.7 million men have college degrees. Women also outpace men in earning graduate degrees (Yen, 2011).

Girls also confront challenges in schools. The rewards they get for completing work, reading and writing well, and minding the teacher reinforce obedience and, conversely, may not encourage girls to think and act independently and to consider when it might be useful to bend rules.

Yet, arguments over whether education is more supportive of women or men miss the larger point just as arguments over whether education is better for one race or another miss the point. By far, the biggest divide in America, including in educational achievement of citizens, is between the rich and poor (Noah, 2012; Stiglitz, 2012). While achievement gaps between males and females and blacks and whites have narrowed, the gap between rich and poor students has grown (Duncan & Murane, 2011; Tavernise, 2012). On standardized tests, the gap between low-income and affluent students' scores has grown by 40% since the 1980s (Travernise, 2012).

The growing chasm between educational achievement by rich and poor students is due, in large measure, to the greater investments of time and other resources that economically well-off parents make in their children. Affluent parents have the luxury of spending more time with very young children. They read and talk to them more than working- and poverty-class parents. It's no surprise that children who are immersed in language from birth develop better language and conceptual skills. Affluent parents also provide their children with enrichments—summer camp, tutors, travel, and SAT preparation classes—that less wealthy parents cannot afford (Brooks, 2012; Noah, 2012). All of those investments in children pay off in schooling where affluent children are more comfortable and more successful.

ALLIE

My grandmother is really smart, but she wasn't able to go to college. Her father sent her four brothers to college, but he said girls didn't need an education. When she was 34, her husband died and she had three kids to support on her own. It surely would have been easier on her if she'd had a degree so she was qualified for a good job instead of the one she had to take.

Race, sex, and economics don't tell the whole story. Personal choices also affect academic performance and success. From elementary school through college, male students spend more time on leisure activities—sports, video games, etc.—than female students (Baenninger, 2011). Choices of how to spend time—studying or

EXPLORING GENDERED LIVES   *A Short History of Gendered Education in America*

Throughout America's history, schools have echoed cultural views of gender. In America's earliest years, women were discouraged from advanced study because it was commonly believed that exposure to higher education might "unsex" women, as an educated woman was "unnatural" (Gordon, 1998). The few women who did pursue education beyond high school usually attended finishing schools, where they learned traditional feminine skills such as embroidery. In the 1800s, some female academies were established to train women as nurses and teachers, two professions considered appropriate for women.

The Morrill Act of 1862 established coeducational state universities and land grant colleges to educate women and men in liberal arts and practical skills. Practical education for men included the study of agriculture and mechanics, whereas practical education for women focused on home economics. By 1870,

30% of U.S. colleges enrolled students of both sexes. In 1920, approximately 70% of U.S. higher education institutions enrolled women and men. The 1920s and 1930s saw the growth of women's colleges that stressed intellectual development, personal independence, and creativity, which was not emphasized for women students in most coeducational institutions.

Throughout most of America's history, many colleges discriminated against women. When more women than men graduated with awards and honors from Stanford University in 1901, the school quickly figured a way to make sure that didn't happen again: Stanford instituted an enrollment ratio of three men to every one woman (Solomon, 1986). Even in the 1960s, many schools accepted only female applicants who were better qualified than male applicants. With passage of Title IX of the Education Act Amendments in 1972, all educational institutions that receive federal funds are required to treat the sexes equally.

EXPLORING GENDERED LIVES   *Gendered Education around the Globe*

The gender gap in education is greatest in sub-Saharan Africa, North Africa, South Asia, and the Middle East. In India, 33 million fewer girls than boys attend school. In rural Africa, only 3 of 10 girls complete elementary school ("Educating Girls," 2005). One barrier to girls' education in sub-Saharan Africa is difficult for Westerners to imagine: lack of toilets. Schools lack toilets and water, so students go to the bathroom behind scrub bushes that allow no sanitation or privacy. This is a barrier for girls when they start menstruating (LaFraniere, 2005).

But there are other countries where girls are more likely than boys to progress through university-level education. In Mongolia, for instance, women make up 60% of students attending universities, and more women than men are top students in faculty opinion (Lin-Liu, 2005). In the Persian Gulf, opportunities for women to attend college have increased remarkably since the 1980s (Zoepf, 2006). Other countries where females are likely to receive good educations are Belgium, France, Canada, Finland, and Norway.

engaging in recreation—contribute to different levels of academic accomplishment. Of course, what at first seem to be quite personal choices are often shaped by other factors. For example, children of affluent parents are more likely than children of less well-off parents to have been exposed to reading and to have acquired pleasure in reading. Children of more affluent parents may also have had mentoring on time management and discipline that helps them regulate their recreational activities in ways that don't undermine academic success.

Females

What about women students? What biases and pressures do they face academically? Despite much effort to eliminate biases against women, not all barriers have disappeared. Women still face biases and barriers in particular fields such as mathematics and natural sciences.

The long-standing belief that females innately have less aptitude and ability in math and science has helped erect barriers to women's participation in science and math education, not to mention barriers to careers in those fields. Twenty years ago, high school boys outscored girls in math, but that is no longer true. Today, male and female high school students perform equally well on math tests. Why the change? Girls used to take fewer advanced math classes than boys, but today they take just as many: With equal training, the sexes do equally well on math tests (Ceci & Williams, 2009). Yet, females progressively drop out of math and science curricula as they advance in their educations.

One reason many women drop out of math and science is that they encounter faculty, as well as peers, who assume that females are less able than males in those fields (Dreifus, 2010). Further, women faculty and scientific and mathematical fields receive fewer resources and lower salaries even when they outperform their male peers (Rivers & Barnett, 2011). A recent study published by National Academy of Sciences (Moss-Racusin, Dovidio, Brescoll, Graham, & Handelsman, 2012) reported that science professors were asked to review applications from students seeking a lab assistant job. The applications were identical except that they were randomly attributed to either a male or a female student. Science professors who believed the applicant was male were more likely to hire the student, offer a higher salary, and offer mentoring than when the professor believed the identical application was submitted by a female student.

SCARLETT

I always liked science. Right from the first grade, it was my favorite subject. The older I got, though, the more I felt odd in my science classes. Especially in college after the required courses, I felt odd. Sometimes, I was the only woman in a class. I was majoring in early education and just took science electives for fun. That changed when I had a woman professor in a course about unsolved problems in biology. She was really good, and so was the course, but to me the main thing was seeing a woman teaching science. That's when I decided to change my major and become a science teacher.

Females in math and sciences may face another gender-related barrier. Because cultural stereotypes of femininity do not include being skilled at science and math, social disapproval may greet women who excel in those fields. Further, the drive and assertiveness required to succeed in historically male fields is inconsistent with social prescriptions for femininity. Consequently, women in the sciences often face a double bind: If they are not extremely successful, they are judged incompetent, but if they are successful, they are often perceived as cold and manipulative and unfeminine (Dean, 2006).

In the United States, males are more likely than females to be encouraged to pursue careers in math and science, whereas females are more likely to be encouraged to enter careers that involve more direct interaction with people (Monastersky, 2005a). But that's not true in some other cultures. For instance, Chinese students of both sexes score better on math tests than American students (Monastersky, 2005b). In Turkey, it's not at all unusual for women students to major in math ("Women and Science," 2005). Observation of other cultures casts doubt over the existence of significant innate sex differences in math and science ability.

Gender-Nonconforming Students

What of students who are not straight males or females? How is the school environment for them? Students who identify as gay, lesbian, bisexual, transsexual, or genderqueer are likely to encounter school practices and policies that range from being confusing to negating their identities.

One problem is the gender binary norm that infuses schools. Bathrooms are labeled with signs for boys and girls. Which one should a transboy use? Which one should a gay student use? Most sports are divided by sex. Should a transgirl play on the girls' or boys' soccer team? Which shower room should she use?

The assumption of heterosexuality that pervades schools as it does other institutions (Meyer, 2009). Books to teach reading in the first grade often involve a family of characters: Mama Bear, Papa Bear, and Baby Bear. In elementary school, children often make cards for Mother's Day and Father's Day. How does that make a child with two mothers or two fathers feel? Novels assigned in literature classes in more advanced grades usually feature heterosexual romances and traditional nuclear families, again proclaiming heterosexuality as normal and right. The presumption of heterosexuality continues throughout education. How should a lesbian go about choosing a college roommate? Must she disclose her sexual orientation to strangers to see if they're okay with it when straight women aren't expected to announce their sexual orientation? In important ways, the personal experience and identity of students who are gay, lesbian, bisexual, or transgendered are at odds with school environments and curricula.

The unspoken norms of the gender binary and heterosexuality aren't a problem for most students. In fact, most students don't even notice that those norms shape school policies and practices. However, if you aren't a straight male or female, the disconnect between your identity and your lived experience and the normative practices of educational settings can be a source of discomfort and alienation.

Gender-Stereotyped Curricula

Although curricular content is less biased than in the past, gender stereotypes persist. Consider how history is taught. Accounts of wars, for instance, focus on battles and military leaders. Seldom noted are the contributions of women either on the battlefields or at home. Who kept families intact and food on the table while men fought? Who manufactured supplies for troops on the front? Chronicles of important events such as the civil rights movement focus on male leaders' speeches and press conferences and obscure the ways in which women contributed to the movements. We are taught about the leadership of Stokely Carmichael, Malcolm X, and the Reverend Martin Luther King Jr., but few of us learn about Ella Baker's pivotal work in organizing neighborhoods in support of civil rights (Parker, 2006; Ransby, 2003) or the activism that took place in African-American beauty shops during the Jim Crow era (Gill, 2010).

The few women who are highlighted in curricula tend to fall into two categories. First, there are women who fit traditional stereotypes of women. For example, most of us learned that Betsy Ross sewed the first American flag. A second group of women highlighted in curricula distinguished themselves on men's terms and in masculine contexts. Mother Jones, for example, was a powerful organizer for unions. Women in this category tend to be represented as exceptional cases—as atypical of women in general. This implies that most women can't do what a few notable ones did. Women such as Ella Baker, who achieve impact in other ways, remain hidden (Spitzack & Carter, 1987).

Historical epochs tend to be taught in terms of their effects on men while neglecting their impact on women and minorities. For instance, textbooks represent the Renaissance as a period of rebirth and progress in human life because it expanded men's options. The Renaissance is *not* taught in terms of its impact in reducing the status and opportunities of most women. The Enlightenment is taught as a time when reason ascended as the surest route to truth and human progress. The Enlightenment is *not* taught as a time when women were considered inferior because they were assumed to have limited capacity to reason. The Industrial Revolution is taught as a time when mechanization of production systems enabled mass production, which propelled factories as the primary workplace for men. The Industrial Revolution is *not* represented in terms of how it changed women's lives, work, and relationships with their husbands.

Even science, which we might think is a highly objective field, has gender stereotypes that can distort how science is taught. For instance, until recently science textbooks routinely misrepresented the process of human reproduction in ways that reflect social views of women and men: The active sperm were described as "invading" the passively waiting egg. When research proved that the egg is very active in controlling which sperm enter it, many science books revised their description of the process (Hammonds, 1998). As this example shows, gender stereotypes can be corrected when evidence disproves them. For this reason, curricula, including those in science, are less gender biased than in the past.

Sexism in education intersects with other forms of discrimination: racism, classism, and heterosexism. Not just any males are presented as the standard: White, heterosexual, able-bodied, middle- and upper-class men continue to be depicted as the norm in textbooks. How often have you studied contributions of lesbians and gays? How frequently did you learn about the lives and contributions of economically disadvantaged people? Have you learned about black women and men in journalism, Asian women and men in music, Hispanic scientists, or African writers? Along with

STONE SOUP   **BY JAN ELIOT**

women, minorities continue to be underrepresented in educational materials, where the reference point has been and remains white, heterosexual, able-bodied, middle- and upper-class males.

Gender-stereotyped curricular material diminishes education for all students. When students learn primarily about straight, white, economically advantaged men and their experiences, perspectives, and accomplishments, they are deprived of understanding the perspectives and contributions of most of the population. On a more personal level, biases in instructional content encourage straight, white, able-bodied, middle-class men to see themselves as able to fulfill high ambitions and affect the course of events, and discourage women and minorities from those self-perceptions (AAUW, 1998; Smith, 2004b).

Athletics

Today's female students enjoy unprecedented opportunities to participate in athlet- ics. In large part, that is due to **Title IX**. There are three basic parts of Title IX as it applies to athletics (Title IX Q & A, 2008):

1. Women must be provided an equitable opportunity to participate in sports as men (not necessarily the identical sports but an equal opportunity to play).

2. Colleges must provide female athletes with athletic scholarship dollars propor- tional to their participation. For instance, if there are 100 male athletes and 50 female athletes at a school that has a $150,000 athletic scholarship budget, female athletes must receive $50,000 in scholarships.

3. Equal treatment includes more than playing time and scholarship. Schools are also required to provide female and male athletes with equivalent equipment and supplies, practice times, travel and daily allowance, tutoring, coaching, locker rooms and facilities, publicity and promotions, recruitment programs, and support services.

Despite Title IX, the playing field still is not exactly even. Male athletes and coaches of men's teams continue to have more support, financial and otherwise, than female athletes and coaches of women's teams. More full scholarships go to male athletes (Hattery, 2012). In addition, male athletes are more likely than female athletes to get academic tutoring and prime schedules and venues for practice. Also, before passage of Title IX, more than 90% of coaches of women's sports were women. Following Title IX's passage, fewer women's sports are coached by women, and all Division I colleges pay male coaches more than women coaches.

HEATHER

This school claims to go by Title IX, but the support for women athletes doesn't even come close to what men get. The school is fair about the number of women it recruits and funds with scholarships, but that's where the equity stops. The men have tutors who basically babysit them through their classes. We are expected to earn our own grades. They have the best practice times on the field; we get the leftover times. They get more travel allowance than we do, and they get a lot more publicity.

Not all colleges and universities receiving federal support actually meet the spirit of Title IX. In fact, a recent report in the *New York Times* (Thomas, 2011) documented a number of deceptive practices that colleges and universities use to appear to comply with Title IX while actually undermining gender equity in athletics. Some schools require women who are cross-country runners to join the indoor and outdoor track teams, which allows the schools to count each runner three times in tallying up the number of women athletes it has. Another deceptive practice that occurs at some Division I schools is counting male players who practice with women as female athletes. Other schools pad the rosters of female athletes by including women who have returned their scholarships or who don't play or by adding to teams when the numbers are counted and then cutting the players after the count is done.

Inequities in supporting athletics have consequences beyond the school years. Girls and women who participate in sports are more likely to pursue additional education and have higher earning power in their 20s and 30s (the latest ages for

EXPLORING GENDERED LIVES   *Generic Maximum Heart Rate*

For years, we've been told that the formula for calculating the maximum heart rate is 220 minus a person's age. Guess what? It turns out that formula isn't accurate for women because it was based on men. To remedy this, researchers at Northwestern Medicine in Chicago studied 5,500 healthy women.

Based on these data, the researchers concluded that the correct formula to calculate women's maximum heart rate is 206 minus 88% of the woman's age. Maybe now women who work out will be less exhausted by effort to meet a rate that is inappropriate for their hearts (Parker-Pope, 2010b).

EXPLORING GENDERED LIVES   Title IX: Fiction and Fact

Although Title IX has been around for more than 30 years, it is still widely misunderstood. Check your understanding of Title IX (Messner, 2002; Neinas, 2002; Suggs, 2005a; Title IX Q & A, 2008).

Fiction: Title IX focuses on athletics.

Fact: Although Title IX has become almost synonymous with athletics, that is a very small part of what the legislation addresses.

Fiction: Title IX is binding on all schools in the United States.

Fact: Title IX is binding only on schools that accept federal funds.

Fiction: Title IX bans sex discrimination only in athletics.

Fact: Title IX bans sex discrimination of all sorts in federally supported schools. This applies to academics as well as athletics.

Fiction: Title IX has reduced opportunities for male college athletes.

Fact: Since the passage of Title IX, college men's sports opportunities have actually increased. Some schools have cut specific men's teams, but overall male athletes have more opportunities.

Fiction: Title IX requires identical athletic programs for males and females.

Fact: Title IX does not require that men's and women's teams receive identical support. Instead, it requires that they receive comparable levels of service, supplies, and facilities. Variations between men's and women's programs are allowed.

Fiction: Because of Title IX, colleges that receive federal funds provide fully equal support to women's and men's sports.

Fact: Compared to male athletes, female athletes receive fewer scholarship dollars, and their teams get fewer dollars for recruiting and operating teams.

Fiction: Most Americans are opposed to Title IX.

Fact: In a recent poll, 82% of Americans said they support Title IX. The poll included all political parties and people with and without children.

Are you satisfied with Title IX as it is currently implemented? If so, why? If not, how do you think it should be modified?

which data are available). They are also more likely to be healthy on many measures, including weight (Parker-Pope, 2010a).

Gender Pressures from Peers

The power of peer pressure is no myth. To be accepted by peers, many students conform to social views of gender (Rudman & Glick, 2008). Schools are a training ground for adulthood, and peer groups are primary agents of gender socialization.

SCOTT

On this campus, Greeks are cool. It took me just a few weeks on campus to figure out that if I wanted to be popular in college, I had to join a fraternity. So I rushed and pledged my first year. I like being part of the group and being considered cool, but I'm still uncomfortable with some of what goes on in the house. Some of the brothers talk

Title IX has created more opportunities for women athletes.

about girls like they're all sluts, and if you don't go along with that talk, you're a jerk.
Same with drinking—you have to drink a lot to be in with the group.

Pressures to Conform to Masculinity

As young boys grow into adolescence, male peer groups reinforce masculine identification. Males often engage in drinking and sexual activity to demonstrate their
masculinity, and they encourage the same in peers (Cross, 2008; Kimmel, 2008).
To be accepted by their peers, some men say and do things as part of the group
that they would never consider doing as individuals.

Male students often enjoy athletic activities since the field and the court are
primary social venues where male students find companionship and camaraderie.
Yet even if male students don't want to play sports or don't have time, they
may perceive peer pressure to play sports either on school or club teams or intra-
mural teams.

Pressures to Conform to Femininity

Female peer groups tend to encourage and reward compliance with feminine
stereotypes. Girls often make fun of or exclude girls who don't wear popular
brands of clothing or who weigh more than what is considered ideal (Adler,
2007; Barash, 2006).

SPENCER

Tuition is nothing compared to what you have to spend to dress well! At this school, it's almost like there is a competition among girls to dress in the latest styles. If you're not wearing the cool boot or not layering the way models do in Marie Claire, you're just out of it. It takes a lot of money to buy all of the clothes and pay for haircuts and manicures. It also takes huge amounts of time that I could spend other ways.

From the earliest years of school through college and graduate school, girls and women report that they experience jeering, lewd suggestions, and unwanted touching. In a national study of girls in 7th to 12th grades, 56% report being harassed (Anderson, 2011). And boys are not exempt: 40% of boys in the same national study reported being harassed at school (Anderson, 2011). While both sexes report being subject to sexual comments, gestures, and jokes, harassment that includes touching or forced sexual activity is more commonly experienced by girls than boys. Yet, the recent Penn State scandal reminds us that boys can be victims of atrocious sexual harassment and assault (Wolverton, 2011).

Sexual discrimination and harassment are not confined to peer interactions. Faculty and coaches may harass and discriminate against women. Ranging from comments on appearance instead of on academic work to offers of higher grades for sexual favors, these actions make women students' sex more salient than their abilities and aspirations. In treating women as sexual objects, such actions tell women students that they are not taken seriously as members of an intellectual community.

BAILEY

It's so unfair how professors treat women. I'm a serious student, and I plan a business career, but my professors have never asked me about my career plans. Even when I bring the subject up, all I get is really superficial stuff—like they really don't want to talk to me. One of my boyfriend's teachers invited him to have coffee and talk about graduate school. My boyfriend didn't even have to ask! They spent over an hour just talking about what he would do after undergraduate school. And my grades are better than his!

For women, the college years offer no reprieve from pressures. Studies of women students at colleges and universities report that they feel two sets of pressures: to be successful as women—attractive, fun to be with, and so forth—and to be smart and academically successful. Women feel compelled to achieve **effortless perfection**: to be beautiful, fit, popular, smart, and accomplished without any visible effort (Dube, 2004; Hinshaw, 2009). Many undergraduate women say they feel enormous pressure to be perfect—to earn high grades, have leadership

EXPLORING GENDERED LIVES *Hooked Up*

Young people, particularly young women, are having more casual sexual contacts than ever before and at earlier and earlier ages, often as early as middle-school. On many college campuses dating has been largely replaced by "hooking up," short-term or even one-time sexual encounters between people who are not interested in romance or commitment (Stepp, 2007). Those who have studied this trend identify several contributing factors:

Fewer men than women attend college, which leads some women to be more competitive in heterosexual interaction (Whitmire, 2008).

Some women feel they must postpone love in order to prepare for and launch careers. Hooking up allows contact without commitment (Stepp, 2007).

Media increasingly teach women—and even very young girls—to view themselves as sexual objects for men. They see these sexual encounters not as sources of experience for themselves, but as sources of sexual pleasure for men. The result is that many young women say sex is something they do to fit in more than for their own pleasure (Levin & Kilbourne, 2008; Levy, 2005).

To what extent do you think the factors identified by researchers account for hooking up?

roles in campus groups, and excel in sports while also being nice, kind, caring, and pleasing to others (Girls Incorporated, 2006). These pressures encourage young women to "equate identity with image, self-expression with appearance, femininity with performance, pleasure with pleasing, and sexuality with sexualization" (Orenstein, 2011b, p. 8).

JACQUIE

College is supposed to be a place for thinking and education, but the bottom line here is that you have to be really attractive if you want to be liked. Brains may get you good grades, but they won't get you friends or dates. Most of the girls I know spend as much time shopping for clothes and fixing their hair and nails as they do studying.

Peer groups on campus may also propel college women into a **culture of romance** (Holland & Eisenhart, 1992). First, many women in college become discouraged by barriers to their academic achievement, such as lack of intellectual mentoring from professors and required readings and class discussions that emphasize important men and men's achievements and give little or no attention to important women and their achievements. The second factor propelling college women into a culture of romance is intense peer pressure that emphasizes attracting men as more important than anything else women can do.

MARIA

My sorority is a great example of the culture of romance. When a girl gets engaged, we throw her in a cold shower and then give her the "warm shower," which is lots of gifts and good wishes. Our newsletter lists alums' marriages and births of children. What it doesn't list and what we don't celebrate is academic achievement or alums' career moves. Aren't those important too?

Gay, lesbian, and transgender students are not exempt from peer pressure. In fact, they are often subjected to more and more strenuous pressures to conform to conventionally gendered identities than are straight students. Bullying of gender nonconforming students can be particularly vicious. In 2010, 18-year-old Tyler Clementi committed suicide when he learned that his roommate Dharun Ravi had sent out Twitter and text messages inviting others to watch a sexual encounter between Clementi and another man. Ravi was tried on 15 charges including hate crime; he was found guilty of a bias crime and using a webcam to spy on Clementi. His sentence was 30 days in jail, three years on probation, and 300 hours of community service (Zernike, 2012).

Clementi is not an isolated case. Estimates are that 53% of LGBT (lesbian, gay, bisexual, and transgender) youth experience abuse and bullying, including cyberbullying (Burney, 2012). Despite the frequency of LGBT bullying, not even 1 in 10 colleges and universities in the United States has LGBT-inclusive policies (Burney, 2012).

Single-Sex Educational Programs

Some educators, scholars, and social commentators think that single-sex schools, or programs in schools, might solve some of the problems we've discussed. For instance, in elementary school, boys generally lag behind girls in reading. If there were no girls in reading classes, teachers might be able to give young boys the help they need to develop reading skills. On campuses where there were no male students, heterosexual women might focus more on academics and less on the culture of romance. Faculty might also be more likely to mentor female students if there were no male students.

Is single-sex education effective? From elementary school through college, heterosexual males and females are more likely to make academics a priority in single-sex schools. If students aren't focused on impressing members of the other sex, won't they study more without worrying about seeming like nerds? The facts on graduates of women's schools are persuasive: Although women's colleges produce only about 5% of all female college graduates, a disproportionate number of women in the U.S. Congress and running top businesses graduated from women's colleges (Salome, 2007; Scelfo, 2006). When The Citadel was all male, its graduation rate was 70%—much higher than the 48% national average (AAUW, 2001).

But critics of single-sex education argue that sex-segregated education isn't the answer to gender inequities in schools. They think a better solution is to make sure that schools support all students equally so that males and females have the same educational opportunities and support. Also, single-sex schools tend to be private and too expensive for most families. Thus, although single-sex schools may benefit children from well-to-do families, they won't do much to help the majority of students (Rivers & Barnett, 2011).

Table 8.1 Gendered Hierarchies at Colleges and Universities

Position	Number of Women	Number of Men	Prestige
Professor	45,571	126,515	most
Associate Professor	56,442	85,622	
Assistant Professor	78,119	86,796	
Instructor	53,546	45,533	least

Gendered Expectations and Pressures Facing Faculty

In addition to being educational institutions, schools are also workplaces, so we want to examine gendered attitudes and practices that affect the faculty who work there. We'll discuss gendered hierarchies, policies, and expectations in American educational institutions. As you will discover, gender dynamics faced by faculty often affect students as well.

Gendered Hierarchies

The more advanced the educational level, the greater the ratio of male to female faculty members. In elementary schools, the vast majority of teachers are female, but most superintendents and assistant superintendents are male. In high schools, female teachers still outnumber male teachers, but the imbalance is less pronounced. At colleges and universities, the number of men increases. Table 8.1 shows that the proportion of women faculty compared to male faculty decreases as prestige of position increases ("The Profession," 2010, p. 20).

The last three decades have seen more women being hired and tenured at colleges and universities, but too many still hit a glass ceiling at the highest level: the rank of full professor (Curtis, 2011; Misra, Hickes, Holmes, & Agiomavritis, 2011). As Table 8.1 shows, men hold approximately three-fourths of full professorships at American colleges and universities. In addition, male faculty still earn more than female faculty, regardless of professional achievement (Curtis, 2010, 2011). At all institutions of higher education, women faculty earn 80.6 cents for every dollar men faculty earn ("Average Salaries," 2012). Only 26.4% of chief administrators of colleges are female, and only 12.6% are members of minority groups ("How College Leaders' Traits," 2012).

Limited numbers of female and minority faculty mean that women and minority students have fewer role models among faculty. Recall cognitive development theory, which we discussed in Chapter 2. This theory notes that we look for models—preferably ones like us in sex, race, and so forth—to emulate as we develop identities. If more men than women are principals and full professors, students may infer that it's normal for men (but not for women) to rise to high levels in education.

MORGAN

With so many male professors, I think it is difficult for some students to feel comfortable getting to know their professors and ask for help. Women are more likely to connect with a female teacher, minorities are more likely to connect with a teacher of their race, etc. Colleges always make a big deal about having a diverse campus, but what about the professors? Where are the female professors? Where are the LGBTQ professors? Where are the professors from other cultures and races?
If colleges want to have a diverse student body, they should also have a diverse faculty that correlates with the students.

Gender Bias in Evaluations

Are fewer women than men hired because of bias or because men are more qualified? Research shows that bias against women influences hiring decisions as well as performance reviews and promotions. Women and minorities are more likely to be hired when the selection process is blind with respect to applicants' sex, race, and other characteristics that sometimes are bases of discrimination (Reskin, 2003). Women are more likely to be hired in computerized application processes that do not identify sex (Richtel, 2000; Sturm, 2001). Hiring committees that are completely or predominantly male tend to hire fewer female faculty than committees with more sex-balanced membership (Valian, 1998; Wilson, 2004b).

Once hired, women faculty continue to face gender biases in evaluation. Researchers have identified three major sources of bias in the evaluation of faculty. First, women's performance tends to be more closely scrutinized and judged by stricter standards than men's. Second, men have to give more convincing demonstrations of incompetence to be judged by others as incompetent. Third, male candidates tend to be judged on whether they show promise, whereas female candidates tend to be judged on accomplishments, a form of bias that is particularly likely to affect hiring and promotion decisions (Wilson, 2004a, 2004b). All in all, different standards are used to evaluate men and women, and the way in which those standards are applied results in men being judged as more competent.

The subtlety of gender bias in evaluation of faculty explains why it is called *invisible hand discrimination* (Haag, 2005). **Invisible hand discrimination** is unwitting discrimination in applying policies that are not inherently biased (Haag, 2005; Wilson, 2004a). It does not happen because a person consciously intends to discriminate or because a policy or practice is inherently discriminatory. The largely unconscious nature of invisible hand discrimination makes it particularly difficult to eliminate.

Consider a few examples of how invisible hand discrimination works. Collegiality is a criterion many universities use when deciding whether to promote faculty members. There is nothing inherently biased about the criterion, as it is reasonable to expect all faculty—men and women—to be civil, courteous, and reasonably easy to work with. So, how might a tenure committee evaluate the collegiality of Professor

Smith, who is known to be very assertive? That often depends on whether Smith is male or female. Research shows that assertiveness in male faculty is likely to be taken as a sign of confidence and intelligence, whereas assertiveness in female faculty is often regarded as antagonistic or confrontational (Haag, 2005). That's invisible hand discrimination.

Another example is the documented tendency to explain women's achievements as resulting from luck or help from others while attributing men's achievements to competence (Heilman, 2001). So, male faculty who publish books may be judged "brilliant" but female faculty may be judged "lucky to have found a supportive editor." That's invisible hand discrimination. Gender biases in evaluation have material consequences, including discrepancies between the salaries paid to women and men faculty.

Gendered Policies and Expectations

Like most employers, colleges and universities are based on the traditional family model, in which the man is employed outside of the home to earn income and the woman takes care of the children and home. Colleges and universities based on that model assume that faculty don't have to worry about domestic life, which is

---

EXPLORING GENDERED LIVES   *Catch-22*

Administrators and other faculty aren't the only ones who engage in gender-biased evaluations. Students evaluate male and female faculty differently. Additionally, Caroline Turner (2003) has found that female faculty of color are frequently challenged and negatively evaluated by students, regardless of teaching ability.

In addition to averaged numerical rankings, written comments on evaluations often reflect sexism and even misogyny. At a Midwestern university where students post comments about faculty on a website, researchers found that it was not uncommon for students to criticize female faculty for appearance, describing them as "ugly," "dorky," or "frumpy." Students made virtually no comments about male professors' appearance. Also, it was commonplace for students to refer to female faculty as "bitches," "whores," and other derogatory names. Although male faculty were occasionally described as "jerks" or "assholes," they were not demeaned to the extent that

female faculty were. The vast majority of explicit sexual comments and derogatory names were directed toward female faculty (Nelson, Trzemzalski, Malkasian, & Pfeffer, 2004).

Michael Messner (2000b) found that, although male faculty are evaluated for their skills and abilities as instructors, women faculty are first evaluated by their gender performance and then by their teaching performance. Women are caught in a catch-22 where they can't win. For example, if a woman tries to assert authority in the classroom by wearing more formal attire and being forceful, she may be seen as being less feminine and, therefore, not performing her appropriate gender role. As a result, students are critical because she is not conforming to their stereotypes of women as feminine, not authoritative. However, if she dresses and acts informally, it reinforces the stereotype that women aren't authorities.

To what extent do you use different criteria to evaluate female and male professors?

the responsibility of the stay-at-home partner. That model, however, does not reflect today's faculty.

Earning Tenure

During the early years of an academic appointment, faculty members have probationary status—they are not permanent faculty until and unless they earn tenure. Thus, the early years require particularly long hours and heavy investments. For women, those years usually coincide with the ideal years for bearing children, a pressure that affects women faculty in ways it does not affect male faculty. The tenure schedule is at odds with the biological clock, which creates tensions for faculty who are also parents (Hayden & O'Brien Hallstein, 2010; Kerber, 2005; Mason, 2007). The fact that this incompatibility affects female faculty more than male faculty may be another form of invisible hand discrimination.

Male faculty members are also penalized if their schools assume that a career is men's principal focus. Many male faculty want to spend time with families, particularly right after a child is born or adopted. Colleges that provide maternity leave but not paternity leave don't support male faculty's involvement in family life. Even so, some male faculty decide to be active partners and parents. Those who do are sometimes penalized professionally for not accomplishing more in terms of research and university service (Kerber, 2005; Mason, 2007).

Service Expectations

The limited number of women faculty generates another problem: excessive responsibilities for service and mentoring. Faculty committees are ubiquitous at universities, and committees are expected to be diverse—that is, to include women, men, and faculty of different races. Thus, the few women and minority faculty are asked to serve on more committees than their white male peers. The same goes for advising students, particularly women and minority students. If there is only one minority woman on the faculty of a department, she's likely to be besieged by requests from the majority of graduate and undergraduate students who are women of color.

SUMMARY

Today both sexes face gender-based issues, expectations, and biases in educational institutions. Males, especially boys in the early years of schooling, are disadvantaged by a system that doesn't accommodate their developmental status. As males progress through school, they are more likely than women students to attract faculty mentors, particularly in graduate and professional school. For female students, the reverse sequence is more common. They tend to be quite successful through high school and perhaps college, but they often hit barriers when they enter graduate and professional school, particularly in math and sciences.

The peer culture on college campuses further encourages male and female students to conform to particular gender ideals, which can limit personal and professional development. Male peer cultures tend to link masculinity with drinking, aggression, and sexual activity. Female peer cultures too often encourage campus women to participate in a culture of romance and to attempt to meet the impossible ideal of effortless perfection.

We also looked at gender biases and pressures experienced by faculty. Both men and women are disadvantaged by current leave policies that make it nearly impossible to be both a good faculty member and a good parent. Further, male faculty often feel they cannot take family leave because doing so would lead others to perceive them as not living up to expectations of men. Discrimination in hiring, promotion, and salaries continues to be a problem at colleges and universities across the nation, as does the disparate expectations for service that women and men faculty members face.

Our examination warrants a mixed report card for America's schools. Discrimination and disadvantage based on sex and gender have been greatly reduced for students, but gendered dynamics persist at all grade levels. There has been uneven and limited progress for faculty.

KEY TERMS

The terms following are defined in this chapter on the pages indicated, as well as in alphabetical order in the book's glossary, which begins on page 283. The text's companion website (**http://www.cengage.com/communication/wood/genderedlives11e**) also provides interactive flash cards and crossword puzzles to help you learn these terms and the concepts they represent.

culture of romance 177   *invisible hand discrimination 180*
effortless perfection 176   *Title IX 172*

GENDER ONLINE

1. Learn more about Title IX by visiting: **http://www.titleix.info**

2. Information about the United Nations' education initiative for girls can be found at: **http://www.ungei.org/**

3. Online search terms: "effortless perfection," "peer pressure," "single-sex education."

REFLECTION AND DISCUSSION

1. Talk with male and female athletes on your campus to find out the extent to which they perceive that your school complies with Title IX.

2. If you could make three changes in elementary schools, with the goal of making them work better for boys and girls, what changes would you make?

3. Reread the material I present in the box Exploring Gendered Lives: Catch-22 on page 181. If your campus has a student-run website for evaluating faculty (often only students can access these), read the evaluations of male and female faculty. To what extent do you see patterns similar to those described in the box?

4. What is your opinion on the desirability of single-sex schools? What do you see as the advantages and disadvantages both for students in the schools and for society?

RECOMMENDED RESOURCES

1. Peg Tyre. (2008). *The Trouble with Boys: A Surprising Report Card on Our Sons, Their Problems at School, and What Parents and Educators Must Do.* New York: Crown. This book, which was a reference for the chapter, gives a thoughtful summary of barriers boys and men face in educational institutions. The book is written for general audiences.

2. Laura Sessions Stepp. (2007). *Unhooked: How Young Women Pursue Sex, Delay Love and Lose at Both.* New York: Penguin/Riverhead. Stepp's book gives in-depth portraits of young college women who participate in the "hook up culture" that is part of many campuses today.

The doors we open and close each day decide the lives we live.
—FLORA WHITTENMORE

Gendered Close Relationships

Knowledge Challenge:

- To what extent are talking and sharing activities important for creating and sustaining intimacy?
- Do women or men typically fall in love faster?
- Are heterosexual or homosexual relationships more equitable?

Perhaps you have found yourself in situations such as those that Mark and Paige describe on the next page. For Mark, as for most people socialized into masculinity, communicating is important when you need to address an issue or solve a problem, but he doesn't see the point in talking extensively about small stuff. For Paige, it's incomprehensible that Ed can work on his paper when there is tension between them. If Paige and Mark do not figure out that their gendered viewpoints are creating misunderstandings, they will continue to experience frustration in their relationships.

In this chapter, we will focus on gender dynamics in close relationships. To begin our discussion, we will consider masculine and feminine ways of experiencing and expressing closeness. Then, we'll explore gendered patterns in friendships and romantic relationships to appreciate different ways that people build and communicate closeness.

The Meaning of Personal Relationships

Of the many relationships we form, only a few become really personal. These are the ones that occupy a special place in our lives and affect us most deeply. **Personal relationships** are those in which partners depend on each other for various things from affection to material assistance. In personal relationships, partners expect affection, companionship, time, energy, and assistance with the large and small issues in life. Also, partners in personal relationships regard each other as unique individuals who cannot be replaced. If a casual friend moves, a replacement may be found; if a business associate goes to another company, we can find a new work colleague; if your golfing buddy relocates, you can find another golfing partner. When a personal partner leaves or dies, however, the relationship ends, although we may continue to feel connected to the person who is no longer with us.

MARK

Sometimes I just don't know what goes on in Ellen's head. We can have a minor problem—like an issue between us, and it's really not serious stuff. But can we let it go? No way with Ellen. She wants "to talk about it." And I mean talk and talk and talk and talk. There's no end to how long she can talk about stuff that really doesn't matter. I tell her that she's analyzing the relationship to death, and I don't want to do that. She insists that we need "to talk things through." Why can't we just have a relationship, instead of always having to talk about it?

PAIGE

Honestly, I almost left my boyfriend when we had our first fight after moving in together. It was really a big one about how to be committed to our relationship and also do all the other stuff that we have to do. It was major. And after we'd yelled for a while, there seemed to be nothing else to do—we were just at a stalemate in terms of conflict between what each of us wanted. So Ed walked away, and I sat fuming in the living room. When I finally left the living room, I found him working away on a paper for one of his courses, and I was furious. I couldn't understand how he could concentrate on work when we were so messed up. How in the world could he just put us aside and get on with his work? I felt like it was a really clear message that he wasn't very committed.

Models of Personal Relationships

Differences in masculine and feminine orientations to close relationships usually—but not always—coincide with male and female approaches to relationships. Yet, researchers disagree about what the differences mean. Some scholars argue that masculine orientations are inferior to feminine ones, while others think that the two styles are different yet equally valid. We'll consider each of these viewpoints.

The Male Deficit Model

Because our society views women as interpersonally sensitive, it is widely assumed that feminine ways of interacting are "the right ways." Sharing the cultural assumption that women are better than men at relating to others, a number of researchers claim that a masculine style of building and maintaining relationships is inadequate.

This view, **the male deficit model**, maintains that men are less skilled in developing and sustaining personal relationships.

The central assumption of the male deficit model is that personal, emotional talk is the hallmark of intimacy. With this assumption in mind, researchers began to study how women and men interact in close relationships. A classic investigation (Caldwell & Peplau, 1982) measured the intimacy of same-sex friendships by the amount of intimate information disclosed between friends. As women generally self-disclose more than men, it is not surprising that the researchers concluded that women were more intimate than men. Based on this line of research, men were advised to learn to express themselves more openly.

EDWIN

I don't have any problem being emotionally sensitive or expressing my feelings. I may not go on forever about my feelings, but I know what they are, and I can express them fine. It's just that the way I express my feelings is different from the way most girls I know express their feelings. I'm not dramatic or sentimental or gushy, but I have ways of showing how I feel. Not dramatic or sentimental or gushy, but I have ways of showing how I feel.

The tendency to privilege feminine ways of relating and disparage masculine ways was strengthened by one of the men's movements we discussed in Chapter 4. Male feminists thought that men were generally emotionally repressed and would be enriched by becoming more aware and expressive of their feelings, and many men worked to develop and express emotions more openly.

Much academic and popular sentiment still holds that many men are deficient in their ability to express emotions and to care. A number of publications in the late 1990s and early part of this century state that personal disclosures are the crux of intimacy, that women have more intimate relationships than men do, that boys' friendships lack the emotional depth of girls' friendships, and that males focus on activities to avoid intimacy (Burleson, 1997; Oliker, 2001).

The assumption underlying the male deficit model is that verbal, emotional expressiveness and personal disclosures are the best ways to create closeness. Gradually, however, a few researchers began to question this assumption, leading to a second interpretation of different ways people create and express closeness.

The Alternate Paths Model

The **alternate paths model** proposes that there are different and equally valid paths to closeness. This model agrees with the male deficit model that gendered socialization is the root of differences between feminine and masculine styles of relating. It departs from the deficit model, however, in two important ways. First, the alternate paths model does not presume that masculine people lack feelings or emotional depth. Rather, the alternate paths explanation suggests that masculine socialization leads most men to find it uncomfortable to verbally express some feelings and, further, that it limits men's opportunities to practice emotional talk.

Second, the alternate paths model argues that masculine people do express closeness, but in an alternate way than feminine people do. According to this model, masculine and feminine ways of expressing closeness are different, and the two ways are equally valid.

The alternate paths model challenges the research used to support the male deficit model. In Western culture, she suggests, we use a "**feminine ruler**" to define and measure closeness (Cancian, 1987, 1989). Using a specifically feminine ruler (emotional talk) misrepresents masculine modes of caring in the same way that using male standards to measure women's speech misrepresents women's communication.

Influenced by this viewpoint, Scott Swain (1989) studied men's close friendships. He discovered that many men develop a closeness "in the doing"—a connection that grows out of doing things together. Following Swain's lead, other studies showed that men's friendships can be as close as women's, but closeness between men generally doesn't grow primarily out of emotional talk and self-disclosure and it is not primarily expressed in those ways (Clark, 1998; Sherrod, 1989). Research has also shown that father–son relationships are built largely on doing things together (Morman & Floyd, 2006). For many men, like Paige's boyfriend, talking about problems may be less effective than diversionary activities to relieve stress (Metts, 2006a; Riessman, 1990).

Yet, it would be a mistake to think that women don't do things with friends and men don't talk with friends. In a study of how men and women communicate support, men tended to engage in emotional as well as instrumental forms of communication. Similarly, women friends enjoy doing things together and helping each other out. In general, most men engage in less explicit emotional communication, yet most men do experience and express emotions in a range of ways (Chapman & Hendler, 1999). Further, as Paul Wright (2006) notes, many of the activities in which men engage enhance emotional closeness. Camping, for instance, provides a rich opportunity to share thoughts and feelings.

The gender of the person needing support may be as important as the gender of the person offering support. Communication scholars Jerold Hale, Rachael Tighe, and Paul Mongeau (1997) report that women engage in more sensitive comforting messages than men do. However, both sexes are more sensitive when trying to comfort women than when trying to comfort men. Further, men offer more sensitive comforting communication in response to major stresses, whereas women tend to provide sensitive comfort for both major and minor stresses.

From this research, we may conclude that masculine individuals less often express their feelings in feminine ways, just as feminine individuals less frequently express theirs in masculine ways. Note that we are discussing the frequency with which the sexes engage in particular behaviors. We are not saying that each sex engages exclusively in either instrumental or expressive behavior. As we've seen, there's a lot of overlap.

Gendered Styles of Friendship

Let's begin by noting that there are many similarities between the friendships of most men and most women. Both sexes value close friends and invest in them. Also, both sexes engage in instrumental and expressive modes of building and

DOING/INSTRUMENTAL   DIALOGUE/EXPRESSIVE

Figure 9.1

Modes of Building and Expressing Affection

expressing closeness, although they differ in the extent to which they use each (Monsour, 2006). Against the backdrop of commonalities in approaches to friendship, there are some differences in how women and men typically—but not invariably—build friendships and interact within them. As you read about these differences, keep in mind that they are not absolute dichotomies. Most of us engage in both styles, although a majority of women more often engage in feminine style and a majority of men more often engage in masculine style. Figure 9.1 makes the point that dialogue and doing are on a continuum, rather than exclusive categories. Most of us fall in-between the ends of the continuum.

As early as 1982, Paul Wright noted that women tend to engage each other face to face, whereas men usually interact side by side. By this, Wright meant that women are more likely than men to communicate directly and verbally with each other to share themselves and their feelings. Men more typically engage in activities that do not involve facing each other. Wright's observation gives us a foundation for exploring the qualities of friendship between women, between men, and between men and women.

Feminine Friendships: Closeness in Dialogue

Regardless of race, ethnicity, sexual orientation, or economic status, a majority of women regard talk as the primary way to build and enrich friendships (Braithwaite & Kellas, 2006; Wood, 2011a; Wright, 2006). Consequently, many women share their personal feelings, experiences, fears, and problems in order to know and be known by each other. In addition, women talk about their daily lives and activities to connect with one another. To capture the quality of women's friendships, Caroline Becker (1987) described them as "an evolving dialogue" through which initially separate worlds are woven together.

To know each other in depth, women friends typically confide personal feelings and disclose intimate information (Braithwaite & Kellas, 2006; Hall, 2011; Metts, 2006b; Reisman, 1990; Walker, 2004). Consistent with feminine socialization's encouragement of permeable ego boundaries, communication between women friends also tends to be empathic, expressive, and supportive (Campbell, 2002; Kuchment, 2004).

JANICE

One of the worst things about being female is not having permission to be selfish or jealous or not to care about a friend. Usually, I'm pretty nice; I feel good for my friends when good things happen to them, and I want to support them when things aren't going well. But sometimes I don't feel that way. Like right now, all my friends and I are interviewing for jobs, and my best friend just got a great offer. I've had 23 interviews and no job offers so far. I felt good for Sally, but I also felt jealous. I couldn't talk about this with her, because I'm not supposed to feel jealous or to be selfish like this. It's just not allowed, so my friends and I have to hide those feelings.

Because most women are socialized to be attentive, emotionally supportive, and caring, it is difficult for many women to deal with feelings of envy and competitiveness toward friends. It is not that women don't experience envy and competitiveness but rather that they may think it's wrong to have such feelings (Simmons, 2002, 2004). Many women also find it difficult to override socialization's message that they are supposed to be constantly available and caring. The bottom line is that the responsiveness and caring typical of women's friendships can both enrich and constrain people.

It is not unusual for women friends to talk explicitly about their relationship. The friendship itself and the dynamics between the friends are matters of interest and discussion (Winstead, 1986). Many women friends are comfortable stating affection explicitly or discussing tensions within a friendship. The ability to recognize and talk about problems allows women to monitor and improve their friendships.

A final quality typical of women's friendships is breadth. With close friends, women tend not to restrict their disclosures to specific areas but invite each other into many parts of their lives. Because women talk in detail about varied aspects of their lives, women friends often know each other in complex and layered ways.

In summary, many women's friendships give center stage to communication, which fosters disclosure, verbal expressiveness, depth and breadth of knowledge, and attentiveness to the evolving nature of the relationship. Many women feel deeply connected to friends even when they are not physically together.

EXPLORING GENDERED LIVES — *When Focusing on Feelings Makes Us Feel Bad*

Women who pay attention to their feelings are able to work through feelings. But there may be a down side.

Research shows that women generally have a greater tendency than men to brood about bad feelings. Excessive brooding can lead women to get stuck in unhappy feelings and to spiral downward emotionally into depression (Nolen-Hoeksema, 2003).

Some studies have found that extended discussion of problems may actually heighten anxieties rather than reduce them (Kershaw, 2008). Researchers have coined the term *co-rumination* to refer to frequent or excessive talk—face-to-face, e-mail, IMs, text messaging, and posting on social networks—between friends about the same problem. A second danger of talking excessively about problems is emotional contagion in which the person listening to another's problem feels the anxieties and depression as if it is her own.

To what extent do you find talking with friends about problems heightens your anxiety? Have you ever experienced emotional contagion?

Masculine Friendships: Closeness in the Doing

Beginning in childhood, friendships between males often revolve around shared activities, particularly sports. Scott Swain's (1989) phrase "closeness in the doing" captures the chief way that many men build friendships. More than two-thirds of the men in Swain's study described activities other than talking as the most meaningful times with friends. Engaging in sports, watching games, and doing other things together cultivate camaraderie and closeness between men. When men do talk, they are likely to talk about activities—reminisce about great games they attended, recall pranks they played or had played on them, and psych themselves up for upcoming activities. Whereas women tend to look for confidantes in friends, men more typically seek companions (Chethik, 2008; Inman, 1996; Swain, 1989; Walker, 2004; Wood & Inman, 1993). Neil Chethik (2008) explains that women are more likely to share feelings, whereas men are more likely to share space. As a reminder, we're discussing tendencies, not absolute dichotomies. Of course, women friends sometimes share space and activities, and men friends sometimes talk and confide in each other.

KEITH

My best friend and I almost never sit and just talk. Mainly, we do things together, like go places or shoot hoops or watch games on TV. When we do talk, we talk about what we have done or plan to do or what's happening in our lives, but we don't say much about how we feel. I don't think we need to. You can say a lot without words.

Growing out of the emphasis on activities is a second feature of men's friendships: an instrumental focus. Many men like to do things for people they care about (Cancian, 1987; Sherrod, 1989); their friendships involve instrumental reciprocity. For example, one helps the other repair his car, and the other provides assistance with a computer problem—an exchange of favors that allows each man to hold his own while helping the other.

A third feature of men's friendship is typically indirect talk about serious feelings. Many men find it uncomfortable to disclose feelings explicitly to other men (Burleson, Holmstrom, & Gilstrap, 2005). If they mention serious emotional issues, they often engage in "joke talk" (Fisher, 2009), which couches serious feelings in humor. Rather than verbally expressing sympathy or support for a male friend who is hurting, a man is more likely to use joke talk to say he cares indirectly or to suggest diversionary activities that take the friend's mind off his troubles (Cancian, 1987; Riessman, 1990).

LEE

I don't know what girls get out of sitting around talking about problems all the time. What a downer. When something bad happens to me, like I blow a test or break up with a girl, the last thing I want is to talk about it. I already feel bad enough. What I want is something to distract me from how lousy I feel. That's where having buddies really matters. They know you feel bad and help you out by taking you out drinking or starting a pickup game or something that gets your mind off the problems. They give you breathing room and some escape from troubles; girls just wallow in troubles.

Fourth, men's friendships often involve "covert intimacy" (Swain, 1989). Male friends tend to signal affection by teasing one another, engaging in friendly competition, and exchanging playful punches and backslaps. Most males learn very early in life that physical displays of affection between men are prohibited except in specific situations such as sports. Compared to women friends, reports Kory Floyd (1997), men "simply communicate affection in different, more 'covert' ways so as to avoid the possible ridicule that more overt expression might invite" (p. 78).

Finally, men's close friendships are often, although not always, more restricted in scope than women's close friendships. Men tend to have different friends for various spheres of interest (Wright, 1988). Thus, Jim might play racquetball with Mike, work on cars with Clay, and enjoy collaborating with Zach on work projects. Because men tend to focus friendships on particular activities, they may not share as many dimensions of their lives with friends as women tend to do. Overall, then, men's friendships emphasize shared activities, instrumental demonstrations of affection, covert intimacy, and defined spheres of interaction.

In summary, gender-linked communication patterns characterize most same-sex friendships. Women tend to rely on personal communication to share themselves

Closeness in dialogue is common in friendships between women.

and their lives and build friendships. Men more typically create and express closeness by sharing activities and interests and by doing things with and for each other. In other words, men tend to bond nonverbally through sharing experiences, whereas women typically become intimate through communicating verbally. These gender-linked tendencies, however, are not absolute, and men's and women's friendship styles are not dichotomous. As we've noted, most men engage in some expressive communication and most women engage in some instrumental communication.

Friendships between Women and Men

Friendships between the sexes pose unique challenges and offer special opportunities for growth. Because our culture so heavily emphasizes gender, it is difficult for women and men not to see each other in sexual terms. Even when cross-sex friends are not sexually involved, an undertone of sexuality often permeates their friendship (Halatsis & Christakis, 2009). In addition, misunderstandings may arise as the result of the different gendered speech communities into which male and female friends were socialized.

Despite these difficulties, many women and men do form friendships with each other and find them rewarding (West, Anderson, & Duck, 1996). For many women, a primary benefit of friendships with men is companionship that is less emotionally intense than that with women friends. For men, an especially valued benefit of closeness with women is access to emotional and expressive support, which tends to be less overtly expressed in friendships between men. African-American men report that friendships with women are personally affirming and provide a context for them to practice interpersonal skills (White, 2006).

EMILY

Last week Jay came by my place to talk. I've known Jay for a year—we're both in band—but we're not close friends or anything. He told me his parents are divorcing and he was really, really upset. He said it just tore him up, and he was crying and everything. Later, I saw Jay's closest friend Rob and asked how Jay was doing with his parents' divorce, but Rob didn't know a thing about it. I thought it was really strange that Jay hadn't told his closest friend but told me.

Many men say they receive more emotional support and therapeutic release with women than with men friends. Women also say they receive more emotional support from women than from men friends (Burleson, Holmstrom, & Gilstrap, 2005). In cross-sex friendships, men generally talk more and get more attention, response, and support than they offer. A majority of both sexes report that friendships with women are closer and more satisfying than those with men (Koesten, 2004). This may explain why both sexes tend to seek women friends in times of stress and why both women and men are generally more comfortable self-disclosing to women than to men (Monsour, 2006).

Gendered Romantic Relationships

Nowhere are gendered roles as salient as in heterosexual romantic relationships. The cultural script for romance is well known to most of us (Metts, 2006a; Mongeau, Serewicz, Henningsen, & Davis, 2006):

- Feminine women and masculine men are desirable.
- Men should initiate, plan, and direct most activities in a relationship.
- Women should facilitate conversation, generally defer to men, but control sexual activity.
- Men should excel in status and earning money, and women should assume primary responsibility for the relationships.

As we will see, this script continues to be played out in many heterosexual relationships.

Developing Romantic Intimacy

Personal ads offer insight into what heterosexual men and women seek in romantic partners. Ads written by men looking for women often place priority on stereotypically feminine physical qualities, using words such as *attractive, slender, petite*, and *sexy*. Women's ads for male partners tend to emphasize status and success and include words such as *ambitious, professional*, and *successful*. In reality, as in personal ads, our views of desirable partners often reflect cultural gender expectations—success and status in males, beauty and nurturing tendencies in females. That may explain why, in online communication, men are more likely than women to misrepresent their personal assets (e.g., financial worth), and women are more likely than men to misrepresent their weight (Hall, Park, Song, & Cody, 2010).

The conventional heterosexual dating script calls for men to take the initiative. Although many people claim they don't accept this pattern, most heterosexuals still conform to it. However, there are exceptions. There tends to be less role playing between gay men and even less between lesbian women (Patterson, 2000; Rutter & Schwartz, 1996).

Is one sex more romantic than the other? Contrary to popular belief, research indicates that men tend to fall in love faster and harder than women. Men tend to express love in more impulsive and sexualized ways than women, whose styles of loving are more pragmatic and friendship-focused (Bierhoff, 1996; Hendrick & Hendrick, 1986, 1996; Riessman, 1990). For instance, men may see love as taking trips to romantic places, spontaneously making love, and surprising their partners. Women more typically think of extended conversations, sharing deep feelings, and physical contact that isn't necessarily sexual.

Although the double standard regarding sexual activity is less rigid than in the past, women and men who are sexually adventurous continue to be judged differently. Even in an era known for hook ups, women who have sex with a lot of men are judged more harshly than men who have sex with a lot of women. Research also shows the sexes have different primary motives for engaging in sex. Women more often say intimacy and commitment are their reasons, whereas men more often say they are motivated by lust and a desire for physical pleasure (Meston & Buss, 2009; Peter & Valkenburg, 2010).

Women are more likely than men to focus on relationship dynamics—a pattern that holds regardless of sexual orientation (Metts, 2006a, 2006b; Patterson, 2000). Lesbian partners tend to take mutual responsibility for nurturing and supporting relationships (Goldberg & Perry-Jenkins, 2007). Gay men, conversely, are less likely to focus on nurturing the relationship and providing emotional leadership (Kurdek & Schmitt, 1986b; Patterson, 2000; Wood, 1993b). Gay men's commitment to romantic relationships tends to be more closely linked to intangible investments such as time, effort, and self-disclosure, whereas straight men's commitment to romantic relationships tends to be more closely tied to tangible investments such as money and possessions (Lehmiller, 2010).

Committed heterosexual relationships, in general, continue to reflect many traditional gender roles endorsed by the culture (Canary & Wahba, 2006; Wood, 2009a). Men tend to be perceived as the head of the family and are expected to be the major breadwinner; women tend to assume primary responsibility for domestic labor and child care; and men tend to have greater power in families. As we've noted in earlier chapters, these perceptions are increasingly at odds with reality: A majority of women work outside of the home, and nearly one-third of women in heterosexual partnerships earn more money than their male partners (Coonz, 2012; Ream, 2012).

Because gender distinctions are less salient, many gays and lesbians are not as bound by roles typical in heterosexual couples. Both gay and lesbian commitments often resemble best-friend relationships with the added dimensions of sexuality and romance. Following the best-friends model, long-term lesbian relationships tend to be monogamous and high in emotionality, disclosure, and support, and partners have the most equality of all types of relationships (Huston & Schwartz, 1996; Parker-Pope, 2008).

KARIN

In Annie's and my relationship, gender roles are pretty interesting. She's more femme than I am, but she also maintains our cars. I'm the one you would think of as the masculine partner if you saw us and I make more money, but I like cooking and baking and Annie doesn't. We've already agreed that I'll stay home with a child when we have one. We're equal when it comes to making decisions, and we take equal responsibility for keeping the house clean.

Gendered Patterns in Committed Relationships

Gendered orientations influence four dimensions of long-term love relationships: modes of expressing care, needs for autonomy and connection, responsibility for relational maintenance, and power. As we will discover, these dynamics are influenced by the distinctive styles and priorities emphasized by masculine and feminine socialization.

What does my girlfriend want? That's all I want to know. She says, if I really loved her, I'd want to be together and talk all the time. I tell her all I do for her. I fix her car when it's broken; I give her rides to places; I helped her move last semester. We've talked about marriage, and I plan to take care of her then, too. I will work all day and overtime to give her a good home and to provide for our family. But she says, "Don't tell me what you do for me," like do is a bad word. Now, why would I do all this stuff if I didn't love her? Just tell me that.

Gendered Modes of Expressing Affection

As we have seen, the masculine mode of expressing affection is primarily instrumental and activity-focused, whereas the feminine mode is more emotionally expressive and talk-focused. Women often feel hurt and shut out if men don't want to discuss feelings and the relationship. Conversely, some men feel resentful or intruded on when women push them to be emotionally expressive.

For many women, ongoing conversation about feelings and daily activities is a primary way to express and enrich personal relationships (Peretti & Abplanalp, 2004; Wood, 2011a). The masculine speech community in which most men are socialized, however, defines solving problems and achieving goals as reasons to talk. Thus, unless there is a problem, men often find it unnecessary to talk about a relationship, whereas many women feel that ongoing talk keeps problems from developing. Generally, men are more likely to express caring by doing things for and with their partners. Thus, the different genders may not recognize each other's ways of communicating care.

The cultural bias favoring feminine modes of expressing love is illustrated by a classic study (Wills, Weiss, & Patterson, 1974). The researchers wanted to know how husbands' demonstrations of affection affected wives' feelings. To find out, they instructed husbands to engage in different degrees of affectionate behavior toward their wives, and then the wives' responses were measured. When one wife showed no indication of receiving affection, the researchers called the husband to see if he had followed instructions. Somewhat irately, the husband said he certainly had—he had thoroughly washed his wife's car. Not only did his wife not experience this as affection, but the researchers themselves concluded that he had "confused" instrumental with affectionate behaviors. Doing something helpful was

entirely disregarded as a valid way to express affection! This exemplifies the cultural bias toward feminine views of loving. It also illustrates a misunderstanding that plagues many heterosexual love relationships.

SHARON

Most of this course has been a review of stuff I already knew, but the unit on how men and women show they love each other was news to me. I'm always fussing at my boyfriend for not showing me he cares. I tell him he takes me for granted and if he really loved me he'd want to talk more about personal, deep stuff inside him. But he bought me a book I'd been wanting, and a couple of weeks ago he spent a whole day fixing my car because he was worried about whether it was safe for me—I thought of that when we talked about the guy in the experiment who washed his wife's car. I guess he has been showing he cares for me, but I haven't been seeing it.

Gay and lesbian couples tend to share perspectives about how to communicate affection. Gay men generally engage in more emotional and intimate talk than straight men but less than women of any sexual orientation. Lesbians, on the other hand, generally share responsibility for taking care of a relationship and build the most expressive and nurturing communication climates of any type of couple (Goldberg & Perry-Jenkins, 2007; Patterson, 2000). Lesbian partners' mutual attentiveness to nurturing and emotional openness may explain why lesbians report more satisfaction with their romantic relationships than gays or heterosexuals do (Goldberg & Perry-Jenkins, 2007).

Gendered Preferences for Autonomy and Connection

Autonomy and connection are two basic needs of all humans. We all need to feel that we have both personal freedom and meaningful interrelatedness with others. Yet, gender affects how much of each of these we find comfortable. Masculine individuals tend to want greater autonomy and less connection than feminine people, whose relative priorities are generally the reverse.

Desires for different degrees of autonomy and connection frequently generate friction in close relationships. Many couples are familiar with a pattern called *demand-withdraw* (Caughlin & Vangelisti, 2000; Wegner, 2005). In this pattern, one partner feels distant and tries to close the distance by engaging in intimate talk, and the other partner withdraws from a degree of closeness that stifles his or her need for autonomy. The more one demands talk, the more the other withdraws; the more one withdraws from interaction, the more the other demands talk. Both men and women are likely to withdraw when partners demand or request change; however, the intensity of withdrawal is greater when a woman requests change in a man than when a man requests change in a woman (Sagrestano, Heavey, & Christensen, 1998). Socialized toward independence, masculine individuals tend to be more comfortable when they have some distance from others, whereas feminine people tend to be more comfortable with close connections. Ironically, the very thing that creates closeness for one partner impedes it for the other.

JEFF

I get really frustrated talking about relationships with girls I've dated. It seems like they feel a need to discuss the relationship every time we're together. I don't get the point. I mean, why talk about a relationship if everything's going along fine? Why not just be in the relationship and enjoy it?

KARIN

I don't know why straight women put up with partners who don't work on their relationship. Angie and I both invest a lot of time and emotion in taking care of our relationship because it matters to both of us. I talk to straight friends and hear them complaining about how their partners never even notice the relationship. I would never settle for that.

More hurtful than the demand-withdraw pattern itself, however, are partners' tendencies to interpret each other according to rules that don't apply to the other's behavior. For instance, to think that a man who wants time alone doesn't love his partner is to interpret his withdrawal according to a feminine ruler. Similarly, to perceive a woman as intrusive because she wants intimate conversation is to judge her by masculine standards. Although the demand-withdraw pattern may persist in relationships, we can eliminate the poison of misinterpretation by respecting different needs for autonomy and connection.

Gendered Responsibility for Relational Health

Lesbian couples tend to share responsibility for their relationships. Because most lesbians, like most heterosexual women, learn feminine ways of thinking and acting, both partners tend to be sensitive to interpersonal dynamics and interested in talking about their relationship and working through problems (Canary & Whaba, 2006; Schwartz & Rutter, 1998; Wood, 1993e).

Against the standard set by lesbians, heterosexual couples do not fare as well in distributing responsibility for relational health. In heterosexual relationships, both men and women tend to assume that women have primary responsibility for keeping relationships on track (Canary & Wahba, 2006; Cubbans & Vannoy, 2004; DeMaris, 2007; Stafford, Dutton, & Haas, 2000).

The expectation that one person should take care of relationships burdens one partner with the responsibility of keeping a relationship satisfying. In addition, it is difficult for one person to meet this responsibility if the other person doesn't acknowledge and work on matters that jeopardize relational health. The partner who is expected to safeguard the relationship may be perceived as a nag by the one who fails to recognize problems until they become very serious. Not surprisingly, research shows that the highest level of couple satisfaction exists when both partners share responsibility for the relationship (Cubbans & Vannoy, 2004; DeMaris, 2007).

Gendered Power Dynamics

Historically, the person who makes the money or the most money has had the greater power in heterosexual romantic relationships, and that person traditionally has been the male. As you might predict, problems fostered by believing that men should be more powerful are not prominent in lesbian relationships. Conversely, in some gay relationships partners constantly compete for status and dominance (Kurdek & Schmitt, 1986a, 1986b; Rutter & Schwartz, 1996).

As we noted in Chapter 7, the belief that men should be the primary breadwinners doesn't match reality for the growing number of two-worker households in which the woman earns as much as or more than the man. Among minorities, women are twice as likely as minority men to earn college degrees and the greater incomes that degrees tend to generate (Goodman, 2006; Wilson, 2007). Currently, more than a million men are unemployed, and that's not counting men who held sales jobs (another 300,000) (Marin & Dokoupil, 2011).

People who adhere to traditional views of gender in relationships are more likely to experience a decrease in both self-esteem and marital satisfaction if the woman earns more money (Helms, Prouiz, Klute, McHale, & Crouter, 2006; Waismel-Manor & Tolbert, 2010). Men whose fathers were actively involved in home life, sometimes as the primary home-maker, are more likely to see home-making as compatible with masculinity. Women and men who had mothers who were successful in the paid labor force tend to see a woman's career success as consistent with femininity (Cose, 2003).

ERNEST

As a male who was reared by a single mother, I see women differently from most of the white men I know. I and a lot of blacks see women as our equals more than most white men do. We treat the women in our lives with a lot more respect than middle-class white males. Men who were raised by a single mother understand women and their plight better than most white men. We know we and black women are in it together.

EXPLORING GENDERED LIVES | "I Promise Not to Exasperate My Husband." NOT!

When Veronica Mendez and Gustavo Garcia married in Mexico City in 2006, their vows were not the same as those their parents took. Since 1859, the Epistle of Melchor Ocampo has been the official law for marriage ceremonies. According to the epistle, brides vow not to exasperate their new husbands, and grooms vow to treat their new wives with "the magnanimity and generous benevolence that the strong must have for the weak" (Dellios, 2006, p. 16A). Ten years of lobbying were required to get Mexico's Congress to pass a resolution urging judges not to include the epistle in marriage services.

In heterosexual relationships, the belief that men have more power than women is often reflected in the distribution of labor in the home. Although the majority of heterosexual families today have two wage earners, the housework and the care of children, parents, and other relatives continue to be done primarily by women (Coontz, 2012; Medved, 2009; Schiebinger & Gilmartin, 2010; Sheehy, 2010; Wood, 2011b, 2011c). In fact, some men who don't have jobs in the paid labor force and whose female partners work outside the home engage in less child care and home maintenance than do men who have jobs in the paid labor force (Dokoupil, 2009). As a point of comparison, unemployed women spend twice as much time on child care and housework as employed women do (Dokoupil, 2009).

The reasons for women's and men's unequal contributions to domestic labor are complex. Al DeMaris and Monica Longmore (1996) have identified three primary reasons. The first is gender ideology. Men and women with more traditional beliefs about gender are more likely than people with less traditional gender beliefs to perceive it as appropriate for women to do most of the domestic labor. The second reason is women's alternatives to a relationship. Women who have desirable alternatives to their current relationships have more leverage to persuade their partners to participate more in domestic labor. The third reason is equity. Most people prefer equitable relationships—ones in which they and their partners invest relatively equally and in which both partners benefit equally. The extent to which partners are committed to equity affects how they divide domestic chores. These three reasons often interact. For instance, women with more traditional gender ideology may perceive it as equitable for them to do the bulk of housework, whereas women with less traditional beliefs about gender may perceive it as inequitable for them to do more housework than their partners. Cultural factors may also affect the three reasons DeMaris and Longmore identified.

Dubbing the extra domestic labor that women typically do the **"second shift,"** sociologist Arlie Hochschild (2003) reports that the majority of wives employed outside the home have a second-shift job in the home. Child care is a big part of the second shift for many women. Mothers with college educations spend an average of 21.2 hours a week with their children and mothers with less education spend 15.2 hours.

Today's fathers are also spending more time with their children than did their own fathers. College-educated fathers spend an average of 9.6 hours a week with their children, and less educated fathers spend an average of 6.8 hours a week with children. That's more than double the amount of time fathers in 1977 spent with children. Fathers under 29 years of age spend more time with children than older fathers do (Council on Contemporary Families, 2010; Parker-Pope, 2010c; Ramey & Ramey, 2009).

As Lynn Hallstein (2008) points out, many women think that because becoming a mother is a choice, they are responsible for the consequences of that choice. In other words, many women who continue working in the paid labor force after becoming mothers accept the idea that they have to figure out how to manage motherhood and a career. They are reluctant to ask their workplaces to make accommodations and they often find their partners are not willing to invest equal time and effort in parenting. Further, they may feel as much pressure to succeed at mothering as at their job (Hallstein, 2010).

Dads at Work

Dads care about their work, and by work they mean both the work they get paid for and the work of being a dad. More than in past eras, many men today want to be full parts of their families and communities. Compared to dads, a decade ago (Bland, 2012):

54 percent take their kids to school once or twice a month, up from 38 percent

45 percent attend class events, up from 34 percent

41 percent visit their child's classroom once or twice a month, up from 30 percent

59 percent attend school-based parents meetings, up from 47 percent

28 percent volunteer at school, up from 20 percent

75 percent help kids with extracurricular activities, up from 71 percent

78 percent help with homework, up from 74 percent

77 percent attend parent–teacher conferences, up from 69 percent

Why do today's dads work so hard at parenting? In their own words (Bland, 2012):

"I know it sounds a bit clichéd, but they do grow up fast, so I want to spend time with them."

"I just want to be part of her life. I want to be there for her."

"It just feels good being with the kids."

"I just feel if you're going to be a parent, you should be there."

Men still do less housework than women (Council on Contemporary Families, 2010). In part, this may reflect masculine socialization, which typically doesn't emphasize developing skills in domestic chores. Because girls are often socialized to perform more traditionally "feminine" tasks such as laundry, cooking, and dusting, they typically have developed skill in these tasks by the time they set up an adult household. In addition, many women have higher standards for housekeeping than their male partners. This may lead women to criticize how their male partners perform the tasks and to redo or take over tasks that their male partners aren't performing to the women's satisfaction (Wiesmann, Boeije, van Doorne-Huiskes, & den Dulk, 2008). Responses like these understandably discourage men from being active in homemaking. Men may also feel that it's not fair for their partners to expect them to comply with housekeeping standards they don't endorse. Only when couples agree on a standard for housekeeping is it fair to expect both partners to follow that standard.

GLORIA

I'm a mother and a professional and a part-time student, but I am not the only one who takes care of my home and family. That's a shared responsibility in our home. My daughter and son each cook dinner one night a week, and they switch off on chores like laundry and vacuuming. My husband and I share the other chores 50-50. Children don't resist a fair division of labor if their parents model it and show that it's expected of them.

We should also note that much of the work women do in the home is generally more taxing and less gratifying. For instance, whereas many of the contributions men typically make are sporadic, variable, and flexible in timing (e.g., mowing the lawn), the tasks women typically do are repetitive, routine, and constrained by deadlines (Canary & Wahba, 2006; Hochschild with Machung, 2003). Women are also more likely to do multiple tasks simultaneously (e.g., helping a child with homework while preparing dinner). Whereas mothers tend to be constantly on duty, fathers more typically take responsibility for irregular tasks such as fixing broken appliances and car maintenance. Fathers are also more likely than mothers to engage in occasional fun child-care activities, such as trips to the park.

AIKAU

My mother works all day at her job. She also cooks all of the meals for the family, does all of the housework, and takes care of my younger brother and sister. When my mother goes out of town on business, she fixes all of the family meals and freezes them before she leaves. She also arranges for day care and cleans very thoroughly before she leaves. My father expects this of her, and she expects it of herself.

It's interesting to trace changes in men's participation in child care and household tasks. In the 1960s and earlier, few men did much to care for home and children. Between the mid-1970s and the mid-1980s, men's contributions increased considerably—and then stagnated at that level (Bronstein, 2004; Hochschild & Ehrenreich, 2003).

The recession that began in 2008 has propelled changes in men's involvement in home life. Between 2008 and 2010, millions of Americans lost jobs, and the majority of them were men. Currently, nearly 20% of men between the age of 25 and 54 are unemployed. This is the highest percentage of unemployed men during earning years since 1948 when the labor bureau began keeping track (Brooks, 2010; Marin & Dokoupil, 2011). As a consequence, many men who are out of work have become stay-at-home dads while their partners have become sole breadwinners. One estimate is that 2 million fathers (1 in 15) are currently stay-at-home dads (Yen, 2011). The shift from fast-and-furious deal making and command decision making to picking children up from school and entertaining them is difficult. Laid off after 20 years in a Fortune 500 company, Andrew Emery says, "It was a big part of my identity; it's who you are. It took me a long time to fill in the blank when people asked me what I do" (Kershaw, 2009, p. E6). Yet, after the initial adjustment, many men find great satisfaction in being full-time fathers (Noelle, 2012). In fact, many of them are hoping to find reemployment in careers that enable them to spend more time with their children (Kershaw, 2009).

Another way in which women's contributions to home life have been greater is in terms of **psychological responsibility**—the responsibility to remember, plan, and make sure things get done (Hochschild, 2003). Partners may agree to share responsibility for taking children to doctors, but typically the woman remembers

---

EXPLORING GENDERED LIVES *Scientists and the Second Shift*

In 2009, Carol Greider got the call every scientist dreams of: The voice at the other end of the line was in Stockholm and told her she had won the Nobel Prize in Physiology or Medicine. Where was Dr. Greider when she got the call? In her lab? Writing a scientific paper? Nope, she was folding laundry, one of the many home responsibilities she assumes.

Greider isn't alone. According to a 2010 study of scientists in the United States, female scientists do twice as much cooking, cleaning, and laundry

as male scientists (Schiebinger & Gilmartin, 2010). And then there's child care. Dr. Greider, for example, has two school-age children, and she takes much of the responsibility for going to their sports events, taking them to and from play dates, and so forth. And that's in addition to the 56 hours spent in paid labor in an average week (Laster, 2010; Philipsen, 2008).

Can you think of ways to reduce the second shift that many women experience?

EXPLORING GENDERED LIVES *Fathering in Other Species*

Most human fathers may engage less in child care than human mothers, but fathering is a big time pursuit in many species (Angier, 2010). Among birds, males and females usually share the tasks of sitting on eggs to hatch them and fetching insects for the baby birds. In certain species of birds, such as emus and rheas, the males exclusively tend the nest.

And birds aren't the only active fathers. Male pipefish and seahorses become pregnant and give birth. Some primates also emphasize the role and status of fathers. Male Barbary macaques, for example, appear with infants to increase their standing in their social groups.

Can you think of reasons why males of other species might be more engaged fathers?

---

when inoculations are due, schedules appointments, and keeps track of whose turn it is to take the child. Similarly, partners may share responsibility for preparing meals, but women usually take on the responsibilities of planning menus, keeping an inventory of supplies, making shopping lists, and going to the grocery store. All of this planning and organization is a psychological responsibility that is often not counted in couples' agreements for sharing the work of a family.

The consequences of the second shift are substantial. Women who do most of the homemaking and child-care tasks are often extremely stressed, fatigued, and susceptible to illness (Babarskiene & Tweed, 2009; Hochschild, 2003), and they are at a disadvantage in their paid work because they are drained by responsibilities at home (McDonald, Phipps, & Lethbridge, 2005). Frustration, resentment, and conflict are also likely when one person in a partnership bears the double respon- sibilities of jobs inside and outside the home (Chethik, 2008; Cubbans & Vannoy, 2004; DeMaris, 2007; Erickson, 2005). Similar stress has been found in single fathers who work a second shift.

Another clue to power dynamics is how couples manage conflict. Masculine individuals (whether female or male) tend to use more unilateral strategies to

EXPLORING GENDERED LIVES   *The Mommy Myth*

Many American women today are brought up to expect motherhood to be an idyllic experience in which mothers and children spend their days engaged in happy adventures (Douglas & Michaels, 2004). This ideal mother loves being with her children, never wants time away from them, and certainly never raises her voice to the little darlings. Unfortunately, a lot of women find that real, day-to-day mothering is very different from the myth. Many young mothers are overwhelmed by what they are expected to do and, simultaneously, they feel guilty that they aren't doing enough, doing it well enough, or enjoying the bliss of motherhood (Hallstein, 2010b).

Judith Warner (2005) says the expectations of American mothers today are a recipe for the perfect madness. There is no way that any normal human being can be as endlessly patient and as engaged as many of today's mothers feel they should be. Because it is impossible to meet these expectations, many mothers feel inadequate and guilty. Warner, Douglas, and Michaels think that a number of factors projected by the media play a big role in creating and sustaining the mommy myth. Television programs and films often show the mythical woman who "has it all"—being a perfect mother and a successful professional. Working mothers in high-profile careers are featured in magazine and newspaper stories. Compounding media is the relentless quest for perfection that characterizes American culture—whatever we do, we should do it perfectly. One way to address this, say Douglas and Michaels, is to learn what the mommy myth is and to name every instance of it you see.

EXPLORING GENDERED LIVES   *Global Nannies*

Two careers plus children may be too much! Many two-worker families find they can't fulfill all their responsibilities at home and in the workplace. One solution is to hire someone else to take care of the home, an option increasingly chosen by many dual-earner families. For the many people who want to minimize the cost of hiring full-time help for the home, the cheapest domestic labor is women from underdeveloped countries who will work for a fraction of the cost that Americans will. That solves one problem but creates another. Each year, millions of women leave Mexico, the Philippines, and other relatively poor countries to become maids and nannies for well-to-do families in the United States. Poor countries become even poorer as women migrate to the United States to work here rather than in their home countries. The result is a "care deficit" in countries that already have too few resources (Bronstein, 2004; Hochschild & Ehrenreich, 2003; Hondagneu-Sotelo, 2007).

engage in and to avoid conflicts. They are more likely than feminine people to issue ultimatums, to refuse to listen or discuss an issue, or to assert that the partner is blowing things out of proportion, thus enacting the masculine tendency to maintain independence and protect the self. Feminine individuals more typically defer or compromise to reduce tension, and they employ indirect strategies when they do engage in conflict, which is consistent with feminine speech communities' emphasis on maintaining equality and building relationships (Rusbult, 1987;

Stafford, Dutton, & Haas, 2000). As you might expect, the tension between masculine and feminine ways of exerting influence is often less pronounced in lesbian relationships, where equality is particularly high. For gay partners, power struggles are common and are sometimes a continual backdrop for the relationship (Kurdek & Schmitt, 1986b).

Finally, gendered power dynamics underlie violence and abuse, which are means of exercising dominance over others. We will cover the topic of violence in detail in Chapter 12, but we also need to acknowledge here that intimate partner violence is one manifestation of gendered power dynamics in romantic relationships. Not confined to any single group, violence cuts across race, ethnic, and class lines. Researchers estimate that at least 28% and possibly as many as 50% of women suffer physical abuse from partners, and even more suffer psychological abuse (Wood, 2001b).

Violence is inflicted primarily by men, most of whom have been socialized into masculine identities (Johnson, 2006; Wood, 2004). In the United States, every 12 to 18 seconds a woman is beaten by a man; four women each day are reported beaten to death; and women are 600% more likely to be brutalized by an intimate partner than are men (Wood, 2001b). Convincing evidence that violence is connected more closely to gender than to sex comes from a study by Edwin Thompson (1991). Based on reports from 336 undergraduates, Thompson found a high degree of violence in dating relationships. Sex alone, however, did not explain the violence. Thompson discovered that violence is linked to gender, with abusers—both male and female—being more masculine and less feminine in their gender orientation. This led Thompson to conclude that physical aggression is associated with the traditionally masculine emphasis on control, domination, and power.

We've seen that personal relationships reflect the expectations and orientations encouraged by feminine and masculine socialization. Gender differences surface in how partners express and experience closeness, preferences for autonomy and connection, the distribution of responsibility for maintaining relationships, and power dynamics.

SUMMARY

Gendered ideas continue to shape friendships and romantic relationships. Yet, today many people feel that traditional gender roles aren't satisfying or realistic. As people discover the limits and disadvantages of traditional gender roles, they are experimenting with new ways to form and sustain relationships and their own identities within those relationships. For instance, some men choose to be stay-at-home dads because they find greater fulfillment in nurturing a family than in pursuing a career in the paid labor force. Some women discover that they are more effective and more fulfilled by work outside the home than by work inside it. And many people balance home and paid work in ways that transcend traditional roles. Examples such as these remind us that we can edit cultural scripts, using our own lives to craft alternative visions of women, men, and relationships.

KEY TERMS

The terms following are defined in this chapter on the pages indicated, as well as in alphabetical order in the book's glossary, which begins on page 283. The text's companion website (**http://www.cengage.com/communication/wood/genderedlives11e**) also provides interactive flash cards and crossword puzzles to help you learn these terms and the concepts they represent.

alternate paths model 187	*personal relationships 185*
feminine ruler 188	*psychological responsibility 202*
male deficit model 187	*second shift 200*

GENDER ONLINE

1. Look at personal ads on Match.com or eharmony.com. To what extent do the characteristics sought in men and women conform to gender stereotypes?

2. Online search terms: "cross-sex friends," "psychological responsibility," "second shift," "dual-worker families."

REFLECTION AND DISCUSSION

1. Reread the quotation on the opening page of this chapter. How could you apply this quotation to the idea of building and sustaining personal relationships?

2. Do you find more value in the male deficit or the alternate paths model of closeness? How does the model you prefer affect your behaviors and your interpretations of others' behaviors?

3. To what extent are gendered patterns of interaction described in this chapter present in your current or past romantic relationships?

4. Expand your communication repertoire. If you have relied primarily on talk to build closeness, see what happens when you do things with friends. If your friendships have tended to grow out of shared activities, check out what happens if you talk with friends without some activity to structure time.

RECOMMENDED RESOURCES

1. Julia Wood and Chris Inman. (1993). In a different mode: Recognizing male modes of closeness. *Journal of Applied Communication Research, 21* (pp. 279–295). This is the article that introduced the alternate paths model of closeness. At the time that we wrote the article, Chris Inman and I were team-teaching a course in gender and communication.

2. Sandra Metts. (2006). Gendered communication in dating relationships. In B. J. Dow & Julia T. Wood (Eds.), *The Sage Handbook of Gender and Communication* (pp. 25–40). Thousand Oaks, CA: Sage.

The last of the human freedoms is to choose one's attitudes.
—Victor Frankl

10

Gendered Organizational Communication

Knowledge Challenge:

- How much is the pay gap between women and men for full-time work?
- What is the glass escalator?
- To what extent are quotas consistent with affirmative action?

The Augusta National Golf Club has refused to admit women since it was established. This policy kept women from competing in one of the biggest tournaments, the Masters, and—even more important—from networking with other corporate executives on the Augusta Club's grounds. As chair of the National Council of Women's Organizations, Martha Burk (2005) thought this was discrimination, so in 2003 she sent Hootie Johnson, Augusta's chair, a letter asking him the club's membership to women. When Johnson refused, Burk organized and led a protest against the club. The protest did not open Augusta's grounds to women.

Fast forward nine years. In 2012, IBM named Ginni Rometty its CEO. Because IBM is one of three corporate sponsors of the Masters, its CEOs have always been invited to join to the club. Not this time. As of April 2013, Rometty has not been offered membership (Jinks & Helvar, 2012). In August 2012, however, Augusta did admit its first two women: Former Secretary of State Condoleeza Rice and financier Darla Moore (Greene, 2012).

The discrimination practiced by Augusta National Golf Club is rare (Dana, 2012). Yet more subtle gender inequities and dynamics persist in the workplace. In this chapter, we will, first, examine gender stereotypes that affect how women and men are perceived and treated in the workplace. Next, we'll consider how gendered dynamics in formal and informal networks can result in inequitable treatment of women and men. Finally, we'll consider ways to redress sex and gender discrimination.

Gendered Stereotypes in the Workplace

Social expectations of the sexes influence how we act and treat others in professional contexts. Often we're not even aware that we are using stereotypes to perceive others. We'll identify stereotypes of women and men that operate in professional contexts.

Stereotypes of Women

Women in the workforce are often classified according to one of four roles, each of which reflects a deeply gendered stereotype: sex object, mother, child, or iron maiden (Kanter, 1977; Wood & Conrad, 1983).

Sex Object

This stereotype defines women in terms of their sex or sexuality. Frequently, it leads to judgments of women workers based on their appearance and actions. We saw examples of this stereotype in the 2008 Presidential Primary. Some commentators described Republican Vice Presidential candidate, Governor Sarah Palin, as "a babe," and "hot." When Hillary Rodham Clinton campaigned in the Democratic Primary, she too was described in terms of her sexuality; however, Senator Clinton was criticized for not being sexy and feminine enough (Mandziuk, 2008).

MAGGIE

I worked at Hooters for a while. They had a manual you are given when you are hired at Hooters. It explains to you their discrimination policy and says they can discriminate based on age, weight, and level of attractiveness. They also have makeup and hair policies. Hair must be worn down and it must be done (curled or straightened), jewelry and tattoos are not allowed. Makeup is required.

The experience that Maggie describes at Hooters is not unusual. The Equal Employment Opportunity Commission (EEOC) sued Abercrombie & Fitch, charging the company for discriminating against job applicants based on race. The EEOC attorney claimed that Abercrombie & Fitch hired only women who were "white, young, and physically fit." The company paid 50 million dollars to settle the case ("Hiring Hotties," 2012). But is all discrimination illegal? No. Federal law forbids discrimination based on sex, race, national origin, disability, and religion. There is no law that prohibits a company from discriminating based on attractiveness. In fact, some companies argue that attractiveness of staff is a bona fide job qualification. Playboy Clubs and Chippendales make the case that attractiveness is essential in all staff.

Stereotyping women as sex objects contributes to sexual harassment, which roughly half the women who work outside the home have experienced. Harassing women is particularly prevalent in the military (Herbert, 2009a; Smith, 2006), as exemplified by the Tailhook and Aberdeen scandals in the 1990s, in which male military personnel mauled, violated, and verbally harassed female personnel. When The Citadel, a private military school in South Carolina, began admitting women, sexual assaults proliferated. According to a study that The Citadel itself conducted, 20% of the female cadets experienced sexual assault even years after women began being admitted (Smith, 2006). Pentagon data for one year, 2008, show a 25% increase in assaults reported by women serving in Iraq and Afghanistan (Herbert, 2009a). Incidents such as these stem from viewing women as sex objects.

The sex-object stereotype is also used to define and harass gays, lesbians, and transgender people. Like heterosexual women, gays and lesbians are often perceived primarily in terms of their sexuality and their conformity—or lack of conformity—to conventional gender roles.

MILISSA

Women can use the sex-object stereotype to their advantage. I pay for my education by being an exotic dancer, and I make better money than any other student I know. A lot of people think all exotic dancers are sluts, but that's not true. There's no difference between me using my body to fund my education and an athlete's using his or her body to fund his or her education. Same thing.

Mother

In institutional life, the stereotype of women as mothers has both figurative and literal forms. The figurative version of this stereotype is expressed when others expect women employees to take care of the "emotional labor" for everyone—to smile, exchange pleasantries, prepare coffee and snacks, and listen to, support, and help others.

Stereotyping women as mothers is one basis of job segregation by gender, a subtle and pervasive form of discrimination. Approximately 75% of women in the paid labor force are in traditionally female jobs or positions that support others (Beck, 2011; Goddess & Calderón, 2006; Watt & Eccles, 2008). Called "pink collar" positions, these are clerks, secretaries, administrative assistants, and so forth, whose job, like that of a mother, is to take care of others. Although at least half of the paid workforce in the United States is female, only 4% of the top 1,000 companies have women as CEOs (Coontz, 2012), only one-third of board members of Fortune 500 companies are women, and women make up less than 18% of senior managers, 15% of corporate boards, and less than 20% of Congress (Beck, 2011). Female managers earn only 73% of what their male counterparts earn (Coontz, 2012). The jobs that most women have—assisting and supporting others—generally have the least prestige and the lowest salaries.

The woman-as-mother stereotype also has a literal form. Women employees who have or plan to have children are often perceived as less serious professionals than male employees or than female employees who aren't mothers. In one experiment, two résumés were created for fictitious female job applicants. The résumés were identical in most respects—successful track record, uninterrupted career

EXPLORING GENDERED LIVES   *Can Women (and Men) Have It All?*

A story in the *Atlantic* magazine reignited a long-standing debate: Can women have it all? The story was written by Anne-Marie Slaughter (2012), who resigned from her job as director of policy planning at the State Department. In that job, her boss was Hillary Clinton; she went to events with Obama, and mingled with foreign dignitaries. It was, in short, a dream job for a foreign-policy scholar like Slaughter. But she was worried about her 14-year-old son who was having some difficulties at home and at school. Slaughter was held up as a shining example of a woman who had it all: glamorous, high-prestige career, and a family. Yet in the *Atlantic* article, she told the world that she couldn't have it all and she chose family.

Holding down the other side of the debate—that women *can* have it all—is Sheryl Sandberg, COO of Facebook. Intent on getting more women in high-level professional positions, Sandberg posts video pep talks that urge women to aim "higher-harder-faster" to succeed (Kantor, 2012). In her 2013 book, *Lean In*, she urges women to take charge of their lives, change circumstances that impede them, and never cut back on the ambition to climb the professional ladder.

Slaughter says that women can't have it all until and unless institutional structures change in ways that make it possible to be a good parent and a good worker simultaneously. Sandberg says women simply need to take control of their own lives.

Beyond the media hype is the stubborn fact that few people—male or female—have it all. Historically and even today, most men have not had it all—they've put their main energy into careers and enjoyed successes there while sacrificing many of the pleasures that come with prioritizing family. Maybe most of us can have some or most of it, but few women or men will have total career fulfillment and total family fulfillment.

history. The only difference was that one résumé noted that the applicant was active in the Parent-Teacher Association, a tip-off that the applicant was a mother, while the other résumé did not mention the PTA. The applicant whose résumé mentioned the PTA was 44% less likely to be hired (Andronici & Katz, 2007; Coontz, 2012; Goodman, 2007). Men who are fathers are not judged as less committed or competent; in fact, fatherhood tends to improve perceptions of male workers' commitment (Andronici & Katz, 2007).

It is illegal to treat mothers differently than other applicants or workers. Despite this law, stereotypes and their consequences persist (Bobbitt-Zeher, 2011). Each year the Equal Employment Opportunity Commission (EEOC) receives thousands of complaints of pregnancy-based discrimination. Women also experience discrimination once they are mothers. Professor of Law, Joan Williams (2010) coined the term **maternal wall** to refer to unexamined assumptions held by coworkers and superiors about how women will behave once they become mothers. Coworkers may resent a new mother if she gets family leave or a priority in scheduling (Wood & Dow, 2010). For example, a supervisor may assume that mothers are always available to their children. Based on this assumption, the supervisor may encourage Lynn Hall to cut back on her hours and quit traveling. Later, when the supervisor is looking for someone with experience in different regions the company serves, the supervisor notes that Ms. Hall is not qualified and attributes this to her being a mother.

CHARLOTTE

I know the mother role all too well. Before coming back to college, I worked as an adjuster for an insurance company. In my office, there were eleven men and one other woman, Anne. I'll bet there weren't more than 10 days in the 3 years I worked there that one of the guys didn't come in to talk with me or Anne about some personal problem. Sometimes, they wanted a lot of time and sympathy; sometimes, they just wanted a few minutes, but always it was Anne and me they came to—never one of the guys. What really burns is that they went to each other to consult about professional matters, but they never came to Anne and me about those. They treated us like mothers, not colleagues.

Child

A third stereotype sometimes imposed on women is that of child, or pet—cute but not to be taken seriously. This stereotype reflects a view of women as less mature and less competent than adults. Stereotyping women as children is sometimes expressed as "protecting" women. A few years ago, a company tried to bar all female employees of childbearing age from positions that exposed them to lead, because such exposure may affect fetuses. (It may also affect sperm, but men were not barred from the jobs.) Even if women did not intend to have children, the company insisted on "protecting" them from the dangers of these jobs, which, incidentally, were higher-paying jobs in that company. The policy was struck down when a court ruled that the company was wrong in treating adult women as children instead of respecting their ability to assess risks and make their own choices.

One argument against allowing women in combat is that they should be protected from the gruesome realities of war. This is ironic, as women have been killed in every war fought by our nation. In the military, combat duty is virtually essential

EXPLORING GENDERED LIVES *In and Out of Stereotypes*

In 2009, the Army consolidated its drill schools into a single campus. At the same time, the Army appointed the first woman to be in charge of basic training for enlisted soldiers.

Meet Sergeant Major Teresa L. King, the eighth of 12 children, who began her Army career as a postal clerk. Those who have worked with Sergeant Major King say she's perfect for the job. Colonel John Bessler, who was her commander when she went

through basic training, describes her as "confident, no nonsense, but compassionate about what's right for the soldier" (Dao, 2009, p. A22). Others who've worked with King say she is gruff, yet shows surprising tenderness toward her soldiers. She is petite in stature yet can do 34 push-ups and 66 sit-ups, each in less than two minutes. In other words, King manages to conform to some expectations of femininity while defying others.

for advancement to the highest levels (Hall, 2012). In 2012, the Army did decide that women could serve in combat battalions in areas such as personnel, intelligence, medical, and mechanics. "Protecting" women from challenging work often excludes them from experiences required for promotion and raises, as well as from the personal development that comes with new challenges.

Iron Maiden

If a woman is not perceived in terms of one of the three stereotypes we've discussed, she may be perceived as fitting a fourth. A woman who is independent, ambitious, directive, competitive, and sometimes tough may be labeled an "iron maiden." She is generally perceived as competent but unlikeable and unfeminine (Heilman & Okimoto, 2007; O'Neill & O'Reilly, 2011; Rudman & Glick, 2008). Hillary Clinton shows how this stereotype can be imposed on a woman. During the 2008 Democratic Primary, polls consistently showed that many people considered her experienced and competent but cold, insensitive, and unlikeable—qualities that violate expectations for femininity. Because Clinton does not fit into the conventional views of women and femininity, she was referred to as "ice queen," "ball breaker," and "castrating bitch" (Phelan, Moss-Racusin, & Rudman, 2007; Rudman & Glick, 2008, p. 162).

EXPLORING GENDERED LIVES *Gendered Wages*

Today, women earn approximately 80 cents for every dollar a man earns. In some professions, the gap is even greater. For instance, male physicians make 26% more than women who work the same amount and in the same specialty (Esteves-Sorenson & Snyder, 2012). But averages don't tell the whole story. Women in the top 20% of the workforce have made most of the gains, whereas women in the lower half are paid about what they were 30 years ago. The difference isn't fully accounted for by training, experience, or performance. In other words, sex discrimination continues to affect what people are paid for the work they do.

In an effort to correct gender discrimination in wages, Congress passed the Lilly Ledbetter Fair Pay Act in 2009. Lilly Ledbetter worked 19 years as a supervisor at a Goodyear Tire and Rubber plant in Alabama. As she approached retirement, someone anonymously left her a pay schedule that showed she was making significantly less than men in the same position she held. Ledbetter sued, but the Supreme Court ruled against her because the law stated that she had to file her suit within 180 days of the first occurrence of pay discrimination (Abrams, 2009; Collins, 2009a). Ledbetter, of course, did not know that her pay was less for all those years. The Lilly Ledbetter Fair Pay Act states that wage discrimination occurs whenever an employee receives discriminatory pay.

Gender discrimination in wages is not a small matter. As the chart below shows, over time the difference in pay can grow to $22,232 a year (Winik & Massey, 2009).

	Age 15–24	Age 25–44	Age 45–64
Women	23,357	41,558	44,808
Men	26,100	55,286	67,040

These four stereotypes define women in terms of sex and gender instead of job qualifications and performance. Some career women report that they escape being classified according to the stereotypes by being very careful not to be unfeminine yet not to act "too much like women" (O'Neill & O'Reilly, 2011).

Stereotypes of Men

Within institutional settings, men are also stereotyped in ways that reflect cultural views of masculinity and men's roles. Three stereotypes of men are particularly prevalent in organizations: sturdy oak, fighter, and breadwinner.

Sturdy Oak

The sturdy oak is a self-sufficient pillar of strength who is never weak or reliant on others. The stereotype of the sturdy oak can hinder men in professional contexts. When others communicate that they think it is unmanly to admit doubts or ask for help, male workers may rule out consulting others for advice or assistance. When others discourage men from collaborating and supporting coworkers, men may feel forced to act independently (Rudman & Fairchild, 2004). One result can be decision making that is faulty because of lack of important input.

Fighter

Cultural stereotypes also cast men as fighters—brave warriors who go to battle, whether literally in war or metaphorically in professional life. Childhood training to be aggressive, to "give 'em hell," and to win at all costs translates into professional expectations to beat the competition. There is no room for being less than fully committed to the cause, less than aggressive, or less than ruthless in defeating the competition. Because fighters are not supposed to take time from work for family, men who do so risk disapproval from coworkers. Although many men working outside the home say they would like to spend more time with their families (Philipsen & Bostic, 2010; Schmidt, 2010), many fear that doing so would lead coworkers to see them as less than fully invested in work.

> **GABE**
>
> *A man at the place where I work part-time asked for family leave when his wife had a baby. Our manager gave him two weeks—he had to by company policy—but he really put the guy down behind his back. I heard him kidding with some of the other managers, saying did the guy think he was a mother or something? Nobody has ever said anything when a woman took family leave.*

Breadwinner

Perhaps no other stereotype so strongly defines men in our society as that of breadwinner. Within organizations, stereotyping men as breadwinners has been used to justify paying them higher wages than women. Being the primary or sole breadwinner for a family is central to how our society has historically judged men, as well as how many men judge themselves. Because others expect men to focus on earning money, men who ask for family leave are often viewed as insufficiently competitive, and they may not advance as far or as quickly as male workers who don't make family commitments visible (Coontz, 2012). Men who tie their identity and worth to earning power are in danger in an uncertain economy where job security is not assured.

The stereotypes of women and men don't match the reality of today's workplace. Most women in the paid labor force do not fit any of the four female stereotypes, and most men in the paid labor force can't be neatly classified as one of the three male stereotypes.

Masculine Norms in Professional Life

Because men historically have dominated institutional life, masculine norms infuse the workplace. We'll examine two masculine norms that pervade the workplace.

Masculine Images of Leaders

The skills required to manage and lead are widely associated with communication traits that are cultivated more in masculine speech communities than in feminine ones—assertiveness, independence, competitiveness, and confidence. To the extent that women engage in traditionally feminine communication, they may not be recognized as leaders or marked for advancement in professional settings.

The answer isn't for women to act masculine. As we've seen, women who use assertive and instrumental communication may be branded "iron maidens" (Bennett, Ellison, & Ball, 2010). Coworkers who hold gender stereotypes may negatively

EXPLORING GENDERED LIVES *If She's A He, He's Better and Paid Better Too!*

For years, researchers have tried to figure out whether differences in judgments of men and women in the workplace are due to sex biases or other variables. Finally, a group of scholars came up with a surefire way to test whether a person's sex affects judgments of competence (Schilt, 2007, 2010; Schilt & Wiswall, 2008; Wentley, Schilt, Windsor, & Lucal, 2008). They studied coworkers' perceptions and pay rates for people who were first one sex and then the other sex and continued to do the same job. By studying transsexuals, Schilt and Wiswall eliminated variables, even personality variables, other than sex. They found that men who become women earn, on average, 32% less after they transitioned.

In one study (Schilt & Wiswall, 2008), the authors described a particular case: Susan was an attorney who transitioned to being a man and took the name Thomas. Thomas stayed at the same firm and one of the other lawyers at the firm mistakenly thought that Susan had left and Thomas had been hired to replace her. The other lawyer told one of the senior partners in the firm that Susan had been incompetent but her replacement (Thomas) was excellent.

evaluate women—but not men—who communicate assertively and who demand results.

Growing research shows that women don't need to act masculine to be effective leaders. Subordinates judge male and female leaders to be equally effective, and judge both masculine and feminine styles of communication to be important in leaders (Eagly & Carli, 2007; Fletcher, Jordan, & Miller, 2000). The most effective leadership style appears to incorporate both relationship-building and instrumental qualities. In fact, Fortune 500 companies that have strong records of promoting women to executive levels outperform other Fortune 500 companies. Beginning in 2001, 200 Fortune 500 companies were tracked. Those that promoted more women had higher overall profits and revenue than the industry average. The 10 firms that promoted the most women showed the highest profits (Adler, 2009; Beck 2011).

TARA

When I first started working, I tried to act like the men at my level. I was pleasant to people, but I didn't talk with coworkers about my life or their lives. I did my work, led my team with firm, directive communication, and stressed results. When I had my first performance review, I got great marks on achieving tasks, but there was serious criticism of "my attitude." A number of people—both my peers and staff I supervised—complained that I was unfriendly or cold. People criticized me for not caring about them and their lives. I pointed out to my supervisor that nobody made those complaints about men, and she told me that I couldn't act like a man if I wanted to succeed in business.

Let's also remind ourselves that we develop new skills, including communication and leadership skills, as we navigate new circumstances. Standpoint theory claims that, as we find ourselves in different contexts that make different demands, we develop new ways of thinking, communicating, and performing identity, including gender. If this is true, then as women enter into contexts that include masculine communication, they should become proficient in new skills. Similarly, as men interact with coworkers who use feminine communication styles, men should develop skills in collaboration and support. A study by Patrice Buzzanell and Kristen Lucas (2006) shows exactly that: both women develop new communication skills that are needed for effectiveness on the job. All of us can develop communication skills when we find ourselves in positions that require abilities not emphasized in our early socialization.

Outdated Norms for Career Paths

The view of a normal career path is out of sync with the needs and identities of today's workers. Career paths are typically regarded as linear progressions. A new employee takes a beginning position and works up the ladder by demonstrating commitment and competence at each level. Career paths are also typically thought of as being full-time. A serious professional works 50 or more hours a week.

The assumption that serious careers are linear and full-time reflects social relations of previous eras in which most professionals were men who had stay-at-home wives to care for the home and children. Today, most women and men work outside of the home. Few people can afford full-time maids and nannies, so the responsibilities of taking care of home and family are not easily met when both partners work outside of the home.

Increasing numbers of people—both male and female—are arguing that organizations should be more flexible to accommodate the realities of today's families (Coontz, 2012; Philipsen & Bostic, 2010; Williams, 2010). Why must everyone be at work by 8 or 9 a.m.? Why can't employers provide paid leave for family care? Why can't people take breaks of several months or years within a serious career? Why can't employees work part-time when there are young children or other family members who need attention and nurturing? Why can't organizations (at least large ones) provide on-site day care?

Beneath these questions lies a gender issue: Women's careers suffer more than men's when there are children or other family members who need care. When couples decide to have children, it is usually the woman who accommodates, often by taking time off from work. Most women don't want to quit work when they have children, but the inflexibility of the workplace and the inability or unwillingness of male partners to take half of the responsibility for parenting leaves women little choice (Coontz, 2012; Goodman, 2008a; Stone, 2007).

Some women choose to continue to work full-time after having a child or children. Recent research conducted over three decades (Wills & Brauer, 2012) reports that working mothers tend to be happier and healthier than stay-at-home mothers. Equally important, the research shows that overall children of working mothers are as emotionally balanced, socially adjusted, and academically accomplished as those of stay-at-home mothers.

Although most women who leave paid labor to care for children plan to return to the workforce in a few years, many run into barriers when they are ready to return to work outside of the home. Many mothers can't find jobs when they are ready to return to work. Either employers prefer to hire women who are not mothers or the break from work leads employers to perceive mothers as less committed workers (June, 2010; Williams, 2010). Even those who do find jobs often discover that they don't have access to prestigious career ladders because colleagues and supervisors perceive working mothers as less than fully committed to their careers (Hayden & O'Brien Hallstein, 2010; Stone, 2007; Wood & Dow, 2010). Further, taking a few years off from work tends to reduce women's earning power.

Perhaps you are thinking that people who step off the traditional career path should expect to be less well compensated than those who follow it. If so, we would expect career losses to be experienced by both women and men who step out of full-time work for a period of time. That's not the case. A recent report (Carter & Silva, 2010) shows that only women experience negative consequences for stepping off the traditional track. Studying the careers of top M.B.A. graduates in countries such as the United States, Asia, Canada, and England, researchers found that men who step off the traditional full-time career track do not necessarily take cuts in pay or position when they return to full-time work, but women do.

I'll admit I was against having a woman promoted to our executive board, but I'll also admit that I was wrong. I thought Linda wouldn't fit in or have anything to add. I voted for a junior male who I thought would fit in with the rest of us executives. But Linda is just superb. What I like most about having her in our group is that she's a real consensus builder, and nobody else is. Linda's first concern always seems to be finding common ground among us, and she has an absolutely amazing lack of ego invested in decisions. I'm not sure it's flattering to admit this, but the guys in the group, including me, operate from ego. Sometimes, winning a point is more important than crafting the best decision. Linda moves us away from that mindset.

Outdated norms for work life aren't a problem only for women. Many men, too, find them overly rigid and restrictive. Increasing numbers of men want jobs that allow them to be actively involved in parenting, home life, and communities (Beck, 2011). A recent poll found that 72% of men between 18 and 29 want a relationship in which both partners work and both care for the home and family, but only 30% of men who have that desire manage to achieve it (Coontz, 2013). Rigid workplace policies and expectations are the primary reason most men can't be as engaged in home and family life as they would like.

Gendered Patterns in Organizations

Organizations have both formal and informal practices. Formal practices include policies regarding leaves, work schedules, performance reviews, who reports to whom, who authorizes and evaluates whom, and so on. Informal practices include normative behaviors and understandings that are not covered by explicit policies: what is required to be on the fast track, gossiping and exchanging information, advising, mentoring, and so forth. As we will see, both formal and informal networks often entail gendered dynamics.

Formal Practices

Leave Policies

In 1993, the Family and Medical Leave Act (FMLA) was passed so that U.S. employees could take up to 12 weeks of unpaid leave to care for new babies or sick family members. In 2010, President Obama announced family leave was extended to workers in same-sex relationships who need time to care for a partner's child (Pear, 2010). Since the act was passed, more than 50 million Americans have taken family leave. The act, however, doesn't cover all workers. Only companies with 50 or more workers are required to grant family leaves, and some employees can be exempted from leave—FMLA covers only about 60% of employees in companies with 50 or more employees. The minimum required leave is

12 weeks. Some individual states, however, do require companies with fewer than 50 employees to grant family and medical leave, and some states require paid family leave.

The FMLA is not a complete solution to the tension between work and family. Because FMLA does not require that companies pay workers who take leaves, many workers cannot afford a leave even if they qualify for it. When time must be taken for families, it is usually a woman who takes it. The mother stereotype of women combines with the breadwinner stereotype of men to create a situation in which it is difficult for men to become full partners in raising children (June, 2010).

The United States has the humiliating distinction of being the only rich country that does not provide paid family leave to mothers (Beck, 2011). In fact, only four countries in a survey of 173 countries that do not guarantee paid maternity leave to any working mother. The other three countries that do not guarantee paid maternity leave are Liberia, Papua New Guinea, and Swaziland (Crary, 2008). Further, 81 countries surveyed give working fathers the right to paid paternity leave (Coontz, 2013). The lack of real support that businesses in the United States provide to employees forces many workers to choose between taking care of families and earning income. The lack of institutional support also influences some workers' career choices. Some workers are opting out of careers that don't provide support for families (Moe & Shandy, 2010; Quinn, 2010; Quinn & Litzler, 2009; Trower & Quinn, 2009).

Work Schedules

Another way in which organizations reflect outdated career models is rigid working schedules. Increasingly, the 9-to-5 model of the workday is giving way to the expectation that 7 or 8 a.m. to 7 or 8 p.m. is normal for "really committed professionals." Obviously, this model—or even the 9-to-5 model—doesn't accommodate families with young children. Even if parents can afford day care, children are sometimes too sick to attend; day care centers also may be closed for a day or more, making it necessary for a parent to take responsibility for child care. Women are more likely than men to take time off to care for children, a pattern that reflects and reinforces gendered assumptions that women put families first and men put careers first.

Employers in the United States say they can't afford to provide family-friendly policies such as paid leave and flexible schedules. However, all other wealthy countries have figured out how to afford policies that allow workers to also be good parents. In fact, providing more leave time and flexible working hours can actually save employers money because doing so is less expensive than training replacement employees (Beck, 2011; Quinn, 2010).

Informal Practices

In addition to formal policies, organizations operate with a number of informal, unwritten understandings that can make or break careers. Through a range of normative practices, some organizations emphasize gender differences, define one sex or gender as standard, or extend different opportunities to women and men.

EXPLORING GENDERED LIVES | *Work–Life Balance for All*

Work–life balance is important for all workers, yet most of the attention has focused on the professional class of workers (Villano, 2011). That's ironic since they already enjoy many benefits that enhance work–life balance. Most professionals know their work hours well in advance; they can come in late or leave early to deal with emergencies; and they can take breaks when they wish.

Low-wage workers often have none of those advantages. They have no flexibility about when they start and stop work. They often don't know their work schedules in advance, so they can't plan day care and other aspects of their lives. They have no emergency leave. They can't even choose when to take breaks. Rigid schedules, inflexibility, and unpredictability add substantial stress to low-wage earners' lives. As many of these workers, put it, "I'm one sick child away from losing my job."

The Institute for Workplace Innovation (IWIN) at the University of Kentucky is devoted to finding solutions to these stresses. Its goal is to boost the bottom line, employee health, and work-life fit. A full report from IWIN is available at: **http://www.uky.edu/Centers/iwin/LWPolicyFinal.pdf**

Unwelcoming Environments for Women

In some organizations, language and behavior that emphasize men's experiences and interests are normative (Cheney, Christensen, Zorn, & Ganesh, 2004). Women are generally less familiar and less comfortable with terms taken from sports (*hit a home run, huddle on strategy, ballpark figures, second-string player, come up with a game plan, be a team player, line up, score a touchdown, put it in your court*), sexuality or sex organs (*hit on a person, he has balls, he's a real prick, screw the competition, get into a pissing contest, stick it to them;* calling women employees "hon" or referring to women generally in sexual ways), and the military (*battle plan, mount a campaign, strategy, plan of attack, under fire, get the big guns*). Intentional or not, language related to sports, sexuality, and the military binds men into a masculine community in which some women feel unwelcome (Beck, 2011).

There can be resistance to—and occasionally outright hostility toward—women who enter fields in which men predominate. Women may be given unrewarding assignments, isolated from key networks of people and information, and treated stereotypically as sex objects, mothers, or children. Each of these techniques contributes to a communication climate that defines women as "not real members of the team."

The Informal Network

Relationships among colleagues are important in creating a sense of fit and providing access to essential information that may not come through formal channels (Barreto, Ryan, & Schmitt, 2009). Because men have predominated in the workplace, many informal networks are largely or exclusively male, giving rise to the term *old boy network*. Hiring and promotion decisions are often made through informal communication within these networks. For example, while golfing, Bob tells Nathan about a job candidate; later that candidate stands out later in Nathan's mind when he reviews applications for a job.

Images Bazaar/Getty Images

The informal network provides information and opportunities

EXPLORING GENDERED LIVES   *The Virtual Informal Network*

A senior technology executive named Josephine recently gave this advice to younger women in her field: "If you want to be in the loop, get yourself a male alias" (Rose, 2008, p. 7G). There's a story behind that advice. Years earlier when she began working at a startup tech company, she asked her boss to call her "Finn," short for Josephine. She was routinely included on e-mails to and from colleagues in other locations. The e-mails to Finn were peppered with crude language and sexist comments and jokes, but they also contained under-the-radar information about markets, investments, and people in the field. E-mails to Josephine contained only general information and didn't provide the inside scoop that allowed Finn to be in the know and to use her knowledge to advance.

Do you think it's professionally smart for women to have male aliases? Do you think it's ethical?

Women tend to be less involved than men in informal networks. Sometimes they are not invited to be part of the network or not made to feel welcome if they try to participate. When only one or two women are in a group, they stand out as different and unlike most of the employees. Only when a group reaches a critical mass does it have critical mass, that is, sufficient size not to be marginalized. A sense of difference is also reported by transgender people and people of color (Allen, 2006; Connell, 2010). In the face of communication that defines them as outsiders, women and racial and sexual minorities may avoid informal networks and thus lose out on these key sources of information and support.

Mentoring Relationships

A **mentor** is an experienced person who guides the development of a less-experienced person. In the workforce, mentors are usually older employees who help younger employees build careers. A mentor is at least helpful, and sometimes indispensable, to career advancement. Women and minorities are less likely than white men to have mentors.

Several factors account for the low number of women and minority workers who have the benefit of mentors. First, the numbers game works against them. Lower numbers of women and minorities in senior positions means that there are few who might counsel new female and/or minority employees. Men are sometimes reluctant to mentor young women for a variety of reasons: They may fear gossip about sexual relations; they may assume that women are less serious than men about careers; or they may feel less comfortable with women than with men. Not mentoring women and minorities perpetuates the status quo, in which white men get more help than women and minorities in climbing the corporate ladder.

In an effort to compensate for the lack of networks and mentors available in existing organizations, some professional women have formed their own networks, in which women share ideas, contacts, strategies for advancement, and information. In addition to furnishing information, these networks provide women with support and a sense of belonging with other professionals like themselves. As men and women become accustomed to interacting as colleagues, they may become more comfortable mentoring one another and forming sex-integrated communication networks.

Another challenge in professional settings is **workplace bullying**, which is repeatedly acting toward a person or persons in ways that humiliate, intimidate, or otherwise undermine the target's professional credibility (Einarsen, Hoel, Zapf, & Cooper, 2010; Fox & Lituchy, 2012). Workplace bullying may be overt (ridiculing someone's work in front of others) or covert (spreading rumors), or both. When persistent, it can interfere with the target's ability to be effective in doing his or her job.

Women are more frequently the targets of workplace bullying by both men and women. Males who bully tend to target men and women in roughly equal numbers. Women who bully, however, disproportionately target women (Fox & Lituchy, 2012). One reason for woman-on-woman bullying may be that, from the early years, girls are taught to evaluate and critique other girls (Workplace Bullying Institute, 2009).

> **TANGIA**
>
> *Where I used to work, the boss was always dropping in on the men who held*
> *positions at my level, but he never dropped in to talk with any of the women at*
> *that level. He also had a habit of introducing males in our division to visitors*
> *from the main office, but he never introduced women to them. It was like there*
> *was a closed loop and we weren't part of it.*

Glass Ceilings and Walls

Many women hit the **glass ceiling**, an invisible barrier that limits the advancement of women and minorities (Barreto et al., 2009; Beck, 2011). Women's progress is often impeded by subtle discrimination. It might be the stereotype of women as mothers that leads an executive to assume that a working mother would not be interested in a major new assignment that could advance her career. It might be seeing a woman in sexual terms so that her competence is overlooked. It might be misinterpreting an inclusive, collaborative style of communication as lack of initiative. These stereotypes can create a glass ceiling—an invisible barrier—that keeps women out of the executive suite.

But glass ceilings may be only part of the problem. The term **glass walls** is a metaphor for sex segregation on the job, in which women are placed in "pink collar" positions that require skills traditionally associated with women (assisting, organizing, counseling, human relations) (Watt & Eccles, 2008). Typically, such

| EXPLORING GENDERED LIVES | *The Glass Escalator* |

When Michael Alquicira couldn't find a job, he went back to school to become a dental assistant. After serving in the army, Daniel Wilden enrolled in nursing school. Unhappy with his job as a data consultant, John Cook also trained to be a nurse. So did Dexter Rodriguez. These men are part of a growing trend for men to work in occupations dominated by women (Dewan & Gebeloff, 2012). Men of all races and ages are participating in this job shift, and more than a third of them have college degrees.

There are multiple reasons for the switch. One is economics. During the recession, cutbacks were particularly severe in jobs typically filled by men. A second reason is that increasing numbers of men want jobs that allow them more time with families. A third reason may be that men in predominantly female careers often advance more quickly and get paid more than their female peers. The **glass escalator** is invisible advantage that accelerates men's success in female-dominated spheres of work (Crosby, Williams, & Biernat, 2005; Williams, 2010). Although the glass escalator seems to help all men in women-dominated fields, it is most helpful to white men (Wingfield, 2009).

jobs do not include career ladders, on which doing well at one level allows advancement to the next. In essence, many of the positions that women are encouraged to take have no advancement paths (Ashcraft, 2006; Coontz, 2012).

Workplace discrimination—whether subtle or blatant—makes it more difficult for some people to get hired, get paid fairly, and advance. This is why there have been repeated efforts to stop discrimination. Assessing those efforts is the final topic in this chapter.

Efforts to Redress Gendered Inequity in Institutions

Five efforts to reduce discrimination are equal opportunity laws, affirmative action policies, quotas, goals, and diversity training. It is important to understand these methods of redressing inequities and the differences among them so that we can evaluate arguments for and against them and decide our own positions. Although this chapter focuses specifically on the workplace, these remedies apply to both professional and educational settings, the two contexts in which efforts to end discrimination have been most pronounced.

Equal Opportunity Laws

Laws prohibiting discrimination began with the landmark legal case *Brown v. Board of Education of Topeka, Kansas*, which was tried in 1954. In that case, the U.S. Supreme Court overturned the "separate but equal" doctrine that had allowed separate educational systems for white and black citizens.

Since the Brown decision, the United States has passed other **equal opportunity laws**. The two main ones are Title VII of the Civil Rights Act (1964), which prohibits discrimination in employment, and Title IX (1972), which forbids discrimination in educational programs that receive federal aid. Other antidiscrimination laws are Title IV of the 1964 Civil Rights Act, the Women's Educational Equity Acts of 1974 and 1978, an amendment to the 1976 Vocational Education Act, and the Lilly Ledbetter Fair Pay Act, passed in 2009.

Equal opportunity laws focus on discrimination against *individuals*. In other words, complaints filed with the EEOC must claim that a particular person has suffered discrimination because of sex, race, or other criteria named in laws. Equal opportunity law does not ask whether a group (e.g., women or Hispanics) is underrepresented or is treated inequitably. Instead, it is concerned solely with discrimination against individuals.

Equal opportunity laws focus on *present* practices, so historical patterns of discrimination are irrelevant. For example, a university with a record of denying admission to women is not subject to suit unless a particular individual can prove she personally and currently suffered discrimination on the basis of her sex.

The scope of Title IX was weakened in 1984 when the Supreme Court narrowed its application from whole institutions to specific programs that receive federal money.

Affirmative Action Policies

President Lyndon B. Johnson used his 1965 commencement address at Howard University to announce a new policy that would address historical prejudice, which equal opportunity laws ignored. He said, "You do not take a person who for years has been hobbled by chains and liberate him, bring him to the starting line of a race, and then say, 'you are free to compete with all the others.'"

Affirmative action is based on three key ideas. First, because discrimination has systematically restricted the opportunities of *groups* of people, remedies must apply to entire groups, not just to individuals. Second, to compensate for the legacy of discrimination, there must be *preferential treatment* of qualified members of groups that have suffered discrimination. Third, the effectiveness of remedies is judged by *results*, not intent. If hiring and admissions policies don't result in a greater presence of women and minorities, then they are ineffective in producing equality.

Some people think that aiming for greater numbers of women and minorities in companies and academic programs results in excluding better-qualified white males. Yet, the claim that affirmative action deprives whites of admission to schools is challenged by a study by William Bowen, president of the Mellon Foundation and former president of Princeton, and Derek Bok, former president of Harvard University (1998). After analyzing grades, SAT scores, and other data for 93,000 students of all races, Bowen and Bok found that eliminating affirmative action would raise whites' chances of admission by a mere 1.5%.

Many people do not realize that affirmative action includes two important limitations. First, affirmative action policies recognize the *limited availability* of qualified people from historically underrepresented groups. Because of long-standing discriminatory practices, fewer women and minorities may be qualified for certain jobs and academic programs.

Second, affirmative action aims to increase the number of *qualified* members of historically marginalized groups. It does not advocate admitting, hiring, or promoting women and minorities who are not qualified. To understand how affirmative action policies work, it's important to distinguish between *qualified* and *best qualified*. Consider an example: Jane Evans and John Powell are candidates for the last opening in a medical school that requires a 3.2 undergraduate grade point average and a score of 1200 on the medical aptitude exam. Jane's undergraduate average is 3.4, whereas John's is 3.6. On the entrance exam, she scores 1290, and he scores 1300. Although his qualifications are slightly better than hers, both individuals clearly meet the school's requirements, so both are qualified. Under affirmative action guidelines, the school would admit Jane because she meets the qualifications and does so despite historical patterns that discourage women from studying science and math.

Affirmative action attempts to compensate for the effects of a history of bias by giving preference to individuals whose qualification was achieved despite obstacles and discrimination. As Thomas Shapiro (2007) points out, one reason that many blacks are economically less well-off than Caucasians is that "one generation passes advantage and disadvantage to the next" (p. 133). Thus, whites who owned property in the 1700s passed it along to their children who passed it along to their children and so forth. Blacks who were slaves owned no land, so they could not pass it on to future generations.

JOHNSON

I've never done anything to discriminate against members of other races, so I don't think I should have to step aside so they can have special advantages now. I don't owe them anything, and I earned everything I've got.

SHERETTA

I get so ripped off when I hear white guys badmouth affirmative action. They don't know what they're talking about. They speak totally from their self-interest and their ignorance. One thing that white guys say a lot is that they didn't hold blacks down in the past, so they shouldn't be penalized today. To that, I'd like to say they sure as hell don't mind taking a heap of advantages they didn't earn, like good schools and clothes and financial support. Do they think they earned those things? How do they think their daddies and granddaddies earned them? I'll tell you how: off the labor of black people that they were holding back, that's how.

Ever since affirmative action policies were enacted, public debate about them has been vigorous. A key issue is whether affirmative action is effective: Does it result in hiring and admitting more members of historically underrepresented groups? Do those hired and admitted succeed?

Let's look at two key studies of the effectiveness of affirmative action. One study examined the records of students admitted to medical schools under affirmative action and a matched sample of students admitted using standard admission criteria (Dreier & Freer, 1997). Students admitted under affirmative action did equally well in their residencies and became equally successful physicians. Further, black men who graduated from selective schools were more likely than their white peers to become civic and community leaders (Bowen & Bok, 1998). A study of law students (Mangan, 2004) produced similar findings. Even though minority students began their professional study with lower grades and standardized scores, they wound up being just as successful in their careers as white students.

The Supreme Court has issued a number of rulings that clarify and refine affirmative action. In 2003, the Court ruled that race cannot be *the deciding factor*, but it may be a factor in admissions decisions because universities have "a compelling interest in a diverse student body" ("In Their Words," 2003, p. 5A).

In late June 2007, the Court ruled that public school districts cannot use race as a basis for assigning students to elementary and secondary schools. The vote was close—five justices voting to invalidate both schools' plans and four voting to allow them. The four justices who dissented from the ruling wrote an opinion that emphasized the compelling need to continue efforts to ensure diversity at all levels of education.

In June of 2013, the Supreme Court considered the latest challenge to affirmative action. The case was *Fisher v. University of Texas*. Abigail Fisher, a white student, alleged that she was denied admission to the University of Texas at Austin because of race-conscious admissions criteria. In a 7 to 1 decision, the Court left intact an earlier ruling that racial diversity in college admissions may be a compelling state interest.

LAKISHA

I don't know how anyone can say the playing field is even today. It's not. I'm the first in my family to go to college. Actually, I'm the first to finish high school. My school didn't have SAT prep courses. My parents didn't know how to help me with my homework or apply to colleges. I didn't have any of the breaks that most students at this college did. So don't tell me the playing field is even. If it weren't for affirmative action, I wouldn't even be on the playing field!

In 2005, the Supreme Court ruled that individuals who report suspected sex discrimination are protected from retaliation under federal law (Lipka, 2005). Without this protection, many people would not report suspected discrimination.

There is growing interest in revising affirmative action to give preference based on socioeconomic status rather than race-ethnicity (Kahlenberg, 2010, 2012). Supporters of preference based on socioeconomic factors argue that "race-based affirmative action treats the symptoms but not the root causes of an underlying social problem" (Espenshade, 2012, p. 25A). People who are economically disadvantaged face numerous barriers to advancement in education and the job market. For instance, a white high school student from a working- or poverty-class family who has a 3.6 grade point average and a 1200 on the SAT has worked against significant disadvantages and, thus, may merit some preferential treatment over more affluent students.

Protection for transgender workers is also underway. In 2009, President Obama authorized attorneys to begin drafting policy guidelines that prohibit workplace discrimination against transgender employees working in the federal government (Rutenberg, 2009). The new guidelines will be in the handbook for federal managers and supervisors and will explicitly warn against discriminating against transgender employees. In 2012, the EEOC ruled that it is illegal to discriminate against a person because the person is transgender (McKinley, 2012).

Quotas

Perhaps the most controversial effort to redress discrimination is the **quota**. Building on affirmative action's focus on results, a quota specifies that a number or percentage of women or minorities must be admitted, hired, or promoted. For instance, a company might stipulate that 30% of promotions must go to women. A binding quota requires a specified number or percentage of women regardless of issues such as merit. If there are not enough qualified women to meet the 30% quota, then women who lack qualifications must be promoted.

A famous case relevant to quotas was brought in 1978, when Alan Bakke sued the University of California at Davis's medical school for rejecting him, a white male, in favor of less-qualified minority applicants. Bakke won his case on the grounds that he had been a victim of "reverse discrimination" because the University of California at Davis violated his Fourteenth Amendment right to equal protection under the law. However, the Court did not outlaw the use of race as one factor in admissions decisions. It only ruled that schools may not set aside specific numbers of spaces for minorities. In other words, the Court allowed race to be a factor as long as it didn't result in a rigid quota. As we noted earlier, this position was reaffirmed in 2003, when the Supreme Court ruled that race can be one factor in admissions decisions but that no factor, including race, can be set as a quota or given a set advantage.

Seven states have banned race-conscious admissions policies. Arizona, California, Florida, Michigan, Nebraska, New Hampshire, and Washington state currently forbid racial preferences in admissions to colleges (Espenshade, 2012). California was

EXPLORING GENDERED LIVES ## When Quotas Raise Questions—and When They Don't

Some people think it's unfair to reserve places for women and minorities. They advocate evaluating all applicants on individual merit. It's interesting that questions aren't raised about a long-standing quota system that has benefited white and male students. Many, if not most, universities have legacy policies, which accord preferential consideration to the children of alumnae and alumni. For example, in recent years, Harvard admitted 40% of legacy applicants but only 11% of the total applicants. Princeton had an overall acceptance rate of 9%, but it accepted 42% of legacy applicants. It's unlikely the legacy applicants were substantially stronger academically since they had lower SAT scores and grade point averages than the overall entering class (Kahlenberg, 2010).

Do you approve of schools giving preferential treatment to children of alumni?

the first state to ban affirmative action in admissions. Ten years after California enacted the ban, only 2% of first-year students at UCLA were black—the smallest percentage in 30 years (Lewin, 2007).

NICOLA

The quota system is the only thing that can work. The laws aren't enforced, so they don't help, and affirmative action is just a bunch of talk. I've watched both my parents be discriminated against all of their lives just because of their skin color. All the laws and pledges of affirmative action haven't done a damned thing to change that. Quotas cut through all of the crap of intentions and pledges and say point-blank there will be so many African Americans in this company or this school or whatever. That's the only way change is ever going to happen. And when I hear white guys whining about how quotas are unfair to them, I want to throw up. They know nothing about unfair.

Goals

A goal is different from a quota, although the two are frequently confused. A **goal** is a stated intention to achieve representation of minorities or women. For instance, a company could establish the goal of awarding 30% of its promotions to women by the year 2015. But goals do not require results. If the company awarded only 10% of its promotions to women by 2010, there would be no penalty; the company could simply announce a new goal: to award 30% of its promotions to women by 2020. There are no penalties for not achieving goals.

Ironically, both quotas and goals can work against women and minorities. The numbers specified by quotas and goals can be interpreted as a maximum number of women and minorities rather than a minimum. In our example, the 30% number could be used to keep more than 30% of promotions from going to women, even if 40% of qualified applicants were women.

TYRONE

I resent the way so many people at this school assume that any minority student is here only because of affirmative action or quotas. I've heard people say that if it weren't for racial quotas, there wouldn't be anyone here who isn't white. One of my suitemates even said to my face once that, since he hadn't had a quota to get him in here, he had to bust his butt to get into this school. I asked him what his SAT score was. He said 1080. I told him mine was 1164; then I walked out.

Goals and quotas can work against women and minorities in a second way. When goals or quotas are in effect, members of institutions may assume that women and minorities got in only because of their sex or race. When this happens, individual women and people of color are not regarded as capable members of the school, business, or trade. Regardless of their qualifications, women and minorities may be perceived as underqualified.

Diversity Training

A final remedy for persistent discrimination—one that is often combined with one of the other four—is diversity training, which aims to increase awareness of and respect for differences that arise from distinct standpoints shaped by a range of factors including race, economic circumstances, ethnicity, sexuality, and religion. This strategy assumes that many people are unaware of how their comments and behavior could be offensive to women, members of minority races, and people who have nontraditional gender identities.

Of course, not everyone cares about inequities, and many people are unwilling to make changes, especially changes that may limit their own privileges. Thus, an important drawback of diversity training is that it requires strong personal commitment from participants.

Efforts to deal with discrimination are evolving. As America continues to become a truly equal society, we are likely to see new ways of addressing persisting inequities.

SUMMARY

In this chapter, we have considered a variety of ways in which institutional life intersects with cultural understandings of gender and communication. Cultural views of masculinity and femininity seep into the formal and informal life of organizations.

Yet, current views of gender won't necessarily be future views. You and your peers will make up and define the workplaces of the future. One of the challenges for your generation is to remake our institutions so that all of us can live and work in humane and fair ways.

KEY TERMS

The terms following are defined in this chapter on the pages indicated, as well as in alphabetical order in the book's glossary, which begins on page 283. The text's companion website (**http://www.cengage.com/communication/wood/genderedlives11e**) also provides interactive flash cards and crossword puzzles to help you learn these terms and the concepts they represent.

affirmative action 224	*goal 228*
equal opportunity laws 223	*maternal wall 210*
glass ceiling 222	*mentor 221*
glass escalator 223	*quota 227*
glass walls 222	*workplace bullying 221*

GENDER ONLINE

1. To learn more about efforts to reduce discrimination in the workplace, visit the Equal Employment Opportunity Commission's homepage: **www.eeoc.gov**.

2. Online search terms: "affirmative action," "glass escalator," "Lilly Ledbetter."

REFLECTION AND DISCUSSION

1. Have you observed instances of classifying women or men workers and men into stereotypes identified in this chapter? How might workers resist being stereotyped?

2. Now that you understand distinctions among equal opportunity laws, affirmative action, goals, quotas, and diversity training, how do you evaluate each?

3. Interview some people involved in careers to learn how much they rely on informal networks. To what extent do women and men professionals report that they are equally welcomed into informal networks in their organizations and fields?

4. Talk with staff in the admissions office at your school to learn about admissions policies and enrollment of women and men, whites and minorities. What is your opinion of your school's policies?

RECOMMENDED RESOURCES

1. Dennis K. Mumby. (2006). Introduction. In B. Dow & J. T. Wood (Eds.), *Handbook of Gender & Communication* (pp. 89–95). Thousand Oaks, CA: Sage. This essay introduces four surveys of current research on gendered aspects of the workplace.

2. Patrice Buzzanell and Kristen Lucas. (2006). Gendered stories of career. In B. Dow & J. T. Wood (Eds.), *Handbook of Gender & Communication* (pp. 161–178). Thousand Oaks, CA: Sage. This essay provides an excellent overview of material, psychological, and communicative influences on women's career opportunities and career experiences.

3. Peggy McIntosh. (2007). White privilege: Unpacking the invisible knapsack. In M. Andersen & P. H. Collins (Eds.), *Race, Class & Gender* (pp. 98–102). Belmont, CA: Thomson Wadsworth. This classic article makes visible white privileges that are normalized.

The media we use and the stories they tell help to make us who we are.
—Maria Mastronardi

11

Gendered Media

Knowledge Challenge:

- In what ways do women and men differ in their use of social media?
- To what extent do media portrayals of relationships shape expectations for real relationships?
- To what extent are social media effective for political organizing?

February 23, 2012: Sandra Fluke, a law student at Georgetown University, appears at a hearing convened by Democrats and testifies that her school's health insurance policies have a harmful impact on women because they do not cover contraception.

February 27, 2012: CNS news proclaims "Sex-crazed co-eds going broke buying birth control, student tells Pelosi hearing."

February 29, 2012: Rush Limbaugh uses his show to call Fluke a slut. He says, "It makes her a slut, right. She wants to be paid to have sex."

March 1, 2012: Limbaugh adds fuel to the fire, saying, "If we are going to pay for your contraceptives, we want you to post the videos so we can watch."

March 1–3, 2012: Online, outrage over Limbaugh's comments is widely expressed. The blogosphere condemns his sexist, crude attack on Fluke.

March 3, 2012: Limbaugh posts a statement saying he regrets his "insulting word choices."

March 7, 2012: More than 45 advertisers withdraw from Limbaugh's show.

March 8 and beyond: Fluke is deluged with offers to speak, appear at political rallies and women's events, and job offers (Cottle, 2012; The Week, 2012).

This episode teaches us a lot about media and gender. One lesson is that media call things to our attention. If CNS and Limbaugh had not attacked Fluke, most of us would never have heard of her. A second lesson is that media can be disciplined. When blogs, social networking sites, TV broadcasts, and newspapers censured Limbaugh for his unfair and no-holds-barred attack on Fluke, Limbaugh had to back down. Public opinion and advertisers forced Limbaugh to issue a minimalist apology. A third lesson is that social media play an increasingly significant role in negotiating issues related to gender.

In this chapter, we explore how mass and social media influence understandings of gender and how social media in particular function as key contemporary sites of education, criticism, and activism.

Media Saturation of Cultural Life

People today are the most media-saturated and media-engaged people in history. Mass media are woven into our everyday lives. Nearly all (98.9%) of American homes have at least one television, and the average American home has more televisions than people—3.3 televisions and fewer than three people per household, and at least one of those televisions is on 8 hours and 21 minutes a day (Media Trends Track, 2010; Vivian, 2011).

Television is only one form of mass media. We watch films and read newspapers and magazines. Advertisements, which make up nearly half of some magazines, tell us what products we need to meet cultural prescriptions for desirability. While walking, driving, or biking, we listen to radio and podcasts while also taking in an endless procession of billboards that advertise various products, services, people, and companies.

In addition, we rely on social media to connect with others, shop, and find out what's happening. Most of us text and go online to chat with friends, collaborate, and participate in online communities. In addition, many of us become not just consumers, but producers of media as we create personal blogs and podcasts and post videos on YouTube. Over a quarter of teens today (28% of boys, 26% of girls) shoot and share videos online (Teens and Online Video, 2012). Across all ages, the average person spends 53 hours a week engaging with all forms of media, 38.5 hours a week on social networking sites (Kendall, 2011).

CECE

Media don't influence what I think or how I dress or act. I can see that a lot of people follow whatever they see online or on TV or films, but I think independently. Sure, I go online and read magazines to see what's in style, but I decide for myself how I like to dress and act and everything else.

Media Impacts

Like Cece, many people believe others are affected by media but they are immune to media effects or influences. In fact, that belief is so prevalent that it has a name: **third person effect**, which is the belief that media affect others more than they affect us (Davison, 1983). However, research shows that most of us are not immune to influence from mass and social media (Douglas, 2010a, b). In this section, we'll discuss three important ways that media are related to gendered attitudes and behaviors: (1) Media set the agenda; (2) media regulate images of women and men; and (3) media motivate us to consume.

ANDREW

Anyone who thinks media don't influence people just needs to spend five minutes on this campus. Everyone dresses alike and everyone changes how they dress when the media hawks new styles. Guys all wear the low slung jeans that nearly fall off their butts. All the girls wear pants so tight they look like they're painted on. Check out shoes. Check out hairstyles. Check out colors. Whatever the fashion gods say is in is what everybody wears. Tattoos? Earrings? If we're told they're cool, we all get them.

Set the Agenda

According to media scholars, a primary impact of media is **agenda setting**, the process by which media tell us what we should attend to. Mass media and some web-based media have the ability to direct large audience's attention to particular issues, events, and people (Vivian, 2010). In setting the agenda, media may not tell us *what* to think, but they are extremely successful in telling us what to think *about*—which issues, events, and people merit our attention; and which aspects of people and events are most important. A story on the front page of the newspaper seems more important than one on an inside page; an issue that is discussed on multiple blogs seems more consequential than an issue mentioned by only one blogger. The outrage against Limbaugh was fueled by blogs and print and online newspapers covering and responding to the unfolding drama. It *became* an issue to think about because media put it on our agenda.

The term **gatekeeper** refers to people and groups that control which messages get through to audiences of mass media. Gatekeepers include editors, owners, bloggers, producers, and advertisers. The gatekeepers for newspapers and news programs shape our perceptions by deciding which issues to spotlight, which points of view get a hearing, and how to depict women, men, people of diverse sexual orientations and gender identities.

An example of gatekeeping comes from media coverage of wars. Newspapers routinely feature poignant pictures of teary-eyed children watching mothers go to war, while online polls ask, "Should a woman leave her baby to go to war?" Perhaps this is a reasonable question to ask about any parent, but the media tend to ask it only about mothers and not about fathers. By doing this, media make parenting central to how we think about women and peripheral to how we think about men.

Regulate Images of Women and Men

Acting as gatekeepers, media regulate the images of men and women that reach us. In turn, this can affect our views of what women and men are supposed to be, feel, think, and do. In regulating images of gender, media underrepresent women as

---

EXPLORING GENDERED LIVES *The Geena Davis Institute*

When actress Geena Davis was watching TV with her young daughter, she was stunned by how few female characters there were. Wanting strong role models for her daughter and other young girls, Davis persuaded the Annenberg School for Communication and Journalism to undertake the largest ever study of gender representations in film and TV. The Annenberg study found that there is one female character for every three male characters (the same ratio as in 1946) and females make up a mere 17% of characters in group scenes. These findings led to the establishment of the Geena Davis Institute at the Annenberg School. The Institute's goals are research, education, and advocacy for gender equity in media representations.

Visit the Geena Davis Institute at **http://www.thegeenadavisinstitute.org /index.php**

---

well as minorities, and they portray both sexes primarily in stereotypical ways that reflect and reproduce conventional views of gender.

Underrepresent Women and Minorities Although women outnumber men in the population, media do not give them equal visibility, particularly as substantive characters. The Geena Davis Institute, which studies gender representations in media states bluntly, "Statistically, there has been little forward movement for girls in media in six decades. For nearly 60 years, gender inequality on screen has remained largely unchanged and unchecked" (Gender in Media, 2012).

Whether it is prime-time TV, children's cartoons, or newscasts, males outnumber females. Roughly 70% of major characters in top-grossing films are males (Jamieson, More, Lee, Busse, & Romer, 2008; Smith, Granados, Choueiti, Erickson, & Noyes, 2010). Despite exceptions such as Alicia Florrick in *The Good Wife*, the majority of women characters on television shows are depicted in interpersonal and secondary roles (Butsch, 2011; Merskin, 2011; Sharp, 2011). Even supposedly liberated TV women such as those in *Sex and the City* focus more on fashion and relationships than on careers or political and social issues (Gerhard, 2011; Lorie, 2011).

Women are rarely presented as authorities in news programming. Males make up 66% of quoted material in newspapers and 75% of sources on major news shows (Farhi, 2012). Further, even on issues where it would be reasonable to think women have more expertise than men—birth control, abortion, and Planned Parenthood—men are the primary sources. Women make up less than one-third of the sources for stories on women's rights (Farhi, 2012). The lack of inclusion of qualified women sources was glaringly obvious after the 9/11 attacks. The ranking member of the Senate Subcommittee on Aviation Operations, Safety, and Security, Kay Bailey Hutchison, was not asked to appear once on a news show. Neither was Nancy Pelosi, the highest ranking Democrat on the House Intelligence Committee.

Media also underrepresent and often negatively portray minorities. Analysis of popular G-rated movies from 1990 to 2005 showed that 85.5% of characters were white, 4.8% were black, and 9.7% were of all other ethnicities combined (Smith & Cook, 2006). Black characters are featured more in television programs, although they are too often portrayed as lazy or criminal (Dixon, 2006; Ramasubramanian, 2010). Similarly, mass media underrepresent Asian Americans, Native Americans, and Hispanics (Stroman & Dates, 2008). Asian women are too often portrayed either as silent and exotic or as ruthless and evil while Asian men are typically portrayed as asexual and either subordinate or villainous (Balaji & Worawongs, 2010; Zhang, 2010).

Portray Men Stereotypically

The majority of men on prime-time television are independent, strong, aggressive, and in charge. Television programming for all ages disproportionately depicts men, particularly white, heterosexual men, as serious, confident, competent, and powerful (Walsh & Ward, 2008). Popular films such as *Drive*, *Thor*, and *The Fast and the Furious* (the whole series) present extreme stereotypes of masculinity: hard, tough, independent, sexually aggressive, unafraid, violent, totally in control of all emotions, and—above all—in no way feminine. Media also portray males as sexually active yet seldom represent them as taking responsibility for sexual safety or pregnancies (Butsch, 2011; Hust, Brown, & L'Engle, 2008; L'Engle & Jackson, 2008).

Equally interesting is how males are *not* typically portrayed. The most obvious misrepresentation is the scarcity of nonwhite men and nonwhite versions of masculinity. With the exception of hip-hop and rap music, white masculinity remains the norm—the unspoken and unquestioned standard for all men. Also, men are seldom shown nurturing others or doing housework. There has been little media effort to accurately portray men's increasing involvement in home life and child care.

Yet, traditional representations of men are not the whole story. Media offer some more complex portrayals of men—portrayals in which male characters combine qualities traditionally associated with masculinity and qualities traditionally associated with femininity or in which characters do not fit neatly into any of the existing gender-sexuality categories. Spiderman is kind and gentle when not ousting evildoers. Tom Hanks played a loving father in *Extremely Loud and Incredibly Close*; the three men in TNT's *Men of a Certain Age* support each other in dealing with emotional issues (Steinberg, 2011); males in *Glee* and *The Big Bang Theory* deal with emotional issues and friendship; and the Jonas Brothers and Justin Bieber embody a version of masculinity that is not afraid of feelings and relationships; in his video "Retrospect for Life," Common showed a young, pregnant black woman who faced single motherhood until the father returned to stay with her. In focusing on a gay man who appears normatively masculine in all ways except his sexual orientation, Carly Rae Jepsen's video, *Call Me Maybe*, forwards nontraditional images of both gay sexuality and desirable masculinity. And in 2012, Frank Ocean, an African-American rap artist with strong links to the R&B traditions, offered a stunningly ambiguous, fluid image of sexuality.

As important as alternative images of men are, they are exceptions in mass media. Media scholars Deborah Borisoff and Jim Chesebro (2011) report that the version of masculinity that predominates in films and music features "social control and domination by force, a power orientation, and physical strength and determination as the means to achieve social status and prestige" (p. 77).

Portray Women Stereotypically

Media continue to portray girls and women primarily in ways consistent with traditional stereotypes. Media show female characters shopping, grooming, being emotional, talking about and flirting with men, being sexual, and engaging in domestic activities (Smith et al., 2010; Walsh & Ward, 2008). Even when films or television programs feature strong, competent women characters such as those on *Law and Order*, they are usually very attractive, heterosexual, and sensitive to others and relationship dynamics. Also there is an increasing trend for media to portray women and even young girls in highly sexualized ways (Gender in Media, 2012).

Like media representations of men, those of women tend to assume that whiteness is both the norm and the ideal. In media for adults, depictions of black women often rely on negative stereotypes of mammies, jezebels, matriarchs, and welfare mothers (Brooks & Hébert, 2006). Media's preference for white norms for female attractiveness explains why many black women in advertising and programming have light skin and straight hair. Asian women and Latinas are usually represented as exotic and sexualized (Brooks & Hébert, 2006; Zhang, 2010). Amy Hasinoff's (2008) analysis of *America's Next Top Model* provides further evidence of media's normalization of whiteness. Hasinoff found that judges described women of color as having "an exotic look" or "an urban vibe," but described white women as "classic" and "American" (p. 334). In *Liquorice*, rapper Azealia Banks critiques such fetishized fantasies of black women.

The most traditional stereotype of woman is sex object, and that continues to dominate media. Highly sexual portrayals of women and, increasingly, girls of all races pervade programming, advertising, and music videos (Brooks & Hébert, 2006; Geena Davis Institute, 2010; Walsh & Ward, 2008). The feminine ideal is young, extremely thin (Harrison, 2008; Smith et al., 2010), preoccupied with appearance, men, and shopping.

JILL

I hate reading magazines or watching TV anymore. All they tell me is what's wrong with me and what I should do to fix it. I think my butt is too big; my roommate has decided hers is too little. Doesn't anybody have a butt that is right? Same for breasts. I wonder if I should have breast enlargement surgery. It sounds stupid, but I keep thinking that I would look better and be more popular. I pluck my eyebrows and wax my legs and streak my hair. I wonder if it will ever be okay for women to look like they really look!

Media's sexualization of women and girls has reached new levels (Gender in Media, 2012; Newsome, 2011). Even animated films feature female characters with impossibly small waists and large breasts (King, Lugo-Lugo, & Bloodsworth-Lugo, 2011). Animated films and other films aimed at children are "teaching machines" through which children learn about race, gender, and sexuality (King et al., 2011). Ironically, even as media encourage girls to model themselves after hypersexualized female characters, media also send the message that girls and women—and not boys and men—are responsible for consequences of sexual activity (Butsch, 2011; Hust et al., 2008; L'Engle & Jackson, 2008).

Makeover reality shows are especially blatant in extolling stereotyped images of attractiveness in women ("The Big Reveal," 2009). Judges on *America's Next Top*

Model lavish praise on anorexic contestants and call normal-sized contestants "plus sized." Makeover shows shine the spotlight on women who are willing to undergo multiple cosmetic surgeries to meet unrealistic and unhealthy ideals for feminine beauty (Weber, 2009). The message for women is clear: Your worth is based on your attractiveness. If you aren't gorgeous, then it's your job to make yourself over until you are (Bodey & Wood, 2009; Newsome, 2011; Weber, 2009).

An example of media's gender stereotyping comes from news coverage of the 9/11 attacks on America. There were approximately three male victims for every one female victim, but media gave far more coverage, especially visual, to female victims. Why? Because showing women victims conformed to social perceptions of women as passive victims, whereas showing men as victims would be inconsistent with social perceptions of men. Media also showed women grieving, mourning, and emoting. On the other hand, media virtually erased women's acts of heroism immediately following the 9/11 attacks. Women were involved in rescuing and providing medical help to victims, but they were nearly absent in coverage of the heroism displayed by Americans following the attacks (Faludi, 2007).

Media juxtapose images of "good" and "bad" women to dramatize differences in the consequences that befall good and bad women. "Good women" are pretty, deferential, faithful, and focused on home and family. Subordinate to men, they are usually cast as victims, angels, martyrs, and loyal helpmates and they tend to enjoy good lives. Cinderella wins the Prince because she is a beautiful, passive, "good" woman.

"Bad" women appear as the witch and evil stepmother in children's stories and programming and as the bitch, slut, and iron maiden in adult media. Bad women usually come to unhappy ends—they die, are banished into the black forest, or simply disappear. The mean stepmother loses because she is a bad woman.

In recent years, media have featured some women characters that depart from tradition. For instance, Alicia Florrick is strong and powerful in *The Good Wife*, and the women on *Law and Order* and *The Closer* are fierce and able. Turning to media for children and young adults, Princess Merida, the first central female character in a Pixar film, and Katniss in *Hunger Games* are resourceful archers and passionate, highly competent people. Whereas Disney princesses have historically passively awaited rescue by males, the new princesses have the self-confidence and skills to rescue themselves (Alexander, 2012). These images of women are a

AP Photo/Disney/Pixar

Media often combine traditional and progressive images of gender such as strength and sexuality in a female character.

departure from traditional media stereotypes in some ways. And yet, Florrick, Katniss, Princess Merida, and the women on *Law and Order* and *The Closer* are white, slender, pretty, and sexy. What at first appear to be radically different images of women are still entwined with some very familiar, very traditional images.

Gendered Images in Advertising

The stereotypical portrayals of women and men we've discussed appear not only in films, games, and programs but also in advertising. For several reasons, advertising's influence on our views of gender may be even more powerful than that of programmed media content (Berger, 2011; Kilbourne, 2010). First, advertisements on TV, in magazines, on billboards, on the Internet, and so forth are repeated multiple times, so we are exposed repeatedly to the messages. Second, a majority of ads emphasize visual images, which we tend to analyze less critically than verbal claims. Third, advertising can affect us significantly because we think we're immune to it. Yet, research suggests differently—ads do affect what people purchase and what they consider attractive, feminine, masculine, and so forth. We buy not just products but also the images that advertisers teach us to associate with products (Berger, 2011; Kilbourne, 2007, 2010).

Consistent with traditional views of masculinity, advertising generally portrays men as independent, successful, engaged in activities, and strong. The men in ads tend to be tall and muscular, and they are shown as being in control. Men's dominance is also emphasized by positioning. In commercials and print ads, men are usually shown positioned above women, and women are more frequently pictured in varying degrees of undress (Geena Davis Institute, 2010). Such nonverbal cues represent men as powerful and women as vulnerable and submissive. The message to men is that this is the ideal of masculinity. These unrealistic images can contribute to negative self-images for men with normal bodies and to extreme, sometimes dangerous behaviors aimed at achieving the false ideals.

KALEB

What burns me up is those programs and commercials that show men as absolute idiots. One of the worst is that one where the mother gets sick, and the kids and husband just fall apart without her to fix meals and do laundry. Give me a break. Most guys can do the basic stuff just as well as women, and I'm tired of seeing them made into jokes anytime they enter a nursery or kitchen.

The dominance of males who are shown in ads is paralleled by the authority of men who are not shown, but are heard as the voices of authority. For example, women do more housework than men, so presumably they know more about the products for cleaning. Yet Mr. Clean tells them how to keep their homes spotless. In many commercials for laundry detergent and bathroom cleaning supplies a man's voice is used to explain the superiority of the product that is being sold. Male **voice-overs** reinforce the cultural view that men are authorities and women depend on men to tell them what to do.

REGINA

The ad that just kills me is the one where a woman is cleaning her carpet with whatever product is being advertised—something you sprinkle on your rug and then vacuum up. This woman is dancing around with her vacuum and seems deliriously happy—like this is what she most loves to do in the world. We may do cleaning, but only a total bimbo would get ecstatic about it. That ad makes women look silly and stupid and trivial.

Central to advertising is sexual objectification of women. Women, usually with minimum clothes and in highly sexual poses, are used to sell everything from jeans to fishing line (Kilbourn, 2010; Zimmerman & Dahlberg, 2008). The women in the ads have faces, bodies, and hair that are impossible for 99% of women. By linking unrealistic images of women with products, advertisers try to convince women that the product will make them like the women in the ads. At the same time, ads try to convince men that if they buy the right car, the sexy woman shown in ads will be sitting next to them in it.

Advertising plays a key role in promoting appearance and pleasing others as foci of women's lives. Advertising tells women to color their hair, lose weight, and get rid of wrinkles. It warns them that their legs must be smooth, nails must be flawlessly manicured, and shoes must be sexy. And it advises them to look adoringly at men, to live for men's gaze, and not to look too powerful. The implicit promise of ads is that if women use the right products and imitate the models' poses, they will be irresistible. All that stands between being attractive and living the life of her dreams is a woman's commitment to fix, improve, repair, rejuvenate, disguise, and correct some or all parts of her appearance and personality.

The influence of ads is more subtle when ads don't stand out because they are blurred with content. One way this happens is when an advertiser pays for an ad in

EXPLORING GENDERED LIVES Miss Representation

Jennifer Newsome set out to make a documentary film that links media's misrepresentations of women to the underrepresentation of women in positions of power and influence. The film provides an informed, stunning critique of media (both content and advertising) that encourages girls and women to focus on appearance and pleasing men rather than achieving real power in their lives. In 2011, she premiered her film, *Miss Representation*, at Sundance in 2011. A showing at prestigious Sundance would be an unbeatable triumph for most filmmakers, but it was just the start of *Miss Representation's* phenomenal success.

Since the showing at Sundance, *Miss Representation* has attracted over 50,000 Facebook fans and over 2,000 social action partners from as far away as Israel. Followers receive weekly action alerts on how to spread the message, from calling out sexist Super Bowl ads on social media under the hashtag #notbuyingit or talking to men in their lives about the social impact of the *Sports Illustrated Swimsuit Edition*.

The film is in such demand that online services listed it as "long wait" for months after the DVD was released. Copies of the film have been shown in venues ranging from classes to the World Bank headquarters and Britain's House of Parliament.

Learn more about the film and activism associated with it by visiting: **http://www.missrepresentation.org/**

a magazine, and, in return, the magazine gives **complimentary copy**—one or more articles that increase the market appeal of its product (Turner, 1998). A soup company that places an ad might be given a three-page story on how to prepare meals using that brand of soup. A second way in which advertising and content are blurred is **product placement**, showing or mentioning a particular brand or product in a show, story, film, or other form of media. For example, red glasses with the Coca-Cola logo are in front of the judges on *American Idol*.

If complimentary copy and product placement blur the line between advertising and content, **immersive advertising** completely erases the line. Immersive advertising incorporates a product or brand into actual storylines in books, television programs, and films (Lamb & Brown, 2006). For instance, Naomi Johnson (2007, 2010, 2011) critically analyzed romance novels marketed to young girls. She found that storylines in series such as *A List* and *Gossip Girl* revolved around buying products such as La Perla lingerie and Prada bags and relying on services to glamorize the face and body. The characters' identities were defined by particular products and services.

Prevalent in media of all types are images of desirable men as strong, aggressive, and dominant and of desirable women as young, thin, sexual, and vulnerable. Whereas men are seldom shown nude or partially nude, women routinely are (Gender in Media, 2012). Women appearing as sex objects and men appearing as sexual aggressors are common in many music videos and video games (think Lara Croft). Winning in some of the most popular video games requires violence, including violence against women (Ivory, 2008). In carrying to extremes the stereotyped images of masculinity as aggressive and femininity as passive, these portrayals encourage us to see violence as erotic.

Mainstream hip-hop, rap, and especially gangsta rap also carry messages about relationships between women and men. They most often portray women as sex

EXPLORING GENDERED LIVES   *Is Censorship the Answer?*

Should we ban violent, misogynistic media that celebrate violence against women? Even those who are most outraged by the objectification and sexism of media seldom advocate censorship. The U.S. Constitution provides strong protections of freedom of speech, and for good reason. The problem with censoring is that somebody decides what all of us can watch, hear, and see. Who has the right to make this decision for all of us?

A better answer may be to demand that media offer us multiple, diverse images of women and men. Instead of banning what we don't like, perhaps we work to enlarge the range of ways in which people and relationships are portrayed. Acting on this idea, Marta Lamas in Mexico founded Debate Feminista, a periodical that provides alternatives to mainstream South American views of gender (Navarro, 2005).

Under what conditions, if any, would you support censorship of media?

objects—frequently only particular body parts instead of whole women—and portray men as egocentric, insensitive abusers of women (Collins, 2007). Along with the disrespect of women, much of rap and gangsta rap glorifies violence. The glorification of violence is evident in the title of 50 Cent's album, *The Massacre*; it's apparent in gang-style rivalries that resulted in the deaths of Tupac Shakur and Notorious B.I.G. Patricia Hill Collins (2007) notes that the "pimp-playa-bitch-ho" representations "encourage youth who listen to rap music, watch hip-hop music videos and chase the latest hip-hop fashions to think of themselves in these terms" (p. 74).

TIFFANY

It makes black guys angry when I say it, but I think gangsta rap is totally sexist and destructive. Some of my girlfriends say they like rap and don't take the anti-woman lyrics personally. The way I see it, though, calling women bitches and whores is as hateful as you can get. It totally disses women. If black men talk that way about black women, how can we respect ourselves or expect others to?

Motivate Us to Consume

Media encourage us to consume. In fact, some media analysts say that the primary purpose of media is to convince us we need to own more things, buy more products and services, spend, spend, spend. Television, films, music, the Internet, and advertising in all of those media, encourage us to think that owning the right things will make us sexy, cool, and desirable. If we buy certain clothes, we'll look sexy. If we drink certain drinks, we'll be cool. If we undergo certain surgeries, we'll be beautiful. If we shop in certain stores, we'll be with it.

When we see perfect bodies in magazines and on television, we may feel our body is not good enough. When we watch *Extreme Makeover*, we witness someone being transformed from ordinary looking to extraordinary looking, and we learn it's possible (and good) to transform ourselves. Advertising plays on that insecurity

EXPLORING GENDERED LIVES   *Hip-Hop without the Misogyny*

"I love hip-hop, but it upsets me that young boys treat girls like objects. I feel like I don't have a voice," said 17-year-old Tempestt Young (Dawson, 2005, p. 18). So she became a key organizer for the 2005 Feminism and Hip-Hop Conference, which was attended by more than 2,000 people, including music industry professionals. Young is just one of many young black women who have decided to change the game in hip-hop (Morgan, 1999).

Young is not alone. In 2005, *Essence*, a leading magazine aimed at blacks, announced it was sponsoring a year-long campaign called "Take Back the Music" to challenge and change the antiwoman stance of much rap music (Childress, 2005). Women students at historically black Spelman College chimed in by voting male rap artist Nelly as "Misogynist of the Month." The women had long resented the antiwoman attitudes in his songs, but it was the last straw when he released "Tip Drill," an urban slang term for a woman who has an attractive body but an unattractive face (Farrell, 2004). Al Sharpton added his support by asking the FCC to ban rappers who disrespect women (Childress, 2005). Many of those who protest rappers like Nelly point to progressive rappers such as Mos Def and Common who, they say, "resist dick-swinging bravado" ("Ms. Musings," 2004, p. 13). Queen Latifah insists that rap can maintain its strong, distinctive character without demeaning women.

Do you think rap and gangsta rap music can maintain its character without disparaging women?

by telling us that if we buy a certain product or have a certain procedure, we will look better. If a man drinks Michelob, he'll get the gorgeous woman that is with the man in the Michelob ad. If women buy clothes at Abercrombie and Fitch, we'll look like the cover girl on *Marie Claire.*

The whole purpose of advertising is to convince us that buying whatever is advertised will make us happier, more attractive, more successful, and so forth (McRobbie, 2009). It's understandable to wish we weighed a little more or less, had better-developed muscles, and never had pimples or cramps. What is not reasonable is to regard normal, functional bodies as unacceptable or defective. Yet, this is precisely the perception cultivated by the predominant media portrayals of women and men.

Buying products to improve ourselves is not restricted to women. Media also tell men that they are deficient but can fix that by buying something. The body-building trend has created unrealistic and unhealthy ideals for masculine bodies. The desire to have a very muscular body appears to be linked to the increasing abuse of steroids among men. Although media's idealization of extreme musculature and strength is not the only cause of steroid use, we should not dismiss the influence of portrayals of muscle-bound men as ideal (Lindgren & Lélièvre, 2009).

Normal changes in men's sexual vigor are also represented as problems to be solved by buying the right products. In recent years, Viagra, Levitra, and Cialis have become blockbuster drugs, making millions for the companies that can solve the "problem." The "problem," of course, was not a problem until drug companies decided they could make money by transforming normal changes in male sexual vitality into problems.

Media have convinced millions of American women that what every reputable medical source considers "normal body weight" is really abnormal and cause for severe dieting (Levin & Kilbourne, 2008; National Institute of Mental Health,

2010). Similarly, facial lines, which both women and men acquire, now can be removed so that we look younger—a prime goal in a culture that glorifies youth.

You might be surprised to know that only in the last century has women's underarm and leg hair been viewed as unattractive. Beginning in 1915, a sustained marketing campaign persuaded women that underarm hair was unsightly and socially incorrect. (The campaign against leg hair came later.) *Harper's Bazaar*, an upscale magazine, launched the crusade against underarm hair with a photograph of a woman whose raised arms revealed clean-shaven armpits. Underneath the photograph was this caption: "Summer dress and modern dancing combine to make necessary the removal of objectionable hair" (Adams, 1991). By 1922, razors and depilatories were firmly ensconced in middle America. In recent years, the hair removal campaign has targeted men—promoting the clean (usually waxed) chest as the ideal of masculinity. With that, companies expand the market of people who will pay for products and services that increase their profits.

To achieve constructed and arbitrary ideals, many women continue to endure surgery that sometimes leads to disfigurement and loss of sensation. Surgeries to enlarge breasts, remove fat, and reshape faces are common among women. In addition, surgeries to conform to white ideals of beauty are also on the rise. In 2006, one of the most popular plastic surgeries for Asians was surgery to transform eyes from ovals, typical of Asians, to orbs, typical of Caucasians. For African Americans, surgery to make the nose less broad was the number-one procedure (Cognard-Black, 2007).

Media images encourage us to measure up to impossible ideals. When we fail, as inevitably we must, we feel bad about our bodies and ourselves. Accepting media messages about our bodies and ourselves, however, is not inevitable: Each of us has the ability to reflect on the messages and resist those we consider inappropriate or harmful.

CHRISTI

When I used to diet, I remember thinking that I was in control. I believed what all the ads said about taking charge of myself, exerting control. But I was totally not in control. The advertisers and the companies making diet products were in control. So was society with the idea that "you can't be too thin" and that it's more important for girls to look good (read "thin") than to feel good (read "not hungry"). Society and its views of women were in control, not me. I was totally a puppet who was just doing what they told me to do.

Consequences of Gendered Media

The images that media advance are not innocent; they have consequences. Throughout our discussion of media's effects on people, we've hinted at harms. Let's now look more closely at two specific ways that media's unrealistic images of gender can affect us adversely.

Normalize Unrealistic Standards

Media's unrealistic images of men, women, and relationships encourage us to see ourselves, by comparison, as inadequate. Media, including advertising, bombard us with unrealistic images of women, men, and relationships—images that few real people can ever achieve but that nevertheless make us feel less good about ourselves. Regardless of how many products we buy and how many surgeries we have, few of us are going to look like Eva Mendes, Beyonce, Tatum Channing, or Chris Hemsworth. In fact, even those celebrities don't really look like they appear in magazines and on-screen.

Because media portrayals of relationships are also unrealistic, they are flawed standards for assessing our own relationships. Most of us encounter problems in our relationships that cannot be solved in 30 minutes (minus time for commercial interruptions). Most of us will not be able to pursue a demanding career and still be as relaxed and available to family and friends as media characters are. And most of us will not have a rich, charming, and incredibly attractive man or woman fall in love with us. Yet the portrayals in media create expectations, and if we have unrealistic expectations of what relationships are and can be, we are likely to be dissatisfied with real, healthy relationships.

Media efforts to pathologize natural bodies can be very dangerous. As we have seen in previous chapters, the emphasis on excessive thinness contributes to severe and potentially lethal dieting and eating disorders. Nonetheless, most of the top female models are skeletal. Seeing anorexic models as the ideal motivates many college women to diet excessively in an effort to force their bodies to fit a socially constructed ideal that is unrealistic and unhealthy. Dangers—including heart attack, stroke, and liver disease—also exist for men who use steroids or diet in an effort to meet the ideal masculine form promoted by media.

You might think that we know the difference between fantasy and reality, and we don't use media images as models for our own lives. Research, however, suggests that the unrealistic ideals in popular media do influence how many of us feel about ourselves. For centuries, the people of Fiji were a food-loving society. People enjoyed eating and considered fleshy bodies attractive in both women and men. All that changed in 1995, when television stations in Fiji began to broadcast American television programs. Within three years, many Fijian women began to diet and developed eating disorders. When asked why they were trying to lose weight, young Fijian women cited very thin characters on American television programs as their model (Becker, Burwell, Gilman, Herzog, & Hamburg, 2002).

Normalize Violence against Women

Gendered violence is so pervasive that all of Chapter 12 is devoted to it. Yet, it would be irresponsible not to mention violence in the context of media. Although it would be naïve to claim that media *cause* violence, there is evidence that violence in media contributes to increasing violence in real life. Research shows that, after watching sexually explicit films that degrade women (not just sexually explicit films), men become more dominant toward women with whom they interact

(Mulac, Jansma, & Linz, 2003). Studies have also shown that men who watch music videos and pro wrestling are more likely to believe that forcing a partner to have sex is sometimes okay (Browne & Hamilton-Giachritis, 2005; Ensslin & Muse, 2011; Kaestle, Halpern, & Brown, 2007). When we continually see violence in media, we may come to view it as a normal and increasingly acceptable as part of ordinary life (Kilbourne, 2010; Yao, Mahood, & Linz, 2010).

RYAN

Some pretty wild stuff goes down in online worlds. There are virtual rapes like when one avatar asks another to go swimming and then forces sex or tries to—sometimes exits the game. I can't decide if virtual rape or assault or whatever is really rape or just part of the game.

Video games push the envelope of mediated violence because they invite players not just to watch violence (as with films and TV) but to engage virtually in violence, including violence against women (Bugeja, 2010; Ivory, 2008; Romer, 2008). In *Grand Theft Auto: San Andreas*, players earn points by having sex with prostitutes and then killing them. Within the game was a hidden scene in which players could use a joystick to control a character that is having sex with a nude woman. When a website published instructions for unlocking the scene, the video's rating went immediately from M (Mature) to AO (Adults Only)—but not before more than six million copies had been sold (Levy, 2005).

Several theories about gender development offer insight into the relationship between mediated violence and real-life violence. Social learning theory claims we engage in behaviors that are rewarded and avoid behaviors that are punished. What happens when boys and men watch music videos that show men being rewarded for exploiting and violating women? Cognitive development theory focuses on our use of role models on which to base our behaviors and identities. If girls and women watch programs and videos in which women allow or invite violence against them, are they more likely to think they should accept violence to be desirable women? Symbolic interactionism highlights the importance of social views in shaping individuals' identities. When disrespect toward women and "pimp-ho" versions of male–female relationships pervade music videos, is it any wonder some of those views may get inside our own heads?

The culture that is part of some gaming communities supports psychological violence. At the 2012 Cross Assault video game tournament, Miranda Pakozdi was subjected to what she considered more than the usual "trash talk" that goes along with gaming. She was asked, on camera, what size bra she wore and told to take off her shirt. Her team's webcam focused directly on her breasts for extended periods and her coach leaned over her neck to smell her. She finally forfeited when she overheard a man at the tournament say that sexual harassment is part of the community of fight gamers (O'Leary, 2012).

In sum, media affect us by setting agenda, regulating images of men and women, and motivating us to consume. Yet we also use media, especially social media, for our own reasons and to achieve our own purposes. The final section of this chapter examines how we use social media.

Gender and Social Media

Social media are intimately related to gender and gender issues. Although we still interact with traditional media, most of us also engage in networked individualism (Rainie & Wellman, 2012), which is the use of social media to share experiences, exchange information, educate ourselves, comment on people, events, and issues, and organize group efforts to address gender issues.

Gendered Use of Social Media

There are some differences in how women and men, in general, tend to use social media. Boys and men tend to use media for instrumental purposes more than girls and women do. Matthew texts Carter if he wants to go out to dinner. Carter texts back "yes" and agrees on a time and place. Then they stop texting, having accomplished the task. Boys and men also use social media—games and virtual spaces—more than women do.

Girls and women are also more likely to see phone conversations and texting as ways to massage relationships. Vanessa calls Natalie to see if Natalie wants to go out to dinner. They talk for 5 minutes before Vanessa gets around to asking about dinner. They agree when and where to meet, then talk another 10 minutes before hanging up. Carolyn IMs Michelle to ask what Michelle's doing; she skypes Harrison to let him know she's coming to his game; she texts Daniel to tell him she saw a great film that he would like. Each of these texts conveys the relationship-level meaning that Carolyn cares and is thinking about her friends.

Functions of Social Media

Social media are so seamlessly woven into our lives that we rely on them for everything from checking the weather to shopping to playing games and staying in touch with friends. Clearly, a majority of online activity is unrelated or only indirectly related to gender. However, there are some important intersections between social media and gender. In this section, we'll discuss four functions of social media that are related to gendered attitudes, identities, and activism. We use social media to (1) to network, (2) learn and share information, (3) hold others accountable, and (4) engage in activism (Cox, 2013). As we discuss these functions of social media, keep in mind that they often overlap as when learning about issues motivates activism.

Social Networking

One of the most popular uses of social media is networking. Girls and women are more inclined than boys and men to regard the online environment as a resource for creating and enriching relationships. In their online communities, girls and women share stories and develop friendships (Miller, 2008; Mitra, 2010; Rosenbloom, 2008), and they engage in video chatting more than boys (Teens & Online Video, 2012).

Girls and women are also more likely than boys to use social media as a venue for self-development. Teen girls use their blogs and pages on social networking sites to talk about issues such as pressures to be skinny, drink (or not), have sex (or not), and dress particular ways (Bodey, 2009; Bodey & Wood, 2009). As girls work out what they think and want to do in their online communities, they count on comments from others to clarify their own thinking and gain confidence in their ability to reject gender norms they find troubling.

Yet there is a downside to social networks: They can be—and too often are—used for **cyberbullying**, which includes text messages, comments, rumors, embarrassing pictures, videos, and fake profiles that are meant to hurt another person and are sent by email or posted on social networking sites. Social networking sites such as Facebook have not done much to develop anti-bullying policies; in fact, they encourage subscribers to give up privacy (Bazelon, 2013). According to a recent report (Burney, 2012), 43% of teenagers are subject to some form of cyberbullying. For LGBTQ (Lesbian, Gay Bisexual, Transexual, and Queer) teenagers the percentage is even higher: 53% (Burney, 2012).

Not all boys and girls are equally likely to be victims of cyberbullying (or f2f bullying). Girls, who are victims tend to be more physically developed than others in their age cohort, are perceived as less attractive than peers, or are perceived as more attractive than peers (Anderson, 2011). Girls who are regarded as less attractive are ridiculed for not measuring up to feminine ideals while girls who are very attractive are bullied out of jealousy. One of the more common tactics for bullying girls is to spread rumors that they are sluts.

Boys, especially nonwhite boys, who are perceived as feminine are most likely to be victims of cyberbullying (Anderson, 2011, Burney, 2012). Collapsing distinctions between gender and sexuality, and reflecting both sexist and homophobic attitudes, bulliers belittle them for not being sufficiently masculine. In fact, positing comments that a boy is gay is a common form of cyberbullying.

Online bullying and harassment are not inconsequential. Many 7th to 12th graders report having trouble sleeping, being sick, and not wanting to go to school (Anderson, 2011;). More serious consequences are also possible.

- 15-year-old Amanda threw herself in front of a bus when she could face no more of the cruel posts on her Facebook wall.
- 13-year-old Rachel hanged herself after an anonymous text saying she was a slut was circulated through her school.
- 14-year-old Jamey killed himself after an anonymous text saying he was gay became a widely spread rumor.
- 15-year-old Phoebe took the advice of a cyberbullier who told her to hang herself.
- 14-year-old Megan committed suicide when information she confided to a person who posed as a friend was turned against her online.
- 18-year-old Tyler jumped off a bridge after his roommate Ravi urged friends and Twitter followers to watch via his hidden webcam Tyler having sex with a man.

Cyberbullying differs from f2f bullying in two key ways. First, it can be and often is perpetrated anonymously. Through fake accounts and other online maneuvers, an individual can post horribly hurtful messages and photos without ever being accountable for her or his actions. When asked why people were so cruel online, one young boy explained, "You can be as mean as you want on Facebook" (Hoffman, 2010, p. A12). Second, cyberbullying has no necessary stopping point. The school-yard bully pretty much stayed on the school yard. Thus, a victim could escape by going home or visiting a friend. Online bullying can follow the victim anywhere 24-7. It is unremitting.

Learning and Sharing Information

The online world has boundless sources of news and information about gender issues. For instance, strong interest in gender issues led online newspaper, Huffington Post, to create a section devoted to news for women (**http://www.huffingtonpost com/women/**), which offers everything from blogs on work–life balance and love to reports on women's health and perspectives on political issues and candidates. Many women who are interested in issues related to women's lives regularly check in with Jezebel (**http://jezebel.com/**) and Feministing (**http://feministing .com/**). College students across the United States have formed an informal online network to share information and strategize about sexual assault on campuses (Pérez-Peña, 2013).

The National Organization for Men against Sexism (**http://www.nomas.org/**) provides information on issues in men's lives as well as issues in women's lives that matter to men who care about women. Likewise, the National Organization for Women (**http://www.now.org/**) provides news on political matters relevant to gender equity.

In addition to sites, twitter updates and RSS feeds are ways to stay on top of information as it unfolds. Signing up to follow particular individuals allows you to get the latest buzz as soon as it's out. For example, Michael Kaukfman (@GenderEQ) blogs and tweets about issues in men's lives. Following Rachel Maddow (@maddow) keeps you tuned into her views on politics and politicians.

EXPLORING GENDERED LIVES *Challenging the Insecurity Factory*

In 2007, Anna Holmes had had enough of women's magazines that function as an "insecurity factory"—making women feel insecure about their bodies, clothes, and behaviors and then advising women to "fix" the insecurity by buying various products. Holmes decided to do something. She founded **Jezebel.com**, a women's interest blog, which criticizes digitally altered pictures that present unrealistic ideals of beauty, offers common sense advice on matters such as how to dress for internships, calls out sexism in media and in celebrities, and identifies inexpensive alternatives to products hyped in most women's magazines. With 37 million page views a month and about 200,000 distinct visitors each day, **Jezebel.com** has established its niche (Mascia, 2010).

There are also online communities that provide information and support related to specific issues. There online sites for people who have or are concerned about eating disorders (e.g., **http://www.healthfulchat.org/eating-disorders-chat-room .html**), male victims of sexual abuse (e.g., **http://www.rainn.org/get-information /types-of-sexual-assault/male-sexual-assault**), surviving rape (e.g., **http://www .aftersilence.org/**), and human rights relevant to gender (e.g., **http://www.ips.org /institutional/global-themes/human-rights-and-gender-issues/**).

Providing information about gender issues is not restricted to big organizations and high-profile reporters. Social media allows ordinary individuals to document what's happening in their communities and broadcast those reports (Cox, 2013). For instance, Ihollaback, is an online grassroots effort to end street harassment that you'll read more about in Chapter 12. On Ihollaback's site (**http://www.iholla back.org**), women who are harassed can post photos and stories, thereby documenting the harassment and the harasser.

Holding Others Accountable

Mass media have historically been voices against corrupt, immoral, or harmful actions by powerful interests. The long-airing *Sixty Minutes* television show often exposed corporate and political misconduct as have courageous journalists throughout history. Picking up this function of traditional media, social media have emerged as vital forces in holding corporations and other powerful interests accountable for sexism and gendered violence.

EXPLORING GENDERED LIVES *Watch Out for Sparks*

Eighth grader Julia Bluhm was sick of air-brushed, digitally altered photos of women in her *Seventeen* magazine. She sparked change by turning to her online network of activists at SPARK. It didn't take her long to get 84,000 signatures, and that led to a meeting with executives at *Seventeen* (Considine, 2012). Following the meeting, Ann Shoket, *Seventeen's* editor, announced that every member of the staff had signed a Body Peace Treaty in which they promise the magazine will "never change girls' body or face shapes" and will include exclusively images of "real girls and models who are healthy" (Haughney, 2012).

Two other Sparkers, 23-year-old Stephanie Cole and 22-year-old Bailey Shoemaker Richards, took issue with Lego's new line of products for girls called Friends, which included sets for building a hair salon and cupcake shop. They sent Lego a letter with 56,000

signatures, saying that Friends are "insulting and condescending" (Consandine, 2012). Lego is considering their objection.

SPARK is a girl-fueled activist group that works to end the sexualization of women and girls in media. In the SPARK community, girls 13 and older work together and partner with other organizations to develop and implement strategies to challenge media's hyper-sexualization of girls and women.

SPARK was started by college professors in 2010 to empower young girls to fight against the unrealistic images of girls and women that media create. Overseeing SPARK are experienced activists, who mentor the young girls and connect them with SPARK's network of 60-plus partners including Girls Inc., and NOW.

Visit SPARK at: **http://www.spark summit.com/**

Activism

Social communities are fertile ground for cultivating activism. A number of large and small national organizations use social media sites to get their messages to the public by creating their own pages and posting action alerts. The film, *Miss Representation*, which we discussed on page 240, was widely discussed on Facebook, and followers of the film received online action alerts telling them how they could participate in spreading the film's message.

An example of simultaneously cultivating activism is Amy Poehler's *Smart Girls at the Party* Series (**http://www.smartgirlsattheparty.com/**), which includes interviews with young feminists (some are under 5-years-old) who give a contemporary, cool face to girl power and gender equity.

Social media are ideal platforms for activism that challenges representations of women and men that we find unacceptable. For instance, the Super Bowl routinely features some ads that are sexist—sometimes demeaning men, sometimes women. Within days of the broadcast each year, viewers post satirical responses to them on YouTube. Each of these videos raises others' awareness and calls out the advertisers for sexism.

Social media allow fast organizing in response to fast-moving issues. An example of this happened in February, 2012. The Susan G. Komen for the Cure, the largest and best-funded breast cancer organization in the United States, announced it was defunding Planned Parenthood. Many people were outraged that a foundation, which pledged to support women's health, would stop funding Planned Parenthood, which provides breast cancer screening and other health services to women. The protest of the Komen Foundation's action happened online and it was fierce. The Komen Foundation was intensely criticized by high-profile women's groups, politicians and public health advocates. At the same time, individuals and group made record donations to Planned Parenthood to show support of its mission (Harris & Belluck, 2012). Within just a few days, Komen reversed its stand and announced it would continue funding Planned Parenthood; shortly thereafter three of its top executives resigned (Sun & Kliff, 2012).

As we have seen, social media allow us to communicate in multiple ways that are related to gendered attitudes, identities, and activism. We use social media to network, learn and share information, hold others accountable, and engage in activism.

SUMMARY

From children's cartoons to video games and online virtual communities, media influence how we perceive men and women, in general, and ourselves, in particular. The historical trend of emphasizing gender-stereotyped roles and images continues today and is sometimes challenged by alternative images of women, men, and relationships. Below the surface, however, most media—both content and advertising—continue to reflect traditional views of women and men. Media representations of gender foster unrealistic gender ideals in men and women, encourage us to pathologize normal human bodies and functions, and normalize violence against women.

Understanding the overt and subtle gender messages in media empowers us to be more critical consumers. As individuals and citizens, we have a responsibility to criticize media representations that demean men and women and that contribute to attitudes that harm us and our relationships. Social media have become a primary platform for education about media's unrealistic images of the sexes, holding corporate interests responsible for more accurate and healthy representations of women and men, and organizing political activism.

Media need you and me. If we refuse to buy their messages and products, they will change. In fact, they *have* changed in response to consumers' criticism and demands. Criticism of dangerously thin fashion models led to new standards that require models to have a body mass index that is within the healthy range. Responding to public demand, Nike launched a campaign that celebrated normal-sized bodies. Dove developed a line of ads that positively portrayed women of all ages, races, and sizes. *Seventeen* magazine promised to change how it represents girls when Julia Bluhm presented a petition signed by 84,000 young girls that *Seventeen* wants as subscribers. Changes such as these don't just happen. They happen when we demand them.

KEY TERMS

The terms following are defined in this chapter on the pages indicated, as well as in alphabetical order in the book's glossary, which begins on page 283. The text's companion website (**http://www.cengage.com/communication/wood/genderedlives11e**) also provides interactive flash cards and crossword puzzles to help you learn these terms and the concepts they represent.

agenda setting 233	*immersive advertising 240*
complimentary copy 240	*product placement 240*
cyberbullying 247	*third person effect 232*
gatekeeper 233	*voice-overs 239*

GENDER ONLINE

1. If you want to learn more about gender and media, or if you want to become active in working against media that devalue women, visit these websites:

   Media Watch: **http://www.mediawatch.com**

   Off Our Backs: **http://www.offourbacks.org**

   Girls, Women Plus Media Project: **http://www.mediaandwomen.org**

   The Geena Davis Institute: **http://www.thegeenadavisinstitute.org/index.php**

2. Visit this website: **http://www.genderads.com**. Does it help you understand how advertisers use gender ideals to sell products and images of how we are supposed to be?

3. If you'd like to learn more about cosmetic surgery to reshape eyelids, view this documentary: **http://www.rawstory.com/rawreplay/2011/02/western -eyes-asian-women-contemplate-eyelid-surgery/**

4. Watch Johanna Blakley's TED talk: Social Media and the End of Gender: **http://www.ted.com/talks/johanna_blakley_social_media_and_the_end_ of_gender.html**. Do you agree with her claim that social media is breaking down gender categories?

5. Online search terms: "third person effect," "gender and media," "agenda setting."

REFLECTION AND DISCUSSION

1. Some people think that the violence in some rap music and video games is harmless. Other people think it encourages, or normalizes, violence in real life. Where do you stand on this issue? Reread Ryan's commentary on page 245. Do you think virtual sexual assault is real assault of "just part of the game"?

2. Watch children's programming on Saturday morning. Are male characters more prominent than female characters? What differences, if any, do you see in the activities and appearances of male and female characters?

3. Bring print and online advertisements to class, and discuss the images of women, men, and relationships in them. Are they realistic? Are they healthy? What are your options as a consumer?

4. Watch prime-time coverage of sports on ESPN or another channel (during the Olympics, most channels have extensive sports programming). Make a record of how much time is devoted to women's and men's sports and how often reporters comment on male and female athletes' dress and appearance. Are the patterns you identify consistent with those discussed in this chapter?

5. You have just read about how social media can be used to challenge social views of gender, sex, and sexual orientation. Think about the ways that you personally use social media. Do you use them to inform your gender, to speak out, or for other reasons? Now imagine how you might engage social media to be part of shaping what gender means.

RECOMMENDED RESOURCES

1. **http://www.about-face.org** This is an excellent site for getting information and taking action. **About-face.org** is devoted to media literacy about gender and self-esteem. Among its features is an ever-changing list of "Top Ten Offenders," which shows ads that destructively stereotype women and men and, in some cases, condone violence toward women. About-Face provides the addresses of companies featured in each ad so you can contact the companies directly.

2. **http://www.genderads.com** This site offers education on how to analyze ads critically.

3. *Miss Representation.* This 90-minute documentary on the hypersexualized representations of girls and women in media premiered at the 2011 Sundance Festival. Jennifer Siebel Newsom is the writer, director, and producer.

The world is a dangerous place to live, not because of the people who are evil, but because of the people who don't do anything about it.

—ALBERT EINSTEIN

12

Gendered Power and Violence

Knowledge Challenge:

- How common are false reports of rape?
- Would victims of intimate partner violence be safer leaving abusive partners?
- What difference can individuals make in reducing gendered violence?
- In the United States, every nine seconds a woman is beaten by an intimate partner; at least three women are murdered by their husbands or boyfriends every day.
- In some countries, it is not uncommon for female fetuses to be aborted and for female infants to be neglected until they die.
- More than three million girls a year are subjected to genital surgery.
- Someone is sexually assaulted every two minutes in the United States.
- Although males experience sexual assault, they are unlikely to report it.

This chapter focuses on the distressing topic of gendered violence. In the pages that follow, we will discuss the nature and extent of gendered violence and identify social structures, practices, and attitudes that allow it. We will also ask how we can be part of reducing gendered violence in our communities and around the world.

The Social Construction of Gendered Violence

Many people explain gendered violence by saying that the perpetrators are sick individuals. It's true that isolated incidents of violence may occur because of individual pathologies. However, individual pathologies can't explain why violence is

253

pervasive and why it is disproportionately inflicted on certain groups. Widespread violence against particular groups reflects social views and values.

The Many Faces of Gendered Violence

What comes to mind when you hear terms such as *gendered violence* and *sexual violence*? Most people think of rape, intimate partner violence, and perhaps **sexual harassment**. That trilogy of abuses, however, doesn't include many forms of gendered violence. **Gendered violence** refers to physical, verbal, emotional, sexual, and visual brutality that is inflicted disproportionately or exclusively on members of one sex. In the following pages, we'll discuss seven forms of gendered violence.

Gender Intimidation

Gender intimidation occurs when members of one sex are treated in ways that make them feel humiliated, unsafe, or inferior because of their sex (Kramarae, 1992). All of us feel unsafe at times. Gender intimidation, however, exists when members of one sex are treated in ways that lead them to feel more vulnerable or unsafe than members of the other sex.

Gender intimidation includes lewd remarks made in public spaces. A number of women students at my university often take longer, less-direct routes around campus to avoid workers who assault them with sexual comments and suggestions. They have to alter their routines and schedules to avoid being intimidated as they walk to classes.

EXPLORING GENDERED LIVES *Hollaback!*

Tired of having strangers comment on your body? Hollaback! is a grassroots organization that started in New York City when seven women decided to use social networking and crowd sourcing to tackle the problem of street harassment. There are now Hollaback! sites in 12 international cities, and more are being planned. Hollaback! encourages victims of street harassment to shoot the harassers—with cameras. The photos can then be posted, along with the photographer's comments, on Holla-back!'s site: **http://www.ihollaback.org**.

Women in India came up with a similar response to street harassment. "Eve-teasing" is what Indians call street harassment, in which men whistle at, leer at, touch, and stalk women. Unwilling to continue tolerating Eve-teasing, a group of Indian women created Blank Noise— blank for the silence that has surrounded Eve-teasing; noise for breaking the silence. Blank Noise has developed several responses to Eve-teasing. One is posting "Unwanted" photos of perpetrators or telling stories on the action heroes site: **http://actionheroes.blanknoise .org/**. Another is "Did You Ask for It?," a collection of items of clothing worn by women who were Eve-teased. The fact that most of the items are very modest testifies that women's dress is not the cause of Eve-teasing (Girish, 2007).

<hr/>

I think gay-bashing is a kind of gender intimidation. I've been a victim of insults and really gross remarks just because I'm gay. I'll be just walking along minding my own business, and someone will shout "fag" at me or even come at me screaming, "We don't want any queers around here." When I go into bathrooms on campus, I usually see gay-bashing graffiti. I have to tolerate these hassles strictly because I'm gay. That makes it gender intimidation.

<hr/>

Tim's commentary highlights another form of gender intimidation: humiliating or disrespecting gays and trans people or people suspected of being gay or trans. The person becomes a target simply because others assume she or he is not straight.

Sexual Assault

Sexual assault is any sexual activity that occurs without the informed consent of at least one of the people involved. One type of sexual assault is rape, which will happen to one in six women and one in thirty-three men will be raped in their lifetimes (Statistics, 2009). Yet, what *rape* means isn't as clear-cut as you might think. For many years, marital rape was not recognized as a crime in the United States. It was assumed that once a woman married, she didn't have the right not to consent to sex with her husband. Some countries still don't recognize married women's right to not consent to sex with their husbands. Only in 2009 did Afghanistan change its laws so that married women do not have to consent to sex with their husbands (by law, married women still must do housework!) ("Law on Marital Rape Revised," 2009).

Since the 1920s, rape in the United States was defined as carnal knowledge of a female forcibly and against her will. According to this definition, a man who is forced to have sex with another man has not been raped nor has a woman who is forced to engage in oral sex. In 2012, the F.B.I. definition of rape was expanded to include male victims and non-vaginal violation. The 2012 definition of rape is the "penetration, no matter how slight, of the vagina or anus with any body part or object, or oral penetration by a sex organ of another person without the consent of the victim" (Savage, 2012, p. A10). This means that all forms of penetration of females and males are now defined as rape.

Sexual assault occurs whenever one person doesn't give **informed consent** for sexual activity. Informed consent can be given only by an adult who has normal mental abilities, who is not being coerced, and whose judgment is not impaired by alcohol, other drugs, or circumstances. Informed consent cannot be given by children.

Sexual assault is not confined to civilian contexts. In 2011, more than 24 women and 2 men filed a federal class-action lawsuit against the current and former Defense Secretaries. They claim that servicemen are allowed to get away with sexual abuse ranging from obscene verbal attacks to gang-rape. They also claim that victims are either involuntarily discharged or told to continue to serve with the men who violated them while those men are not even reprimanded. Current Defense Secretary Robert Gates has acknowledged that sexual assault is a substantial problem in the U.S. military (Hefling, 2011; Nocera, 2013).

When people think of rape, they think about strangers jumping out of bushes at night. But that's not how it usually happens. Most of the women in my victims' support group were raped by friends or dates—guys they knew and trusted. In some ways, that's worse because it makes you afraid to trust anyone.

Sexual assault is prevalent on college campuses. One-third of undergraduate women report one or more unwanted sexual interactions, ranging from kissing to intercourse, during a single year; one-half of college women in their senior year reported one or more unwanted sexual interactions during their college careers (Crown & Roberts, 2007). On college campuses, as elsewhere, most assaults, including rape, are not between strangers. In fact, 73% of rape victims know their assailant (Statistics, 2009). Kate Harris (2009, 2011) interviewed women who had engaged in nonconsensual sex with acquaintances or dates. She found that many of these women felt confused because they couldn't associate "rape" with friends. For that reason, they seldom called the nonconsensual sex "rape."

I think people blame rape victims because we like to think there was a reason that someone was raped. They were alone, or it was late at night, or they dressed suggestively, or they drank too much. If we can find a reason why someone was raped, then we think we're safe if we don't go out alone or drink too much or whatever. But really we should start teaching people how to not rape as opposed to how to not get raped. We have to educate ourselves and take a stand! Stop yourself the next time you call a girl a slut, or judge a girl for what she's wearing, or assume that a man isn't capable of feeling, or being an ally.

One reason that rapes are common at colleges and universities is the existence of what researchers call a campus "rape culture" (Burnett, Mattern, Herakova, Kahl, Tabola, & Bornsen, 2009; Sanday, 2007). Many people, including college students, believe rape myths (Burnett et al., 2009; Meyer, 2010; Yeater, Treat, Viken, & McFall, 2010) such as women say "no" when they mean "yes"; some women enjoy rape because it fulfills their sexual fantasies; men can't help themselves when they become aroused; and nice girls don't get raped (Burnett et al., 2009).

I went to a club with some friends, and we were dancing in a circle. I was wearing this great top that makes me feel really sexy and pretty. This guy I had met once pulled me out of the group and started to dirty dance. Then he groped me, my genitals. I backed off, and he said "What?" like he hadn't done anything wrong.

I know he violated me, but I can't help thinking that maybe I was "asking for it" because I was wearing a sexy outfit and all. I know my mother would say I was asking for it because I was dressed in a sexy way.

AUSTIN

What do girls expect if they go to a club where hookups happen, and they're wearing revealing clothes that are meant to excite and provoke guys, and they are dancing suggestively? It's like sending out an invitation to a guy. So why, when a guy accepts, do they blame him for responding to their invitation?

Saying that rape happens because of the way a woman is dressed or dances or where she goes is **blaming the victim**: holding a person responsible for the harm that another person has inflicted. The commentaries by Carrie and Austin offer examples of how both men and women, including women who are victims, can blame the victim.

In 2008, the United Nations officially designated rape a "weapon of war" after the release of a report by the humanitarian group, Refugees International, which documented the systematic use of rape as a means of ethnic cleansing in Darfur. The government-backed Janjaweed military routinely rape women without fear of consequence because Sudanese laws harshly punish women who have sex—even against their wills—outside of marriage (Boustany, 2007). In Zimbabwe, hundreds of women have been raped by opposition soldiers. Some of the rape victims are children who have not even reached puberty; others are pregnant women

EXPLORING GENDERED LIVES *Sexual Assault of Men*

Recent media stories have brought to light the extent to which boys and men are victims of sexual assault. On June 22, 2012, Penn State's Assistant Football coach, Jerry Sandusky, was found guilty of 45 counts of sexual abuse of 10 young boys over a 15-year period. Earlier the same month, The *New York Times* Magazine published the story of sexual abuse of both boys and girls that occurred at the very prestigious private Horace Mann School in New York City (Anderson, 2012; Kamil, 2012). And cases of Catholic priests' and bishops' abuses of young boys are constantly in the news.

In each of these cases, as in most cases of abuse of boys, the victims stayed silent for years. There are many reasons for male victims' silence. One is that, like women victims, they don't want the public scrutiny that reporting brings. In addition, men have distinct reasons not to speak up. Richard Gartner (2005, 2012), a psychotherapist who works with male victims of childhood abuse, says that male victims put their emotions in a "deep freeze" because they believe that "real men should be resilient and certainly not victims" (2012, p. A23). Another reason some male victims stay silent is that they fear others might think they are gay because a man engaged in sexual activity with them. Many turn to alcohol or other drugs to deal with the pain and shame of what happened to them.

Despite social pressures, some male victims are refusing to stay silent. In recent years, men have filed between 15% and 20% of claims of sexual harassment (Mattioli, 2010).

EXPLORING GENDERED LIVES   *The Victim*

One of my students adapted this story from one he found on the Web. A version of the story was posted on the Men Ending Rape site at **http://www .menendingrape.org/Rape.**

Bob Smith was robbed by John Jones. Jones was caught, and Smith pressed charges. Following is the transcript of the defense attorney's cross-examination of Mr. Smith.

"Mr. Smith, were you held up on the corner of 16th and Locust by Mr. Jones?"

"Yes."

"Did you struggle with Mr. Jones?"

"No."

"Why not?"

"He had a gun to my head and told me he'd kill me if I didn't give him my wallet."

"So you decided to comply with his demands instead of resisting. Did you at least scream for help?"

"No. I was afraid."

"Is it true that, earlier on the evening of the alleged robbery, you gave money to some friends who asked for it?"

"Yes."

"Isn't it true that you often give money to others?"

"Yes, I like to help people I care about."

"In fact, don't you have quite a reputation for generosity—for giving money away? How was Mr. Jones supposed to know you didn't want to give him money? I mean, you give it away to lots

of people, so why shouldn't Mr. Jones have assumed you would give him some?"

"What are you getting at?"

"Never mind. When did the robbery take place?"

"About 11 p.m."

"11 p.m.? You were out walking alone at 11 p.m. at night? You know it's dangerous to be out on the streets alone at night. Why were you there at that time of night?"

"I just felt like walking home instead of taking a cab."

"Okay. What were you wearing?"

"A suit. I'd worked late at the office, gone out with friends, and was walking home."

"A suit. An expensive suit, right?"

"Well, yes. It is a very nice suit. What's your point?"

"So, you were walking around a deserted street late at night in an expensive suit that practically advertised you had money. The way you were dressed was really provocative, isn't that so? In fact, we could think that, being dressed that way and out on the streets alone late at night, you were asking to be robbed."

Why do you think some people would not think Mr. Smith asked to be robbed but might think a woman wearing sexy clothes and out late at night asked to be raped?

(Zukerman, 2009). Increasingly, males are also victims of rape in the Congo. Oxfam, Human Rights Watch, and the United Nations estimate that war in the Congo and Rwanda has resulted in hundreds of thousands of female rape victims, and rape is now a weapon used to humiliate and demoralize men (Gettleman, 2009a). According to Pulitzer Prize winning journalists, Nicholas Kristof and Sherryl WuDunn (2009), 90% of women and girls over the age of three were sexually abused during civil wars in Liberia and 75% of women in some areas of the Congo have been raped. Kristof and WuDunn report that "In one instance, soldiers raped a three-year-old girl and then fired their guns into her. When surgeons saw her, there was no tissue left to repair" (p. 84).

Sexual assault includes forced prostitution, also called sexual slavery. During World War II, the Japanese forced women to be "comfort women" for Japanese soldiers. They had sex with 20 to 30 Japanese soldiers a day. The repeated and

The Many Faces of Gendered Violence **259**

sometimes brutal rapes caused some of these women to become sterile. Many committed suicide (Onishi, 2007).

Sexual slavery is not confined to history. Even today, in countries such as India, Pakistan, Bangladesh, and Nepal, girls are sold by their families or kidnapped and forced to be prostitutes (Kristof & WuDunn, 2009; Owen, 2007). It is estimated that 1.8 million girls and women, some who have not even gone through puberty, are trafficked each year (Kristof, 2011a). Of those, 50,000 to 100,000 are trafficked into the United States (Goddess & Calderón, 2006). Virgins bring particularly high prices since some men with HIV/AIDS believe that having sex with a virgin will cure them (Norlund & Rubin, 2010). The men pass their lethal disease to the girl or woman who is the sex slave.

EXPLORING GENDERED LIVES *Corrective Rape*

Jeremy Schaap is an Emmy-award winning journalist and a national news correspondent. He created a documentary video on "corrective rape" in South Africa. Corrective rape is rape of lesbians to punish them for being lesbian and correct their sexual orientation. Preceding and during the rape, the women are usually beaten, often brutally. Lesbian soccer players have been particular targets of corrective rape. In addition to humiliating victims, corrective rapists claim they are teaching the victims to act like a woman and want sex with men. I am providing a link to Schaap's documentary so that you can view the video, but please be aware that it is very disturbing: **http://espn.go.com/video/clip?id=5181871.**

EXPLORING GENDERED LIVES *Myths and Facts about Rape*

Myth	Fact
Rape is motivated by sexual urges.	Rape is an aggressive act used to dominate another person.
Most rapes occur between strangers.	More than 75% of rapes are committed by a person known to the victim.
Most rapists are African-American men, and most victims are European-American women.	More than three-fourths of all rapes occur within races, not between races.
False reports of rapes are frequent.	False reports of rapes constitute only 2% of all reported rapes.
The way a woman dresses affects the likelihood that she will be raped.	Most rapes are planned in advance, without knowledge of how victims will be dressed.
Women who don't drink too much are alert enough to protect themselves from being raped.	Date rape drugs such as Rohypnol, GHB (gamma hydroxybutyric acid), and Ketamine have no color, smell, or taste, so you can't tell if you are being drugged. The drugs can make you become weak and confused—or even pass out—so that you are unable to refuse sex or defend yourself.

Intimate Partner Violence

The Centers for Disease Control's (CDC) 2011 report states that one in four U.S. women has been violently attacked by husbands or boyfriends, and one in seven men has been violently attacked by wives or girlfriends. **Intimate partner violence** is physical, mental, emotional, verbal, or economic power used by one partner against the other partner in a romantic relationship. Intimate partner violence is also on the rise in dating relationships, including those of very young people. Nearly 10% of high-school students report being physically hurt by a girlfriend or boyfriend, and one in three high-school students reports psychological violence from a girlfriend or boyfriend (Hoffman, 2012).

PAULA

The worst thing I ever went through was being stalked by my ex-boyfriend. We'd dated for about a year when I broke up with him. He was so jealous—wouldn't let me go out with friends or anything, so I just decided to end the relationship. But he didn't want it to end. He followed me around campus, showed up at movies when I was out with other guys, and called at all hours of the night. Sometimes, he would tell me he loved me and beg to get back together; other times, he would threaten me. I finally called the police, and that put an end to his terrorism.

Intimate partner violence is experienced and perpetrated by both sexes and by gays, lesbians, straights, and transgender people. The CDC (2011) reports that one in three women and one in seven men in the United States have experienced physical aggression, and approximately 48% of each sex reports experiencing psychological aggression. Lesbian, gay, and transgender people report roughly the same rates as heterosexuals (Douglas, 2012; Pear, 2012).

In 2009, President Obama's administration recommended that political asylum be granted to a Guatemalan woman, Rody Alvarado, who had come to the United States to escape a brutally abusive husband. Married at 16, she was routinely the target of her husband's violence. He beat and kicked her, dislocated her jaw, pistol whipped her, and threatened her with a machete (Preston, 2009a, b). The administration's recommendation was ground breaking because it recognizes that intimate partner violence is a basis for asylum.

Intimate partner violence typically follows a cyclical pattern (Johnson, 2006). In the first stage, the perpetrator experiences mounting tension. Perhaps the individual has problems at work or feels insecure or frustrated. As tension mounts, verbal and emotional abuse may occur. In the second stage, there is a violent explosion involving physical assault—kicking, beating, throwing the victim against a wall, cutting, or shooting. The third stage in the cycle of abuse is called remorse because the perpetrator typically acts ashamed, apologizes, and promises never to do it again. In the fourth stage, the honeymoon phase, the abuser acts lovingly and often brings gifts to the battered partner. The apologies of stage three and the loving acts of stage four often revive the victim's faith in the abuser and the possibility of a loving relationship. If they convince victims to stay, the cycle continues.

EXPLORING GENDERED LIVES | *The Cycle of Intimate Partner Violence*

Stage 1: Tension builds, and the abusive partner blames the other for problems or for not being supportive. Typically, the abuser begins psychological battering with insults, threats, taunts, and intimidation. Especially in chronically abusive relationships, victims learn to spot cues, to become extremely compliant, and to placate the partner. This seldom helps, because the abuser is looking for an excuse to relieve frustration by exerting power over another.

Stage 2: Tension erupts into physical violence, which may be severe and even lethal.

Stage 3: The abuser appears contrite and remorseful. The abuser may apologize to the victim and promise it will never happen again. The victim sees the "good person" inside and remembers what led to commitment or marriage.

Stage 4: The abuser acts devoted to convince the victim that the abuse was an aberration that will not recur—even if it has repeatedly. And then the whole cycle begins anew.

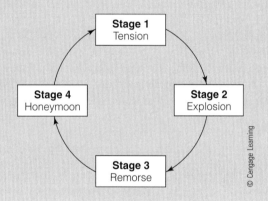

© Cengage Learning

BRICE

Growing up, I saw my father shove Mom around whenever he was having a rough time at work. Sometimes, it was more than shoving—he would actually hit her. Always, the next day he would be Mr. Nice, and things would go along fine for a while until he got upset about something else; then it would start all over again. I hated him because of what he did to her, and I swore I would never be like him. But last year, when I was going through a really rough time, the girl I was dating kept nagging me, and I hauled off and hit her. I never thought I could do that.

Brice's experience, as presented in his commentary, is not unusual. In our families of origin, we learn what is normal and allowable in relationships between men and women. What we learn in families, however, need not be the blueprint for our lives. We can choose not to repeat destructive patterns that we have observed in our families.

There are general differences in the type of violence committed by women and men. Women who abuse most often verbally abuse or push, slap, or shove partners. In contrast, abusive men are more likely to use their bodies, weapons, and even acid to commit assaults (Johnson, M., 2006, 2008). Although both sexes may engage in violence, men more often inflict moderate to severe physical injuries. Men who perpetrate physical violence tend to justify their violence by overestimating how common such behavior is or underestimating the damage their violence does (Olson & Rauscher, 2011). Men who inflict physical violence also overestimate the commonness of what they do by two to three times the actual rates (Neighbors, Walker, Mbilinyi, O'Rourke, Edleson, Zegree, & Roffman, 2010).

Men tend to use physical aggression to gain or sustain self-esteem, to win the respect of others, and to maintain control over people and situations. In Asian countries such as Pakistan and Cambodia, some men use acid to punish women who refuse to be subservient to men. When Naeema Azar, a Pakistani woman, wanted to divorce her husband, he poured acid on her face. The acid blinded her and burned away an ear, her eyelids, and flesh on her face. Acid burnings are seldom prosecuted (Kristof, 2008).

Women and men between 18 and 25 years old are equally likely to engage in relational aggression in friendships. However, in romantic relationships, women exceed men in engaging in this kind of aggression, which is intentionally designed to hurt romantic partners by manipulating social relationships (Goldstein, 2011).

Increasingly, stalking is recognized as a form of intimate partner violence. Stalking is repeated, intrusive behavior that is uninvited and unwanted, that seems obsessive, and that makes the target concerned for her or his safety (Cupach & Spitzberg, 2011). Stalking is particularly common on campuses because it is easy to monitor and learn others' routines. Further, tweeting and updates on social networking sites such as Facebook give stalkers more ways to learn about (potential) victims' habits and current whereabouts.

EXPLORING GENDERED LIVES   Myths and Facts about Violence between Intimates

Myth	Fact
Victims of battering can just leave the abusive relationship.	Many victims of battering have nowhere to go and no means of supporting themselves and their children.
Abuse of intimates often stops on its own.	Abuse of intimates seldom stops without intervention or other radical measures.
Abuse is confined primarily to the working and poverty classes.	Abuse occurs in relationships between members of the upper and middle classes as well as members of the working and poverty classes.
Victims of battering would be safer if they left abusive relationships.	Victims of battering are most likely to be murdered by abusive partners if they try to leave.

Sexual Harassment

Sexual harassment is unwelcome verbal or nonverbal behavior of a sexual nature that links academic or professional standing or success to sexual favors or that interferes with work or learning.

Prior to the 1970s, the term *sexual harassment* was not used (Wise & Stanley, 1987). Once sexual harassment was named, those who were targets of it had a way to define their experience and demand institutional and legal redress. Although women are the predominant targets and men the predominant harassers, the Supreme Court has recognized that either sex can be the target or perpetrator and that people can be harassed by people of their own sex.

Two broad categories of sexual harassment are widely recognized today: *quid pro quo harassment* and *hostile environment harassment.*

Quid Pro Quo

Quid pro quo harassment is the actual or threatened use of professional or academic rewards and/or punishments to gain sexual compliance from a subordinate or student. *Quid pro quo* is a Latin phrase that means "this for that." For instance, a professor might promise a student a good grade in exchange for a date, or a manager might offer a subordinate a promotion in exchange for sex. Quid pro quo harassment may also involve punishing someone for not providing sexual favors. For example, a manager might withhold a promotion from an employee who refuses to have sex.

Quid pro quo sex depends on power differences. The person seeking sexual favors must have some kind of power over the other person—the power to assign a grade, give a promotion, or control wages. Quid pro quo harassment works because of this power difference—the person with less power may be reluctant or unable to say "no." Men who are inclined to engage in sexual harassment tend to blame victims more than men who are not inclined to engage in sexual harassment (Key & Ridge, 2011).

Hostile Environment

Hostile environment harassment is unwelcome conduct of a sexual nature that interferes with a person's ability to perform a job or to gain an education, and/or conduct that creates a hostile, intimidating, or offensive working environment because of sexualized conduct. Both women and men have brought suits for hostile environment sexual harassment. In one case, a jury awarded $3.75 million to a male prison guard whose employer did nothing to stop a female coworker who harassed him by calling his home, following him at work, and making repeated sexual comments to him ("Sexually Harassed Male," 1999).

A hostile environment may be created by lewd remarks, language that demeans one sex, hanging pinups, and circulating rumors about an individual's real or speculated sexual activities. Particularly common is sexual banter or suggestions. In addition, a hostile environment may be created when members of one sex (usually women) are disrespected, demeaned, ignored, and/or told directly or indirectly that they aren't welcome.

A hostile environment is created by a pattern of behavior. A single action, even if it is unwelcome and inappropriate, is unlikely to meet the legal standard for sexual harassment. Instead, there must be a pervasive pattern of unwelcome conduct related to a person's sex, and that pattern must create conditions that are so intolerable a reasonable person would resign (Greenhouse, 2004). This standard ensures that isolated misconduct, which might be deliberate or inadvertent, doesn't result in excessive penalties.

In 2006, the U.S. Supreme Court issued an important ruling that offers further protection to victims of sexual discrimination of all sorts. The plaintiff, White, sued a company because, after she complained about sexist statements made by her supervisor, she was reassigned to less desirable duties and then suspended. The Court ruled that a company cannot suspend or reassign workers who complain about sexist treatment because such retaliatory actions would discourage other workers from complaining about sexist treatment and, thus, would undercut laws protecting workers against sexual harassment (Andronici & Katz, 2007).

Genital Surgery

Some people have never heard of genital surgery (also called genital mutilation and genital cutting). Of those who have, many think it is an ancient procedure that is no longer practiced. Yet, genital surgery continues to be practiced in many parts of the world today. More than three million girls a year are subjected to female genital mutilation (Kristof, 2011b). I'll warn you in advance that you may find the pages that follow very disturbing.

Male Circumcision

Male circumcision is the removal of the sheath, or prepuce, of the penis. In many countries, including the United States, male babies are routinely circumcised. The rationale for male circumcision is that it makes it easier to keep the penis clean and reduces the likelihood of infections (Bakalar, 2009). Yet some people view male circumcision as a form of genital mutilation that is unnecessary, dangerous, and painful. Believing that parents should not be able to impose circumcision on a boy, a group of citizens got a measure banning circumcision of boys under 18 on the November 2012 ballot (Hindery, 2011). The measure did not pass.

Sunna

The word **sunna** comes from the Arabic word for "religious duty" (Trangsrud, 1994). Sunna, or female circumcision, is practiced primarily in African countries. It is usually performed on girls between the ages of 4 and 14, although it is sometimes performed on infants (Johnson, A., 2008). Sunna involves removing both the sheath and the tip of the clitoris. Sunna is not equivalent to male. Removal of the foreskin of a penis doesn't preclude a man's sexual pleasure, but removal of the prepuce and tip of the clitoris eliminates or reduces women's sexual pleasure. Sunna also has greater potential for medical complications.

To Circumcise or Not to Circumcise: That Is the Question

In 1999, 63% of Western males were circumcised whereas only 55% of Western males were circumcised a decade later (Rabin, 2012). Why the change? Questions about the health benefits of removing the foreskin from the penis have stoked opposition to the procedure in the United States and many European countries. In addition, some critics of circumcision consider it cruel and unethical to subject an infant to involuntary surgery to remove a healthy body part.

In 2012, the influential American Academy of Pediatrics stopped short of recommending circumcision, but noted research suggests the procedure may offer some protection against HIV infection from female sexual partners and reduce urinary tract infections and penile cancer. These benefits are balanced against complications that occur in 1 in every 500 circumcisions and result in 100 deaths annually (Circumcision, 2012; Rabin, 2012).

And then there's the pain of the surgery. Traditionally, circumcision is performed without anesthesia, and some religions ban even local anesthesia. When Berlin announced all circumcisions must be conducted in sterile environments with as little pain as possible, Muslims and Jews marched in protest, claiming this interfered with their religious freedom ("Circumcision," 2012). Some Austrian provinces have prohibited state hospitals from performing circumcisions, and the Royal Dutch Medical Society discourages the procedure.

Excision or Clitoridectomy

A second type of female genital surgery is excision or **clitoridectomy**, in which the entire clitoris and parts of the labia minora are removed. This operation greatly diminishes women's ability to experience sexual pleasure, so it is thought to reduce the likelihood that a woman will be sexually active before marriage or unfaithful after marriage. Of lesser concern to those who endorse the practice is that it often has medical complications and increases pain and danger in childbirth.

You might be surprised to learn that clitoridectomies were performed in the United States and Europe as late as the twentieth century to "cure" masturbation and prevent orgasm, which was considered an "ailment" that good women didn't have (Dreifus, 2000). Reminding us again of the power of social constructions of gender, the belief that women should be sexually "pure" was, and still is, used to justify mutilating women.

Infibulation

The most radical form of genital surgery is **infibulation**. In this operation, which is usually performed on girls between ages five and eight, the clitoris and labia minora are removed. Next, the flesh of the labia majora is scraped raw and sewn together to form a hood over the vagina, with a small opening left for urination and menstruation (Kristof, 2011b), and the girl is kept immobile for 10 days. When a female who has been infibulated marries, an opening is cut to permit intercourse. Sometimes the opening is deliberately made extremely small to increase male sexual pleasure, although it makes intercourse painful for women. Husbands may order their wives resewn when they travel or to prevent pregnancy.

Genital surgery is performed by people with little or no medical training who operate in unsanitary conditions and without anesthesia. The immediate consequences may include excruciating pain, hemorrhage, tetanus, gangrene, blood poisoning, and fractured bones from the force needed to hold girls down during the operation. Long-term consequences include sterility, agonizing pain during intercourse, difficulty delivering babies, permanent incontinence, and stillbirths of babies who cannot emerge through birth canals that have been scarred and deformed by genital operations (Browne, 2003/2004).

Cultural traditions change only when members of the culture resist them. In China, for centuries women's feet were bound. Yet, this practice was eliminated in a mere 17 years (1895–1912) in urban China when progressive Chinese citizens launched an education campaign against foot binding. Also critical to ending the practice was associations of fathers who refused to bind their daughters' feet and prohibited their sons from marrying women whose feet had been bound (Lorber, 1997). When enough fathers made these commitments, women with unbound feet became suitable as marriage partners.

Gender-Based Murder

Consider two facts: (1) When both sexes are given adequate care, there are more females than males in the population; and (2) in many countries today, men substantially outnumber women. How can both of these facts be true? Because millions of females are killed before or after birth.

One way to reduce the number of women is to selectively abort female fetuses. If a female child is born, cultures that don't value females condone female infanticide, the active or passive killing of female children. Active female infanticide is sometimes practiced by smothering a newborn female or drowning her in a bucket of water kept by the birthing bed. More passive methods of female infanticide include feeding girl babies little or nothing and denying them essential medical care (Patel, 2006).

Women who survive to adulthood aren't necessarily safe. **Femicide** is the killing of women. In many places, including India, Pakistan, Albania, Mexico, and United Arab Emirates, adult women are killed. Governments do little to investigate cases of women who are found dead or who simply disappear (de Alba & Guzmán, 2010; Panther, 2008). Femicide also takes the form of dowry deaths, or bride burnings. Some groups in India still follow the custom in which a woman's parents give a sum of money or other goods to the man who marries their daughter. After the marriage, the new husband sometimes makes demands for additional payments from the bride's parents. If the demands aren't met, the husband's family may hold the bride near the cooking stove until her sari catches fire and she burns to death. The husband is then free to get another wife and another dowry. Hundreds of thousands of women have been victims of bride burning. Currently, it's estimated that there is a dowry death in India every 1 hour and 44 minutes. Tim Muehlhoff (2007), a communication professor at Biola University, went to India to interview women about gender relations in their culture. Repeatedly women told him that the largest wing in hospitals was the burn unit, which is where women who have "accidents" in the kitchen go for help.

Reproductive Violence

Reproductive violence is coerced or discriminatory infringement on reproductive rights. It includes force or exploitation that inhibits an individual's free choice of whether, when, and with whom to reproduce, to become a parent and to parent existing children (Ross, 2009). In America's early history, these rights were denied to slaves. Any children they bore were legally the "property" of the slave owner; so enslaved mothers, many of whom were raped by slave owners for economic gain, had no legal claim to parentage (Roberts, 1997).

Denying minority women's rights to motherhood and reproductive self-determination didn't end with slavery. In the twentieth century, the United States saw in the emergence of eugenics, a set of reproductive strategies to "improve" society by reducing the births of "undesirable" people and increasing the births of "desirable" people. The history of eugenics reveals that those designated undesirable were almost always low-income, socially marginalized minorities (Solinger, 2005). State-funded programs in the United States forcibly and involuntarily sterilized numerous women who were immigrants, minorities, lesbians, poor, or disabled (Roberts, 2009; Solinger, 2005).

Reproductive violence also includes state-forced abortions as in the case of Feng Jianmei, whose story appears in the Exploring Gendered Lives box on this page.

EXPLORING GENDERED LIVES *Forced Abortion*

When 23-year-old Feng Jianmei learned she was pregnant in 2012, she and her husband were worried. They already had one child, which is the allowed limit under China's one-child policy. Local officials fined Feng $6,300, but she had given all of her money to her mother-in-law for cancer treatment. When Feng couldn't pay the fine, she was beaten, dragged into a van, and taken to a hospital where she was forced to sign a document that she couldn't read because she was blindfolded. She was then given injections that forced abortion of her seven-month fetus.

When photos of Feng lying beside the bloody, dead fetus were posted online, there was a public outcry, which forced the Chinese government to suspend three officials and apologize to Feng. Yet the government also called Feng and her husband traitors and beat her husband who fled the region. Feng could not join him because she was detained in the hospital.

In another case, Pan Chunyan was eight months pregnant when she was abducted from a store. After four days of confinement, she was forced to put her thumbprint on a document to attest that she agreed to have an abortion. Hours after being injected with a drug, Pan's fetus emerged, black and blue and dead. Ms. Pan's husband says they paid the fine for having more than one child, but Pan was subjected to forcible abortion anyway (Wong, 2012).

Other forms of reproductive injustice do not involve the clear-cut violence of eugenics, forced abortion, and slavery, but do severely constrain decisions about reproduction. For example, the link between racism and regulation of reproductive rights is obvious in programs in the United States in the 1930s that promoted free birth control to minority women and women with low incomes in lieu of a range of social services aimed at poverty reduction, access to health care and education (Dorothy Roberts 2001; Gordon, 2007; Roberts, 1997). Even today, poor and minority women are targeted with population reduction strategies. Project Prevention, a U.S. charity, pays women with drug or alcohol addictions $300 cash to be sterilized or agree to long-term contraception (Kristof, 2012).

One in famous infringement on reproductive rights involved Norplant, a long-term, implanted contraceptive that came on market in the early 1990s. Within days of Norplant's entry into the market, prominent publications such as the *Philadelphia Inquirer* (Kimelman, 1990), *The Richmond-Times Dispatch* (Journalistic Thought Police, 1990), and *Newsweek* (Alter, 1990) published editorials noting that the new contraceptive might "curb the expansion of an underclass" (Journalistic Thought Police, 1990, p. A12). Every state and the District of Columbia made Norplant available to poor women (Roberts, 1997). In some instances, judges offered women the "choice" between having Norplant implanted and serving jail terms (Bigham, 1991). However, states refused to pay to remove Norplant when women wanted to conceive and even when they experienced serious medical complications (Roberts, 1997). Because Norplant is a foreign object, the body reacts, sometimes violently, to its implantation. Known potential side effects of Norplant include migraine headaches, nerve injury, ovarian cysts, phlebitis, significant weight gain, and gallbladder disease (Norplant, 2012).

It is notable that both the American Medical Association and the American Bar Association oppose state or judicial efforts to coerce a woman to use any method of contraception or sterilization. Even Dr. Sheldon Segal, the originator of Norplant, stated, "I am totally and unalterably opposed to the use of Norplant for any coercive or involuntary purpose. It was developed to improve reproductive freedom, not to restrict it" (Norplant, 1994).

Natalie Fixmer-Oraiz (2013), who studies contemporary reproductive politics, has illuminated other intrusions on reproductive rights that disproportionately impact poor women. One example is commercial surrogacy. Women with sufficient wealth who cannot conceive or carry a child or who choose not to be pregnant can hire women to carry a pregnancy to term. In one sense, this is a win-win situation: Women who cannot give birth are able to become mothers, and women who are desperately poor are able to earn income by carrying a child. Without denying the mutual benefit, we should also recognize the power dynamics involved (Fixmer-Oraiz, 2013). The surrogate mothers often have no other means of earning income so their "choice" to be surrogates is deeply constrained. Some surrogate mothers are required to live in supervised gestational dormitories, leaving their own children and family for nine months, and to agree to caesarian births so that the birth date is convenient for the hiring woman. If the surrogates later have other children by vaginal delivery, the prior caesarian delivery may cause complications, including ones that are life-threatening. Thus, in "choosing" to be surrogates, women may give up rights to protect their ability to carry and give birth to their own children (Jaiwal, 2012). Should being poor mean losing the right to control your reproductive rights?

The gendered violence we've discussed is not inevitable. Throughout this book, we have seen that what is considered acceptable or normal is socially constructed. In the next section of this chapter, we discuss social processes that allow or encourage gendered violence.

The Social Foundations of Gendered Violence

Although particular individuals commit violent acts and should be held responsible for them, causes are broader than individual psychology. To unravel cultural forces that cultivate tolerance for gendered violence, we will consider how media, institutions, and language normalize gendered violence.

The Normalization of Violence in Media

As we noted in Chapter 11, violence is customary—not unusual—in films, on MTV and television programs, and in popular music and video games. Gangsta rap includes lyrics that refer to women as "hos" (whores) and "bitches" and glorify killing for sport, which reflects a widespread and deeply ensconced cultural ideology that esteems violence, including rape. Newspaper coverage of rape often includes extraneous and irrelevant information about what a victim was wearing or where she was when she was assaulted.

On her *Huffington Post* blog, Soraya Chemaly (2012) wrote, "On any given day you can, if you chose, participate in an entertaining pop culture rape happening. Last week started with Salon's Glenn Greenwalk making jokes about President Obama **raping nuns** and in December, **#ItAintRapeIf**, a fun Twitter hash tag was trending. You can find **popular TV shows and movies** and lists of **music with rapey lyrics** to hyper-real, 3-D **video games** like **RapeLay** (which went viral last year), in which players help the hero rape a mother and her two daughters.... Not quite convinced? How about the '**Who Would You Rape?**' University of Vermont fraternity survey?"

Pornography often includes violence against women that may encourage those who consume it to think violence in real relationships is acceptable. Before going further with this discussion, we need to distinguish pornography from **erotica**. Pornography is not simply sexually explicit material. Rather, it is material that favorably shows subordination and degradation of individuals by presenting sadistic behaviors as pleasurable, pain as enjoyable, and forced sex as positive. Erotica, on the other hand, depicts consensual activities that are desired by and pleasurable to all parties.

The Normalization of Violence by Institutions

Many of the basic structures and institutional practices of Western culture uphold violence, including violence toward women. They do this by refusing to interfere in domestic disputes, praising men for aggression, advising victims not to prosecute batterers, and encouraging victims to fulfill social prescriptions for femininity by standing by their men.

Family

One of the most important institutions shaping cultural consciousness, including perspectives on violence, is the family. In families where violence exists, daughters and sons may grow up assuming that violence is part of marriage.

In some countries, cultural norms maintain that men have a right to abuse women and that women should tolerate abuse and remain loyal. Some African-American and Asian-American women don't report intimate partner violence because doing so would disrupt family cohesiveness and fuel negative stereotypes of their race (Dasgupta, 2007; Meyers, 2004).

Law Enforcement

For many years, police officers were often reluctant to intervene in violence in families, believing that was a private matter. Significant efforts to educate law enforcement officers, as well as judges, have led to greater willingness to hold perpetrators accountable. Also, laws have been passed that increase victims' and potential victims' ability to protect themselves. Despite this progress, the current legal system does not offer sufficient safeguards for victims (Johnson, M., 2008). The laws governing restraining orders, for example, need to be strengthened so that people can get protection before tragedy happens.

Language

Another cultural practice that reflects and sustains tolerance of violence is the use of language that obscures the seriousness of the issue. Much of the language used to describe violence between intimates conceals the brutality of what happens. Why do newspapers and news programs use inappropriately gentle terms, such as *domestic dispute* or *spousal conflict*, to camouflage acts such as smashing women's faces with fists and hammers, slashing women with knives, and breaking bones by throwing or stomping on women (Lamb, 1991, 1999)?

Responsibility for violence is also diminished by passive language that fails to name aggressors—for example, "The battery occurred on Sunday," "Women are abused frequently," or "Many women are beaten." The horror of intimate partner violence is also diminished when the language of love is used to describe physical abuse. Media accounts of battering of women often include phrases such as "He loved her too much," "She was the victim of love," and "It was love that went too far" (Meyers, 1994, 2004).

Cultural acceptance of gendered violence is supported—subtly and overtly, deliberately and inadvertently—by a number of social practices and institutions. But violence is not innate, and acceptance of it is not inevitable. Individual attitudes and cultural ideologies can be transformed.

Resisting Gendered Violence: Where Do We Go from Here?

I suspect that this chapter has been as distressing for you to read as it was for me to research and write. However, if we are only distressed about the extent of gendered violence, we will not lessen it. We must ask how we can be agents of change who resist gendered violence and who compel revisions in cultural attitudes toward it.

Personal Efforts to Reduce Gendered Violence

Each of us can do something to lessen gendered violence. The most basic personal choice is to decide that you will not engage in or tolerate violence in your relationships. You can also make conscious choices about the language you use. You can heighten others' awareness by using language that accurately represents the ugliness and inhumanity of violent actions.

Another choice, one emphasized by Mentors in Violence Prevention, is to refuse to be a silent bystander. In 2009, a homecoming dance in Richmond, California, turned into a horrific tragedy when a 15-year-old girl was beaten and gang-raped for hours. More than a dozen people watched during this extended attack, yet none of them chose to intervene to stop the brutal assault ("California," 2009). You can make a different choice; you can speak out against violence and intervene in situations such as the one in Richmond, California.

There are other ways you personally can take a stand against gendered violence. You might volunteer to work with victims of violence. Most campuses and communities have a number of women's groups that offer outreach programs to educate citizens about violence toward women. Men on many campuses work to get other men involved in combating violence toward women. Becoming a community educator is a way to be an agent of change. You can also make a personal statement by writing or calling in to object to magazine stories, radio programs, and televisions shows that present violence as normal or acceptable. If you are a parent or plan to be one, you can teach your children that nobody has a right to touch them in a violent or sexual way without their permission. And all children should learn that it is wrong to be violent toward others or to coerce others into sexual activities.

For too many years, people have looked away from sexual harassment and violence between intimates. We've pretended not to see bruises, looked the other way when there was on-the-job harassment. If you suspect that a friend or colleague is experiencing violence, don't tell yourself, "It's none of my business." It is your business. Speaking up to support someone who is being harmed is a concrete way to use your voice to resist violence.

Social Efforts to Reduce Gendered Violence

We must also change cultural practices and structures. Here, too, there are many ways to be an agent of change. You can vote for tax increases to underwrite education and counseling. If you have skills as an educator or administrator, you can design and implement educational programs. You can also get involved with international efforts to reduce.

Many organizations work against violence, and they welcome volunteers and financial support. For example, Southeast Asian women formed *Saheli*, which protests dowry deaths. *Saheli* was successful in getting a law passed that requires thorough investigation of any "accidental death" of a woman during the first seven years of marriage. Eve Ensler (2000, 2001), who won the coveted Obie award for her play, *Vagina Monologues*, has founded V-day (Ensler, 2004). This organization works to stop all kinds of violence against women, including rape, incest, female genital mutilation, and sexual slavery.

Gendered violence, particularly violence against women, is pervasive. As Bob Herbert (2009a) recently commented after a man gunned down nine women, killing three, "there would have been thunderous outrage if someone had separated potential victims by race or religion and then shot, say, only the blacks, or only the whites or only the Jews. But if you shoot only the girls or only the women— not so much of an uproar.... We should take particular notice of the staggering amounts of violence brought down on the nation's women and girls each and every day for no other reason than *because they are female*" (p. A17).

Sometimes, when I am overwhelmed by the extent of violence against women, I inspire myself by reading accounts of resistance by women and girls in cultures that radically degrade women. In India, a group of women formed *Vimochana*, an organization that helps battered women get legal assistance. In addition to responding to the symptoms of violence (battered women), *Vimochana* tackles the structural causes of it by organizing consciousness-raising groups that help women work together to redefine battering and dowry murders as unacceptable. Asian men have formed "Men Oppose Wife Abuse" to end intimate partner violence (Cuklanz & Moorti, 2009). Chilean women are risking imprisonment and death to demand that *desaparecidas*, "disappeared women," be returned. If women in India and Chile can claim a voice in resisting violence, you and I can, too.

I want to close this chapter with a story that highlights the horrific nature of gendered violence and gives us an inspiring example of personal dignity, courage, and commitment to making change happen. The Exploring Gendered Lives box on the next two pages presents this story.

Refusing to Be Defeated

Mukhtar Mai

ARIF ALI/AFP/Getty Images

In 2002, when Pakistani Mukhtar Mai was 32, her 12-year-old brother was accused of having sexual relations with the daughter in a higher-caste family. The village council found him guilty and decided to punish his family by sentencing Mukhtar to be gang-raped. A group of men stripped her, carried out the sentence, and then forced her to walk home naked while 300 villagers watched. A woman who has been raped in Pakistan is dishonored (Minhas, 2009), so Mukhtar was expected to commit suicide.

She didn't. Instead, she fought back—and not just for herself. She prosecuted her rapists in another court that convicted them and awarded her $8,300. She used that money to start two schools in her village, one for boys and one for girls. Mukhtar believes that education is the best way to change the attitudes that led a council to order her to be gang-raped and led her neighbors to commit the assault. *New York Times* columnist Nicholas Kristof (2005a, b, c, d) brought the case to the world's attention and continually updated the story. On March 3, 2005, a Pakistani appeals court overturned the death sentences of six of the men convicted of attacking her and set five of them free to live in her neighborhood. The Pakistani authorities placed Mukhtar under house arrest and refused to let her leave the country.

In June 2005, the Pakistani Supreme Court yielded to international pressure and freed Mukhtar from house arrest. She returned to her village, where she continues her efforts to provide educational opportunities to children. But

Mukhtar is far from safe. She lives under threats on her life, yet continues her work providing education to Pakistanis and supporting Pakistani women who want to prosecute rapes and acid attacks. In 2011, Pakistan's Supreme Court freed five of the six men who were imprisoned for gang-raping Mukhtar (Shah, 2011).

Mukhtar's story is presented in her autobiography, *In the Name of Honor* (Mai, Cuny, Kristof, & Coverdale, 2006) and in "Shame," a documentary produced by Showtime in 2007.

SUMMARY

We can do much to reduce gendered violence in our personal lives and to contribute to broader changes in the social structures and practices that sustain cultural acceptance of gendered violence. We need to work together to provide safe refuges for victims of violence and to provide counseling to both victims and abusers. In addition, we need to develop educational programs that teach very young children that violence toward others is unacceptable. These and other changes in social structures and practices can reform cultural attitudes toward gendered violence. The changes will not be easy, but they are possible. Continuing to live with pervasive and relentless violence is not acceptable. In the time it has taken you to read this chapter, at least one woman has been raped and at least two have been beaten by a friend, lover, or family member. We need to be part of changing this.

KEY TERMS

The terms following are defined in this chapter on the pages indicated, as well as in alphabetical order in the book's glossary, which begins on page 283. The text's companion website (**http://www.cengage.com/communication/wood/genderedlives11e**) also provides interactive flash cards and crossword puzzles to help you learn these terms and the concepts they represent.

blaming the victim 257
clitoridectomy 265
erotica 269
femicide 266
gender intimidation 254
gendered violence 254
hostile environment harassment 263
infibulation 265
informed consent 255

intimate partner violence 260
male circumcision 264
pornography 269
quid pro quo harassment 263
reproductive violence 267
sexual assault 255
sexual harassment 254
sunna 264

GENDER ONLINE

1. For more information, go to the National Coalition Against Domestic Violence's site at **http://www.ncadv.org**.

2. These are organizations that provide up-to-date information on ways you can help stop gendered violence around the world. For starters, try these websites: Office of Violence Against Women: **http://www.usdoj.gov/ovw**; National Domestic Violence Hotline: **http://www.ndvh.org**.

3. To learn more about men who are committed to stopping men's violence, visit this website: **http://menstoppingviolence.org**.

4. The Department of Justice has a special office that focuses exclusively on violence against women. Its website is: **http://www.ovw.usdoj.gov**. You might want to pay particular attention to the "Campus Grants" link, which is a relatively new feature that emphasizes dealing with and reducing violence against women on campuses.

5. Online search terms: "bride burning," "informed consent," "sexual harassment."

6. "The Invisible War" is a 2012 feature-length documentary about sexual assault in the military in which 35 former soldiers and sailors recount being raped and otherwise sexually assaulted while in the military. **Warning**: This film is disturbing.

REFLECTION AND DISCUSSION

1. Invite an attorney to talk with your class about your state's laws concerning rape charges and trials. What counts as rape in your state? What insights can the attorney offer about juries' attitudes toward plaintiffs who bring rape charges? Are juries equally sympathetic toward plaintiffs who bring charges of stranger versus acquaintance rape?

2. Conduct a survey to see if students on your campus believe the rape myths discussed in this chapter.

   • On the left-hand side of a sheet of paper, type the five myths about rape that are listed in the Exploring Gendered Lives: Myths and Facts about Rape box. To the right of the statements, type five categories of answer: strongly agree; somewhat agree; not sure; somewhat disagree; strongly disagree.

   • Make 15 copies of the sheet. Use two different colors of paper; give one color to women students and the other color to men students. Ask the students to respond anonymously. Ideally, members of the class should poll students at different places, such as the library, the student center or union, a fraternity house, and so forth.

   • Compile and analyze the data gathered by all the students in your class.

3. Is bombing abortion clinics and killing medical professionals who provide abortion reproductive violence? If bombings and threats of them discourage medical professionals from performing abortions or if fear of harm discourages women from going to clinics, is that interference with their right to choose whether, when and with whom to reproduce?

RECOMMENDED RESOURCES

1. Mukhtar Mai, Nicholas Kristof, and Neil Coverdale. (2006). *In the Name of Honor*. New York: Simon Schuster/Atria. This is Mukhtar Mai's autobiography.

2. *Shame* (2007). Showtime, Producer. This is the documentary on Mukhtar Mai's schools and her commitment to social change.

3. Nicholas Kristof and Sherryl WuDunn. (2009). *Half the Sky*. New York: Knopf.

If you don't like something, change it.
—MAYA ANGELOU

Looking Backward, Looking Forward

Throughout this book, you've seen that you have choices in who you are, how you act, what you buy, what and whom you support, what and whom you get involved with. If you don't like Bratz dolls, buy American Girl dolls, or design a new doll. If you don't have any interest in Free Men and NOMAS, join the Good Men Project, or create your own group. If you don't like the sexualization of women and girls, refuse to buy products that feature ads demeaning women. If you reject violence, get involved in Men Can Stop Rape or one of the many other antiviolence groups. It's up to you.

You choose how to define and perform your personal sex and gender identities. You can invest time, energy, and some money to have a buff muscular body or a slender, waxed body. You can dress ultra femme, grunge, metrosexual, or retro. You can follow social norms for women's and men's communication, you can reject them, or you can revise them to suit your style. It's up to you.

You also choose how and how much to engage in the ongoing cultural conversation about gender. You entered this conversation at a particular moment—one long after people fought for women's rights to vote and own property, one long after men were almost always primary breadwinners for their families. The moment at which you entered this conversation is also before the playing field—whether in sports, politics, or salaries—is truly even, before marriage is based on their two people's love and commitment rather than their sexual orientation, before American organizations have established policies that make it possible for all workers simultaneously to do their jobs and care for their families.

The conversation about gender is not limited to any single place. It is carried on in living rooms, blogs, legislative chambers, classrooms, church groups, zines, music videos, barbershops, newspapers, personal relationships, video games, and boardrooms. It is a conversation in which each generation edits what's been said before and adds new themes and modes of communication to the dialogue.

What you've learned in this book and your class will affect how you participate in the ongoing conversation about gender, communication, and culture. Throughout this book, I've encouraged you to think critically about current views of gender and to challenge those that limit our individual and collective lives. In the years ahead, you and others of your generation will revise what gender means. Given the profound impact of gender on personal and cultural life, this is no small responsibility.

Creating the Future

TAFT

I wonder if it's possible that we'll see a movement for gender equality that involves a lot of men and women. It seems to me that it would be good for us to work together instead of in separate movements. After all, a lot of the issues men face have to do with women and vice versa. Couldn't we get a lot more accomplished by talking with each other and combining forces to work for change?

In shaping the future, you individually and your generation collectively will decide how to respond to social practices that produce differences in the quality of life and opportunities available to various groups in our culture.

You will have opportunities to influence policies and laws that affect work–life balance. Do you plan to take a voice on public issues, such as laws to ensure family leave policies for men and women who work outside the home? Do you plan to make commitments within your personal relationships that lead to greater gender equity than has traditionally characterized relationships? In the places you work, will you speak out for policies that provide equitable opportunities, working environments, and rewards for women and men and straights and gender-nonconforming workers? In influencing government and business policies regarding families, your generation will play a critical role in redesigning institutional practices that have an impact on every citizen.

Defining Masculinity and Femininity

If you are a man, how do you define masculinity for yourself? What do your actions say about what it means to be a man? How do they shape others' views of manhood? If you have children, will you define active fathering as integral to

---

EXPLORING GENDERED LIVES   *Remaking Ourselves*

Freedom ... is characterized by a constantly renewed obligation to remake the *self*, which designates the free being.

—Jean Paul Sartre (1966)

masculinity? Will you assume a fair share of responsibility for housework and child care?

You may want to rethink the long-standing connection between masculinity and breadwinning. Many men in your generation will form relationships with women who earn higher salaries and have more professional prestige. This offers new challenges and—equally—new opportunities for defining masculinity. Through your personal and collective choices, your generation will author its own vision—or visions—of manhood.

If you are a woman, how do you define femininity for yourself? How does your embodiment of femininity affect others' views of what women are and can be? If you have children, how will you define mothering and, if you have a partner, parenting? Will your view of men be affected by whether they earn more or less money than their partners? How do your behaviors and appearance reinforce or challenge unrealistic media images of women? The femininity that you personally embody and perform adds to the range of images of women that is available to everyone.

Responding to Differences

Growing out of what we have discussed is perhaps the most urgent challenge for your generation: to enlarge recognition of and respect for differences that include, yet go beyond differences between men and women. Diversity can be a source of cultural strength or divisiveness, and you will influence which it is in the future. Will you respect men who give up careers to be homemakers and primary parents *and* men who find fulfillment in intense professional commitment? Will you encourage your sons and daughters to be caring and strong? Will you work and socialize with trans people? Your answers to these questions will be found not in what you say in this moment, but in how you live your life.

As your generation remakes social meanings of women, men, gender identity, sexual orientation, and differences among people, you will simultaneously influence our collective vision of who we are as a culture. Our country has always included people of varied gender identities, sexual orientations, sexes, socioeconomic classes, and races. Yet, the melting-pot metaphor that has long been used to describe America encourages people to erase their differences—including facets of their identity that they cherish—and become alike in order to assimilate into a single, homogeneous culture. The painful divisions in our society suggest that the melting pot is an inappropriate ideal for us. It no longer works—if indeed it ever did.

Perhaps it is time to abandon the melting-pot metaphor and inaugurate a new one that acclaims differences as valuable and desirable, one that remakes the cultural ideal to include all citizens instead of trying to remake diverse citizens to fit a single, narrow ideal. Maybe your generation will replace the melting-pot metaphor with one that recognizes commonality that is in harmony with real and valuable differences among people. In her history of the second wave of feminism in the United States, Flora Davis (1991) used the metaphor of a salad bowl to describe our society. She pointed out that a salad consists of many different ingredients that retain their individual tastes, textures, and colors and at the same time contribute to a whole that is more complex, interesting, and enjoyable than the individual parts or some fusion of those parts. The Reverend Jesse Jackson offered the metaphor of our nation as a family quilt made up of patches of various colors and design. Another metaphor is that of a collage, in which distinct patterns stand out in their individual integrity while simultaneously contributing to the character and beauty of the whole. If your generation is able to affirm diversity in sex, race, class, ethnicity, sexuality, and sexual orientation, then you will have inaugurated a bold new theme in the cultural conversation—one with the potential to make our society richer and more equitable for all.

Taking a Voice

You cannot escape participating in the ongoing conversation about gender. Just as speaking out is a choice, so, too, is silence. You can't avoid having influence. Instead, your only options are to decide what influence you will exert and how and where you will do it. In his study of how people respond to toxic chemical disasters, Michael Reich (1991) identified three ways in which citizens affect public awareness, public policy, and redress for victims of chemical disasters. Translating his ideas to our concern with gender, we can identify three forms of influence on cultural views of gender: direct power, agenda setting, and voice.

Direct power is the ability to make others do what they would not do on their own. If you become an executive or own a company, you will have many opportunities to establish policies that affect family leave, work schedules, and criteria for promotion. If you have children, you will exercise direct power when you encourage or discourage playing with particular toys and engaging in various kinds of activities. As a citizen, you exercise direct power by voting, supporting candidates, and entering politics yourself.

A second form of power is agenda setting. If you pursue a career in advertising, public relations, popular music, or journalism, you will have opportunities to shape the public agenda. You can also participate in agenda setting by blogging and calling in to talk shows to state your opinions and to get issues on the public agenda. Likewise, you can engage in agenda setting in your professional and social relationships by calling out issues that operate covertly to sustain gender inequities.

The third way to exercise power is through voice—communicating with others and engaging in everyday acts of principled resistance. One means of enacting voice is adopting a traitorous identity, which we discussed in Chapter 4. Queer performative work, which we first discussed in Chapter 2, is another means of using voice to challenge conventional categories of sex, gender, and sexuality. Other examples of voice come from third-wave feminists who challenge sexist attitudes and practices in everyday life. They challenge peers who unthinkingly say, "That's so gay"; they refuse to diet excessively to meet unrealistic and unhealthy ideals of femininity; they call out acquaintances who make racist, sexist, and homophobic comments; and they participate in protests and rallies.

It's important to realize that voice and resistance are processes. We notice outcomes such as a protest, rally, or strike. But those visible results grow out of prolonged processes of listening, reading, reflecting, and talking with others. We are often cultivating our voices in quiet moments. Making time to think about issues is part of developing a strong voice.

In speaking about the financial crisis, President Obama observed that some of us are to blame for the crisis, but all of us are responsible for it. Those words apply equally to other facets of our lives, including gender. We are all responsible. We owe it to ourselves and to each other to take responsibility for our shared future.

The future is open. You and others in your generation will decide what it becomes. Your choices—in personal, social, civic, and professional life—will shape the meaning of gender and the character of our collective world. Because society is a human creation that we continuously remake, your capacity for being an agent of change is great. So is your responsibility.

> *The most radical step you can take is your next one.*
> **James Baldwin**

REFLECTION AND DISCUSSION

1. What do you see as the future of women's and men's movements? Will new kinds of movements emerge? Will men and women come together in a single movement?

2. After reading this book and completing the course it accompanies, how do you now define feminism? Has your view changed at all as a result of your studies this term?

3. If you could write the script, how would you define masculinity and femininity in the year 2050? What would each gender be like? Or would there be no need for two distinct genders? Or would there be more than two? How would culture change if your script for gender were endorsed by everyone?

4. The textbook closes by discussing metaphors for the United States that might replace the melting-pot metaphor. What metaphor would you advocate?

Glossary

affirmative action Collective term for policies that go beyond equal opportunity laws to redress discrimination. Assumes that historical patterns of discrimination against groups of people justify the preferential treatment of members of those groups; focuses on results, not on the intent of efforts to redress inequities; and attempts to increase the number of qualified members of minorities in education and the workplace, commensurate with their availability.

agenda setting Process by which media tell us to what we should attend.

alternate paths model A relationship theory according to which masculine and feminine ways of creating and expressing closeness are viewed as different from each other and equally valid.

androgyny Combination of qualities society considers both masculine and feminine. Androgynous people tend to identify with and enact qualities socially ascribed both to women and to men.

antifeminism A movement opposing any measures that advance women's equality, status, rights, or opportunities; also called the *backlash against feminism*.

antisuffrage movement A movement that aimed to prevent women from gaining the right to vote in the United States. Opposition to women's suffrage was evident as early as 1848 and was formalized in organizations by 1911.

artifact A personal object that influences how we see ourselves and how we express our identities.

backlash A countermovement that seeks to repudiate and contain feminism by arguing two contradictory claims: (1) that women

have never had it so good, so there is no longer any need for feminism; and (2) that feminism has caused serious problems in women's lives and family relationships. Also called *antifeminism*.

benevolent sexism Paternalistic attitude that describes women affectionately but assumes they aren't competent to do particular tasks.

biological theory The theory that biological characteristics of the sexes are the basis of differences in women's and men's thinking, communicating, feeling, and other functions.

blaming the victim Holding a harmed person responsible for the harm inflicted on him or her by another person.

cis Prefix that designates someone whose gender identity is consistent with what society considers appropriate for the sex assigned at birth.

clitoridectomy Removal of the entire clitoris. Part or all of the labia minora may also be removed. Also called *excision*.

cognitive development theory A developmental theory according to which children participate in defining their genders by acting on internal motivations to be competent, which in turn lead them to seek out gender models that help them to sculpt their own femininity or masculinity.

communication A dynamic, systemic process in which meanings are created and reflected in and through humans' interactions with symbols.

complimentary copy An article or section of writing about an advertiser's product or service that is placed in a magazine by the publisher at no cost to the advertiser, to increase the market appeal of the product or service.

content level of meaning The literal meaning of communication. Content-level meanings are the formal, or denotative, meanings of messages.

critical theories Identify and challenge to inequities and problems in social life.

cultural feminism The viewpoint that women and men differ in fundamental ways, including biology, they have different abilities and skills, and they are entitled to different rights.

culture The structures and practices, especially those relating to communication, through which a particular social order is produced and reproduced by legitimizing certain values, expectations, meanings, and patterns of behavior.

culture of romance Created when forces in higher education encourage women students to regard being attractive to men as more important than academics and career preparation.

cyberbullying It includes text messages, comments, rumors, embarrassing pictures, videos, and fake profiles that are meant to hurt another person and are sent by email or posted on social networking sites.

ecofeminism A movement that integrates the intellectual and political bases of feminist theorizing with ecological philosophy. The specific oppression of women is seen as a particular instance of a larger ideology that esteems violence and domination of women, children, animals, and the Earth.

effortless perfection The pressure felt by many women students at colleges to be beautiful, fit, popular, smart, and accomplished, all without visible effort.

ego boundary Psychologically, the point at which an individual stops and the rest of the world begins; an individual's sense of the line between herself or himself and others. Ego boundaries range from permeable (a sense of self that includes others and their issues, problems, and so on) to rigid (a sense of self as completely distinct from others).

equal opportunity laws Laws that prohibit discrimination on the basis of race, color, religion, sex, or national origin. Equal opportunity laws seek to protect *individual* members of groups that have been targets of discrimination; they redress only current discrimination, not historical bias.

erotica Depictions of sexual activities that are agreed to and enjoyed by the parties participating in the activities.

essentializing The reduction of a phenomenon to its essential characteristics, which are generally presumed to be innate or unchangeable. To essentialize the sexes is to imply that all women are alike in basic respects, that all men are alike in basic respects, and that the two sexes are distinct from each other because of fundamental, essential qualities.

excision See *clitoridectomy*.

father hunger From the mythopoetic men's movement, men's yearning to be close to other men and to build deep, enduring bonds with them; based on the mythopoetic belief that most young boys have distant relationships with the primary man in their lives—the father—and that the hunger for meaningful contact with men, of which they were deprived in youth, continues throughout life.

Fathers 4 Justice A British fathers' rights group that relies on the two rhetorical strategies of humor and dramatic stunts to raise public awareness about the custody rights of separated and divorced fathers.

femicide The killing of girls and women.

feminine ruler Measuring closeness, or intimacy in a way that gives priority to behaviors more typical of women than of men.

Free Men A branch of the men's movement that seeks to restore the traditional image of men by celebrating and encouraging the qualities of competitiveness, independence, and ruggedness in men.

gatekeeper Person or group that controls which messages get through to audiences of mass media.

gender Also called gender role. A social, symbolic construction that expresses the meanings a society associates with biological sex. Gender varies across cultures, over time within any given society, and in relation to other genders.

gender constancy A person's understanding, which usually develops by age three, that her or his sex is relatively fixed and unchanging.

gender identity A person's private sense of, and subjective experience of, his or her own gender.

gender intimidation The treatment of members of one sex in ways that make them feel humiliated, unsafe, or inferior because of their sex.

gender-linked language effect Asserts that differences between women's and men's communication are influenced by a variety of factors including topics, speaker status, salience of gender in a communication situation, and other people present.

gender schema An internal mental framework that organizes perceptions and directs behavior related to gender.

gender schema theory Claims that cognitive processes are central to our learning what gender means in our culture and to learning how to perform our gender competently. Related to *cognitive development theory*.

gendered violence Physical, verbal, emotional, sexual, or visual brutality inflicted disproportionately or exclusively on members of one sex. Includes gender intimidation, sexual assault, violence between intimates, sexual harassment, genital mutilation, and gender-based murder.

glass ceiling An invisible barrier, made up of subtle, often unconscious prejudices and stereotypes, that limits the opportunities and advancement of women and minorities.

glass escalator An invisible advantage that accelerates men's success in female-dominated spheres of work.

glass walls A metaphor for sex segregation on the job. Glass walls exist when members of a group, such as women, are placed in positions based on stereotypes of that group. Typically, such positions do not entail advancement ladders.

goal A stated intention to achieve a defined representation of minorities or women.

Good Men Project A multifaceted effort to stimulate a national conversation about what it means to be a good man today.

haptics Touch as a form of nonverbal communication.

hermaphrodite A person who possesses aspects of physical genitalia from both sexes. Currently, *intersexual* is the preferred term.

heternormativity The assumption that heterosexuality is normative and all other sexual identities are abnormal.

hostile environment harassment Conduct that has sexual overtones and that interferes with a person's ability to perform a job or gain an education or that creates a hostile, intimidating, or offensive working environment.

immersive advertising Incorporating a particular brand or product into entertainment.

infibulation Removal of the clitoris and labia minora and subsequent joining of the lips of the labia majora so that they fuse together.

informed consent Consent given by a legal adult with normal mental abilities whose judgment is not impaired by circumstances, including alcohol or other drugs.

intersexed Having both male and female biological sexual characteristics.

intimate partner violence The use of physical, mental, emotional, verbal, or economic power by one partner against the other partner in a current or past romantic relationship.

invisible hand discrimination The inadvertent application, in discriminatory fashion, of policies that are not inherently biased.

kinesics Facial and body movements; one type of nonverbal communication.

liberal feminism A form of feminism that maintains that women and men are alike in important respects and that women should have the same economic, political, professional, and civic opportunities and rights as men. NOW (the National Organization for Women) is the best-known organization representing liberal feminism.

liking The dimension of relationship-level meaning that expresses affection for another.

male circumcision Removal of the sheath, or prepuce, of the penis.

male deficit model A relationship theory according to which men are deficient in forming and participating in close relationships; holds that most men's ways of experiencing and expressing closeness are not simply different from, but inferior to, those of women.

male feminists Men who believe that women and men are alike in important respects and that the sexes should enjoy the same privileges, rights, opportunities, and status in society. Male feminists join liberal women feminists in fighting for equitable treatment of women. In addition, many male feminists seek to rid themselves of what they regard as toxic masculinity promoted in men by socialization, and to develop sensitivities more typically inculcated in women. Also called *profeminist men.*

male generic language Words and phrases that are claimed to refer to both women and men yet are denotatively masculine; for example, the word *man* used to refer to all human beings.

masculinist A category of men's movement that sees men as oppressed and seeks to preserve men's freedom from women and feminization.

maternal wall Unexamined assumptions held by coworkers and superiors about how women will behave once they become mothers.

matriarchal Of or pertaining to matriarchy, "rule by the mothers." The term *matriarchy* is generally used to refer to systems of ideology, social structures, and practices that are created by women and reflect the values, priorities, and views of women as a group.

men's rights activists Members of a men's movement whose goal is to restore traditional roles for men and women and, with that, the privileges men have historically enjoyed.

mentor A more experienced person who helps a less experienced person develop.

Mentors in Violence Prevention (MVP) A male antiviolence program that educates men about socialization that links masculinity to violence and aggression; motivates men to reject violence in themselves and in other men; emphasizes role of bystander.

Million Man March A branch of the men's movement that began with a march in Washington, DC, in 1995, in which black men atoned for sins and committed themselves to spiritual transformation and political action. Annual marches were also held in subsequent years.

Million Woman March A grassroots gathering of African-American women launched in Philadelphia in 1997 to celebrate and foster solidarity among black women.

minimal response cues Nominal indicators of listening or attending. "Um" and "yeah" are minimal response cues.

multiracial feminism A branch of the women's movement that is concerned with race and the racial oppression of women.

mythopoetic movement A branch of the men's movement headed by poet Robert Bly and active in the 1990s. Mythopoetics believe that men need to rediscover their distinctively masculine modes of feeling, which they regard as rooted largely in myth.

NOMAS (National Organization for Men Against Sexism) An activist men's organization that promotes personal, political, and social changes that foster equality of men and women and gay and straight people through workshops and informal group discussions, public speaking, educational outreach programs, and enactment of traitorous identities.

nonverbal communication All elements of communication other than words themselves. Estimated to carry 65 to 93% of the total meaning of communication; includes visual, vocal, environmental, and physical aspects of interaction.

paralanguage Vocal cues that accompany verbal communication, such as accent, volume, and inflection.

patriarchal Of or pertaining to patriarchy, "rule by the fathers." The term *patriarchy* generally refers to systems of ideology, social structures, and practices created by men, which reflect the values, priorities, and views of men as a group.

performative theory Claims that identity, including gender, is not something individuals have, but rather something they do through performance or expression.

personal relationships Connections in which partners are interdependent, consider each other irreplaceable, and are strongly and specifically connected to each other as unique individuals.

physical appearance Aspects of personal appearance; often evaluated according to cultural standards.

polarized thinking Conceiving things in terms of opposites (e.g., good or bad, right or wrong).

pornography Written, oral, or visual material that favorably shows subordination and degradation of individuals by presenting sadistic behaviors as pleasurable, pain as enjoyable, and forced sex as positive. Distinct from erotica, which depicts consensual activities desired by and pleasurable to all parties.

power Dimension of relationship-level meaning that expresses the degree to which a person is equal to, dominant over, or deferential to others.

power feminism A movement that emerged in the 1990s as a reaction to feminist emphasis on women's oppression. Urges women to take the power that is theirs and to reject seeing themselves as victims of men or society.

product placement Showing or mentioning a particular brand or product in a show, story, film, or other form of media.

profeminists See *male feminists.*

Promise Keepers Begun in 1990, a Christian branch of the men's movement that calls men together to pray and commit to Christ-centered living.

proxemics Space and the human use of space, including personal territories.

psychodynamic theory The theory that family relationships, especially between mother and child during the formative years of life, have a pivotal and continuing impact on the development of self, particularly gender identity.

psychological responsibility The responsibility to remember, plan, think ahead, organize, and so forth. In most heterosexual relationships, even when physical labor is divided between partners, women assume greater psychological responsibility for the home and children.

qualitative research methods Aim to understand the nature or meaning of experiences, which cannot be quantified into numbers.

quantitative research methods Way of gathering data that can be quantified and analyzing the data to draw conclusions.

queer performative theories Integration of queer and performative theories into a perspective on performances as means of challenging and destabilizing conventional cultural categories and the values attached to them.

queer theory Critique of conventional categories of identity and cultural views of "normal" and "abnormal," particularly in relation to sexuality. Queer theory argues identities are not fixed, but fluid.

quid pro quo harassment Actual or threatened use of professional or academic rewards or punishments to gain sexual compliance from a subordinate or student.

quota A particular number or percentage of women or minorities who must be admitted to schools, hired in certain positions, or promoted to certain levels in institutions.

radical feminism A branch of feminism that grew out of New Left politics and demanded the same attention to women's oppression that New Left organizations gave to racial oppression and other ideological issues. Radical feminists pioneered revolutionary communication techniques such as consciousness raising, leaderless group discussion, and guerrilla theater.

relationship level of meaning The nonliteral meaning of communication. Expresses how a speaker sees the relationship between self and other. May provide cues about how to interpret the literal meaning of a message, for instance, as a joke.

reproductive violence Coerced or discriminatory infringement on reproductive rights. It includes force or exploitation that inhibits an individual's free choice of whether, when, and with whom to reproduce, become a parent, and parent existing children.

responsiveness The dimension of relationship-level meaning that expresses attentiveness to others and interest in what they say and do.

revalorism Feminist group that focuses on valuing traditionally feminine skills, activities, and perspectives and their contributions to personal, interpersonal, and cultural life.

role Social definitions of expected behaviors and the values associated with them; typically internalized by individuals in the process of socialization.

second shift The work of homemaking and child care performed by a member of a dual-worker family after and in addition to that person's job in the paid labor force.

separatism Feminist group that believes that, because patriarchal culture cannot be changed or reformed, women who find it oppressive must create and live in their own women-centered communities separate from the larger culture.

sex A personal quality determined by biological and genetic characteristics. *Male*, *female*, *man*, and *woman* indicate sex.

sexual assault Sexual activity to which at least one participant has not given informed consent.

sexual harassment Unwelcome sexualized conduct that is linked to the target's academic or professional standing.

sexual orientation A person's preferences for romantic and sexual partners.

social learning theory Theory that individuals learn to be masculine and feminine (among other things) by observing and imitating others and by reacting to the rewards and punishments others give in response to imitative behaviors.

speech community A group of people who share assumptions regarding how, when, and why to communicate and how to interpret others' communication.

standpoint theory A theory that focuses on the influence of gender, race, class, and other social categories on circumstances of people's lives, especially their social positions and the kinds of experiences fostered within those positions. According to standpoint theory, political consciousness about social location can generate a standpoint that affects perspective and action.

stereotype A broad generalization about an entire class of phenomena, based on some knowledge of limited aspects of certain members of the class.

sunna Genital mutilation involving removal of the sheath and tip of the clitoris. Also called *female circumcision*.

symbolic interactionism The theory that individuals develop self-identity and an understanding of social life, values, and codes of conduct through communicative interactions with others in a society.

territoriality An aspect of proxemics; the sense of personal space that one does not want others to invade.

theory A way to describe, explain, and predict relationships among phenomena.

third person effect The belief that media affect others more than they affect us.

third-wave feminism An emergent movement asserting that feminism for the current era is not just an extension of second-wave feminism. Aims (1) to be inclusive of diverse peoples; (2) to use personal life and personal action for political impact; and (3) to work to build coalitions with other groups that struggle against oppression.

Title IX The section of the Educational Amendment of 1972 that makes it illegal for schools that accept federal funds to discriminate on the basis of sex.

traitorous identity A group member's criticism of particular attitudes and actions—for example, sexist jokes—that are accepted and normative within the group.

transgendered Individual who feels that her or his biologically assigned sex is inconsistent with her or his true sexual identity.

transsexual Individual who has had surgery and/or hormonal treatments to make his or her body more closely match the sex with which he or she identifies.

transvestites People who enjoy wearing clothing of the other sex.

voice-over A technique used in audiovisual media, particularly television commercials; over the action on the screen, viewers hear a voice that makes claims about the product, gives advice, or explains the action.

White Ribbon Campaign (WRC) An international group of men who work to end men's violence against women.

womanism Activism started by black women to define oppression as resulting from both race and sex. The womanist movement arose out of dissatisfaction with mainstream feminism's predominant focus on white, middle-class women and their interests.

women's rights movement From the mid-1800s to the 1920s, a movement that focused on gaining basic rights for women, such as the rights to vote, to pursue higher education, and to enter professions.

workplace bullying Repeatedly acting toward a person or persons in ways that humiliate, intimidate, or otherwise undermine the target's professional credibility.

References

Abrams, J. (2009, January 23). Bill lifting limits on equal-pay lawsuits clears Senate. *Raleigh News & Observer*, p. 6A.

Acitelli, L. (1988). When spouses talk to each other about their relationship. *Journal of Social and Personal Relationships, 5*, 185–199.

Adams, C. (1991, April). The straight dope. *Triangle Comic Review*, p. 26.

Adler, J. (2007, March 12). The great sorority purge. *Newsweek*, p. 47.

Adler, R. (2009, March–April). Profit, thy name is ... woman? *Miller-McCune*, pp. 33–35.

Alexander, B. (2012, June 22). Macdonald's the "Brave" girl. *USA Today*, pp. 1D, 2D.

Allen, B. (2006). Communicating race at Weigh Co. In J. T. Wood & S. W. Duck (Eds.), *Composing relationships: Communication in everyday life* (pp. 156–165). Belmont, CA: Thomson.

Allis, S. (1990, Fall). What do men really want? *Time*, pp. 80–82.

Almaguer, T. (1993). Chicano men: A cartography of homosexual identity and behavior. In H. Abelove, M. Barale, & D. Halperin (Eds.), *The lesbian and gay studies reader* (pp. 255–273). London: Routledge.

Alter, J. (1990, December 31). One well-read editorial. *Newsweek*, pp. 85, 86.

American Association of University Women (AAUW). (1991). *Shortchanging girls, shortchanging America*. Washington, DC: Greenberg-Lake Analysis Group.

American Association of University Women (AAUW). (1998). *Gender gaps: Where schools still fail our children*. Washington, DC: American Association of University Women Educational Foundation.

American Association of University Women (AAUW). (2001). *Beyond the "gender wars": A conversation about girls, boys, and education*. Washington, DC: American Association of University Women Educational Foundation.

American Society for Aesthetic Plastic Surgeons. (2012). *Celebrating 15 years of trustworthy plastic surgery statistics*. Retrieved from http://www.surgery.org/media/news-releases/celebrating-15-years-of-trustworthy-plastic-surgery-statistics

Andelin, H. (1975). *Fascinating womanhood*. New York: Bantam.

Andersen, M., & Collins, P. H. (Eds.). (2007a). *Race, class, and gender: An anthology* (6th ed.). Belmont, CA: Thomson.

Andersen, P. (2006). The evolution of biological sex differences in communication. In K. Dindia & D. Canary (Eds.), *Sex differences and similarities in communication* (pp. 117–135). Mahwah, NJ: Erlbaum.

Anderson, J. (2011, November 7). National study finds widespread sexual harassment of students in grades 7 to 12. *The New York Times*, p. A10.

Anderson, J. (2012, July 5). Alumni criticism grows over Horace Mann's response to reports of sexual abuse. *The New York Times*, pp. A14, A15.

Anderson, K., & Leaper, C. (1998). Meta-analyses of gender effects on conversational interruption: Who, what, when, where, and how. *Sex Roles, 39*, 225–252.

Andronici, J. F., & Katz, D. S. (2007, Winter). Scaling the maternal wall. *Ms.*, pp. 63–64.

Angier, N. (2007a, May 1). For motherly X chromosome, gender is only the beginning. *The New York Times*, pp. Dl, D6.

Angier, N. (2007b, June 12). Sleek, fast and focused: The cells that make dad dad. *The New York Times*, pp. D1, D6.

Angier, N. (2010, June 15). Paternal bonds, special and strange. *The New York Times*, pp. D1, D2.

Anzaldúa, G. (1999). *Borderlands/la frontera: The new mestizo*. San Francisco: Spinsters/Aunt Lute.

Anzaldua, G. (2002, October 11). Beyond traditional notions of identity. *The Chronicle of Higher Education*, pp. B11–B13.

Anzaldua, G., & Keating, A. (Eds.). (2002). *This bridge called home*. New York: Routledge.

Archer, J., & Coyne, S. (2005). An integrated review of indirect, relational, and social aggression. *Personality and Social Review, 9*, 212–230.

Aronowitz, T., Rennells, R. E., & Todd, E. (2005). Heterosocial behaviors in early adolescent African American girls: The role of mother-daughter relationships. *Journal of Family Nursing, 11*, 122–139.

Arroyo, A., & Harwood, J. (2012). Exploring the causes and consequences of engaging in fat talk. *Journal of Applied Communication Research, 40*, 167–187.

Ashcraft, K. (2006). Back to work: Sights/sites of difference in gender and organizational communication studies. In B. Dow & J. T. Wood (Eds.), *Handbook of gender and communication* (pp. 97–122). Thousand Oaks, CA: Sage.

Average salaries of full-time faculty members, 2011-2012. (2012, August 31). *The Chronicle of Higher Education*, p. 6.

Babarskiene, J., & Tweed, R. (2009). Marital adjustment in post-Soviet Eastern Europe: A focus on Lithuania. *Personal Relationships, 16,* 647–658.

Babel, C., & Kwan, S. (Eds.). (2011). *Embodied resistance: Challenging the norms, breaking the rules.* Nashville, TN: Vanderbilt University Press.

Baenninger, M. (2011, October 7). For women on campus, access doesn't equal success. *The Chronicle of Higher Education,* p. A26.

Bagemihl, B. (2000). *Biological exuberance: Animal homosexuality and natural diversity.* Boston: St. Martin's Press.

Bakalar, N. (2006, June 13). Men are better than women at ferreting out that angry face in a crowd. *The New York Times,* p. D5.

Bakalar, N. (2009, March 27). Circumcision is found to curb two S.T.D.'s. *The New York Times,* p. A17.

Baker, J. (2006). *Sisters: The lives of America's suffragists.* New York: Hill and Wang.

Balaji, M., & Worawongs, T. (2010, June). The new Suzie Wong: Normative assumptions of white male and Asian female relationships. *Communication, Culture & Critique, 3,* 224–241.

Bandura, A. (2002). Social cognitive theory of mass communication. In J. Bryant & D. Zillmann (Eds.), *Media effects: Advances in theory and research* (2nd ed., pp. 121–153). Mahwah, NJ: Erlbaum.

Bandura, A., & Walters, R. H. (1963). *Social learning and personality development.* New York: Holt, Rinehart & Winston.

Banks, I. (2000). *Hair matters: Beauty, power, and black women's consciousness.* New York: New York University Press.

Barash, D. (2002, May 24). Evolution, males, and violence. *The Chronicle of Higher Education,* pp. B7–B9.

Barash, D., & Lipton, J. (2002). *Gender gap: The biology of male-female differences.* New Brunswick, NJ: Transaction Publishers.

Barash, S. (2006). *Tripping the prom queen.* New York: St. Martin's Griffin.

Barnett, R., & Rivers, C. (1996). *She works, he works: How two-income families are happier, healthier, and better off.* San Francisco: HarperCollins.

Barnett, R., & Rivers, C. (2004). *Same difference: How gender myths are hurting our relationships, our children, and our jobs.* New York: Basic Books.

Barres, B. (2006, July). Does gender matter? *Nature, 442,* 133–136.

Barreto, M., Ryan, M., & Schmitt, M. (Eds.). (2009). *The glass ceiling in the 21st century.* Washington, DC: American Psychological Association.

Barrett, J. (2004, May 10). No time for wrinkles. *Newsweek,* pp. 82–85.

Barry, K. (1998). Radical feminism. In W. Mankiller, G. Mink, M. Navarro, B. Smith, & G. Steinem (Eds.), *The reader's companion to U.S. women's history* (pp. 217–218). New York: Houghton Mifflin.

Bartlett, N. B., & Vasey, P. L. (2006). A retrospective study of childhood gender-atypical behavior in Samoan fa'afafine. *Archives of Sexual Behavior, 35,* 559–566.

Basow, S. A. (1990). Effects of teacher expressiveness: Mediated by sex-typing? *Journal of Educational Psychology, 82,* 599–602.

Basow, S. A., & Rubenfeld, K. (2003). "Troubles talk": Effects of gender and gender-typing. *Sex Roles, 48,* 183–187.

Batman scales wall near palace balcony. (2004, September 14). *Raleigh News & Observer,* p. A2.

Baumgardner, J., & Richards, A. (2000). *Manifesto: Young women, feminism, and the future.* New York: Farrar, Straus & Giroux.

Bazelon, E. (2013). *Sticks and stones: Defeating the culture of bullying and rediscovering the power of character and empathy.* New York: Random House.

Bearak, B. (2009, August 26). Inquiry about sprinter's sex angers South Africans. *The New York Times,* p. A6.

Beatie, T. (2008). *Labor of love: The story of one man's extraordinary pregnancy.* Boston: Seal.

Beck, B. (2011, November 26). Closing the gap. *The Economist,* pp. 3–20.

Beck, R. (2008, January 23). When they couldn't even vote. *Raleigh News & Observer,* p. A14.

Becker, A., Burwell, R., Gilman, S., Herzog, D., & Hamburg, P. (2002). Eating behaviours and attitudes following prolonged exposure to television among ethnic Fijian adolescent girls. *British Journal of Psychiatry, 180,* 509–514.

Becker, C. S. (1987). Friendship between women: A phenomenological study of best friends. *Journal of Phenomenological Psychology, 18,* 59–72.

Begley, S. (2009, June 29). Don't blame the cavemen. *Newsweek,* pp. 50–62.

Belluck, P. (2011, September 13). Fatherhood cuts testosterone, study finds, for good of the family. *The New York Times,* pp. A1, A3.

Bem, S. L. (1983). Gender schema theory and its implications for child development: Raising gender-aschematic children in a gender-schematic society. *Signs, 8,* 598–616.

Bem, S. L. (1993). *The lenses of gender: Transforming the debate on sexual inequality.* New Haven, CT: Yale University Press.

Benenson, J., Del Bianco, R., Philippoussis, M., & Apostoleris, N. (1997). Girls' expression of their own perspectives in the presence of varying numbers of boys. *International Journal of Behavioral Development, 21,* 389–405.

Bennett, J., Ellison, J., & Ball, S. (2010). Are we there yet? *Newsweek*, pp. 42–46.

Bennetts, L. (2012, March 12). A long way to go. *Newsweek*, p. 5.

Beren, S., Hayden, H., Wilfey, D., & Grilo, C. (1996). The influence of sexual orientation on body dissatisfaction in adult men and women. *The International Journal of Eating Disorders*, 20, 135–141.

Berger, A. (2011). *Ads, fads, and consumer culture*. Lanham, MD: Rowman & Littlefield.

Berger, E. (2006). *Raising kids with character*. New York: Rowman & Littlefield.

Bergeron, C. (2009, November 2). A few "Good Men": Authors spread wisdom of manhood. *Metrowest Daily News*. Retrieved from http://www.metrowestdailynews.com/news/x16594 94253/A-few-Good-Men-Authors-spread-wisdom-of-manhood?zc_p=0

Bernstein, A. (1999, February 1). Why the law should adopt more family leave. *Business Week*, p. 48.

Bernstein, F. (2004, March 17). On campus, rethinking Biology 101. *The New York Times*, pp. 9-1, 9-6.

Bianchi, S., Robinson, J., & Milkie, M. (2006). *Changing rhythms of American family life*. New York: Russell Sage Foundation.

Bierhoff, H. (1996). Heterosexual partnerships: Initiation, maintenance and disengagement. In A. E. Auhagen & M. von Salisch (Eds.), *The diversity of human relationships* (pp. 173–196). New York: Cambridge University Press.

The big reveal. (2009, October 29). *The Chronicle of Higher Education*, p. B18.

Bigham, J. (1991, January 11). Birth control order stands until appeal. *The Oregonian* [Portland, Oregon], p. A16.

Bilefsky D. (2008, June 25). *Albanian custom fades: Woman as family man*. Retrieved July 7, 2008, from http://www.nytimes.com/2008/06/25/world/Europe/25virgins.html?ex=137213 2800&en=8668ba514ff6f5fd&ei=5124&partner=permalink&exprod=permalink

Birdwhistell, R. (1970). *Kinesics and context*. Philadelphia: University of Pennsylvania Press.

Blackless, M., Charuvastra, A., Derryek, A., Fausto-Sterling, A., Lauzanne, K., & Lee, E. (2000). How sexually dimorphic are we? Review and synthesis. *American Journal of Human Biology*, 12, 151–166.

Blades, J., & Rowe-Finkbeiner, K. (2006). *The motherhood manifesto*. New York: Nation Books.

Blum, D. (1997). *Sex on the brain: The biological differences between women and men*. New York: Penguin.

Blum, D. (1998). The gender blur: Where does biology end and society take over? *Utne Reader*, 45–48.

Bland, K. (2012, June 29). *Dad on duty*. Retrieved from http://www.azcentral.com/arizonarepublic/news/articles/2009/06/21/20090621dadtoday06210.html

Blow, C. (2012, June 23). Bullies on the bus. *The New York Times*, p. A19.

Bly, R. (1990). *Iron John: A book about men*. Reading, MA: Addison-Wesley.

Bobbitt-Zeher, D. (2011). Gender discrimination at work: Connecting gender stereotypes, institutional policies, and gender composition of workplace. *Gender & Society*, 25, 764–786.

Bocella, K. (2001, January 31). Eating disorders spread among minority girls, women. *Raleigh News & Observer*, p. 5E.

Bodey, K. (2009). *Exploring the possibilities of self work: Girls speak about their lives*. Ph.D. Dissertation. Department of Communication Studies, The University of North Carolina, Chapel Hill.

Bodey, K. R., & Wood, J. T. (2009). Whose voices count and who does the counting? *Southern Communication Journal*, 74, 325–337.

Bond, J. T., Thompson, C., Galinsky, E., & Prottas, D. (2002). *Highlights of the national study of the changing workforce: Executive summary, Vol. 3*. Washington, DC: Families and Work Institute.

Bonnett, A. (1996). The new primitives: Identity, landscape and cultural appropriation in the mythopoetic men's movement. *Antipode*, 28, 273–291.

Bonnett, C. (2007, May 13). What's up with mom? *Raleigh News & Observer*, pp. 23A–24A.

Boodman, S. (2007, March 15). Eating disorders strike men. *Raleigh News & Observer*, pp. IE, 3E.

Bordo, S. (1997). *Twilight zones: The hidden life of cultural images from Plato to O. J.* Berkeley: University of California Press.

Bordo, S. (2004). *Unbearable weight: Feminism, western culture, and the body*. Berkeley: University of California Press.

Borenstein, S. (2010, January 14). Ladies first? Chromosomes say no. *Raleigh News & Observer*, p. 4A.

Borisoff, D., & Chesebro, J. (2011). *Communicating power & gender*. Long Grove, IL: Waveland.

Boston Women's Health Club Book Collective. (1976). *Our bodies/ourselves* (2nd ed.). New York: Simon & Schuster.

Boustany, N. (2007, July 4). Rape called a weapon in Sudan. *Raleigh News & Observer*, p. 7A.

Bowen, W., & Bok, D. (1998). *The shape of the river*. Princeton, NJ: Princeton University Press.

Braithwaite, D., & Kellas, J. (2006). Shopping for and with friends: Everyday communication at the shopping mall. In J. T. Wood & S. W. Duck (Eds.), *Composing relationships: Communication in everyday life* (pp. 86–95). Belmont, CA: Thomson/Wadsworth.

Breines, W. (2006). *The trouble between us: An uneasy history of white and black women in the feminist movement.* New York: Oxford University Press.

Brizendine, L. (2007). *The female brain.* New York: Doubleday/Broadway.

Bronstein, Z. (2004, Spring). Nowhere woman. *Dissent,* pp. 90–97.

Brooks, D. (2010, February 16). The lean years. *The New York Times,* p. A23.

Brooks, D. (2012, July 10). The opportunity gap. *The New York Times,* p. A19.

Brooks, D. E., & Hebert, L. P. (2006). Gender, race and media representation. In B. Dow & J. T. Wood (Eds.), *Handbook of gender and communication* (pp. 297–317). Thousand Oaks, CA: Sage.

Brown, L. (1997). *Two-spirit people.* Binghamton, NY: Haworth Press.

Brown, L. M., Lamb, S., & Tappan, M. (2009). *Packaging boyhood.* New York: St. Martin's Press.

Browne, K. (2003/2004, Winter). Fighting fistula. *Ms.,* p. 20.

Browne, K., & Hamilton-Giachritsis, C. (2005). The influence of violent media on children and adolescents: A public-health approach. *Lancet, 365,* 702–710.

Bryant, A., & Check, E. (2000, Fall/Winter). How parents raise boys and girls. *Newsweek,* pp. 64–65.

Bugeja, M. (2010, February 25). Avatar rape. *Inside Higher Ed.* Retrieved from http://www.insidehighered.com/views/2010/02/25/bugeja

Bulik, C., & Taylor, N. (2005). *Runaway eating.* New York: Rodale Books.

Burk, M. (2005). *Cult of power: Sex discrimination in corporate America and what can be done about it.* New York: Scribner.

Burleson, B. (1997, November). *Sex-related differences in communicative behavior: A matter of social skills, not gender cultures.* Paper presented at the National Communication Convention, Chicago.

Burleson, B. R., Holmstrom, A. J., & Gilstrap, C. M. (2005). Guys can't say that to guys: Four experiments assessing the normative motivation account for deficiencies in the emotional support provided by men. *Communication Monographs, 72,* 468–501.

Burn, J. (1996). *The social psychology of gender.* New York: McGraw-Hill.

Burnett, A., Mattern, J., Herakova, L., Kahl, D., Jr., Tabola, C., & Bornsen, E. (2009). Communicating/muting date rape: A co-cultural theoretical analysis of communication factors related to rape culture on a college campus. *Journal of Applied Communication Research, 37,* 435–465.

Burney, M. (2012, March 15). Standing up to bullies. *The Chronicle of Higher Education* [Supplement: Diverse: Issues in Higher Education], pp. 50–53.

Buss, D. (1994). *The evolution of desire: Strategies of human mating.* New York: Basic Books.

Buss, D. (1995). Evolutionary psychology: A new paradigm for psychological science. *Psychological Inquiry, 6,* 1–30.

Buss, D. (1996). The evolutionary psychology of human social strategies. In E. Higgins & A. Druglanski (Eds.), *Social psychology: Handbook of basic principles* (pp. 3–38). New York: Guilford.

Buss, D. (1999). *Evolutionary psychology: The new science of the mind.* Boston: Allyn & Bacon.

Buss, D., & Kenrick, D. (1998). Evolutionary social psychology. In D. Gilbert, S. Fiske, & G. Lindzey (Eds.), *The handbook of social psychology* (4th ed., Vol. 2, pp. 982–1026). Boston: McGraw-Hill.

Butaine, R., & Costenbader, V. (1997). Self-reported differences in the experience and expression of anger between girls and boys. *Sex Roles, 36,* 625–637.

Butler, J. (1990). Performative acts and gender constitution: An essay in phenomenology and feminist theory. In S. Case (Ed.), *Performing feminisms: Feminist critical theory and theater* (pp. 270–282). Baltimore: Johns Hopkins University Press.

Butler, J. (1993a). *Bodies that matter: On the discursive limits of "sex."* New York: Routledge.

Butler, J. (1993b). *Gender trouble: Feminism and the subversion of identity.* New York: Routledge.

Butler, J. (2004). *Undoing gender.* London: Routledge.

Butsch, R. (2011). Ralph, Fred, Archie, Homer, and the king of Queens: Why television keeps recreating the male working-class buffoon. In G. Dines & J. Humez (Eds.), *Gender, race, and class in media: A critical reader* (3rd ed., pp. 101–109). Los Angeles: Sage.

Buzzanell, P. M., & Lucas, K. (2006). Gendered stories of career: Unfolding discourses of time, space, and identity. In B. Dow & J. T. Wood (Eds.), *Handbook of gender and communication* (pp. 161–178). Thousand Oaks, CA: Sage.

Caldwell, M., & Peplau, L. (1982). Sex differences in same-sex friendship. *Sex Roles, 8,* 721–732.

California: Gang rape is investigated. (2009, October 27). *The New York Times,* p. A21.

Callimachi, R. (2007, February 5). Here, women woo, men wait. *Raleigh News & Observer,* p. 10A.

Campbell, A. (2002). *A mind of her own.* Oxford: Oxford University Press.

Campbell, K. K. (1989a). *Man cannot speak for her: I. A critical study of early feminist rhetoric.* New York: Praeger.

Campbell, K. K. (1989b). *Man cannot speak for her: II. Key texts of the early feminists.* New York: Greenwood.

Campbell, K. K. (Ed.). (1993). *Women public speakers in the United States: A bio-critical sourcebook*. Westport, CT: Greenwood.

Campbell, K. (2005). Agency: Promiscuous and protean. *Communication and Critical/Cultural Studies, 2*, 1–19.

Canary, D., & Wahba, J. (2006). Do women work harder than men at maintaining relationships? In K. Dindia & D. Canary (Eds.), *Sex differences and similarities in communication* (2nd ed., pp. 359–377). Mahwah, NJ: Erlbaum.

Cancian, F. (1987). *Love in America*. Cambridge, MA: Cambridge University Press.

Cancian, F. (1989). Love and the rise of capitalism. In B. Risman & P. Schwartz (Eds.), *Gender and intimate relationships* (pp. 12–25). Belmont, CA: Wadsworth.

Cantos, L. (2004). De ambiente: Queer tourism and the shifting boundaries of Mexican male sexualities. In J. Spade & C. Valentine (Eds.), *The gender kaleidoscope* (pp. 521–531). Belmont, CA: Thomson/Wadsworth.

Carter, N. M., & Silva, C. (2010). *Broken promises*. New York: Catalyst.

Cassidy, T. (2004, July 5). Proper whites? *Raleigh News & Observer*, p. 3B.

Caughlin, J., & Vangelisti, A. (2000). An individual differences explanation of why married couples engage in the demand/withdraw pattern of conflict. *Journal of Social and Personal Relationships, 17*, 523–551.

Caughlin, P., & Caughlin, P. (2005). *No more Christian nice guy*. Minneapolis, MN: Bethany House.

Ceci, S. J., & Williams, W. M. (Eds.). (2007). *Why aren't more women in science?* Washington, DC: American Psychological Association.

Ceci, S. J., & Williams, W. M. (2009). *The mathematics of sex*. New York: Oxford University Press.

Centers for Disease Control (CDC). (2011). *National intimate partner and sexual violence survey: 2010 summary report*. Retrieved from http://www.cdc.gov/ViolencePrevention/pdf/NISVS_Report2010-a.pdf

Chang, A., Sandhofer, C., & Brown, C. (2012). Gender biases in early number exposure to preschool-aged children. *Journal of Language and Social Psychology, 30*, 440–450.

Channell, C. (2002). The Tatau: A bridge to manhood. *Faces, Places, and Culture*, 18–22.

Chapman, M., & Hendler, G. (Eds.). (1999). *Sentimental men: Masculinity and the politics of affect in American culture*. Berkeley: University of California Press.

Chaudhry, L. (2005, November 21). Babes in Bushworld. *In These Times*, pp. 38–39.

Chemaly, S. (2012, January 6). *Definition of rape: 7 ways to rethink how we approach sexual assault*. Retrieved from http://www.huffingtonpost.com/soraya-chemaly/definition-of-rape_b_1190255.html

Cheney, G., Christensen, L., Zorn, T., & Ganesh, S. (2004). *Organizational communication in an age of globalization*. Prospect Heights, IL: Waveland.

Chernik, A. F. (1995). The body politic. In B. Findlen (Ed.), *Listen up: Voices from the next generation of feminists* (pp. 75–84). Seattle: Seal Press.

Chesler, E. (1992). *Woman of valor: Margaret Sanger and the birth control movement in America*. New York: Simon & Schuster.

Chesley, N. (2011). Stay-at-home fathers and breadwinning mothers: Gender, couple dynamics, and social change. *Gender & Society, 25*, 642–664.

Chethik, N. (2001). *FatherLoss: How sons of all ages come to terms with the deaths of their dads*. New York: Hyperion.

Chethik, N. (2008). *VoiceMale: What husbands really think about their marriages, their wives, sex, housework and commitment*. New York: Simon & Schuster.

Childress, S. (2005, May 9). Anti-misogyny message. *Newsweek*, p. 13.

Chodorow, N. J. (1978). *The reproduction of mothering: Psychoanalysis and the sociology of gender*. Berkeley: University of California Press.

Chodorow, N. J. (1989). *Feminism and psychoanalytic theory*. New Haven, CT: Yale University Press.

Chodorow, N. J. (1999). *The power of feelings: Personal meaning in psychoanalysis, gender, and culture*. New Haven, CT: Yale University Press.

Christopher, K. (2012). Extensive mothering: Employed mothers' constructions of the good mother. *Gender & Society, 26*, 73–96.

Circumcision. (2012, September 15). *The Economist*, pp. 57–58.

Clarey, C., & Kolata, G. (2009, August 21). Gold is awarded, but dispute over runner's sex intensifies. *The New York Times*, p. B9.

Clark, R. A. (1998). A comparison of topics and objectives in a cross section of young men's and women's everyday conversations. In D. J. Canary & K. Dindia (Eds.), *Sex differences and similarities in communication: Critical essays and empirical investigations of sex and gender in interaction* (pp. 303–319). Mahwah, NJ: Erlbaum.

Clift, E. (2003). *Founding sisters and the nineteenth amendment*. New York: John Wiley & Sons.

Clinton, K. (2001, May). Unplugged: Surrendered wives. *The Nation*, p. 17.

Cloud, J. (2008, October 7). If women were more like men: Why females earn less. *Time Online*. Retrieved October 7, 2008, from http://www.time.com/time/nation/article/0,8599,1847194,00.html

Cognard-Black, J. (2007, Summer). Extreme makeover: Feminist edition. *Ms.*, pp. 46–49.

Colapinto, J. (2006). *As nature made him.* New York: HarperPerennial.

Cole, J. B., & Guy-Sheftall, B. (2003). *The struggle for women's equality in African American communities.* New York: Random House.

Collins, G. (2009a, January 29). Lilly's big day. *The New York Times,* p. A21.

Collins, G. (2009b). *When everything changed: The amazing journey of American women from 1960 to the present.* New York: Little, Brown, & Co.

Collins, P. H. (1986). Learning from the outsider within. *Social Problems, 33,* 514–532.

Collins, P. H. (1998). *Fighting words: Black women and the search for justice.* Minneapolis: University of Minnesota Press.

Collins, P. H. (2007, Spring). The lust generation. *Ms.,* pp. 73–74.

Coltrane, S. (1996). *Family man: Fatherhood, housework, and gender equity.* New York: Oxford University Press.

Connell, C. (2010). Doing, undoing, or redoing gender? Learning from the workplace experiences of transpeople. *Gender & Society, 24,* 31–55.

Consandine, A. (2012). Saying "no" to picture perfect. *The New York Times.* Retrieved from http://www.nytimes.com/2012/05/17/fashion/saying-no-to-picture-perfect.html?r=1

Considine, A. (2012, May 16). Saying "no" to picture perfect. *The New York Times.* Retrieved from http://www.nytimes.com/2012/05/17/fashion/saying-no-to picture-perfect.html?_r=1

Coontz, S. (2013a). Gender equality. *The New York Times,* pp. 1, 6, 7.

Coontz, S. (2013b). Why gender equality stalled. *The New York Times,* pp. 1, 6, 7.

Cooper, A. (2006, November–December). One of the guys: Transgender performance artist Scott Turner Schofield explores gender issues for the average Joe. *Utne Reader,* pp. 34–35.

Cose, E. (1997, October 13). Promises. *Newsweek,* pp. 30–31.

Cose, E. (2003, March 3). The black gender gap. *Newsweek,* pp. 46–51.

Cote, J. (1997). A social history of youth in Samoa: Religion, capitalism, and cultural disenfranchisement. *International Journal of Comparative Sociology, 38,* 207–222.

Cottle, M. (2012, May 28). Thank you, Rush Limbaugh! *Newsweek,* pp. 18–19.

Council on Contemporary Families. (2010). *Unconventional wisdom.* Retrieved April 14, 2010, from http://www.contemporaryfamilies.org/all/unconventional-wisdom-issue-3.html?=unconventional+wisdom

Cowley, G. (2003a, June 16). Why we strive for status. *Newsweek,* pp. 66–70.

Cowley, G. (2003b, September 8). Girls, boys, and autism. *Newsweek,* pp. 40–50.

Cox, M., & Aim, R. (2005, February 28). Scientists are made, not born. *The New York Times,* p. A25.

Cox, J. R. (2013). *Environmental communication and the public sphere* (3rd ed.). Thousand Oaks, CA: Sage.

Crary, D. (2008, December 8). Family-friendly laws face uncertain times. *Raleigh News & Observer,* p. 7A.

Crawford, B. J. (2007). Toward a third-wave feminist legal theory: Young women, pornography and the praxis of pleasure. *Michigan Journal of Gender & Law, 14,* 99.

Cronk, L. (1993). Parental favoritism toward daughters. *American Scientist, 81,* 272–279.

Crosby, F., Williams, J., & Biernat, M. (2005). The maternal wall. *Journal of Social Issues, 60,* 675–682.

Cross, G. (2008). *Men to boys: The making of modern immaturity.* New York: Columbia University Press.

Crouch, R. (1998). Betwixt and between: The past and the future of intersexuality. *Journal of Clinical Ethics, 9,* 372–384.

Crown, L., & Roberts, L. (2007). Against their will: Young women's nonagentic sexual experiences. *Journal of Social and Personal Relationships, 24,* 385–405.

Crowston, K., & Kammeres, E. (1998). Communicative style and gender differences in computer-mediated communications. In B. Ebo (Ed.), *Cyberghetto or cybertopia* (pp. 185–202). Westport, CT: Praeger.

Cubbans, L. A., & Vannoy, D. (2004). Division of household labor as a source of contention for married and cohabiting couples in Metropolitan Moscow. *Journal of Family Issues, 25,* 182–185.

Cuklanz, L. M., & Moorti, S. (Eds.). (2009). *Local violence, global media.* New York: Peter Lang.

Cupach, W., & Spitzberg, B. (2011). Unilateral union: Obsessive relational intrusion and stalking in a romantic context. In D. O. Braithwaite & J. T. Wood (Eds.), *Casing interpersonal communication* (pp. 157–164). Dubuque, IA: Kendall-Hunt.

Curtis, J. W. (2010, Spring). "Faculty salary equity: Still a gender gap?" *On campus with women* (Association of American College and Universities), p. 1. Pay Equity (event). Retrieved from http://www.aacu.org/ocww/volume39_1/feature.cfm?section=2

Damaske, S. (2011). A "major career woman"? How women develop early expectations about work. *Gender & Society, 25,* 409–430.

Dana, R. (2011, December 19). All I want for Christmas is a brand-new face. *Newsweek,* pp. 13–15.

Dana, R. (2012, April 16). Cherchez la femme. *Newsweek,* p. 13.

Dao, J. (2009, September 22). Drill sergeant at heart, she ascends to a top spot in the Army. *The New York Times*, pp. A1, A22.

Dasgupta, S. D. (Eds.). (2007). *Body evidence: Intimate violence against South Asian women in America*. New Brunswick, NJ: Rutgers University Press.

Davies-Popelka, W. (2011). Mirror, mirror on the wall. In D. O. Braithwaite & J. T. Wood (Eds.), *Casing interpersonal communication* (pp. 25–32). Dubuque, IA: Kendall Hunt.

Davis, F. (1991). *Moving the mountain: The women's movement in America since 1960*. New York: Simon & Schuster.

Davison, K., & Birch, L. (2001). Weight, status, parent reaction, and self-concept in five-year-old girls. *Pediatrics, 107*, 42–53.

Davison, W. P. (1983). The third-person effect in communication. *Public Opinion Quarterly, 47*, 1–15.

Dawson, I. (2005, Summer). Good rap, bad rap. *Ms.*, p. 18.

De Alba, G. A., & Guzman, G. (2010). *Making a killing: Femicide, free trade, and la frontera*. Austin: University of Texas Press.

Dean, C. (2006, December 19). Women in science: The battle moves to the trenches. *The New York Times*, pp. D6–D7.

D'eaubonne, F. (1974). *Le feminisme ou la mart*. Paris: Pierre Horay.

DeFrancisco, V., & Chatham-Carpenter, A. (2000). Self in community: African American women's views of self-esteem. *Howard Journal of Communication, 11*, 73–92.

Dellios, H. (2006, May 24). Mexican law no longer sees bride as "weak creature." *Raleigh News & Observer*, p. 16A.

DeMaris, A. (2007). The role of relationship inequity in marital disruption. *Journal of Social and Personal Relationships, 24*, 177–195.

DeMaris, A., & Longmore, M. A. (1996). Ideology, power, and equity: Testing competing explanations for the perception of fairness in household labor. *Social Forces, 74*, 1043–1071.

Dennis, A., & Wood, J. T. (2012). "We're not going to have this conversation, but you get it.": Black Mother-Daughter Communication about Sexual Relations. *Women's Studies in Communication, 35*(2), 204–223. doi: 10.1080/07491409.2012.724525

De Ruijter, E., Treas, J. K., & Cohen, P. N. (2005). Outsourcing the gender factory: Living arrangements and service expenditures on female and male tasks. *Social Forces, 84*(1), 305–322.

DeVault, M. (1990). Conflict over housework: A problem that (still) has no name. In L. Kreisberg (Ed.), *Research in social movements, conflict, and change*. Greenwich, CT: JAI Press.

Deveny, K. (2009, June 30). We're bossy—and proud of it. *Newsweek*, p. 58.

Dewan, S., & Gebeloff, R. (2012, May 21). More men enter fields dominated by women. *The New York Times*, pp. A1, A3.

The Diagram Group. (1977). *Woman's body: An owner's manual*. New York: Bantam.

Dixon, T. L. (2006). Psychological reactions to crime news portrayals of black criminals: Understanding the moderating roles of prior news view and stereotype endorsement. *Communication Monographs, 73*, 162–187.

Docter, R. F., & Prince, V. (1997). Transvestism: A survey of 1032 cross-dressers. *Archives of Sexual Behavior, 26*, 589–605.

Dokoupil, T. (2008, September 8). Why I am leaving guyland. *Newsweek*, pp. 70–71.

Dokoupil, T. (2009, March 2). Men will be men. *Newsweek*, p. 50.

Dominous, S. (2005). The fathers' crusade. *The New York Times*, pp. 25–33, 50, 56–58.

Dorothy Roberts. (2001, April–May). *Ms*. Retrieved from http://www.msmagazine.com/apr01/roberts.html

Douglas, S. (2010a). *Enlightened sexism: The seductive message that feminism's work is done*. New York: Times Books.

Douglas, S. (2010b). *The rise of enlightened sexism: How pop culture took us from girl power to girls gone wild*. New York: St. Martin's.

Douglas, S., & Michaels, M. (2004). *The mommy myth: The idealization of motherhood and how it has undermined women*. New York: The Free Press.

Douglas, W. (2012, May 17). House Oks anti-domestic violence bill. *Raleigh News & Observer*, p. 3A.

Dow, B. J. (in press). Televising the revolution: Women's liberation. *Network News*, and 1970.

Dow, B. J., & Condit, C. (2005). The state of the art in feminist scholarship. *Journal of Communication, 55*, 448–478.

Dow, B. J., & Tonn, M. B. (1993). Feminine style and political judgment in the rhetoric of Ann Richards. *Quarterly Journal of Speech, 79*, 286–302.

Dow, B. J., & Wood, J. T. (Eds.). (2006). *The handbook of gender and communication*. Thousand Oaks, CA: Sage.

Dow, B. J., & Wood, J. T. (in press). Repeating history and learning from it: What can slut-walks teach us about feminism? In K. Silva & K. Mendes (Eds.), *The crisis in feminism*. New York: Palgrave.

Dowd, M. (2005, March 20). X-celling over men. *The New York Times*, pp. 4–13.

Doyle, J. (1997). *The male experience* (3rd ed.). Dubuque, IA: Brown & Benchmark.

Doyle, L. (2001). *The surrendered wife: A practical guide for finding intimacy, passion and peace with a man*. New York: Fireside.

Dreier, P., & Freer, R. (1997, October 24). Saints, sinners, and affirmative action. *The Chronicle of Higher Education*, pp. B6, B7.

Dreifus, C. (2000, July 11). A conversation with Nawal Nour. *The New York Times*, p. D7.

Driefus, C. (2010, June 22). A conversation with Elaine Fuchs. *The New York Times*, p. D3.

Dresser, N. (1996). *Multicultural manners*. New York: Wiley.

Dube, K. (2004, June 18). What feminism means to today's undergraduates. *The Chronicle of Higher Education*, p. B5.

Duenwald, M. (2005, March 8). Aspirin is found to protect women from strokes, not heart attacks. *The New York Times*, p. D5.

Duncan, G., & Murane, R. (2011). *Whither opportunity?* New York: Russell Sage Foundation.

Dunn, J. (1999). Siblings, friends, and the development of social understanding. In W. A. Collins & B. Laursen (Eds.), *Relationships as developmental contexts* (pp. 263–279). Mahwah, NJ: Erlbaum.

Durham, M. G. (2008). *The Lolita effect: The media sexualization of young girls and what we can do about it*. New York: Overlook Press.

Dyer, G. (2007, January 26). France gives birth to a trend. *Raleigh News & Observer*, p. 13A.

Eagly, A. H., & Carli, L. L. (2007). *Through the labyrinth: The truth about how women become leaders*. Boston: Harvard Business School Press.

Einarsen, S., Hoel, H., Zapf, D., & Cooper, C. (Eds.). (2010). *Bullying and harassment in the workplace: Developments in theory, research, and practice* (2nd ed.). Boca Raton, FL: Taylor & Francis/CRC.

Eisenberg, N. (2002). Empathy-related emotional responses, altruism, and their socialization. In R. Davidson & A. Harrington (Eds.), *Visions of compassion: Western scientists and Tibetan Buddhists examine human nature* (pp. 131–164). London: Oxford University Press.

Elliott, L. (2009). *Pink brain, blue brain: How small differences grow into troublesome gaps—and what we can do about it*. Boston: Houghton Mifflin-Harcourt.

Ellis, K. M., & Eriksen, K. (2002). Transsexual and transgenderist experiences and treatment options. *The Family Journal, 10*, 289–299.

Ensler, E. (2000). *The vagina monologues: The V-Day edition*. New York: Random House, Villard.

Ensler, E. (2001). *Necessary targets: A story of women and war*. New York: Random House, Villard.

Ensler, E. (2004). *The good body*. New York: Random House: Villard.

Ensler, E. (2011). *I am an emotional creature*. New York: Random House, Villard.

Erickson, R. J. (2005). Why emotion work matters: Sex, gender and the division of household labor. *Journal of Marriage and the Family, 67*, 337–351.

Ensslin, A., & Muse, E. (Eds.). (2011). *Creating second lives: Community, identity, and spatiality as constructions of the virtual*. New York: Routledge.

Espenshade, T. (2012). Action after affirmative action. *Raleigh News & Observer*, p. 25A.

Esteves-Sorenson, C., & Snyder, J. (2012). The gender earnings gap for physicians and its increase over time. *Economic Letters, 116*, 37–41.

Estioko-Griffin, A., & Griffin, P. (1997). Woman the hunter: The Agta. In C. Brettell & C. Sargent (Eds.), *Gender in crosscultural perspectives* (pp. 123–149). Englewood Cliffs, NJ: Prentice Hall.

Faludi, S. (2007). *The terror dream: Fear and fantasy in post-9/11 America*. New York: Metropolitan.

Farhi, P. (2012, June 28). Media often consult men for views on women's issues. *Raleigh News & Observer*, p. 3D.

Farrell, E. F. (2004, June 4). It's getting hot in here. *The Chronicle of Higher Education*, pp. A27–A28.

Fattah, H. (2006, June 30). Kuwaiti women join the voting after a long battle for suffrage. *Raleigh News & Observer*, p. A9.

Fausto-Sterling, A. (2000). *Sexing the body: Gender politics and the construction of sexuality*. New York: Basic Books.

Federman, D. D., & Walford, G. A. (2007, January 15). Is male menopause real? *Newsweek*, pp. 58–60.

Ferraro, S. (2001). Gender affects the course of disease, researchers say. *Raleigh News & Observer*, p. 2E.

Fiebert, M. (1987). Some perspectives on the men's movement. *Men's Studies Review, 4*, 8–10.

Fields, A. (2003). *Katharine Dexter McCormick: Pioneer for women's rights*. Westport, CT: Praeger.

Findlen, B. (Ed.). (1995). *Listen up! Voices from the next feminist generation*. Seattle: Seal Press.

Fisher, H. (2000). *The first sex*. New York: Bantam.

Fisher, H. (2009, October). Intimacy: His & hers. *O: The Oprah Winfrey Magazine*, p. 138.

Fishman, P. M. (1978). Interaction: The work women do. *Social Problems, 25*, 397–406.

Fivush, R., Brotman, M., Buckner, J., & Goodman, S. (2000). Gender differences in parent-child emotion narratives. *Sex Roles, 42*, 223–253.

Fixmer, N. (2003). *Revisioning the political: Feminism, difference, and solidarity in a new generation*. Unpublished master's thesis, University of North Carolina, Chapel Hill.

Fixmer, N., & Wood, J. T. (2005). The political is personal: Difference, solidarity, and embodied politics in a new generation of feminists. *Women's Studies in Communication, 28*, 235–257.

Fixmer-Oraiz, N. (2013). *Maternity in crisis: Con(tra)captive politics in millennial imaginaries.* Ph.D. Dissertation, University of North Carolina, Chapel Hill.

Flanagan, M. (2004). Next level: Women's digital activism through gaming. In G. Liestol, A. Morrison, & T. Rasmussen (Eds.), *Digital media revisited* (pp. 82–106). Cambridge: MIT Press.

Fletcher, J., Jordan, J., & Miller, J. (2000). Women and the workplace: Applications of a psychodynamic theory. *American Journal of Psychoanalysis, 60*, 243–261.

Floyd, K. (1997). Communicating affection in dyadic relationships: An assessment of behavior and expectancies. *Communication Quarterly, 45*, 68–80.

Floyd, K., & Morman, M. (2005). Fathers' and sons' reports of fathers' affectionate communication: Implications of a naive theory of affection. *Journal of Social and Personal Relationships, 22*, 99–109.

Foss, K., Edson, B., & Linde, J. (2000). What's in a name? Negotiating decisions about marital names. In D. O. Braithwaite & J. T. Wood (Eds.), *Case studies in interpersonal communication* (pp. 18–25). Belmont, CA: Wadsworth.

Foss, S., Domenico, M., & Foss, K. (2013). *Gender stories.* Long Grove, IL: Waveland.

Foucault, M. (1978). *The history of sexuality, volume 1: An introduction* (R. Hurley, Trans.). New York: Pantheon.

Fox, S., & Lituchy, T. (Eds.). (2012). *Gender and the dysfunctional Workplace.* Northampton, MA: Edward Elgar Publishing Limited.

France, D. (2006, January & February). Domestic violence. *AARP Magazine*, pp. 84–85, 112–118.

Frawley, T. J. (2008). Gender schema and pre-judicial recall: How children misremember, fabricate, and distort gendered picture book information. *Journal of Research in Childhood Education, 22*, 291–303.

Freed, B., & Freed, D. (2012, July/August). Why won't men get help? *Pacific Standard,* pp. 34–41.

Freeman, E. (2002). *No turning back.* New York: Ballantine.

Friedan, B. (1963). *The feminine mystique.* New York: Dell.

Gallagher, J. (2012). *Black women and politics in New York City.* Urbana: University of Illinois Press.

Galvin, K. (2006). Gendered communication in families. In B. Dow & J. T. Wood (Eds.), *Handbook of gender and communication* (pp. 41–55). Thousand Oaks, CA: Sage.

Gannon, M. (2009). (Director & Producer). *The Good Men: One-hour documentary.* Boston: Good Men Foundation.

Garcia, G. (2008). *The decline of men: How the American male is tuning out, giving up, and flipping off his future.* New York: Harper.

Garloch, K. (2009, September 29). Saving our sons. *Raleigh News & Observer,* p. Dl.

Garrett, W. (2001). Personal communication.

Gartner, R. (2005). *Beyond betrayal: Taking charge of your life after boyhood sexual abuse.* New York: Wiley.

Gartner, R. B. (2012, June 8). A troubled silence. *The New York Times,* p. A23.

Gastil, J. (1990). Generic pronouns and sexist language: The oxymoronic character of masculine generics. *Sex Roles, 23*, 629–643.

Geena Davis Institute. (2010). *Improving gender portrayals in children's media.* Retrieved from http://www.thegeenadavisinstitute.org/research

Gelles, R., & Straus, M. (1988). *Intimate violence.* New York: Simon & Schuster.

Gender gap starts with household chores, study finds. (2006, December 8). *Raleigh News & Observer,* p. 3A.

Gender in Media. (2012). *Research informs & empowers.* Retrieved from http://www.the geenadavisinstitute.org/research

Gerhard, J. (2011). Sex and the City: Carrie Bradshaw's queer postfeminism. In G. Dines & J. Humez (Eds.), *Gender, race, and class in media: A critical reader* (3rd ed., pp. 75–79). Los Angeles: Sage.

Gerson, K. (2010). *The unfinished revolution: Coming of age in a new era of gender, work and family.* New York: Oxford University Press.

Gettleman, J. (2009a, August 5). Latest tragic symbol of an unhealed Congo: Male rape victims. *The New York Times,* pp. A1, A7.

Gettleman, J. (2009b, September 7). Sudanese court to define indecent dress for women. *The New York Times,* p. A5.

Gilenstam, K., Karp, S., & Henriksson-Larsen, K. (2008). Gender in ice hockey: Women in a male territory. *Scandinavian Journal of Medicine & Science in Sports, 18*, 235–249.

Gill, R. (2008). Empowerment/sexism: Figuring female sexual agency in contemporary advertising. *Feminism & Psychology, 18*, 35–60.

Gill, T. (2010). *Beauty shop politics: African American women's activism in the beauty industry.* Urbana: University of Illinois Press.

Gilley, B. J. (2006). *Becoming two-spirit: Gay identity and social acceptance in Indian country.* Lincoln: University of Nebraska Press.

Gilligan, C. (1982). *In a different voice: Psychological theory and women's development.* Cambridge, MA: Harvard University Press.

Gilligan, C., & Pollack, S. (1988). The vulnerable and invulnerable physician. In C. Gilligan, J. V. Ward, & J. M. Taylor (with B. Bardige) (Eds.),

Mapping the moral domain (pp. 245–262). Cambridge, MA: Harvard University Press.

Girish, U. (2007, Spring). Don't "tease" these Eves. *Ms.*, p. 27.

"Girls gone wild" leader pleads guilty. (2006, December 14). *Raleigh News & Observer*, p. 3A.

Girls Incorporated. (2006). *The supergirl dilemma: Girls grapple with the mounting pressure of expectations, Summary findings.* New York: Girls Incorporated.

Givhan, R. (2006, December 11). Thin is not in on runways. *Raleigh News & Observer*, p. 3C.

Glenn, K. (2012, February 10). Little boy blue— and little girls, too? *The Chronicle of Higher Education*, p. B14.

Glover, D., & Kaplan, C. (2009). *Genders* (2nd ed.). New York: Routledge.

Goddess, R., & Calderon, J. L. (Eds.). (2006). *We got issues!* Makawao, HI: Inner Ocean Publishing, Inc.

Goldberg, A., & Perry-Jenkins, M. (2007). The division of labor and perceptions of parental roles: Lesbian couples across the transition to parenthood. *Journal of Social and Personal Relationships, 24*, 297–318.

Goldner, V., Penn, P., Sheinberg, M., & Walker, G. (1990). Love and violence: Gender paradoxes in volatile attachments. *Family Process, 19*, 343–364.

Goldsmith, D., & Fulfs, P. (1999). "You just don't have the evidence": An analysis of claims and evidence in Deborah Tannen's *You Just Don't Understand*. In M. Roloff (Ed.), *Communication Yearbook, 22*, pp. 1–49.

Goldstein, S. (2011). Relational aggression in young adults' friendships and romantic relationships. *Journal of Personal Relationships, 18*, 645–656.

Gonzalez, A., Houston, M., & Chen, V. (2012). *Our voices: Essays in culture, ethnicity, and communication* (5th ed.). Los Angeles, CA: Roxbury.

The Good Men Foundation. Retrieved from http://goodmenproject.com/foundation/

The Good Men Project Magazine. Retrieved from http://goodmenproject.com

The Good Men Project on Tumbler. Retrieved from http://goodmenproject.tumblr.com/

Goodman, E. (2006, July 10). Boys and girls and school. *Raleigh News & Observer*, p. 11A.

Goodman, E. (2007). Our other office ceiling. *Raleigh News & Observer*, p. 15A.

Goodman, E. (2008a, August 4). How equality's adding up. *Raleigh News & Observer*, p. 9A.

Goodwin, M. H. (1990). *He said, she said: Talk as social organization among black children.* Bloomington: Indiana University Press.

Goodwin, M. H. (2006). *The hidden life of girls.* Maiden, MA: Blackwell Publishing.

Gordon, L. (1976). *Woman's body, woman's right: A social history of birth control in America.* New York: Grossman.

Gordon, L. (1998). Women's colleges. In W. Mankiller, G. Mink, M. Navarro, B. Smith, & G. Steinem (Eds.), *The reader's companion to U.S. women's history* (pp. 642–644). New York: Houghton Mifflin.

Gordon, L. (2007). *The moral property of women: A history of birth control politics in America.* . Chicago: University of Illinois Press.

Gorman, C., & Cole, C. (2004, March 1). Between the sexes. *Newsweek*, pp. 54–56.

Gorski, E. (2003, October 6). Promise Keepers to shift direction under new chief. *Denver Post*, pp. IB, 3B.

Gray, J. (1992). *Men are from Mars, women are from Venus: A practical guide for improving communication and getting what you want in your relationships.* New York: HarperCollins.

Gray, J. (1995). *Mars and Venus in the bedroom: A guide to lasting romance and passion.* New York: HarperCollins.

Gray, J. (1996a). *Mars and Venus in love.* New York: HarperCollins.

Gray, J. (1996b). *Mars and Venus together forever.* New York: HarperCollins.

Gray, J. (1998). *Mars and Venus on a date: A guide for navigating the five stages of dating to create a loving and lasting relationship.* New York: HarperCollins.

Gray, P. (2010). *Fatherhood: Evolution and human paternal behavior.* Cambridge, MA: Harvard University Press.

Gray, P., & Feldman, J. (1997). Patterns of age mixing and gender mixing among children and adolescents at an ungraded democratic school. *Merill-Palmer Quarterly, 43*, 67–86.

Gray, R., II. (Ed.). (2012). *The performance identities of Lady Gaga.* Jefferson, NC: McFarland.

Green, R. (2012). Augusta national ends its ban on women. *Raleigh News & Observer*, pp. 1A, 7A.

Greenhouse, L. (2004, June 15). Rules are set for some harassment cases. *The New York Times*, p. A16.

Greenhouse, S. (2003, July 13). Going for the look, but risking discrimination. *The New York Times International*, p. 10YT.

Gregory, S. (2007, December 10). Head games. *Time*, pp. 69–70.

Griffith, R. (1997, October 17). The affinities between feminists and evangelical women. *The Chronicle of Higher Education*, pp. B6, B7.

Gross, D. (1990, April 16). The gender rap. *New Republic*, pp. 11–14.

Guerrero, L. (1997). Nonverbal involvement across interactions with same-sex friends, opposite-sex friends, and romantic partners: Consistency or change? *Journal of Social and Personal Relationships, 14*, 31–58.

Guerrero, L., Jones, S., & Boburka, R. (2006). Sex differences in emotional communication. In K. Dindia & D. Canary (Eds.), *Sex differences and similarities in communication* (pp. 242–261). Mahwah, MJ: Erlbaum.

Gurian, M. (2006). *The wonder of boys*. New York: Penguin/Tarcher.

Gurian, M., & Stevens, K. (2007). *The minds of boys*. San Francisco: Jossey-Bass.

Guy-Sheftall, B. (2003). African American women: The legacy of black feminism. In R. Morgan (Ed.), *Sisterhood is forever* (pp. 176–187). New York: Washington Square Press.

Haag, P. (2005, February 11). Navigating the new subtleties of sex-discrimination cases in academe. *The Chronicle of Higher Education*, p. B20.

Halatsis, P., & Christakis, N. (2009). The challenge of sexual attraction with heterosexuals? Cross-sex friendship. *Journal of Social and Personal Relationships, 26*, 919–937.

Halberstam, J. J. (1998). *Female masculinity*. Durham, NC: Duke University Press.

Halberstam, J. J. (2011). *The queer art of failure*. Durham, NC: Duke University Press.

Halberstam, J. J. (2012). *Gaga feminism: Sex, gender and the end of normal*. Boston: Beacon.

Hale, J., Tighe, R., & Mongeau, P. (1997). Effects of event type and sex on comforting messages. *Communication Research Reports, 14*, 214–220.

Hall, J. (2006). How big are nonverbal sex differences? The case of smiling and nonverbal sensitivity. In K. Dindia & D. Canary (Eds.), *Sex differences and similarities in communication* (2nd ed., pp. 59–81). Mahwah, NJ: Lawrence Erlbaum.

Hall, J., Park, N., Song, H., & Cody, J. (2010). Strategic misrepresentation in online dating: The effects of gender, self-monitoring, and personality traits. *Journal of Social and Personal Relationships, 27*, 117–135.

Hall, J. A. (2011). Sex differences in friendship expectations: A meta-analysis. *Journal of Social and Personal Relationships, 28*, 723–747.

Hall, K. (2012, May 16). Army opens more jobs to women. *Raleigh News & Observer*, p. 3A.

Hallstein, D. L. O. (2008). Silences and choice: The legacies of white second wave feminism in the new professoriate. *Women's Studies in Communication, 31*, 143–150.

Hallstein, L. (2010a). Public choices, private control: How mediated mom labels work rhetorically to dismantle the politics of choice and white second-wave feminist success. In S. Hayden & D. L. Hallstein (Eds.), *Contemplating maternity in an era of choice* (pp. 5–26). New York: Lexington.

Hallstein, L. (2010b). *White feminists and contemporary maternity*. New York: Palgrave Macmillan.

Halperin, D. (2007). *What do gay men want? An essay on sex, risk, and subjectivity*. Ann Arbor: University of Michigan Press.

Halpern, D. (1996). Public policy implications of sex differences in cognitive abilities. *Psychology, Public Policy, and Law, 2*, 561–574.

Hamilton, M. C. (1991). Masculine bias in the attribution of personhood: People-male, male-people. *Psychology of Women Quarterly, 15*, 393–402.

Hammer, J. (2001). *What it means to be a daddy: Fatherhood for black men living away from their children*. New York: Columbia University Press.

Hammonds, E. (1998). Science and gender. In W. Mankiller, G. Mink, M. Navarro, B. Smith, & G. Steinem (Eds.), *The reader's companion to U.S. Women's history* (pp. 521–522). New York: Houghton Mifflin.

Hanisch, C. (1970). What can be learned? A critique of the Miss America protest. In L. Tanner (Ed.), *Voices from women's liberation* (pp. 132–136). New York: Signet Classics.

Harding, S. (1991). *Whose science? Whose knowledge? Thinking from women's lives*. Ithaca, NY: Cornell University Press.

Harding, S. (1998). *Is science multicultural?* Ithaca, NY: Cornell University Press.

Harper, C. (2007). *Intersex*. Oxford, AL: Berg Publishers.

Harris, A. (Eds.). (2004). *All about the girl*. London: Routledge.

Harris, G., & Belluck, P. (2012, February 1). Uproar as breast cancer group ends partnership with Planned Parenthood. *The New York Times*. Retrieved from http://www.nytimes.com/2012/02/02/us/uproar-as-komen-foundation-cuts-money-to-planned-parenthood.html?r=1&pagewanted=all

Harris, J. (1998). *The nurture assumption*. New York: Simon & Schuster/Free Press.

Harris, J. (2009). *The next problem that has no name: The discourse and politics of "rape."* M. A. Thesis, Department of Communication Studies, The University of North Carolina, Chapel Hill.

Harris, K. (2011a). The next problem with no name: The politics and pragmatics of the word rape. *Women's Studies in Communication, 34*, 42–63.

Harris, K. (2011b). Peanut butter sandwiches: Making sense of acquaintance rape in ongoing relationships. In D. O. Braithwaite & J. T. Wood (Eds.), *Casing interpersonal communication* (pp. 181–285). Dubuque, IA: Kendall-Hunt.

Harrison, C. E. (1988). *On account of sex: The politics of women's issues, 1945-1968*. Berkeley: University of California Press.

Harrison, K. (2008). Adolescent body image and eating in media: Trends and implications for adolescent health. In P. E. Jamieson & D. Romer (Eds.), *The changing portrayal of adolescents in the media since 1950* (pp. 165–197). New York: Oxford University Press.

Hartmann, E. (1993). *Boundaries in the mind: A new psychology of personality*. New York: Basic Books.

Hasinoff, A. (2008). Fashioning race for the free market on American's next top model. *Critical Studies in Media Communication, 25,* 324–343.

Hattery, A. (2012, June 21). Title IX at 40: More work to be done. *USA Today,* p. 7A.

Haughney, C. (2012, July 4). A magazine vows to ease retouching. *The New York Times,* pp. B1, B2.

Hayden, S. (2003). Family metaphors and the nation: Promoting a politics of care through the Million Mom March. *Quarterly Journal of Speech, 89,* 196–215.

Hayden, S., & O'Brien Hallstein, L. (Eds.). (2010). *Contemplating maternity in an era of choice: Exploring discourses of reproduction.* New York: Lexington.

Haynes, J. (2009). Exposing domestic violence in country music videos. In L. Cuklanz & S. Moorti (Eds.), *Local violence, global media* (pp. 201–221). New York: Peter Lang.

Helfling, K. (2011, February 16). Veterans sue over rape cases. *Raleigh News & Observer,* p. 5A.

Hegde, R. (2006). Globalizing feminist research in communication. In B. Dow & J. T. Wood (Eds.), *Handbook of gender and communication* (pp. 433–449). Thousand Oaks, CA: Sage.

Hegel, G. W. F. (1807). *Phenomenology of mind* (J. B. Baillie, Trans.). Germany: Wurzburg & Bamberg.

Heilman, M. E., & Okimoto, T. G. (2007). Averting penalties for women's success: Rectifying the perceived communality deficiency. *Journal of Applied Psychology, 92,* 81–92.

Helms, H., Prouix, C., Klute, M., McHale, S., & Crouter, A. (2006). Spouses' gender-typed attributes and their links with marital quality: A pattern analytic approach. *Journal of Social and Personal Relationships, 23,* 343–364.

Hendrick, C., & Hendrick, S. (1986). A theory and method of love. *Journal of Personality and Social Psychology, 50,* 392–402.

Hendrick, C., & Hendrick, S. (1996). Gender and the experience of heterosexual love. In J. T. Wood (Ed.), *Gendered relationships: A reader.* Mountain View, CA: Mayfield.

Henley, N. M., & LaFrance, M. (1996). On oppressing hypotenses: Or differences in non-verbal sensitivity revisited. In L. Radtke & H. Stam (Eds.), *Power/gender: Social relations in theory and practice: Inquiries in social construction* (pp. 287–311). Thousand Oaks, CA: Sage.

Henry, A. (2004). *Not my mother's sister.* Bloomington: Indiana University Press.

Herbert, B. (2006, October 16). Why aren't we shocked? *The New York Times,* p. A23.

Herbert, B. (2009a, March 21). The great shame. *The New York Times,* p. A17.

Herbert, B. (2009b, August 8). Women at risk. *The New York Times,* p. A17.

Herbert, E. (2010). *Lady Gaga: Behind the fame.* New York: Overlook.

Herdt, G. (1997). *Same sex, different cultures.* Boulder, CO: Westview.

Herrup, M. J. (1995). Virtual identity. In R. Walker (Ed.), *To be real* (pp. 239–252). New York: Anchor.

Hesse-Biber, S. N., & Leavy, P. (2006). *The cult of thinness* (2nd ed.). New York: Oxford University Press.

Hewitt, N. A. (Ed.). (2010). *No permanent waves: Recasting histories of U. S. Feminism.* Piscataway, NJ: Rutgers University Press.

Hindery, R. (2011, May 10). Circumcision ban on ballot in San Francisco. *Raleigh News & Observer,* p. 8A.

Hine, D., & Thompson, K. (1998). *A shining thread of hope: The history of black women in America.* New York: Broadway.

Hines, S. (2006). Intimate transitions: Transgender practices of partnering and parenting. *Sociology, 2,* 353–371.

Hinshaw, S. (with Kranz, R.). (2009). *The triple bind: Saving our teenage girls from today's pressures.* New York: Ballentine.

Hirschfeld, S., & Wolf, S. (2005, May 27). Sex, religion, and politics: New challenges in discrimination law. *The Chronicle of Higher Education,* pp. B10–B14.

Hise, R. (2004). *The war against men.* Oakland, OR: Elderberry Press LLC.

Hochschild, A. (with Machung, A.). (2003). *The second shift: Working parents and the revolution at home* (Rev. ed.). New York: Viking/ Penguin Press.

Hochschild, A., & Ehrenreich, B. (Eds.). (2003). *Global women: Nannies, maids and sex workers in the new economy.* New York: Metropolitan.

Hoffman, J. (2010, June 28). Online bullies pull schools into the fray. *The New York Times,* pp. A13, A14, A15.

Hoffman, J. (2012, June 4). A warning to teenagers before they start dating. *The New York Times,* pp. A12, A13.

Holland, D., & Eisenhart, M. (1992). *Educated in romance: Women, achievement, and college culture.* Chicago: University of Chicago Press.

Holmes, M. (2008). *Gender and everyday life.* New York: Routledge.

Hondagneu-Sotelo, P. (2007). *Domestica: Immigrant workers cleaning and caring in the shadows of affluence.* Berkeley: University of California Press.

hooks, B. (1990). *Yearning: Race, gender, and cultural politics.* Boston: South End Press.

hooks, B. (2000). *Feminist theory: From margin to center* (2nd ed.). Boston: South End Press.

hooks, B. (2002). *Feminism is for everybody*. Boston: South End Press.

Hotties, H. (2012, July 21). *The Economist*, p. 25.

Houghton, J., Bean, L., & Matlack, T. (2009). *The Good Men Project: Real stories from the front lines of modern manhood*. Boston: Good Men Foundation.

How college leaders' traits have changed over 5 years. (2012, August 31). *The Chronicle of Higher Education*, p. 19.

Howry, A., & Wood, J. T. (2001). Something old, something new, something borrowed: Themes in the voices of a new generation of feminists. *Southern Journal of Communication, 66*, 323–336.

Hurlemann, R., Patin, A., Onur, O., Cohen, M., Baumgartner, T., Metzler, S., et al. (2010). Ocytocin enhances amygdala-dependent, socially reinforced learning and emotional empathy in humans. *Journal of Neuroscience, 30*, 4999–5007.

Hust, S. J. T., Brown, J., & L'Engle, K. L. (2008). Boys will be boys and girls better be prepared: An analysis of the rare sexual health messages in young adolescents' media. *Mass Communication & Society, 11*, 3–23.

Huston, M., & Schwartz, P. (1996). Gendered dynamics in gay and lesbian relationships. In J. T. Wood (Ed.), *Gendered relationships: A reader* (pp. 89–121). Mountain View, CA: Mayfield.

Hyde, J. S. (1984). Children's understanding of sexist language. *Developmental Psychology, 20*, 697–706.

Ickes, W. (1993). Traditional gender roles: Do they make and then break our relationships? *Journal of Social Work, 49*, 71–85.

In their words. (2003, June 24). *Raleigh News & Observer*, p. 5A.

Ingraham, L. (1997, July 15). Feminists welcome the Promise Keepers. *Raleigh News & Observer*, p. 11A.

Inman, C. (1996). Friendships between men: Closeness in the doing. In J. T. Wood (Ed.), *Gendered relationships: A reader* (pp. 95–110). Mountain View, CA: Mayfield.

Ivory, J. D. (2008). The games, they are a-changin'. In P. E. Jamieson & D. Romer (Eds.), *The changing portrayal of adolescents in the media since 1950* (pp. 347–376). New York: Oxford.

Jackson, R., & Murali, B. (Eds.). (2011). *Global masculinities and manhood*. Urbana: University of Illinois Press.

Jacobs, T. (2010). *Cyberbullying investigated*. Minneapolis, MN: Free Spirit Publishing.

Jacobson, J. (2001, March 9). Why do so many female athletes enter ACL hell? *The Chronicle of Higher Education*, p. A45.

Jaiwal, S. (2012). Commercial surrogacy in India: An ethical assessment of existing legal scenario from the perspective of women's autonomy and reproductive rights. *Gender Technology and Development, 1*, 1–28.

Jagger, G. (2008). *Judith Butler: Sexual politics, social change and the power of performance*. New York: Routledge.

Jamieson, K. H. (1995). *Beyond the double bind: Women and leadership*. New York: Oxford University Press.

Jamieson, P. E., More, E., Lee, S. S., Busse, P., & Romer, D. (2008). It matters what young people watch: Health risk behaviors portrayed in top-grossing movies since 1950. In P. E. Jamieson & D. Romer (Eds.), *The changing portrayal of adolescents in the media since 1950* (pp. 107–131). New York: Oxford.

Jamieson, P. E., & Romer, D. (Eds.). (2008). *The changing portrayal of adolescents in the media since 1950*. New York: Oxford University Press.

Janeway, E. (1971). *Man's world, woman's place: A study in social mythology*. New York: Dell.

Jegalian, K., & Lahn, B. (2001). Why the Y is so weird. *Scientific American, 284*, 56.

Jinks, B., & Helyar, J. (2012, April 5). IBM faces gender bias at Masters. *Raleigh News & Observer*, pp. 1A, 6A.

Johnson, A. (2008, August 4). One by one, women in Egypt fight female circumcision. *Raleigh News & Observer*, p. 7A.

Johnson, F. (2000). *Speaking culturally: Language diversity in the United States*. Thousand Oaks, CA: Sage.

Johnson, J. W. (1912/1989). *Autobiography of an ex-coloured man*. New York: Vintage-Random.

Johnson, M. (2006). Gendered communication and intimate partner violence. In B. Dow & J. T. Wood (Eds.), *Handbook of gender and communication* (pp. 71–87). Thousand Oaks, CA: Sage.

Johnson, M. (2008). *A typology of domestic violence*. Boston: Northeastern University Press.

Johnson, M. L. (Ed.). (2007). *Third-wave feminism and television: Jane puts it in a box*. New York: Palgrave Macmillan.

Johnson, N. (2007). *All I Want Is Everything: A Feminist Analysis of Consumption in Bestselling Teen Romance Novels*. Ph.D. Dissertation, The University of North Carolina, Chapel Hill.

Johnson, N. (2011). The whole package: Commodifying the self. In D. O. Braithwaite & J. T. Wood (Eds.), *Casing interpersonal communication* (pp. 9–15). Dubuque, IA: Kendall-Hunt.

Johnson, N. R. (2010). Consuming desires: Consumption, romance, and sexuality in best-selling teen romance novels. *Women's Studies in Communication, 33*, 54–73.

Johnson, S. (2005). *Whatever is bad for you is good for you.* New York: Riverhead Hardcover.

Jordan, J. (2004). The rhetorical limits of the "plastic body." *Quarterly Journal of Speech, 90,* 327–358.

Joseph, R. (2000). The evolution of sex differences in language, sexuality and visual-spatial skills. *Archives of Sexual Behavior, 29,* 55–66.

Journalistic Thought Police. (1990, December 27). *Richmond Times-Dispatch,* p. A12.

Julia, M. (Eds.). (2000). *Constructing gender: Multicultural perspectives in working with women.* Belmont, CA: Thomson/Brooks/Cole.

June, A. W. (2010, February 19). Family-friendly policies fall short when professors worry about backlash. *The Chronicle of Higher Education,* p. A12.

Kaestle, C., Halpern, C., & Brown, J. (2007). Music videos, pro wrestling, and acceptance of date rape among middle school males and females: An exploratory analysis. *Journal of Adolescent Health, 40,* 185–187.

Kahlenberg, R. (2010a). *Affirmative action for the rich: Legacy preferences in college admissions.* New York: Century/Foundation.

Kahlenberg, R. (Ed.). (2010b). *Rewarding strivers: Helping low-income students succeed in college.* New York: Century Foundation Press.

Kahlenberg, R. (2012). A new kind of affirmative action can ensure diversity. *The Chronicle of Higher Education,* pp. A29–A30.

Kailey, M. (2006). *Just add hormones: An insider's guide to the transsexual experience.* Boston: Beacon.

Kamil, A. (2012, June 6). Prep-school predators. *The New York Times.* Retrieved from http://www.nytimes.com/2012/06/10/magazine/the-horace-mann-schools-secret-history-of-sexual-abuse.html?pagewanted=all

Kanter, R. M. (1977). *Men and women of the corporation.* New York: Basic Books.

Kantor, J. (2012, June 22). Elite women put new spin on an old debate. *The New York Times,* pp. A1, A14.

Kaschak, E. (1992). *Engendered lives.* New York: Basic Books.

Katz, J. (2000). *MVP trainer's guide for working with male high school students. MVP strategies: Gender violence prevention education and training.* Retrieved November 20, 2007, from http://www.eurowrc.org/05.education/education_en/11.edu_en.htm

Katz, J., & Jhally, S. (1999, May 2). The national conversation in the wake of Littleton is missing the mark. *The Boston Globe,* p. E1.

Katz, J., & Jhally, S. (2000, June 25). Put the blame where it belongs: On men. *The Los Angeles Times,* p. M5.

Kearney, M. C. (2006). *Girls make media.* London: Routledge.

Kaufman, M., & Kimmel, M. (2011). *The guy's guide to feminism.* Berkeley, CA: Seal.

Keen, S. (1991). *Fire in the belly: On being a man.* New York: Bantam.

Kellerman, C. J. (2012, May 22). *17-year-old to Facebook: I exist, and gender identity is also a civil rights issue.* Retrieved from http://www.huffingtonpost.com/cj-kellman/facebook-gender-identity_b_1534832.html?icid=maing-grid10%7Chtmlws-main-bb%7CdlI1%7Csec1_lnk3%26pLid%3D162917

Kendall, D. (2011). *Framing class.* Lanham, MD: Rowman & Littlefield.

Kerber, L. (2005, March 18). We must make the academic workplace more humane and equitable. *The Chronicle of Higher Education,* pp. B6–B9.

Kershaw, S. (2008, September 11). Girl talk has its limits. *The New York Times,* pp. E1, E6.

Kershaw, S. (2009, April 23). Mr. Moms (by way of Fortune 500). *The New York Times,* pp. E1, E6.

Key, C., & Ridge, R. (2011). Guys like us: The link between sexual harassment proclivity and blame. *Journal of Social and Personal Relationships, 28,* 1093–1103.

Kilbourne, J. (2004). The more you subtract, the more you add: Cutting girls down to size. In J. Spade & C. Valentine (Eds.), *The kaleidoscope of gender: Prisms, patterns, and possibilities* (pp. 234–244). Belmont, CA: Thomson/Wadsworth.

Kilbourne, J. (2007). "You talkin' to me?" In M. Andersen & P. H. Collins (Eds.), *Race, class, and gender: An anthology* (6th ed., pp. 228–233). Belmont, CA: Thomson.

Kilbourne, J. (2010a, summer). Sexist advertising, then & now. *Ms,* pp. 34–35.

Kilbourne, J. (Writer). (2010a). *Still killing us softly/4.* Northampton, MA: Media Education Foundation.

Kill, G. (2007, April 11). Too far for Imus, not far enough for us. *Raleigh News & Observer,* p. 11A.

Kimbrell, A. (1991, May/June). A time for men to pull together. *Utne Reader,* pp. 66–71.

Kimelman, D. (1990, December 12). Poverty and Norplant: Can contraception reduce the underclass? *Philadelphia Enquirer,* p. A18.

Kimmel, M. (1996). *Manhood.* New York: Free Press.

Kimmel, M. (2000a). *The gendered society.* Cambridge, MA: Oxford University Press.

Kimmel, M. (2000b, January 12). *What about the boys?* Keynote speech at the Center for Research on Women's 6th Annual Gender Equity Conference, Boston, MA.

Kimmel, M. (2003). Introduction. In M. Kimmel (Ed.) (with Aronson, A.), *The gendered society reader* (pp. 1–6). New York: Oxford University Press.

Kimmel, M. (2005). *Manhood in America*. New York: Oxford University Press.

Kimmel, M. (2008). *Guyland: The perilous world where boys become men*. New York: Macmillan.

King, R., Lugo-Lugo, C., & Bloodsworth-Lugo, M. (2011). *Animating difference*. Lanham, MD: Rowman & Littlefield.

Kinney, T. A., Smith, B. A., & Donzella, B. (2001). The influence of sex, gender, self-discrepancies, and self-awareness on anger and verbal aggressiveness among U.S. college students. *Journal of Social Psychology, 141*, 245–276.

Kirby, E., & Krone, K. (2002). "The policy exists but you can't really use it": Communication and the structuration of work-family policies. *Journal of Applied Communication Research, 30*, 50–77.

Kneidinger, L. G., Kelly-Reid, J., & Ginder, S. (2011). *Enrollment in postsecondary institutions, Fall 2009; graduation rates, 2003 & 2006 cohorts; and financial statistics, fiscal year 2009* (NCES 2011-230). U.S. Department of Education. Washington, DC: National Center for Education Statistics.

Kneidinger, L. M., Maple, T. L., & Tross, S. A. (2001). Touching behavior in sport: Functional components, analysis of sex differences, and ethological considerations. *Journal of Nonverbal Behavior, 25*, 43–62.

Koesten, J. (2004). Family communication patterns, sex of subject, and communication competence. *Communication Monographs, 71*, 226–244.

Kohlberg, L. (1958). *The development of modes of thinking and moral choice in the years 10 to 16*. Unpublished doctoral dissertation, University of Chicago.

Kolata, G. (2012, February 9). Male genes may explain higher heart disease risk. *The New York Times*, p. A13.

Kosova, W. (2007, April 23). The power that was. *Newsweek*, pp. 24–32.

Kovacs, P., Parker, J., & Hoffman, L. (1996). Behavioral, affective and social correlates of involvement in cross-sex friendships in elementary school. *Child Development, 67*, 2269–2286.

Kramarae, C. (1992). Harassment and everyday life. In L. F. Rakow (Ed.), *Women making meaning: New feminist directions in communication* (pp. 100–120). New York: Routledge.

Kristof, N. (2005a, March 5). When rapists walk free. *The New York Times*, p. A27.

Kristof, N. (2005b, June 14). Raped, kidnapped and silenced. *The New York Times*, p. A19.

Kristof, N. (2005c, June 19). A free woman. *The New York Times*, Section 4, p. 13.

Kristof, N. (2005d, June 21). The 11-year-old wife. *The New York Times*, p. A23.

Kristof, N. (2008, December 5). Women the victims, acid the weapon. *Raleigh News & Observer*, p. 17A.

Kristof, N. (2011a, May 26). Raiding a brothel in India. *The New York Times*, p. A27.

Kristof, N. (2011b, May 12). A rite of torture for girls. *The New York Times*, p. A23.

Kristof, N. (2012, May 30). Markets and morals. *The New York Times*, p. A23.

Kristof, N., & WuDunn, S. (2009). *Half the sky*. New York: Knopf.

Kuchment, A. (2004, May 10). The more social sex. *Newsweek*, pp. 88–89.

Kunkel, A., Dennis, R., & Waters, E. (2003). Contemporary university students' ratings of characteristics of men, women, and CEOs. *Psychological Reports, 93*, 1197–1213.

Kunkel, A., Hummert, M., & Dennis, M. (2006). Social learning theory: Modeling and communication in the family context. In D. Braithwaite & L. Baxter (Eds.), *Engaging theories in family communication* (pp. 260–275). Thousand Oaks, CA: Sage.

Kurdek, L. A., & Schmitt, J. P. (1986a). Early development of relationship quality in heterosexual married, heterosexual cohabiting, gay, and lesbian couples. *Developmental Psychology, 22*, 305–309.

Kurdek, L. A., & Schmitt, J. P. (1986b). Interaction of sex-role self-concept with relationship quality and relationship belief in married, heterosexual cohabiting, gay, and lesbian couples. *Journal of Personality and Social Psychology, 51*, 365–370.

Labov, W. (1972). *Sociolinguistic patterns*. Philadelphia: University of Pennsylvania Press.

Lacey, M. (2008, December 7). A lifestyle distinct: The Muxe of Mexico. *The New York Times*, p. WK4.

LaFraniere, S. (2005, December 23). Another school barrier for African girls: No toilet. *The New York Times*, pp. A1, A10.

LaFraniere, S. (2007, July 8). If obesity is beauty, health is a low priority. *Raleigh News & Observer*, p. 20A.

Lakoff, R. (1975). *Language and woman's place*. New York: Harper & Row.

Lamb, S. (1991). Acts without agents: An analysis of linguistic avoidance in journal articles on men who batter women. *American Journal of Orthopsychiatry, 61*, 87–102.

Lamb, S. (Ed.). (1999). *New versions of victims*. New York: New York University Press.

Lamb, S., & Brown, L. (2006). *Packaging girlhood: Rescuing our daughters from marketers' schemes*. New York: St. Martin's Press.

Lamb, S., Brown, L., & Tappan, M. (2009). *Packaging boyhood: Saving our sons from superheroes, slackers, and other media stereotypes*. New York: St. Martin's.

Lang, S. S. (1991, January 20). When women drink. *Parade*, pp. 18–20.

Langer, S. K. (1953). *Feeling and form: A theory of art*. New York: Scribner's.

Langer, S. K. (1979). *Philosophy in a new key: A study in the symbolism of reason, rite and art* (3rd ed.). Cambridge, MA: Harvard University Press.

Lansberg, M. (2000). White Ribbon Campaign: Canadian feminists' uneasy alliance with men challenging violence. *Voice Male*, p. 15.

Laster, J. (2010, January 29). Unlike men, female scientists have a second shift: Housework. *The Chronicle of Higher Education*, p. A10.

Law on marital rape revised. (2009, July 10). *Raleigh News & Observer*, p. 3A.

Lawrence, M. (2011, September 13). *Transgender policy approved*. NCAA. Retrieved from http://www.ncaa.org/wps/wcm/connect/public/NCAA/Resources/Latest+News/2011/September/Transgender+policy+approved

Leaper, C. (Ed.). (1994). *Childhood gender segregation: Causes and consequences*. San Francisco: Jossey-Bass.

Leaper, C. (1996). The relationship of play activity and gender to parent and child sex-typed communication. *International Journal of Behavioral Development, 19*, 689–703.

Leaper, C., & Ayres, M. (2007). A meta-analytic review of gender variations in adults' language use: Talkativeness, affiliative speech, and assertive speech. *Personality & Social Psychology Review, 11*, 328–363.

Lee, S. (1997). *Get on the bus* [Motion picture]. United States: Columbia/Tristar.

Lehmiller, J. J. (2010). Differences in relationship investments between gay and heterosexual men. *Journal of Personal Relationships, 17*, 81–96.

Lelchuk, I. (2007, May 20). Being Mr. Dad. *San Francisco Chronicle Magazine*, pp. 8, 9, 19.

LélièveLindgren, S., & Lélière, M. (2009). In the laboratory of masculinity: Renegotiating gender subjectivities in MTV's Jackass. *Critical Studies in Media Communication, 26*, 393–410.

L'Engle, K., & Jackson, C. (2008). Socialization influences on early adolescents' cognitive susceptibility and transition to sexual intercourse. *Journal of Research on Adolescence, 18*, 353–378.

LePoire, B. A., Burgoon, J. K., & Parrott, R. (1992). Status and privacy restoring communication in the workplace. *Journal of Applied Communication Research, 4*, 419–136.

Levin, D., & Kilbourne, J. (2008). *So sexy, so soon*. New York: Ballantine.

Levy, A. (2005). *Female chauvinist pigs*. New York: Free Press.

Levy, S. (2005, August 1). Sex, secret codes, and videogames. *Newsweek*, p. 14.

Lewin, T. (2007, January 26). Colleges regroup after votes ban race preferences. *The New York Times*, pp. A1, A13.

Lin-Liu, J. (2005, February 4). Mongolia's reverse gender gap. *The Chronicle of Higher Education*, p. A39.

Lipka, S. (2005, April 8). High court expands protections of Title IX. *The Chronicle of Higher Education*, pp. A1, A36.

Logwood, D. (1998, Winter). One million strong. *Hues*, pp. 15–19.

Looy, H., & Bouma, H., III. (2005). The nature of gender: Gender identity in persons who are intersexed or transgender. *Journal of Psychology and Theology, 3*, 166–178.

Lorber, J. (1997). A woman's rights/cultural conflict. *Democratic Left, 2*, 3–5.

Lorber, J. (2001). *Gender inequality: Feminist theories and politics* (2nd ed.). Los Angeles: Roxbury.

Lorie, A. (2011). Forbidden fruit or conventional apple pie? A look at sex and the city's reversal of the female gender. *Media, Culture, and Society, 33*, 35–51.

Louis, C. S. (2010a, April 29). Cosmetic surgery gets a nip and tuck. *The New York Times*, p. E3.

Louis, C. S. (2010b, August 12). This teenage girl uses botox. And, no, she's not alone. *The New York Times*, pp. E1, E3.

Loury, G. (1996, January/February). Joy and doubt on the mall. *Utne Reader*, pp. 70–71.

Lugones, M., & Spelman, E. (1983). Have we got a theory for you! Feminist theory, cultural imperialism, and the demand for "the woman's voice." *Women's Studies International Forum, 6*, 573–581.

Lumsden, L. (2009). "Women's lib has no soul"? Analysis of women's movement coverage in black periodicals, 1968–73. *Journalism History, 35*, 118–130.

Lundy, L. K., Ruth, A. M., & Park, T. D. (2008). Simply irresistible: Reality TV consumption patterns. *Communication Quarterly, 56*, 208–225.

Luster, T., & Okagaki, L. (Eds.). (2005). *Parenting: An ecological perspective* (2nd ed.). Mahwah, NJ: Erlbaum.

Maccoby, E. E. (1998). *The two sexes: Growing up apart, coming together*. Cambridge, MA: Belknap Press of the Harvard University Press.

MacGeorge, E., Gillihan, S. J., Samter, W., & Clark, R. A. (2003). Skill deficit or differential motivation? Accounting for sex differences in the provision of emotional support. *Communication Research, 30*, 272–293.

MacKinnon, C. A. (2005). *Women's lives, men's laws*. Cambridge, MA: Harvard University Press.

Mai, M., Cuny, M., Kristof, N., & Coverdale, L. (2006). *In the name of honor*. New York: Simon & Schuster/Atria.

Major, B., Schmidlin, A. M., & Williams, L. (1990). Gender patterns in social touch: The impact of setting and age. *Journal of Personality and Social Psychology, 58*, 634–643.

Maltz, D. N., & Borker, R. (1982). A cultural approach to male-female miscommunication. In J. J. Gumperz (Ed.), *Language and social identity* (pp. 196–216). Cambridge, UK: Cambridge University Press.

Mandziuk, R. (2008). Dressing down Hillary. *Communication and Critical/Cultural Studies, 5*, 312–316.

Mangan, K. (2004, November 12). Does affirmative action hurt black law students? *The Chronicle of Higher Education*, pp. A35–A36.

Mansfield, H. (2007). *Manliness*. New Haven, CT: Yale University Press.

Mapstone, E. (1998). *War of words: Women and men argue*. London: Random House.

March of Dimes. (2006, October). *Chromosomal abnormalities*. Retrieved November 12, 2007, from http://www.marchofdimes.com/pnhec/4439_1209.asp

Marcus, S. (2007). *Between women: Friendship, desire, and marriage in Victorian England*. Princeton, NJ: Princeton University Press.

Marin, R., & Dokoupil, T. (2011, April 25). Dead suit walking. *Newsweek*, pp. 30–36.

Martin, C. (1997). *Gender cognitions and social relationships*. Paper presented at the meeting of the American Psychological Association, Chicago.

Martin, C., & Ruble, D. (2004). Children's search for gender cues: Cognitive perspectives on gender development. *Current Directions in Psychological Science, 13*, 67–70.

Martin, H., & Finn, S. (2010). *Masculinity and femininity in the MMPI-2 and MMPI-A*. Minneapolis: University of Minnesota Press.

Martz, D., Petroff, A., Curtin, L., & Bazzini, D. (2009). Gender differences in fat talk among American adults. *Sex Roles, 61*, 34–41.

Marx, J. (2004, August 29). He turns boys into men. *Parade*, pp. 4–7.

Marx, K. (1975). *Capital* (Ed. B. Fowles, Vol. 1). New York: Vintage.

Marx, K. (1977). *Early writings*. (Ed. Q. Hoare). New York: Vintage.

Mascia, J. (2010, July 12). A Web site that's not afraid to pick a fight. *The New York Times*, pp. B1, B4.

Mason, M. A. (2007). *Mothers on the fast track: How a new generation can balance family and careers*. Cambridge, MA: Yale University Press.

Mattioli, D. (2010, March 23). More men make harassment claims. *The Wall Street Journal*, p. D4.

May, L. (1998). *Masculinity and morality*. Ithaca, NY: Cornell University Press.

Mazur, E. (1989). Predicting gender differences in same-sex friendships from affiliation motive and value. *Psychology of Women Quarterly, 13*, 277–291.

McCann, C., & Kim, S. (Eds.). (2003). *Feminist theory reader*. London: Routledge.

McClelland, C. (2004, May 14). Man raised as a girl commits suicide at 38. *Raleigh News & Observer*, p. 9B.

McClish, G., & Bacon, J. (2002). "Telling the story her own way": The role of feminist standpoint theory in rhetorical studies. *Rhetoric Society Quarterly, 32*, 27–55.

McCloskey, D. (1999). *Crossing: A memoir*. Chicago: University of Chicago Press.

McDonald, K. (2012). *Feminism, the left, and postwar literary culture*. Jackson: University Press of Mississippi.

McDonald, M., Phipps, S., & Lethbridge, L. (2005). Taking its toll: The influences of paid and unpaid work on women's well-being. *Feminist Economics, 11*, 63–94.

McDonald, T. (2005, June 19). The rite to be men. *Raleigh News & Observer*, pp. 1B, 2B.

McGuffey, S., & Rich, L. (2004). Playing in the gender transgression zone: Race, class, and hegemonic masculinity in middle childhood. In J. Spade & C. Valentine (Eds.), *The kaleidoscope of gender: Prisms, patterns, and possibilities* (pp. 172–183). Belmont, CA: Wadsworth.

McKee, M. (2006, April). Al mousawat (equality) for Iraqi women. *Raising our voices: News from the Global Fund for Women*, n.p.

McKinley, J. (2012, March 25). Ruling extends sex-discrimination protection to transgender woman denied federal job. *The New York Times*, p. A14.

McMahan, D. (2011). Heartland: Symbolic displays of aggression and male masculinity in rural America. *Qualitative Research Reports in Communication, 12*, 51–59.

McRobbie, A. (2000). *Feminism and youth culture*. New York: Routledge.

McRobbie, A. (2009). *The aftermath of feminism: Gender, culture and social change*. Thousand Oaks, CA: Sage.

Mead, M. (1935/1968). *Sex and temperament in three primitive societies*. New York: Dell.

Mealy, L. (2000). *Sex differences: Development and evolutionary strategies*. San Diego: Academic Press.

Mean, L. J., & Kassing, J. W. (2008). "I would just like to be known as an athlete": Maintaining hegemony, femininity, and heterosexuality in female sport. *Western Journal of Communication, 72*(2), 126–144.

Mechling, E., & Mechling, J. (1994). The Jung and the restless: The mythopoetic men's movement. *Southern Communication Journal, 59*, 97–111.

Media Trends Track. (2010). Retrieved April 22, 2010, from http://www.tvb.org/rcentral/media trendstrack/tvbasics/02_TVHouseholds.asp

Medved, C. E. (2009). Crossing and transforming occupational and household gendered divisions of labor. *Communication Yearbook, 33,* 301–341.

Mehrabian, A. (1981). *Silent messages: Implicit communication of emotion and attitudes* (2nd ed.). Belmont, CA: Wadsworth.

Meloy, R. (2006). *The psychology of stalking: Clinical and forensic perspectives* (2nd ed.). New York: Academic Press.

Mernissi, F. (2004). Size 6: The Western woman's harem. In J. Spade & C. Valentine (Eds.), *The kaleidoscope of gender: Prisms, patterns, and possibilities* (pp. 297–301). Belmont, CA: Thomson/Wadsworth.

Merskin, D. (2011). Perpetuation of the hot-Latina stereotype in desperate housewives. In G. Dines & J. M. Humez (Eds.), *Gender, race and class in media: A critical reader* (3rd ed., pp. 27–334). Los Angeles: Sage.

Messner, M. A. (2000a). Barbie girls versus sea monsters: Children constructing gender. *Gender and Society, 7,* 121–137.

Messner, M. A. (2000b). White guy habitus in the classroom: Challenging the reproduction of privilege. *Men and Masculinities, 2,* 457–169.

Messner, M. A. (2001). When bodies are weapons: Masculinity and violence in sports. In D. Vannoy (Ed.), *Gender mosaics* (pp. 94–105). Los Angeles: Roxbury.

Messner, M. A. (2002, December 6). Needed: A fair assessment by a "budgetary umpire." *The Chronicle of Higher Education,* pp. B8–B9.

Messner, M. A. (2005). Still a man's world? Studying masculinities and sport. In M. A. Messner, J. Hearn, & R. W. Connell (Eds.), *Handbook of studies on men & masculinities* (pp. 313–325). Thousand Oaks, CA: Sage Publications.

Messner, M. A. (2007). Masculinities and athletic careers. In M. Andersen & P. H. Collins (Eds.), *Race, class, gender: An anthology* (6th ed., pp. 172–184). Belmont, CA: Thomson.

Messner, M. A., & Sabo, D. F. (2006). Sport in the social construction of masculinity. In S. M. Whitehead (Ed.), *Men and masculinities: Critical concepts in sociology* (pp. 303–316). New York: Routledge.

Meston, C., & Buss, D. (2009). *Why women have sex: Understanding sexual motivations—from adventure to revenge (and everything in between).* New York: Times/Holt.

Metts, S. (2006a). Gendered communication in dating relationships. In B. Dow & J. T. Wood (Eds.), *Handbook of Gender & Communication* (pp. 25–10). Thousand Oaks, CA: Sage.

Metts, S. (2006b). Hanging out and doing lunch: Enacting friendship closeness. In J. T. Wood &

S. W. Duck (Eds.), *Composing relationships: Communication in everyday life* (pp. 76–85). Belmont, CA: Thomson/Wadsworth.

Meyer, A. (2010). Too drunk to say no. *Feminist Media Studies, 10,* 19–34.

Meyer, S. (2009). Creating schools that value sexual diversity. In S. Steinberg (Ed.), *Diversity and multiculturalism: A reader* (pp. 173–192). New York: Peter Lang.

Meyers, D. (2007). *Nature, nurture, and human diversity.* New York: Worth Publishers.

Meyers, M. (1994). News of battering. *Journal of Communication, 44,* 47–62.

Meyers, M. (2004). African American women and violence: Gender, race, and class in the news. *Critical Studies in Media Communication, 21,* 95–118.

Miller, A. N. (2011, February). Men's and women's communication is different—sometimes. *Communication Currents,* p. 1.

Miller, C. (2008, August 14). Woman to woman, online. *The New York Times,* pp. C1, C9.

Miller, J. (2012). Girls face ACL woes. *Raleigh News & Observer,* pp. 1D, 2D.

Miller-Day, M., & Fisher, C. (2006). Communication in mother-adult daughter relationships. In K. Floyd & M. Morman (Eds.), *Widening the family circle: New research on family communication* (pp. 15–38). Newbury Park, CA: Sage.

Million, J. (2003). *Woman's voice, woman's place: Lucy Stone and the birth of the women's rights movement.* Westport, CT: Praeger.

Million Family March picks up where men's march ended 5 years before. (2000, October 14). *Raleigh News & Observer,* p. 6B.

Mills, J. (1985, February). Body language speaks louder than words. *Horizon,* pp. 8–12.

Mills, R., Nazar, J., & Farrell, H. (2002). Child and parent perceptions of hurtful messages. *Journal of Social and Personal Relationships, 19,* 731–754.

Minhas, S. F. (2009). The politics of rape and honor in Pakistan. In L. Cuklanz & S. Moorti (Eds.), *Local violence, global media* (pp. 65–78). New York: Peter Lang.

Mischel, W. (1966). A social learning view of sex differences in behavior. In E. E. Maccoby (Ed.), *The development of sex differences* (pp. 93–106). Stanford, CA: Stanford University Press.

Misra, J., Hickes, L. J., Holmes, E., & Agiomavritis, S. (2011). The ivory ceiling of service work. *Academe, 97,* 22–26.

Mitra, A. (2010). Voices of the marginalized on the Internet: Examples from a website for women of South Asia. In P. Nayar (Ed.), *The new media and cybercultures anthology* (pp. 166–182). Malden, MA: Wiley-Blackwell.

Moe, K., & Shandy, D. (2010). *Glass ceilings & 100-hour couples: What the opt-out phenomenon can teach us about work and family.* Athens, GA: University of Georgia Press.

Moller, L., & Serbin, L. (1996). Antecedents of toddler gender segregation: Cognitive consonance, gender-typed toy preferences and behavioral compatibility. *Sex Roles, 35,* 445–460.

Molloy, B., & Herzberger, S. (1998). Body image and self-esteem: A comparison of African-American and Caucasian women. *Sex Roles, 38,* 631–643.

Monastersky, R. (2005a, March 4). Studies show biological differences in how boys and girls learn math, but social factors play a big role too. *The Chronicle of Higher Education,* pp. A1, A12–A19.

Monastersky, R. (2005b, March 4). Why Chinese students score high in math. *The Chronicle of Higher Education,* p. A19.

Mongeau, P., Serewicz, M., Henningsen, M., & Davis, K. (2006). Sex differences in the transition to a heterosexual romantic relationship. In K. Dindia & D. Canary (Eds.), *Sex differences and similarities in communication* (2nd ed., pp. 337–358). Mahwah, NJ: Lawrence Erlbaum.

Monsour, M. (2002). *Women and men as friends: Relationships across the life span in the 21st century.* Mahwah, NJ: Erlbaum.

Monsour, M. (2006). Gendered communication in friendships. In B. Dow & J. T. Wood (Eds.), *The SAGE handbook of gender and communication* (pp. 57–70). Thousand Oaks, CA: Sage.

Morgan, J. (1999). *When chickenheads come home to roost: My life as a hip-hop feminist.* New York: Simon & Schuster.

Morgan, M. (1973). *The total woman.* New York: Pocket.

Morgan, R. (2003/2004, Winter). Infecting our souls. *Ms.,* p. 95.

Morman, M. T., & Floyd, K. (2002). A "changing culture of fatherhood": Effects on affectionate communication, closeness, and satisfaction in men's relationships with their fathers and their sons. *Western Journal of Communication, 66,* 395–411.

Morman, M. T., & Floyd, K. (2006). The good son: Men's perceptions of the characteristics of sonhood. In K. Floyd & M. T. Morman (Eds.), *Widening the family circle: New research on family communication* (pp. 37–55). Thousand Oaks, CA: Sage.

Morrow, V. (2006). Understanding gender differences in context: Implications for young children's everyday lives. *Children & Society, 20,* 92–104.

Ms. Musings. (2004, Spring). *Ms.,* p. 13.

Muehlhoff, T. (2007, March 18). Personal communication.

Mulac, A. (1998). The gender-linked language effect: Do language differences really make a difference? In D. J. Canary & K. Dindia (Eds.), *Sex differences and similarities in communication: Critical essays and empirical investigations of sex and gender in interaction* (pp. 127–153). Mahwah, NJ: Erlbaum.

Mulac, A. (2006). The gender-linked language effect: Do language differences really make a difference? In K. Dindia & D. Canary (Eds.), *Sex differences and similarities in communication* (pp. 219–239). Mahwah, NJ: Erlbaum.

Mulac, A., Jansma, L., & Linz, D. (2003). Men's behavior toward women after viewing sexually explicit films: Degradation makes a difference. *Communication Monographs, 69,* 311–328.

Murphy, C. (2005). Grass-roots men's ministries growing. *Raleigh News & Observer,* p. 5E.

Murrow, D. (2004). *Why men hate going to church.* Nashville, TN: Thomas Nelson.

Muwakkil, S. (2005, December 19). Jump-starting a movement. *In These Times,* p. 13.

Myers, P. N., & Biocca, F. A. (1992). The elastic body image: The effect of television advertising on body image distortion in young women. *Journal of Communication, 3,* 108–133.

Namaste, V. (2000). *Invisible lives: The erasure of transsexual and transgendered people.* Chicago: University of Chicago Press.

Nanda, S. (2004). Multiple genders among North American Indians. In J. Spade & C. Valentine (Eds.), *The kaleidoscope of gender* (pp. 64–70). Belmont, CA: Thomson/ Wadsworth.

Natalier, K. (2003). 'I'm not his wife': Doing gender and doing housework in the absence of women. *Journal of Sociology, 39,* 253–269.

National Association of Anorexia Nervosa and Associated Disorders. (2010). Retrieved April 22, 2010, from http://www.anad.org/getInformation/abouteatingdisorders

National coalition against domestic violence. (1999). [Website]. Retrieved July 10, 1999, from http: www.ncadv.org

National Domestic Violence Hotline. (n.d.). Abuse in America. *In Break the silence, make the call.* Retrieved December 8, 2005, from http://www.ndvh.org/educate/abuse_in_america.html

National Institute of Mental Health. (2010). Retrieved April 22, 2010, from http://www.nimh.nih.gov/health/publications/eating-disorders/what-are-eating-disorders.shtml

National Institute on Media and the Family. (2007). Retrieved June 8, 2007, from http://www.mediafamily.org/facts/facts_mediaeffect.shtml

Navarro, M. (2005). Mexico: Activism and reflection. *Ms.,* p. 29.

Neighbors, C., Walker, D., Mbilinyi, L., O'Rourke, A., Edleson, J., Zegree, J., et al. (2010). Normative misperceptions of abuse among perpetrators of intimate partner violence. *Violence against Women, 16,* 370–389.

Neinas, C. M. (2002, December 6). Can we avoid unintended consequences for men? *The Chronicle of Higher Education,* p. B8.

Nelson, C., Trzemzalski, J., Malkasian, K., & Pfeffer, K. (2004, April). *Expressions of incompetence, sexual fantasies, and sexualized hostility toward male and female faculty: A qualitative analysis of student comments on an anonymous faculty evaluation Web site.* Presentation at Multicultural Psychology (Psy 493W/Psy 992) Michigan State University, East Lansing, MI.

Newcombe, N. (2002, December 14). Is sociobiology ready for prime time? *The Chronicle of Higher Education,* pp. B10–B11.

Newsome, J. (Writer, director, and producer). (2011). *Miss representation* [Motion Picture]. Los Angeles, US.

Noah, T. (2012). *The great divergence.* New York: Bloomsbury Press.

Nocera, J. (2013). This war is no longer invisible. *The New York Times,* p. A19.

Nolen-Hoeksema, S. (2003). *Women who think too much.* New York: Henry Holt.

Norlund, R., & Rubin, A. (2010, May 31). Escaping marriage, but not lashes. *The New York Times,* p. A4.

Norplant: A new contraceptive with the potential for abuse. (1994, January). Retrieved from http://www.aclu.org/reproductive-freedom/norplant-new-contraceptive-potential-abuse

Norplant. (2012, July 7). *Rx list* (online). Retrieved from http://www.rxlist.com/norplant-drug.htm

Northrup, C. (1995). *Women's bodies, women's wisdom.* New York: Bantam.

O'Leary, A. (2012, August 2). In virtual play, sex harassment is all too real. *The New York Times,* pp. A1, A3.

Oliker, S. (2001). Gender and friendship. In D. Vannoy (Ed.), *Gender mosaics* (pp. 195–204). Los Angeles: Roxbury.

Olson, L., & Rauscher, E. (2011). We'll never be that kind of couple: The variability of intimate violence. In D. O. Braithwaite & J. T. Wood (Eds.), *Casing interpersonal communication* (pp. 149–156). Dubuque, IA: Kendall-Hunt.

Olyslager, F., & Conway, L. (2007, September). *On the calculation of the prevalence of transsexualism.* Paper presented at the WPATH 20th International Symposium, Chicago.

O'Neill, R., & Colley, A. (2006). Gender and status effects in student e-mails to staff. *Journal of Computer Assisted Learning, 22,* 360–367.

O'Neill, O., & O'Reilly, C. (2011). Reducing the backlash effect: Self-monitoring and women's promotions. *Journal of Occupational Psychology.* doi:10.1111/j.2044-8325.2010.02008.x

Onishi, H. (1998). *Women in Japan and the USA: Identity status and its relationship to depression.* Unpublished doctoral dissertation, University of Connecticut.

Onishi, N. (2007, April 28). Japan court rules against sex slaves and laborers. *The New York Times,* p. A5.

Orenstein, P. (2011a). *Cinderella ate my daughter.* New York: Harper.

Orenstein, P. (2011b). Should the world of toys be gender-free? *The New York Times,* p. A21.

Ostrow, N. (2010, May 19). Men, too, suffer postpartum depression. *Raleigh News & Observer,* p. 5A.

Owen, D. (2007, Spring). A tragic tradition. *World Vision,* p. 25.

Painter, N. (1996). *Sojourner Truth: A life, a symbol.* New York: W. W. Norton.

Palomares, N. (2008). Gender salience and language. *Human Communication Research, 34,* 263–286.

Palomares, N. A. (2010). Gender-based language use: Understanding how and why men communicate similarly and differently. In M. B. Hinner (Ed.), *The interrelationship of business and communication* (pp. 74–96). Frankfurt, Germany: Peter Lang.

Panther, N. (2008). *Violence against women and femicide in Mexico.* Saarbruken, Germany: VDM Verlag.

Paoletti, J. (2012). *Pink and blue.* Bloomington: Indiana University Press.

Parker, P. (2006). *Race, gender, and leadership: Re-envisioning organizational leadership from the perspective of African American women.* Mahwah, NJ: Erlbaum.

Parker-Pope, T. (2008, June 10). Gay unions shed light on gender in marriage. *The New York Times,* p. Dl.

Parker-Pope, T. (2010a, February 16). As girls become women, sports pay dividends. *The New York Times,* p. D5.

Parker-Pope, T. (2010b, July 6). Recalibrated formula eases women's workouts. *The New York Times,* p. D5.

Parker-Pope, T. (2010c, April 6). Surprisingly, family time has grown. *The New York Times,* p. D5.

Parks, S. (2010). *Fierce angels: The strong black woman in American life and culture.* New York: Random House.

Parlee, M. B. (1979, May). Conversational politics. *Psychology Today,* pp. 48–56.

Patel, T. (2006). *Sex-selective abortion in India.* Thousand Oaks, CA: Sage.

Patterson, C. J. (2000). Family relationships of lesbians and gay men. *Journal of Marriage and the Family, 62,* 1052–1069.

Paul, P. (2006). *Pornified: How pornography is damaging our lives, our relationships and our families.* New York: Owl Books.

Pear, R. (2009, January 10). House passes 2 measures on job bias. *The New York Times*, p. A13.

Pear, R. (2010, June 22). Gay workers get time to care for partner's sick child. *The New York Times*, p. A13.

Pear, R. (2012, May 17). House vote sets up battle on domestic violence bill. *The New York Times*, p. A19.

Pennington, B. A., & Turner, L. H. (2004). Playground or training ground? The function of talk in African American and European American mother-adolescent daughter dyads. In P. M. Buzzanell, H. Sterk, & L. H. Turner (Eds.), *Gender in applied contexts* (pp. 275–294). Thousand Oaks, CA: Sage Publications.

Peretti, P. O., & Abplanalp, R. R., Jr. (2004). Chemistry in the college dating process: Structure and function. *Social Behavior and Personality, 32*, 147–154.

Pérez-Peña, R. (2013). College groups connect to fight sexual assault. *The New York Times*, pp. A14, A17.

Peter, J., & Valkenburg, P. (2010). Adolescents' use of sexually explicit Internet material and sexual uncertainty: The role of involvement and gender. *Communication Monographs, 77*, 357–375.

Phelan, J. E., Moss-Racusin, C. A., & Rudman, L. A. (2007). *Competent yet out in the cold: Shifting standards reflect backlash toward agentic women.* Manuscript submitted for publication. Cited in Rudman & Glick, 2008.

Phillips, M. (2011, June 13). *These "Slut Walks" prove feminism is now irrelevant to most women's lives.* Retrieved from http://www.dailymail.co.uk/debate/article-2002887/Slut-Walks-prove-feminism-irrelevant-womens-lives.html#ixzz1isfBlzEJ

Philipsen, M. I. (2008). *Challenges of the faculty career for women.* San Francisco: Jossey-Bass, Wiley.

Philipsen, M. I., & Bostic, T. P. (2010). *Helping faculty find work-life balance: The path toward life-friendly institutions.* San Francisco: Jossey-Bass, Wiley.

Piaget, J. (1932/1965). *The moral judgment of the child.* New York: Free Press.

Piepmeier, A. (2009). *Girl zines: Making media, doing feminism.* New York: New York University Press.

Pinsky, L., Erickson, R., & Schimke, R. (Eds.). (1999). *Genetic disorders of human sexual development.* New York: Oxford University Press.

Pinsky, M. (2007, February 2). Churches ramp up to bring in men. *Raleigh News & Observer*, p. 4E.

Pollack, W. (2000). *Real boys: Rescuing ourselves from the myths of boyhood.* New York: Owl Books.

Pollitt, K. (1994). *Reasonable creatures: Essays on women and feminism.* New York: Knopf.

Pollitt, K. (2011, July 18–25). Talk the talk, walk the SlutWalk. *The Nation.* Retrieved from http://www.thenation.com/article/161728/talk-talk-walk-slutwalk

Popenoe, D. (1996). *Life without father.* New York: Free Press.

Porter, B. (2007, Spring). Changing his name. *Ms.*, p. 17.

Powlishta, K., Serbin, L., & Moller, L. (1993). The stability of individual differences in gender typing: Implications for understanding gender segregation. *Sex Roles, 29*, 723–788.

Preston, J. (2009a, July 16). New policy permits asylum for battered women. *The New York Times*, pp. A1, A18.

Preston, J. (2009b, October 30). Officals endorse asylum for abuse. *The New York Times*, pp. A12, A20.

Preves, S. (2004). Sexing the intersexed: An analysis of sociocultural responses to inter-sexuality. In J. Spade & C. Valentine (Eds.), *The kaleidoscope of gender: Prisms, patterns, and possibilities* (pp. 31–45). Belmont, CA: Thomson/Wadsworth.

The profession. (2010, August 27). *The Chronicle of Higher Education*, pp. 20–24.

Promise Keepers: "Men have dropped the ball." (1997, October 1). *USA Today*, p. 14A.

Pruett, M. K., & Pruett, K. (2009). *Partnership parenting.* Cambridge, MA: DaCapo Lifelong Books.

Putney, C. (2003). *Muscular Christianity.* Cambridge, MA: Harvard University Press.

Quinn, K. (2010). Tenure Clock Extension Policies: Who uses them and to what effect? *Journal about Women in Higher Education, 3*, 182–206.

Quinn, K., & Litzler, E. (2009). Turning away from academic careers: What does work-family have to do with it? *Journal about Women in Higher Education, 2*, 66–90.

Rabidue v. Osceola Refining Company. 805F 2nd 611, 626 Cir. (6th Cir. 1986).

Rabin, R. (2012). Benefits of circumcision are said to outweigh risks. *The New York Times*, p. A3.

Rainie, L., & Wellman, B. (2012). *Networked.* Boston: MIT.

Ramasubramanian, S. (2010). Television viewing, racial attitudes, and policy preferences: Exploring the role of social identity and intergroup emotions in influencing support for affirmative action. *Communication Monographs, 77*, 102–120.

Ramey, G., & Ramey, V. A. (2009, August). *The rug rat race.* NBER Working Paper No. wl5284. Retrieved April 6, 2010, from http://ssrn.com/abstract=1459585

Ransby, B. (2003). *Ella Baker and the Black Freedom Movement: A radical democratic vision*. Chapel Hill: University of North Carolina Press.

Rasmussen, J. L., & Moley, B. E. (1986). Impression formation as a function of the sex role appropriateness of linguistic behavior. *Sex Roles, 14*, 149–161.

Ream, Diane Show. (2012, June 25). Aired on NPR 10-11 a.m. EDS.

Reich, M. (1991). *Toxic politics: Responding to chemical disasters*. Ithaca, NY: Cornell University Press.

Reisman, J. M. (1990). Intimacy in same-sex friendships. *Sex Roles, 23*, 65–82.

Reiss, D. (2000). *The relational code: Genetic and social influences on social development*. Cambridge, MA: Harvard University Press.

Renzetti, C. (2008). *Feminist criminology*. New York: Routledge.

Reskin, B. (2003). Including mechanisms in our models of ascriptive inequality. *American Sociological Review, 6*, 1–21.

Retherford, R. D., Ogawa, N., & Matsukura, R. (2001). Late marriage and less marriage in Japan. *Population and Development Review, 27*, 65–102.

Reuther, R. R. (Ed.). (1974). *Religion and sexism: Images of woman in the Jewish and Christian traditions*. New York: Simon & Schuster.

Reuther, R. R. (1983). *Sexism and Godtalk: Toward a feminist theology*. Boston: Beacon.

Reuther, R. R. (2001). Ecofeminism and healing ourselves, healing the earth. In D. Vannoy (Ed.), *Gender mosaics* (pp. 406–414). Los Angeles: Roxbury.

Rich, M. (2008). Music videos: Media of the youth, by the youth, for the youth. In P. E. Jamieson & D. Romer (Eds.), *The changing portrayal of adolescents in the media since 1950* (pp. 78–102). New York: Oxford University Press.

Richtel, M. (2000, February 6). Online revolution's latest twist: Computers screening job seekers. *The New York Times*, p. Al.

Rhode, D. (2010). *The beauty bias: The injustice of appearance in life and law*. New York: Oxford University Press.

Riegle-Crumb, C., & Humphries, M. (2012). Exploring bias in math teachers' perceptions of students' ability by gender and race/ethnicity. *Gender & Society, 26*, 290–322.

Riessman, C. K. (1990). *Divorce talk: Women and men make sense of personal relationships*. New Brunswick, NJ: Rutgers University Press.

Risman, B. J. (1989). Can men mother? Life as a single father. In B. J. Risman & P. Schwartz (Eds.), *Gender in intimate relationships* (pp. 155–164). Belmont, CA: Wadsworth.

Risman, B. J., & Godwin, S. (2001). Twentieth-century changes in economic work and family.

In D. Vannoy (Ed.), *Gender mosaics* (pp. 134–144). Los Angeles: Roxbury.

Rivers, C., & Barnett, R. (2011). *The truth about girls and boys*. New York: Columbia University Press.

Rives, K. (2005, May 22). Keep up appearances. *Raleigh News & Observer*, p. 1A.

Roberts, D. (1997). *Killing the Black body: Race, reproduction, and the meaning of liberty*. New York: Pantheon Books.

Roberts, D. (2009, Summer). Race, gender, and genetic technologies: A new reproductive dystopia? *Signs: Journal of Women in Culture and Society, 34*, 783–804.

Roiphe, K. (1993). *The morning after: Sex, fear, and feminism on campus*. Boston: Little, Brown.

Romaine, S. (1999). *Communicating gender*. Mahwah, NJ: Erlbaum.

Romano, A., & Dokoupil, T. (2010). Men's lib. *Newsweek*. Retrieved from http://www.thedaily beast.com/newsweek/2010/09/20/why-we-need-to-reimagine-masculinity.html

Roosevelt, M. (2010, January 14). When the gym isn't enough. *The New York Times*, pp. E1, E8.

Roscoe, W. (1993). How to become a Berdache: Toward a unified analysis of gender diversity. In G. Herdt (Ed.), *Third sex and third gender: Beyond sexual dimorphism in culture and history* (pp. 329–372). New York: Zone Books.

Rose, B. (2008, June 8). Even the geeks are sexist. *Raleigh News & Observer*, p. 7G.

Rose, N. S. (2007). *The politics of life itself: Biomedicine, power, and subjectivity in the twenty-first century*. Princeton: Princeton University Press.

Rosenbloom, S. (2008, February 21). Sorry, boys, this is our domain. *The New York Times*, pp. E1, E8.

Rosenberg, D. (2007). (Rethinking) gender. *Newsweek*, pp. 50–57.

Rosenthal, E. (2006, October 6). Women face greatest threat of violence at home, study finds. *The New York Times*, p. A5.

Ross, K. (2010). *Gendered media*. Lanham, MD: Rowman & Littlefield.

Ross, L. J. (2009). The movement for reproductive justice: Six years old and growing. *Collective Voices, 4*, 8–9.

Rowe-Finkbeiner, K. (2004). *The F-word: Feminism in jeopardy*. Emeryville, CA: Seal Press.

Rubin, J. Z., Provenzano, F. J., & Luria, Z. (1974). The eye of the beholder: Parents' views on sex of newborns. *American Journal of Orthopsychiatry, 44*, 512–519.

Ruble, D., & Martin, C. (1998). Gender development. In W. Damon (Ed.), *The handbook of child psychology* (pp. 933–1017). New York: Wiley.

Rudacille, D. (2006). *The riddle of gender*. New York: Anchor.

Ruddick, S. (1989). *Maternal thinking: Toward a politics of peace.* Boston: Beacon.

Rudman, L. A., & Fairchild, K. (2004). Reactions to counterstereotypic behavior: The role of backlash in cultural stereotype maintenance. *Journal of Personality and Social Psychology, 87,* 157–176.

Rudman, L. A., & Phelan, J. E. (2007). The interpersonal power feminism: Is feminism good for relationships? *Sex Roles, 57,* 787–799.

Rusbult, C. (1987). Responses to dissatisfaction in close relationships: The exit-voice-loyalty-neglect model. In D. Perlman & S. W. Duck (Eds.), *Intimate relationships: Development, dynamics, and deterioration* (pp. 209–238). London: Sage.

Rutenberg, J. (2009, June 24). Obama team to add protections for transgender federal employees. *The New York Times,* p. A15.

Rutter, V., & Schwartz, P. (1996). Same-sex couples: Courtship, commitment, and context. In A. Auhagen & M. von Salisch (Eds.), *The diversity of human relationships* (pp. 197–226). New York: Cambridge University Press.

Ryan, B. (2004). Identity politics in the women's movement. In J. Spade & C. Valentine (Eds.), *The kaleidoscope of gender: Prisms, patterns, and possibilities* (pp. 104–113). Belmont, CA: Thomson/Wadsworth.

Sagrestano, L., Heavey, C., & Christensen, A. (1998). Theoretical approaches to understanding sex differences and similarities in conflict behavior. In D. J. Canary & K. Dindia (Eds.), *Sex differences and similarities in communication: Critical essays and empirical investigations of sex and gender in interaction* (pp. 287–302). Mahwah, NJ: Erlbaum.

Salome, R. (2007). A place for women's colleges. *The Chronicle of Higher Education,* p. B20.

Samovar, L., Porter, R., & Stefani, L. (1998). *Communication between cultures* (2nd ed.). Belmont, CA: Wadsworth.

Samuels, A. (2008, July 7–14). A new color clash on the catwalk. *Newsweek,* p. 12.

Sanday, P. (2007). *Fraternity gang rape: Sex, brotherhood, and privilege on campus* (2nd ed.). New York: New York University Press.

Sandberg, C. (2013). *Lean in: Women, work, and the will to lead.* New York: Knopf.

Sandberg, S. (2013). *Lean in.* New York: Knopf.

Sandier, B. (2004). The chilly climate: Subtle ways in which women are often treated differently at work and in classrooms. In J. Spade & C. Valentine (Eds.), *The kaleidoscope of gender: Prisms, patterns, and possibilities* (pp. 187–190). Belmont, CA: Thomson/Wadsworth.

Sanger, M. (1914, June). Suppression. *The Woman Rebel,* p. 1.

Sarkela, S. J., Ross, S. R., & Lowe, M. A. (2003). *From megaphones to microphones: Speeches of American women, 1920-1960.* Westport, CT: Praeger.

Sartre, J. P. (1966). *Being and nothingness: An essay in phenomenological ontology.* New York: Citadel.

Savage, C. (2012, January 7). U.S. to expand its definition of rape in statistics. *The New York Times,* pp. A10, A15.

Saxen, R. (2007). *Good eater: The true story of one man's struggle with binge eating disorder.* Oakland, CA: New Harbinger Publications.

Scelfo, J. (2002, December 9). Kneed to know. *Newsweek,* pp. 88, 90.

Scelfo, J. (2006, November 6). Extreme make-overs. *Newsweek,* pp. 56–57.

Schaap, J. (2010). *Corrective rape* (Video shown on ESPN). Retrieved May 10, 2010, from http://espn.go.com/video/clip?id=5181871

Schalet, A. (2011, April 7). Caring, romantic American boys. *The New York Times,* p. A15.

Schalet, A. (2012). *Not under my roof: Parents, teens and the culture of sex.* Chicago: University of Chicago Press.

Schiebinger, L., & Gilmartin, S. K. (2010, January-February). Housework is an academic issue. *Academe,* 39–44.

Schiff, S. (2006, October 13). Desperately seeking Susan. *The New York Times,* p. A27.

Schilt, K. R. (2007, August 11). *Doing gender in open workplace transitions: the power of homosocial reproduction.* Paper presented at the annual meeting of the American Sociological Association, New York.

Schilt, K. R. (2010). *Just one of the guys? Transgender men and the persistence of inequality.* Chicago: University of Chicago Press.

Schilt, K. R., & Wiswall, M. (2008). Before and after: Gender transitions, human capital, and workplace experiences. *Berkeley Electronic Journal of Economic Analysis & Policy.* Retrieved October 28, 2008, from http://www.bepress.com/bejeap/vol8/iss1/art39/

Schmidt, P. (2010, March 26). Male professors face their own challenges in balancing work and home. *The Chronicle of Higher Education,* pp. A8–A10.

Schneider, J., & Hacker, S. (1973). Sex role imagery and use of the generic "man" in introductory texts: A case in the sociology of sociology. *American Sociologist, 8,* 12–18.

Schroeder, L. O. (1986). A rose by any other name: Post-marital right to use maiden name: 1934-1982. *Sociology and Social Research, 70,* 290–293.

Schwalbe, M. (1996). *Unlocking the cage: The men's movement, gender, politics, and American culture.* Cambridge, MA: Oxford University Press.

Schwartz, B. K., & Cellini, H. (Eds.). (1995). *The sex offender: Corrections, treatment, and legal practice* (Vol. *1*, pp. 51–52). Kingston, NJ: Civic Research Institute.

Schwartz, P., & Rutter, V. (1998). *The gender of sexuality*. Newbury Park, CA: Pine Forge Press.

Seattle Times. (2009, July 9). Retrieved from http://seattletimes.nwsource.com/html/books/2009437319_steineml0.html

Sedgwick, E. (1990). *Epistemology of the closet.* Berkeley: University of California Press.

Segrin, C., & Flora, F. J. (2005). *Family communication*. Mahwah, NJ: Erlbaum.

Seligman, K. (2007, May 20). The motherhood movement. *San Francisco Chronicle Magazine*, pp. 10–15, 19.

Sen, J., & Saini, M. (2005). *Are other worlds possible? Talking new politics*. New Delhi, India: Zubaan.

Setoodeh, R. (2006, December 11). Get ready to rumble. *Newsweek*, p. 46.

Sexually harassed male guard awarded $3.75 million. (1999, May 30). *Raleigh News & Observer*, p. 9A.

Shah, S. (2011, April 22). Pakistan frees 5 accused in court-ordered gang rape. *Raleigh News & Observer*, p. 4A.

Shapiro, T. (2007). The hidden cost of being African American. In M. Andersen & P. H. Collins (Eds.), *Race, class, & gender* (6th ed., pp. 127–135). Thousand Oaks, CA: Sage.

Sharp, S. (2011). Disciplining the housewife in Desperate Housewives and domestic reality television. In G. Dines & J. Humez (Eds.), *Gender, race, anmd class in media: A critical reader* (3rd ed., pp. 481–486). Los Angeles: Sage.

Sheehy, G. (2010). *Passages in caregiving*. New York: William Morrow.

Shelton, M. (2008, May-June). Forced into manhood: Males and homesickness at camp. *Camping Magazine*, pp. 41–15.

Shepard, B. (2008). *Queer political performance and protest*. New York: Routledge.

Shepherd, M. E. (2008). *Sex-selective abortion in India*. Amherst, NY: Cambria Press.

Sheridan-Rabideau, M. P. (2009). *Girls, feminism, and grassroots literacies: Activism in the Girlzone*. New York: SUNY Press.

Sherrod, D. (1989). The influence of gender on same-sex friendships. In C. Hendrick (Ed.), *Close relationships* (pp. 164–186). Newbury Park, CA: Sage.

Shimron, Y. (1997, January 22). Men unite to live their faith. *Raleigh News & Observer*, pp. 1A–6A.

Shimron, Y. (2002, July 21). Promise Keepers fill the house—and heart. *Raleigh News & Observer*, pp. 1A, 17A.

Shimron, Y. (2007, May 10). Christians test masculine side. *Raleigh News & Observer*, pp. IB, 7B.

Silverstein, L., Auerbach, C., Grieco, L., & Dunkel, F. (1999). Do Promise Keepers dream of feminist sheep? *Sex Roles, 40*, 665–688.

Simmons, R. (2002). *Odd girl out: The hidden culture of aggression in girls*. New York: Harcourt.

Simmons, R. (2004). *Odd girl speaks out: Girls write about bullies, cliques, popularity, and jealousy*. Orlando, FL: Harvest Books.

Slaughter, A. (2012, June/July). Why women still can't have it all. *Atlantic*. Retrieved from http://www.theatlantic.com/magazine/archive/2012/07/why-women-still-can-8217-t-have-it-all/9020/

Slaughter, A. (2013). Yes, you can. *The New York Times Book Review*, pp. 1, 12–13.

Sloop, J. (2004). *Disciplining gender: Rhetorics of sex identity in contemporary U.S. culture*. Amherst: University of Massachusetts Press.

Sloop, J. (2006). Critical studies in gender/sexuality and media. In B. Dow & J. T. Wood (Eds.), *Handbook of gender and communication* (pp. 319–333). Thousand Oaks, CA: Sage.

Smith, B. (2006, August 24). Women at the Citadel report sexual assaults. *Raleigh News & Observer*, p. 7A.

Smith, D. (2004a, February 8). Gay animals not uncommon. *Raleigh News & Observer*, p. 7A.

Smith, D. (2004b). Schooling for inequality. In J. Spade & C. Valentine (Eds.), *The kaleidoscope of gender: Prisms, patterns, and possibilities* (pp. 183–186). Belmont, CA: Thomson/Wadsworth.

Smith, N. (1998). Guerrilla girls. In W. Mankiller, G. Mink, M. Navarro, B. Smith, & G. Steinem (Eds.), *The reader's companion to U.S. women's history* (p. 250). New York: Houghton Mifflin.

Smith, S., Choueiti, M., & Stern, J. (2012). *Occupational aspirations: What are G-rated films teaching children about the world*. Retrieved from http://www.thegeenadavisinstitute.org/downloads/KeyFindings_OccupAspirations.pdf

Smith, S., & Cook, C. A. (2006). *Gender stereotypes: An analysis of popular films and TV*. Retrieved from http://www.thegeenadavis institute.org/downloads/GDIGM_Main_Findings.pdf

Smith, S., Granados, A., Choueiti, M., Erickson, S., & Noyes, A. (2010). *Changing the status quo: Industry leaders' perceptions of gender in family films*. Retrieved from http://www.thegeenadavisinstitute.org/downloads/Key Findings_StatusQuo.pdf

Socha, T. J., Sanchez-Hucles, J., Bromley, J., & Kelly, B. (1995). Invisible parents and children: Exploring African-American parent-child communication. In T. J. Socha & G. H. Stamp (Eds.), *Parents, children and communication: Frontiers of theory and research* (pp. 127–145). Mahwah, NJ: Erlbaum.

Solebello, N., & Elliott, S. (2011). "We want them to be as heterosexual as possible": Fathers talk about their teen children's sexuality. *Gender & Society, 25,* 293–315.

Solinger, R. (2005). *Pregnancy and power: A short history of reproductive politics in America.* New York: New York University Press.

Solomon, B. (1986). *In the company of educated women.* New Haven, CT: Yale University Press.

Sommers, C. (2000). *The war against boys: How misguided feminism is harming our young men.* New York: Simon & Schuster.

Spence, J., & Buckner, C. (2000). Instrumental and expressive traits, trait stereotypes and sexist attitudes: What do they signify? *Psychology of Women Quarterly, 24,* 44–62.

Spender, D. (1984a). Defining reality: A powerful tool. In C. Kramarae, M. Schultz, & W. O'Barr (Eds.), *Language and power* (pp. 195–205). Beverly Hills, CA: Sage.

Spender, D. (1984b). *Man-made language.* London: Routledge and Kegan Paul.

Spitzack, C., & Carter, K. (1987). Women in communication studies: A typology for revision. *Quarterly Journal of Speech, 73,* 401–423.

Stacey, J. (1996). *In the name of the father: Rethinking family values in a postmodern age.* Boston: Beacon.

Stafford, L., Dutton, M., & Haas, S. (2000). Measuring routine maintenance: Scale revision, sex versus gender roles, and the prediction of relational characteristics. *Communication Monographs, 67,* 306–323.

Stafford, L., & Kline, S. (1996). Women's surnames and titles: Men's and women's views. *Communication Research Reports, 13,* 214–224.

Stampler, L. (2011, April 20). SlutWalks sweep the nation. *Huffington Post.* Retrieved from http://www.huffingtonpost.com/2011/04/20/slutwalk-united-states-city_n_851725.html

Stansell, C. (2010). *The feminist promise.* New York: Random House.

Statistics. (2009). *Rape, Abuse, and Incest National Network.* Retrieved November 22, 2009, from http://www.rainn.org

Stanton, E. C., Anthony, S. B., & Gage, M. J. (Eds.). (1882). *History of woman suffrage* (Vol. *1,* p. 116). New York: Fowler & Wells.

Staples, B. (2005, May 12). How hip-hop music lost its way and betrayed its fans. *The New York Times,* p. A26.

Starling-Lyons, K. (2003, October 21). The gender game. *Raleigh News & Observer,* pp. IE, 3E.

Steinberg, B. (2011). Chevy takes on ambitious role in TNT's "Men" program. *Advertising Age, 82,* 3–22.

Stepp, L. S. (2007). *Unhooked: How young women pursue sex, delay love and lose at both.* New York: Penguin/Riverhead.

Stigliltz, J. (2012). *The price of inequality.* New York: W. W. Norton.

Stobbe, M. (2011, December 15). Survey: 1 in 4 women victims of domestic assault. *Raleigh News & Observer,* p. 6A.

Stobbe, M. (2012, March 22). Move-in before marriage no longer predicts divorce. *Raleigh News & Observer,* p. 4A.

Stone, P. (2007). *Opting out? Why women really quit careers and head home.* Berkeley, CA: University of California Press.

Stonington, J. (2011, December 11). Recession increases number of stay-at-home dads. *The Raleigh News & Observer,* p. 5A.

Straus, S. (2004). Escape from animal house. In J. Spade & C. Valentine (Eds.), *The kaleidoscope of gender* (pp. 462–465). Belmont, CA: Thomson/Wadsworth.

Strauss, V. (2008, May 20). "Boys crisis" in education debunked. *Raleigh News & Observer,* p. 5A.

Streib, L. (2011, September 26). Power and progress. *Newsweek,* pp. 30–33.

Stroman, C. A., & Dates, J. L. (2008). African Americans, Latinos, Asians, and Native Americans in the media. In P. E. Jamieson & D. Romer (Eds.), *The changing portrayal of adolescents in the media since 1950* (pp. 198–219). New York: Oxford.

Strout, E. (2007, February 16). What the stopwatch doesn't tell. *The Chronicle of Higher Education,* pp. A44–A46.

Study reveals new differences between the sexes. (2005, March 17). *The New York Times,* p. A23.

Sturm, S. (2001). Second generation employment discrimination. *Columbia Law Review, 101,* 458–568.

Suggs, W. (2005a, July 1). Gender quotas? Not in college sports. *The Chronicle of Higher Education,* pp. A24–A26.

Sullivan, P. J., & Short, S. E. (2001). *Furthering the construct of effective communication: A second version of the Scale for Effective Communication in Team Sports.* Paper presented at the North American Society for the Psychology of Sport and Physical Activity (NASPSPA), St Louis, MO.

Sun, L., & Kliff, S. (2012, March 21). Komen foundation continues to see fallout from Planned Parenthood controversy. *Washington Post.* Retrieved from http://www.washingtonpost.com/national/health-science/komen-foundation-continues-to-see-fallout-from-planned-parenthood-controversy/2012/03/21/gIQAtfviSS_story.html

Superson, A., & Cudd, A. (Eds.). (2002). *Theorizing backlash: Philosophical reflections on the resistance to feminism.* Oxford, UK: Rowman & Littlefield.

Surrey, J. L. (1983). The relational self in women: Clinical implications. In J. V. Jordan, J. L. Surrey, & A. G. Kaplan (Eds.), *Women and empathy:*

Implications for psychological development and psychotherapy (pp. 6–11). Wellesley, MA: Stone Center for Developmental Services and Studies.

Suter, E., & Oswald, R. (2003). Do lesbians change their last names in the context of a committed relationship? *Journal of Lesbian Studies, 7,* 71–83.

Swain, S. (1989). Covert intimacy: Closeness in men's friendships. In B. J. Risman & P. Schwartz (Eds.), *Gender and intimate relationships* (pp. 71–86). Belmont, CA: Wadsworth.

Swim, J., & Becker, J. (2011). Seeing the unseen. *Psychology of Women Quarterly, 35,* 227–242.

Switzer, J. Y. (1990). The impact of generic word choices: An empirical investigation of age- and sex-related differences. *Sex Roles, 22,* 69–82.

Tannen, D. (1990a). Gender differences in conversational coherence: Physical alignment and topical cohesion. In B. Dorval (Ed.), *Conversational organization and its development* (Vol. XXXVIII, pp. 167–206). Norwood, NJ: Ablex.

Tannen, D. (1990b). *You just don't understand: Women and men in conversation.* New York: Morrow.

Tannen, D. (1995). *Talking 9 to 5: Women and men in the workplace.* New York: Avon.

Tarkan, L. (2009). Fathers gain respect from experts (and mothers). *The New York Times,* pp. D5–D6.

Tavernise, S. (2012, February 10). Rich and poor further apart in education. *The New York Times,* pp. A1, A3.

Tavris, C. (1992). *The mismeasure of woman.* New York: Simon & Schuster.

Tavris, C. (2002, July 5). Are girls really as mean as books say they are? *The Chronicle of Higher Education,* pp. B7–B9.

Taylor, S. (2002). *The tending instinct: How nurturing is essential for who we are and how we live.* New York: Times Books.

Taylor, V., & Rupp, L. (1998). Lesbian organizations. In W. Mankiller, G. Mink, M. Navarro, B. Smith, & G. Steinem (Eds.), *The reader's companion to U.S. women's history* (pp. 330–332). New York: Houghton Mifflin.

Teens and Online Video. (2010, May 3). Pew Center. Retrieved from http://www.pewinter net.org/~/media/Files/Reports/2012/PIP_ Teens_and_online_video.pdf

Teens and Online Video. (2012). *Pew Internet and American Life Project.* Retrieved from http://www.pewinternet.org/Reports/2012/ Teens-and-online-video.aspx

Thomas, K. (2008, July 30). A lab is set to test the gender of some female athletes. *The New York Times,* p. C9.

Thomas, K. (2011, April 26). College teams, relying on deception, undermine gender equity. *The New York Times,* pp. A1, A18.

Thompson, E. H., Jr. (1991). The maleness of vilence in dating relationships: An appraisal of stereotypes. *Sex Roles, 24,* 261–178.

Tichenor, V. (2005). Maintaining men's dominance: Negotiating identity and power when she earns more. *Sex Roles, S3,* 191–205.

Tierney, J. (2010, June 15). Legislation won't close gender gap in sciences. *The New York Times,* p. D4.

Tilsley, A. (2010, July 2). New policies accommodate transgender students. *The Chronicle of Higher Education,* pp. A19–A20.

Timmers, M., Fischer, A. H., & Manstead, A. S. (1998). Gender differences in motives for regulating emotions. *Personality and Social Psychology Bulletin, 24,* 974–985.

Title IX and issues. (2012). Retrieved from http:// www.womenssportsfoundation.org/home/ advocate/title-ix-and-issues/what-is-title-ix/ title-ix-myths-and-facts

Title IX Q & A. (2008). Retrieved October 26, 2008, from http://www.womenssports foundation.org/Content/Articles/Issues/Title% 20IX/T/Title%20IX%20Q%20%20A.aspx

Tootsie. (1994). Burbank, CA: RCA/Columbia Pictures.

Tough guise. (1999). Northampton, MA: Media Education Foundation.

Townsley, N. (2006). Love, sex, and tech in the global workplace. In B. Dow & J. T. Wood (Eds.), *Handbook of gender and communication* (pp. 143–160). Thousand Oaks, CA: Sage.

Traister, R. (2012). *Can modern women have it all?* Retrieved June 25, 2012, from http://www. salon.com/2012/06/21/can_modern_women_ have_it_all/singleton/

Trangsrud, R. (1994). Female genital mutilation: Recommendations for education and policy. *Carolina Papers in International Health and Development, 1,* n.p.

Trebay, G. (2010, January 21). Disaster coverage without having to roll up the sleeves. *The New York Times.* Retrieved from http://www.nytimes. com/2010/01/24/fashion/24tshirt.html?r=1

Troop, D. (2011, October 28). Women's university to reconsider hard line on transgender students. *The Chronicle of Higher Education,* pp. A18–A19.

Trower, C., & Quinn, K. (2009). Generation matters: What department chairs need to know about Gen X and Boomer pre-tenure faculty. *The Department Chair, 20,* 10–12.

Turner, C. S. (2002). Women of color in the academe: Living with multiple marginality. *The Journal of Higher Education, 73,* 74–93.

Turner, C. S. (2003). Incorporation and marginalization in the academy: From border toward center for faculty of color? *Journal of Black Studies, 34,* 112–125.

Turner, R. (1998, December 14). Back in the Ms. Biz. *Newsweek*, p. 67.

Tyre, P. (2006, January 30). The trouble with boys. *Newsweek*, pp. 44–52.

Tyre, P. (2009). *The trouble with boys: A surprising report card on our sons, their problems at school, and what parents and educators must do.* New York: Crown.

Tyre, P., & Scelfo, J. (2006, July 31). Why girls will be girls. *Newsweek*, pp. 46–17.

Udell, E. (2005, May 9). Where are the women? *In These Times*, p. 32.

Ugwu-Oju, D. (2000, December 4). My turn: Should my tribal past shape Delia's future? *Newsweek*, p. 14.

Valenti, J. (2011, June 5). SlutWalks and the future of feminism. *Washington Post.* Retrieved from http://www.washingtonpost.com/opinions/slutwalks-and-the-future-of-feminism/2011/06/01/AGjB9LIH_story_1.html

Valentine, D. (2007). *Imagining transgender: An ethnography of a category.* Durham, NC: Duke University Press.

Valian, V. (1998). *Why so slow? The advancement of women.* Boston: MIT Press.

Villano, D. (2011, September/October). Balancing act. *Miller-McCune*, pp. 22–25.

Vincent, N. (2006). *Self made man: One woman's journey into manhood and back.* New York: Viking.

Vivian, J. (2011). *The media of mass communication* (10th ed.). Boston: Allyn & Bacon.

Voice of the shuttle. (2010). Retrieved March 22, 2010, from http://vos.ucsb.edu/browse.asp?id=1810

Vokey, M., Tefft, B., & Tysiaczny, C. (2013). An analysis of hyper-masculinity in magazine advertisements. *Sex Roles.* doi:10.1007/s11199-013-0268-1

Waddell, L., & Campo-Flores, A. (2007, March 12). A case of gender blues. *Newsweek*, p. 51.

Wade, L. (2009, March 19). Dora the Explorer's makeover. *Sociological Images.* Retrieved from http://thesocietypages.org/socimages/2009/03/19/dora-the-explorers-makeover-gwen-and-i-saw-it-comin/

Wade, N. (2009, September 15). New clues to sex anomalies in how Y chromosomes are copied. *The New York Times*, p. D4.

Wagenheim, J. (1990, September/October). The secret life of men. *New Age Journal*, pp. 40–45, 106–118.

Wagenheim, J. (1996, January-February). Among the Promise Keepers. *Utne Reader*, pp. 74–77.

Waismel-Manor, R., & Tolbert, P. (2010). *Earnings differences in dual earner couples.* International Sociological Association Conference, Gothenburg, Sweden.

Walker, A. (1983). *In search of our mothers' gardens.* New York: Harcourt Brace Jovanovich.

Walker, K. (2004). Men, women, and friendship: What they say, what they do. In J. Spade & C. Valentine (Eds.), *The kaleidoscope of gender: Prisms, patterns, and possibilities* (pp. 403–413). Belmont, CA: Thomson/Wadsworth.

Walker, S. (2007). *Style and status: Selling beauty to African American women.* Lexington, KY: University of Kentucky Press.

Walker, R. (1992, January–February). Doing the third wave. *Ms.*, *12*, pp. 86–87.

Walsh, J. L., & Ward, L. M. (2008). Adolescent gender role portrayals in the media: 1950 to the present. In P. E. Jamieson & D. Romer (Eds.), *The changing portrayal of adolescents in the media since 1950* (pp. 132–164). New York: Oxford.

Warner, J. (2005). *Mommy madness.* New York: Penguin/Riverhead Books.

Wartik, N. (2002, June 23). Hurting more, helped less? *The New York Times*, pp. 15-1, 15-6, 15-7.

Watt, H. M. G., & Eccles, J. S. (Eds.). (2008). *Gender and occupational outcomes.* Washington, DC: American Psychological Association.

Watzlawick, P., Beavin, J., & Jackson, D. D. (1967). *Pragmatics of human communication.* New York: W. W. Norton.

Way, N. (1998). *Everyday courage.* New York: New York University Press.

Way, N. (2010). *Deep secrets: The hidden landscape of boys' friendships.* Cambridge, MA: Harvard University Press.

Weber, B. R. (2009). *Makeover TV: Selfhood, citizenship, and celebrity.* Durham, NC: Duke University Press.

The Week. (2012). Retrieved from http://theweek.com/article/index/225214/rush-limbaugh-vs-sandra-fluke-a-timeline

Wegner, H., Jr. (2005). Disconfirming communication and self-verification in marriage: Associations among the demand/withdraw interaction pattern, feeling understood, and marital satisfaction. *Journal of Social and Personal Relationships*, *22*, 19–31.

Weigel, J. (2010). Are you a good man? *Chicago Tribune.* Retrieved from http://www.chicagotribune.com/features/tribu/ct-tribu-weigel-good-men-20101202,0,6738782.column

Weinman, M., Small, E., Buzi, R., & Smith, P. (2008). Parental communication, self and peers' believes as predictors of condom use among female adolescents attending family planning clinics. *Child and Adolescent Social Work*, *25*, 157–170.

Weiss, D. M., & Sachs, J. (1991). Persuasive strategies used by preschool children. *Sociology*, *97*, 114–142.

Welter, B. (1966). The cult of true womanhood: 1820-1960. *American Quarterly*, *18*, 151–174.

Wentley, T., Schilt, K., Windsor, E., & Lucal, E. (2008). Teaching transgender issues. *Teaching Sociology*, 49–57.

West, C. (2007). Black sexuality: The taboo subject. In M. Andersen & P. H. Collins (Eds.), *Race, class, gender: An anthology* (6th ed., pp. 247–252). Belmont, CA: Thomson.

West, C., & Zimmerman, D. H. (1983). Small insults: A study of interruptions in cross-sex conversations between unacquainted persons. In B. Thorne, C. Kramarae, & N. Henley (Eds.), *Language, gender and society* (pp. 102–117). Rowley, MA: Newbury House.

West, L., Anderson, J., & Duck, S. W. (1996). Crossing the barriers to friendship between women and men. In J. T. Wood (Ed.), *Gendered relationships: A reader* (pp. 111–127). Mountain View, CA: Mayfield.

Weston, K. (1999). *Love makes a family: Portraits of lesbian, gay, bisexual, and transgender parents and their families*. Amherst: University of Massachusetts Press.

Whitaker, S. (2001). Gender politics in men's movements. In D. Vannoy (Ed.), *Gender mosaics* (pp. 343–351). Los Angeles: Roxbury.

White, A. M. (2006). "You've got a friend": African American men's cross-sex feminist friendships and their influence on perceptions of masculinity and women. *Journal of Social and Personal Relationships*, 23, 523–542.

White, A. M. (2008). *Ain't I a feminist? African American men speak out on fatherhood, friendship, forgiveness, and freedom*. New York: State University of New York Press.

White Ribbon Campaign. (n.d.). Retrieved May 20, 2003, from http://www.whiteribbon.com

Whitehead, B. (1997, October 3). Soccer dads march on Washington. *The Wall Street Journal*, p. A10.

Whitmire, R. (2007, July 25). A tough time to be a girl: Gender imbalance on campuses. *The Chronicle of Higher Education*, p. A23.

Whitmire, R. (2011). *Why boys fail*. New York: AMACOM.

Wiesmann, S., Boeije, H., van Doorne-Huiskes, A., & den Dulk, L. (2008). 'Not worth mentioning': The implicit and explicit nature of decision-making about the division of paid and domestic work. *Community, Work & Family*, 11, 341–363.

Wilier, E. (2011). The queen and her bee: Social aggression in female friendship. In D. O. Braithwaite & J. T. Wood (Eds.), *Casing interpersonal communication* (pp. 189–196). Dubuque, IA: Kendall-Hunt.

Williams, J. C. (2010). *Reshaping the work-family debate: Why men and class matter*. Cambridge, MA: Harvard University Press.

Williams, J. J. (2012, January 6). Queer 20: Judith "Jack" Halberstam complicates gender. *The Chronicle of Higher Education*, pp. B13–B15.

Williams, N. (2010, March 11). Is Lady Gaga a feminist or isn't she? *Ms. Blog*. Retrieved from http://msmagazine.com/blog/blog/2010/03/11/is-lady-gaga-a-feminist-or-isnt-she/

Williamson, G., & Silverman, J. (2001). Violence against female partners: Direct and interactive effects of family history, communal orientation, and peer-related variables. *Journal of Social and Personal Relationships*, 18, 535–549.

Wills, J. B., & Brauer, J. R. (2012). Have children adapted to their mothers working, or was adaptation unnecessary? Cohort effects and the relationship between maternal employment and child well-being. *Social Science Research*, 41, 425–443.

Wills, T. A., Weiss, R. L., & Patterson, G. R. (1974). A behavioral analysis of the determinants of marital satisfaction. *Journal of Consulting and Clinical Psychology*, 42, 802–811.

Wilson, E. (1975). *Sociobiology: The new synthesis*. Cambridge, MA: Harvard University Press, Belknap.

Wilson, E. (2010, January 14). The triumph of the size 12's. *The New York Times*, pp. E1, E6.

Wilson, E., & Koo, H. (2010). Mothers, fathers, sons, and daughters: Gender differences in factors associated with parent-child communication about sexual topics. *Reproductive Health*, 7, 7–31.

Wilson, M. (2004, Summer). Closing the leadership gap. *Ms.*, pp. 14–15.

Wilson, R. (2004a, January 23). Louts in the lab. *The Chronicle of Higher Education*, pp. A7, A9.

Wilson, R. (2004b, October 29). Report shows difficulty of sex-discrimination lawsuits. *The Chronicle of Higher Education*, p. A12.

Wilson, R. (2005, October 7). Second sex. *The Chronicle of Higher Education*, pp. A10–A12.

Wilson, R. (2007, January 26). The new gender divide. *The Chronicle of Higher Education*, pp. A36–A39.

Winik, L. W., & Massey, M. (2009, January 18). A new push for equal pay. *Parade*, p. 8.

Wingfield, A. (2009). Racializing the glass escalator: Reconsidering men's experiences with women's work. *Gender & Society*, 23, 5–26.

Winstead, B. A. (1986). Sex differences in same-sex friendships. In V. J. Derlega & B. A. Winstead (Eds.), *Friendship and social interaction* (pp. 81–99). New York: Springer-Verlag.

Wise, S., & Stanley, L. (1987). *Georgie Porgie: Sexual harassment in everyday life*. New York: Pandora.

Wolf, N. (1991). *The beauty myth*. New York: Morrow.

Wolf, N. (1993). *Fire with fire: The new female power and how it will change the 21st century*. New York: Random House.

Wolf, N. (2006, March 12). Wild things. *The New York Times Book Review*, pp. 22–23.

Wolverton, B. (2011, November 18). An icon falls, and a president with him. *The Chronicle of Higher Education*, pp. A1, A3–A6.

Women and Science. (2005, Spring/Summer). *The Stone Center Report*, pp. 9–11.

Wong, E. (2012, July 23). Pressure grows in china to end one-child law. *The New York Times*, pp. A1, A6.

Wood, J. (2013). Becoming gendered: Theories of gendering within families. In M. Fine & H. Fincham (Eds.), *Handbook of family theories: A content-based approach* (pp. 301–315). New York: Routledge.

Wood, J. T. (1993a). Engendered identities: Shaping voice and mind through gender. In D. Vocate (Ed.), *Intrapersonal communication: Different voices, different minds* (pp. 145–167). Hillsdale, NJ: Erlbaum.

Wood, J. T. (1993b). Gender and relationship crises: Contrasting reasons, responses, and relational orientations. In J. Ringer (Ed.), *Queer words, queer images: The (re) construction of homosexuality* (pp. 238–264). New York: New York University Press.

Wood, J. T. (1994). *Who cares: Women, care, and culture.* Carbondale: Southern Illinois University Press.

Wood, J. T. (1996a). Dominant and muted discourses in popular representations of feminism. *Quarterly Journal of Speech, 82*, 171–185.

Wood, J. T. (Ed.). (1996b). *Gendered relationships: A reader.* Mountain View, CA: Mayfield.

Wood, J. T. (1998). *But I thought you meant. Misunderstandings in human communication.* Mountain View, CA: Mayfield.

Wood, J. T. (2001a). A critical response to John Gray's Mars and Venus portrayals of men and women. *Southern Communication Journal, 67,* 201–210.

Wood, J. T. (2001b). The normalization of violence in heterosexual romantic relationships: Women's narratives of love and violence. *Journal of Social and Personal Relationships, 18,* 239–262.

Wood, J. T. (2004). Monsters and victims: Male felons' accounts of intimate partner violence. *Journal of Social and Personal Relationships, 21,* 555–576.

Wood, J. T. (2005). Feminist standpoint theory and muted group theory: Commonalities and divergences. *Women & Language, 28,* 61–64.

Wood, J. T. (2006). Gender, power and violence in heterosexual relationships. In D. Canary & K. Dindia (Eds.), *Sex differences and similarities in communication* (2nd ed., pp. 397–411). Mahwah, NJ: Erlbaum.

Wood, J. T. (2008). Critical, feminist theories of interpersonal communication. In L. A. Baxter & D. O. Braithwaite (Eds.), *Engaging theories in interpersonal communication* (pp. 323–334). Thousand Oaks, CA: Sage.

Wood, J. T. (2009a). Gender as an area of study. In W. Eadie (Ed.), *21st century communication: A reference handbook* (pp. 371–379). Thousand Oaks, CA: Sage.

Wood, J. T. (2009b). Gender differences in communication. In S. Hendrick & C. Hendrick (Eds.), *The encyclopedia of human relationships.* Thousand Oaks, CA: Sage.

Wood, J. T. (2010). The can-do discourse and young women's anticipations of future. *Women & Language, 33,* 103–107.

Wood, J. T. (2011a). He says/she says: Misunderstandings in communication between women and men. In D. O. Braithwaite & J. T. Wood (Eds.), *Casing interpersonal communication* (pp. 59–65). Dubuque, IA: Kendall-Hunt.

Wood, J. T. (2011b). Which ruler? What are we measuring? Thoughts on theorizing the division of domestic labor. *Journal of Family Communication, 11,* 29–49.

Wood, J. T. (2011c). Who's the parent now? In D. O. Braithwaite & J. T. Wood (Eds.), *Casing interpersonal communication* (pp. 197–202). Dubuque, IA: Kendall-Hunt.

Wood, J. T. (2013). Becoming gendered: Theories of gender development in families. In M. Fine & F. Fincham (Eds.), *Family theories: A content-based approach* (pp. 301–315). New York: Routledge.

Wood, J. T., & Conrad, C. R. (1983). Paradox in the experience of professional women. *Western Journal of Speech Communication, 47,* 305–322.

Wood, J. T., & Dow, B. J. (2010). The invisible politics of "choice" in the workplace: Naming the informal parenting support system. In S. Hayden & L. Obrien Hallstein (Eds.), *Contemplating maternity in an era of choice: Contemplating discourses of reproduction* (pp. 203–225). Lanham, MD: Lexington Books.

Wood, J. T., & Inman, C. (1993). In a different mode: Recognizing male modes of closeness. *Journal of Applied Communication Research, 21,* 279–295.

Woolls, D. (2006, September 9). Too-thin models can't walk the catwalk at Madrid fashion show. *Raleigh News & Observer*, p. 3A.

Workplace Bullying Institute. (2009). Retrieved from http://www.workplacebullying.org/2009/05/20/wow-bullying/

Wright, K. (2004, October). Hip-hop kids these days. *The Progressive*, pp. 40–42.

Wright, P. H. (1982). Men's friendships, women's friendships, and the alleged inferiority of the latter. *Sex Roles, 8,* 1–20.

Wright, P. H. (1988). Interpreting research on gender differences in friendship: A case for moderation and a plea for caution. *Journal of Social and Personal Relationships, 5,* 367–373.

Wright, P. H. (2006). Toward an expanded orientation to the comparative study of women's and men's same-sex friendships. In K. Dindia & D. Canary (Eds.), *Sex differences and similarities in communication* (pp. 37–57). Mahwah, NJ: Erlbaum.

Yao, M., Mahood, C., & Linz, D. (2010). Sexual priming, gender stereotyping, and likelihood to sexually harass: Examining the cognitive effects of playing a sexually-explicit video game. *Sex Roles, 62*, 77–88.

Yardley, J. (2008, August 13). In grand Olympic show, some sleight of voice. *The New York Times*, pp. A1, A12.

Yeater, E., Treat, T., Viken, R., & McFall, R. (2010). Cognitive processes underlying women's risk judgments: Associations with sexual victimization history and rape myths. *Journal of Consulting and Clinical Psychology, 78*, 375–386.

Yen, H. (2010a, January 16). More moms become breadwinners. *Raleigh News & Observer*, p. 3A.

Yen, H. (2010b, April 21). Women even with men in degrees. *Raleigh News & Observer*, p. 6A.

Yen, H. (2011, April 27). As more women earn degrees, more men stay home. *Raleigh News & Observer*, pp. 1A, 6A.

Zack, N. (2005). *Inclusive feminism: A third wave theory of women's commonality*. Lanham, MD: Rowman & Littlefield.

Zernike, K. (2012, March 17). Jury finds spying in Rutgers dorm was a hate crime. *The New York Times*, pp. A1, A16.

Zhang, Q. (2010). Asian Americans beyond the model minority stereotype: The nerdy and the left out. *Journal of International and Intercultural Communication, 3*, 20–37.

Zimmerman, A., & Dahlberg, J. (2008). The sexual objectification of women in advertising: A contemporary cultural perspective. *Journal of Advertising Research, 48*, 71–79.

Zimmerman, A., & Geist-Martin, P. (2006). The hybrid identities of gender queer: Claiming neither/nor, both/and. In L. A. Samovar, R. E. Porter, & E. R. McDaniel (Eds.), *Intercultural communication: A reader* (11th ed., pp. 76–82). Belmont, CA: Thomson.

Zinn, M., Hondagneu-Sotelo, P., & Messner, M. (2007). Sex and gender through the prism of difference. In M. Andersen & P. H. Collins (Eds.), *Race, class, gender: An anthology* (6th ed., pp. 147–156). Belmont, CA: Thomson.

Ziv, L. (1997, May). The horror of female genital mutilation. *Cosmopolitan*, pp. 242–245.

Zoepf, K. (2006, April 14). Universities for women push borders in Persian Gulf. *The Chronicle of Higher Education*, pp. A45–A47.

Zukerman, J. C. (2009, March 22). We must stop the rape and terror. *Parade*, pp. 6–7.

Index

lesbians
 See also gay, lesbian, bisexual, or transgendered
  (GLBT); gays
 affection communication and, 197
 as parents, 150
 relational health and, 198
Lethbridge, L., 203
Levin, D., 108, 157, 177, 242
Levitra, 242
Lewin, Kurt, 37
Lewin, T., 228
liberal feminism, 61, 67, 68, 70
liberal ideology
 first wave of women's movements, 62
 second wave of women's movements, 64–71
Liberia, 258
liking, 125
Lilly Ledbetter Fair Pay Act, 212, 224
Limbaugh, Rush, 231
Linde, J., 105
Lin-Liu, J., 168
Linz, D., 245
Lipka, S., 226
Lipton, J., 41
Liquorice, 236
Lituchy, T., 221
Litzler, E., 218
Logwood, D., 68
Longmore, M. A., 200
Looy, H., 26
Lorber, J., 21, 266
Lorie, A., 234
Louis, C. S., 133
Loury, G., 97
Lowe, M. A., 63
Lucal, E., 214
Lucas, K, 215
Lugo-Lugo, C., 236
Lugones, M., 52
Lumsden, L., 67
Luria, Z., 147
Luster, T., 149

M

Maccoby, E. E., 50
MacGeorge, E., 113
machismo, 68
Machung, A., 202
Madonna, 56
Mahatma Gandhi, 81
Mahood, C., 245
Mai, Mukhtar, 273, 274
"maintenance work," 114
Major, B., 125
Malcolm X, 171
male aliases, 220
male circumcision, 264

male deficit model, of personal relationships,
 186–187
male feminism, 83–89
male generic language, 103
Malkasian, K., 181
Maltz, D. N., 110
Mandela, Nelson, 165
Mandziuk, R., 105, 208
Mangan, K., 226
manhood, rites of, 93
mannequins, 156
Mansfield, H., 89
Manstead, A. S., 131
Maple, T. L., 130
Mapstone, E., 107
March for Women's Lives, 72
marginalized groups, 52
Marie Claire, 244
Marin, R., 152, 199, 202
Martin, C., 110
Martin, H., 22
Martínez, Maria José, 40
Martz, D., 108
Marx, J., 85
Marx, Karl, 51
Mascia, J., 248
masculine speech communities, 114–116, 196
masculinist men's groups, 89–97
masculinity
 aggression and, 153
 antifemale directive of, 151
 career paths, 215–217
 closeness of, 191–193
 cultural definition of, 24
 ego boundaries and, 151–155
 expectations of, 244
 false, 85
 friendships among, 191–193
 gender identity and, 146
 gender socialization and, 151–155
 ideal, 151
 of leaders, 214–215
 male feminist views of, 84
 meanings of, 22
 norms in professional life, 214–217
 peer pressure in, 175
 self-reliance and, 155
 sexual activity and, 149
 success and, 152
 in United States, 150
Masculinity and Morality (May), 83
Mason, M. A., 182
The Massacre, 241
Massey, M., 212
Mastronardi, Maria, 231
maternal thinking, 52, 73
maternal wall, 210
Matlack, T, 98
matriarchy, 105
Matsukura, R., 105
Mattern, J., 256
Mattioli, D., 257